Route C171 near Mole Creek, TAS (54 G6)

National Parks iii

Touring Tips & Safety

Road Rules & Driving Tips	viii
Preparing for your Trip	xii
After a Breakdown	xiv
After an Accident	xv
Emergency First Aid	xvi

Tasmania

Tasmania Key Map & Distance Chart	48
Hobart CBD	49
Hobart Region	50
Southern Tasmania	52
Northern Tasmania	54
Launceston Region	56

Queensland

Queensland Key Map & Distance Chart	1
Brisbane CBD	2
Brisbane Throughroads	3
Brisbane Region	4
South-East Queensland	6
Central-East Queensland	8
North Queensland	10
Outback Queensland	12
South-West Queensland	14
Cape York	16

South Australia

South Australia Key Map & Distance Chart	57
Adelaide CBD	58
Adelaide Throughroads	59
Adelaide Region	60
Fleurieu Peninsula	61
South-East South Australia	62
Central-East South Australia	64
North-East South Australia	66
Western South Australia	68

New South Wales

New South Wales Key Map & Distance Chart	17
Sydney CBD	18
Sydney Throughroads	19
Sydney Region	20
Central-East New South Wales	22
North-East New South Wales	24
North-West New South Wales	26
South-West New South Wales	28
South-East New South Wales	30
Canberra CBD (ACT)	31
Canberra Throughroads (ACT)	32

Western Australia

Western Australia Key Map & Distance Chart	69
Perth CBD	70
Perth Throughroads	71
Perth Region	72
South-West Western Australia	74
Central-West Western Australia	76
North Western Australia	78
The Kimberley	80
The Pilbara	82
South-East Western Australia	83

Victoria

Victoria Key Map & Distance Chart	33
Melbourne CBD	34
Melbourne Throughroads	35
Melbourne Region	36
South-West Victoria	38
North-West Victoria	40
North-East Victoria	42
Gippsland Region	44
South-East Victoria	46

Northern Territory

Northern Territory Key Map, Distance Chart & Darwin City	84
Darwin Region	85
The Top End	86
Central Northern Territory	88
Southern Northern Territory	90

Index 92

Legend 112

Quick Find Distance Chart
(Inside back cover)

Bungle Bungle Range, Purnululu NP (81 G13)

Australia Touring Atlas

National Parks

- Camping Area
- Bush Camping
- Picnic Area
- Fireplace/Barbecue
- Toilets
- Showers
- Drinking Water
- Walking Trail
- Ranger Station
- Four Wheel Drive Advisable
- Caravan Access

Queensland

Info Ph (07) 3227 8185
www.env.qld.gov.au/parks_and_forests

Park	Grid
Alton	6 H6
Astrebla Downs	12 G5 No public access
Auburn River	7 C9
Barnard Island Group*	11 E13
Barron Gorge	11 D12
Bendidee	7 H8
Black Mountain	11 B12
Blackbraes	11 H10
Blackdown Tableland	9 H8
Blackwood	8 D5
Bladensburg	13 D9
Blue Lake	5 A8
Boodjamulla	10 G2
Bowling Green Bay	8 A6
Brampton Islands	9 C8
Bribie Island	4 E3
Broad Sound Island	9 E9
Brook Islands*	11 F13 No access
Bulleringa	11 E10 No access
Bunya Mountains	7 E10
Burleigh Head	5 B13
Burrum Coast	7 A12
Byfield	9 G10
Camooweal Caves	10 J1
Cania Gorge	9 K11
Cape Hillsborough	9 C8
Cape Melville	16 H5
Cape Palmerston	9 E9
Cape Upstart	8 A6 Boat access only
Capricorn Coast	9 G11
Capricornia Cays	9 H13
Carnarvon	6 A4
Castle Tower	9 J11 No access
Cedar Bay	11 B12 Walk-in/boat access only
Chesterton Range	6 D2 No access
Chillagoe-Mungana Caves	11 D11
Claremont Isles	16 G4
Cliff Island*	16 H4
Clump Mountain*	11 E13
Coalstoun Lakes*	7 C11
Conondale	4 J1
Conway	9 C8
Crater Lakes*	11 D12
Crows Nest	7 F11
Cudmore	8 G4 No access
Culgoa Floodplain	6 K1
Currawinya	15 J10
Curtis Island	9 H11

Park	Grid
D'Aguilar	4 G6
Daintree	11 C12
Dalrymple	11 J13
Davies Creek	11 D12
Deepwater	9 J12
Denham Group	16 C3
Diamantina	12 F6
Dipperu	8 E7 Scientific – permit access only
Dryander	8 B7 Boat access only
Dularcha	4 F2
Edmund Kennedy	11 F13
Ella Bay	11 E13
Endeavour River	11 A12
Epping Forest	8 F4 Scientific – permit access only
Erringibba	6 F7
Eubenangee Swamp	11 E13
Eudlo Creek	4 F1 No access
Eungella	8 C7
Eurimbula	9 J12
Expedition	6 B5
Fairlies Knob*	7 B11
Family Islands	11 F13
Ferntree Creek*	7 E13
Finucane Island	10 E4
Fitzroy Island	11 D13
Flinders Group	16 H5
Forbes Islands*	16 E4
Forest Den	13 C12
Fort Lytton	4 D7
Forty Mile Scrub	11 F11
Frankland Group*	11 D13
Freshwater	4 F5
Girraween	7 K11
Girringun	11 F13
Glasshouse Mountains	4 F3
Gloucester Island	8 B7
Goneaway	13 F8 No access
Goodedulla	9 G9
Goodnight Scrub	7 B11
Goold Island	11 F13
Great Basalt Wall	11 J12 No access
Great Sandy (Cooloola)	7 D13
Great Sandy (Fraser)	7 B13
Green Island	11 D13
Grey Peaks	11 D13 No access
Halifax Bay Wetlands*	11 G13
Hann Tableland	11 D12 No access
Hasties Swamp*	11 E13
Hell Hole Gorge	15 B10 No access
Hinchinbrook Island	11 F13
Holbourne Islands*	8 B7

iv Queensland continued

Name	Map		Name	Map	
Homevale	8 D7		North East Island	9 E10	
Hope Islands*	11 B12		Northumberland Islands	9 D9	
Howick Group	16 H6		Nuga Nuga	6 A5	
Hull River*	11 F13		Orpheus Island	11 G14	
Idalia	13 H11		Palmerston Rocks*	11 E13	
Iron Range	16 E3		Palmgrove	6 A6	Scientific – permit access only
Isla Gorge	6 B7		Paluma Range	11 G13	Walk-in access only
Japoon*	11 E13		Peak Range	8 F6	
Jardine River	16 C2		Percy Isles	9 E10	
Junee	9 G8		Pioneer Peaks*	9 D8	
Keppel Bay Islands	9 G11		Pipeclay*	7 D13	
Kinrara	11 F12		Piper Islands*	16 E3	
Kondalilla	4 G1		Poona	7 C12	
Kroombit Tops	9 J11		Porcupine Gorge	11 K11	
Kurrimine Beach	11 E13		Possession Island	16 B2	
Lake Bindegolly	15 H10		Precipice	6 B7	No access
Lakefield	16 J5		Quoin Island*	16 E4	
Lamington	5 D14		Ravensbourne*	7 G11	
Lindeman Islands	9 C8		Reliance Creek*	9 D8	
Littabella	9 K12		Repulse Island*	9 C8	
Lizard Island	16 J7		Restoration Island*	16 E4	
Lochern	13 F9		Rundle Range	9 H11	
Magnetic Island	11 G14		Russell River	11 D13	
Main Range	5 K13		Sandbanks*	16 G4	
Mapleton Falls*	7 E12		Sarabah*	5 D13	No access
Maria Creek*	11 E13		Saunders Islands*	16 D3	
Mariala	15 C11	Walk-in access only	Simpson Desert	12 J2	
Mazeppa	8 F5		Sir Charles Hardy Group*	16 D4	
Michaelmas & Upolu Cays	11 C13		Smith Islands	9 C8	
Millstream Falls	11 E12		Snake Range	8 J6	No access
Minerva Hills	8 J6		South Cumberland Islands	9 C9	
Mitchell – Alice Rivers	16 K2		South Island	9 E10	
Molle Islands*	9 B8		Southern Moreton Bay Islands	5 B11	
Moogerah Peaks	5 J13		Southwood	6 G7	
Mooloolah River	4 E1		Springbrook	5 C14	
Moorrinya	8 D2		St Helena Island	4 C7	
Moresby Range*	11 E13		Staaten River	11 C8	
Moreton Island	4 B5		Starcke	16 J6	
Mount Aberdeen	8 B6	No access	Sundown	7 K10	
Mount Archer	9 H10		Swain Reefs	9 E13	
Mount Barney	7 J12		Tamborine	5 D11	
Mount Bauple	7 C12	Scientific – permit access only	Tarong*	7 E10	
Mount Chinghee*	7 J12		Taunton	9 H8	Scientific – permit access only
Mount Colosseum	9 J12		The Palms*	7 F11	
Mount Cook	16 K6		Three Islands*	16 J7	
Mount Coolum*	7 E13		Thrushton	6 G3	
Mount Etna Caves	9 G10		Topaz Road*	11 E13	
Mount Hypipamee	11 E12		Tregole	6 D2	
Mount Jim Crow*	9 G10		Triunia*	4 F1	
Mount Martin *	9 D8		Tully Gorge	11 E13	
Mount O'Connell	9 G10	No access	Turtle Group	16 J6	
Mount Ossa*	9 D8		Undara Volcanic (Undara Lodge)	11 F11	
Mount Pinbarren*	7 D12	No access	Venman Bushland	3 J7	
Mount Walsh	7 C11		Welford	13 H9	
Mount Webb	16 J6		West Hill	9 E9	
Mowbray*	11 C12		White Mountains	11 K12	
Mungkan Kandju	16 G3		Whitsunday Islands	9 B8	
Nairana	8 D5	No access	Wild Cattle Island*	9 J11	No access
Narrien Range	8 G5	No access	Wondul Range	7 H9	
Newry Islands	9 C8		Wooroonooran	11 D13	
Nicoll Scrub	5 B14	No access	Yungaburra*	11 D11	
Noosa	7 D13				

* The National Park is not shown on the map

New South Wales

Info Ph 1300 361 967
www.npws.nsw.gov.au

Park	Map Ref
Abercrombie River	22 J6
Arakwal	25 B14
Bago Bluff	23 A13
Bald Rock	25 C10
Bangadilly	22 K7
Barakee	23 A11
Barool	25 E11
Barrington Tops	23 C10
Basket Swamp	25 C11
Bellinger River	25 G12
Ben Boyd	31 K11
Ben Halls Gap	23 A9 — No access
Benambra	29 K13
Biamanga	31 H11
Bimberamala	30 E6
Bindarri	25 G12
Biriwal Bulga	23 A12
Blue Mountains	21 H9
Bongil Bongil	25 G13
Booderee (Comm. Terr.)	30 D7
Boonoo Boonoo	25 B11
Booti Booti	23 C13
Border Ranges	25 A12
Botany Bay	21 B10
Bouddi	20 B5
Bournda	30 J5
Brindabella	30 D2
Brisbane Water	20 C5
Broadwater	25 C14
Budawang	30 E5
Budderoo	30 B7
Bugong	30 C6
Bundjalung	25 D13
Bungawalbin	25 C13
Butterleaf	25 D10
Capoompeta	25 D10
Carrai	25 H10
Cascade	25 G12
Cataract	25 B11
Cathedral Rock	25 G10
Cattai	20 F6
Chaelundi	25 F11
Clyde River	30 E5
Cocoparra	29 F11
Conimbla	22 H3
Conjola	30 D7
Coolah Tops	22 B7
Coorabakh	23 B12
Cotton-Bimbang	23 A12
Crowdy Bay	23 B13
Culgoa	27 C12
Cunnawarra	25 H10
Deua	30 F5
Dharug	20 E4
Dooragan	23 B13
Dorrigo	25 G12
Dunggir	25 H11
Eurobodalla	30 F6
Fortis Creek	25 D12
Gardens of Stone	22 F7
Garigal	19 C5
Georges River	19 H2
Ghin-Doo-Ee	23 C11
Gibraltar Range	25 E11
Goobang	22 E3
Goonengerry	25 B14
Goulburn River	22 C7
Gourock	30 F4
Gulaga	30 G5
Gundabooka	27 F10
Guy Fawkes River	25 F11
Hat Head	25 J12
Heathcote	21 D11 — No vehicle access
Jerrawangala	30 C6
Jervis Bay	30 C7
Junuy Juluum	25 G11
Kanangra-Boyd	22 H6
Kinchega	26 K3
Kings Plains	25 E9
Kooraban	30 G5
Koreelah	25 A11
Kosciuszko	30 G1
Kumbatine	25 J11
Ku-ring-gai Chase	20 C6
Kwiambal	25 C8
Lane Cove	21 C8
Livingstone	29 H13
Macquarie Pass	30 B7
Mallanganee	25 C12
Mallee Cliffs	28 F4 — No access
Maria	25 J12
Marramarra	20 D5
Maryland	25 A10
Mebbin	25 A13
Meroo	30 E6
Middle Brother	23 B13
Mimosa Rocks	30 H5
Minjary	29 H14
Monga	30 E5
Mooball	25 A14
Morton	30 C6
Mount Clunie	25 A11
Mount Imlay	30 K4
Mount Jerusalem	25 B14
Mount Kaputar	24 F6
Mount Nothofagus	25 A12
Mount Pikapene	25 C12
Mount Royal	23 C10
Mount Warning	25 A13
Mummel Gulf	23 A11
Mungo	28 E5
Murramarang	30 E6
Mutawintji	26 H4
Myall Lakes	23 D12
Nangar	22 F3
Nattai	21 H13
New England	25 G11
Nightcap	25 B13
Nowendoc	23 A10
Nymboi-Binderay	25 F12
Nymboida	25 E11
Oolambeyan	29 G9

vi New South Wales continued

Park	Ref									
Oxley Wild Rivers	25 H10	▲		🏕	🏔	👥		🚶		🚐
Paroo-Darling	26 F6	▲				👥		🚶	🅿	
Popran	20 D4			🏕		👥		🚶		
Ramornie	25 E12		🌲							
Richmond Range	25 B12	▲		🏕		👥		🚶		
Royal	21 C11		🌲	🏕	🏔	👥	🚿	🏊	🚶 🅿	🚐
Saltwater	23 C13			🏕		👥	🚿	🏊	🚶	
Scheyville	20 F6			🏕		👥			🚶	
Seven Mile Beach	30 C7			🏕		👥	🚿	🏊	🚶	
Single	25 F9	No access								
South East Forest	30 J4	▲	🌲	🏕		👥		🚶		🚐
Sturt	26 C1	▲		🏕		👥		🚶		🚐
Sydney Harbour	21 B8			🏕		👥		🏊	🚶	
Tallaganda	30 F4		🌲						🚶	🚐
Tapin Tops	23 B12	▲	🌲	🏕		👥				
Tarlo River	30 B5									🚐
Thirlmere Lakes	21 G13			🏕	🏔	👥			🚶	
Timbarra	25 C11									
Tomaree	23 E11								🚶	
Tooloom	25 A11			🏕	🏔	👥			🚶	
Toonumbar	25 B12	▲		🏕		👥			🚶	🚐
Towarri	23 B8	▲		🏕	🏔	👥				🚐
Turon	22 F6	▲	🌲	🏕		👥			🚶	🚐
Ulidarra	25 G13									🚐
Wadbilliga	30 G4	▲	🌲	🏕		👥				🚐
Wallarah	23 F10								🚶	
Wallingat	23 C12	▲		🏕		👥			🚶	🚐
Warra	25 F10		🌲							🚐
Warrabah	24 G7	▲		🏕	🏔	👥			🚶	🚐
Warrumbungle	24 J3	▲	🌲	🏕	🏔	👥 🚿		🏊	🚶 🅿	🚐
Washpool	25 D11	▲	🌲	🏕	🏔	👥			🚶	
Watagans	23 E9	▲	🌲	🏕	🏔	👥			🚶	🚐
Weddin Mountains	22 H2	▲		🏕	🏔	👥			🚶	
Werakata	23 E10			🏕						
Werrikimbe	25 J10	▲	🌲	🏕	🏔	👥			🚶	🚐
Willandra	29 C8	▲		🏕	🏔	👥 🚿	🏊	🚶 🅿		🚐
Willi Willi	25 J11	▲	🌲	🏕	🏔	👥			🚶	🚐
Woko	23 B11	▲		🏕	🏔	👥			🚶	
Wollemi	20 K4	▲	🌲	🏕		👥			🚶	🚐
Wollumbin	25 A13								🚶	
Woomargama	29 K13	▲	🌲	🏕	🏔	👥			🚶	🚐
Wyrrabalong	20 A2			🏕		👥			🚶	
Yabbra	25 B11									
Yanununbeyan	30 E4		🌲							🚐
Yarriabini	25 H12			🏕	🏔	👥			🚶	
Yengo	20 G1	▲	🌲	🏕	🏔	👥			🚶	
Yuraygir	25 E13	▲	🌲	🏕	🏔	👥		🏊	🚶	🚐

Victoria

Info Ph 13 19 63
www.parkweb.vic.gov.au

Park	Ref									
Alfred	47 C12									
Alpine	43 E11	▲	🌲	🏕	🏔	👥			🚶	🚐
Baw Baw	44 B7	▲		🏕	🏔	👥			🚶	
Brisbane Ranges	36 D2	▲								
Burrowa Pine Mountain	43 B12	▲		🏕		👥			🚶	🚐
Chiltern - Mt Pilot	43 B8		🌲		🏔	👥			🚶	🚐
Churchill	37 E9			🏕	🏔	👥			🚶	
Coopracambra	47 B12		🌲	🏕	🏔					🚐
Croajingolong	47 D12	▲		🏕		👥			🚶	
Dandenong Ranges	37 D10			🏕	🏔	👥		🏊	🚶 🅿	
Errinundra	47 B10		🌲	🏕	🏔	👥			🚶	
French Island	37 J10	▲				👥		🏊	🚶	

Park	Ref									
Grampians	38 C6	▲	🌲	🏕	🏔	👥			🚶 🅿	🚐
Greater Bendigo	39 A12	▲		🏕	🏔				🚶	
Hattah-Kulkyne	40 C5	▲		🏕	🏔	👥		🏊	🚶	🚐
Heathcote-Graytown	39 B13	▲		🏕						
Kinglake	37 A10	▲		🏕	🏔	👥			🚶	
Lake Eildon	42 G5	▲	🌲	🏕	🏔	👥		🏊	🚶 🅿	🚐
Lind	47 C10			🏕	🏔					
Little Desert	38 A3	▲		🏕	🏔	👥			🚶	🚐
Lower Glenelg	38 G3	▲	🌲	🏕	🏔	👥			🚶	🚐
Mitchell River	45 A12	▲	🌲	🏕	🏔				🚶	🚐
Mornington Peninsula	36 K7			🏕	🏔	👥		🏊	🚶 🅿	
Morwell	45 F8			🏕	🏔	👥			🚶	
Mount Buffalo	43 E8	▲		🏕	🏔	👥	🚿		🚶	🚐
Mount Eccles	38 G4			🏕	🏔	👥			🚶	
Mount Richmond	38 H3			🏕	🏔	👥			🚶	
Murray – Sunset	40 D3	▲	🌲	🏕	🏔	👥			🚶	🚐
Organ Pipes	36 B6			🏕		👥			🚶	
Otway	39 K10	▲	🌲	🏕	🏔	👥			🚶 🅿	🚐
Port Campbell	39 J8					👥			🚶	
Snowy River	43 G14	▲	🌲	🏕	🏔	👥			🚶	🚐
St Arnaud Range	39 B9	▲		🏕	🏔	👥			🚶	
Tarra Bulga	45 F8			🏕	🏔	👥			🚶 🅿	
Terrick Terrick	41 J11	▲		🏕	🏔				🚶	🚐
The Lakes	45 D13	▲		🏕						🚐
Wilsons Promontory	44 J7	▲		🏕	🏔	👥 🚿	🏊	🚶 🅿		
Wyperfeld	40 G4	▲	🌲	🏕	🏔	👥		🏊	🚶 🅿	🚐
Yarra Ranges	37 B12			🏕	🏔	👥			🚶	

Tasmania

Info Ph 1300 135 513
www.parks.tas.gov.au

Park	Ref									
Ben Lomond	55 G12	▲	🌲	🏕	🏔	👥		🏊	🚶	🚐
Cradle Mt - Lake St Clair	54 H5	▲		🏕	🏔	👥 🚿	🏊	🚶 🅿		🚐
Douglas-Apsley	55 H13	▲	🌲			👥			🚶	
Franklin-Gordon	52 D5	▲		🏕	🏔	👥			🚶	🚐
Freycinet	55 K14	▲	🌲	🏕	🏔	👥		🏊	🚶 🅿	🚐
Hartz Mountains	53 H8			🏕	🏔	👥			🚶	🚐
Kent Group*		▲		🏕	🏔	👥		🏊	🚶 🅿	
Maria Island	53 E13	▲	🌲	🏕	🏔	👥		🏊	🚶 🅿	
Mole Creek Karst	54 G7	▲	🌲		🏔	👥			🚶	🚐
Mt Field	53 E8	▲	🌲	🏕	🏔	👥		🏊	🚶 🅿	🚐
Mt William	55 D14	▲		🏕	🏔	👥			🚶	
Narawntapu	55 D8	▲		🏕	🏔	👥			🚶	
Rocky Cape	54 C4			🏕	🏔	👥			🚶	
Savage River	54 E4									
South Bruny	53 J10	▲		🏕	🏔	👥			🚶	🚐
Southwest	52 H6	▲	🌲	🏕	🏔	👥		🏊	🚶	🚐
Strzelecki	55 C9	▲		🏕	🏔	👥			🚶	🚐
Tasman	51 J13	▲	🌲	🏕	🏔	👥 🚿			🚶 🅿	
Walls of Jerusalem	54 H6	▲	🌲	🏕		👥			🚶	Walk-in access only

* The National Park is not shown on the map

South Australia

Info Ph (08) 8204 1910
www.environment.sa.gov.au/parks

Park	Ref									
Belair	60 H3			🏕	🏔	👥		🏊	🚶 🅿	
Canunda	63 C13	▲		🏕	🏔	👥		🏊	🚶	
Coffin Bay	64 H5	▲	🌲	🏕		👥			🚶	🚐
Coorong	63 E9	▲	🌲	🏕	🏔	👥			🚶	🚐
Flinders Chase	63 K9			🏕	🏔	👥 🚿	🏊	🚶 🅿		
Flinders Ranges	65 B10	▲		🏕	🏔	👥			🚶 🅿	🚐
Gawler Ranges	64 D5		🌲			👥				
Great Australian Bight Marine	68 K3									
Innes	62 J7	▲	🌲	🏕	🏔	👥 🚿			🚶 🅿	🚐

vii

(continued listings)

Park	Ref
Lake Eyre	67 F8
Lake Gairdner	64 B6
Lake Torrens	65 A9
Lincoln	64 J6
Mount Remarkable	62 G2
Murray River	62 B6
Naracoorte Caves	38 C1
Nullarbor	68 J2
Onkaparinga River	61 D6
Vulkathuna-Gammon Ranges	67 K11
Witjira	66 B5

Western Australia
Info Ph (08) 9334 0333
www.calm.wa.gov.au/national_parks/

Park	Ref
Alexander Morrison	76 H4
Avon Valley	72 E2
Badgingarra	76 H4
Beedelup	73 F14
Boorabbin	75 B10
Brockman	74 J3
Cape Arid	83 J2
Cape Le Grand	75 G14
Cape Range	78 F1
Collier Range	82 K5
D'Entrecasteaux	74 J3
Drovers Cave	76 H3
Drysdale River	81 C11
Eucla	83 G7
Fitzgerald River	75 H9
Francois Peron	76 B2
Frank Hann	75 E10
Geikie Gorge	81 H9
Gloucester	73 F14
Goldfields-Woodland	75 B11
Goongarrie	77 G11
Gooseberry Hill	72 F3
Greenmount	72 F3
Hassell	74 J7
John Forrest	72 F3
Kalamunda	72 F3
Kalbarri	76 D2
Karijini (Hamersley Range)	82 F4
Kennedy Range	78 H2
Leeuwin-Naturaliste	73 K12
Lesmurdie	72 F3
Lesueur	76 H3
Millstream-Chichester	82 D2
Mirima (Hidden Valley)	81 D14
Mitchell River	81 C9
Moore River	74 B2
Mount Augustus	82 J2
Mount Frankland	74 J5
Nambung	74 A1
Neerabup	72 G2
Peak Charles	75 E12
Porongurup	74 J6
Purnululu	81 G13
Rudall River	79 F9
Scott	73 J13
Serpentine	72 F5
Shannon	74 J4
Stirling Range	74 H6
Stockyard Gully	76 H3
Stokes	75 G11
Tathra	76 G4
Torndirrup	74 K7
Tuart Forest	73 H10
Tunnel Creek	81 G8
Walpole-Nornalup	74 K4
Walyunga	72 F2
Warren	73 F14
Watheroo	76 H4
Waychinicup	74 J7
Wellington	73 F10
West Cape Howe	74 K6
William Bay	74 K5
Windjana Gorge	81 G8
Wolfe Creek Crater	79 C13
Yalgorup	72 H7
Yanchep	72 G1

Northern Territory
Info Ph Alice Springs (08) 8951 8250
Darwin (08) 8999 5511
Katherine (08) 8973 8888 www.nt.gov.au/ipe/pwcnt

Park	Ref
Barranyi (North Island)	87 J13
Charles Darwin	84 D3
Davenport Range	89 J10
Djukbinj	85 C3
Dulcie Ranges	91 D11
Elsey	86 H7
Finke Gorge	90 G7
Garig Gunak Barlu	86 B5
Gregory	88 B3
Kakadu (Comm. Terr.)	85 C6
Keep River	88 A1
Lawley River	81 B9
Limmen (Proposed)	87 J10
Litchfield	85 E1
Mary River	85 D4
Nitmiluk (Katherine Gorge)	85 H6
Uluru-Kata Tjuta (Comm. Terr.)	90 J4
Watarrka (Kings Canyon)	90 G5
West MacDonnell	90 F7

Australian Capital Territory
Info Ph (02) 6207 9777
www.environment.act.gov.au/bushparksandreserves/bushparksandreserves.html

Park	Ref
Namadgi	32 K1

The publisher gratefully acknowledges the assistance provided by Australia's rangers and parks office personnel in researching the park facilities.

The following publications offer more detailed information on parks, camps and rest areas around Australia. Some of these publications also refer to the Australia Road Atlas maps within their texts.

- Hema Maps' state-based Camping Atlas products

- Camps Australia Wide by Philip Procter (www.campsaustraliawide.com)

- Highway Guide Around Australia and Highway Guide Across Australia by Paul Smedley (www.highwaymanproductions.com)

- Boiling Billy Publications' assorted camping guides by Craig Lewis and Cathy Savage (www.boilingbilly.com.au)

Hinchinbrook Island, QLD (11 F13)

Australia Touring Atlas

Touring Tips and Safety

The Hema 'Map Patrol' Photo: Splitimage

Road Rules and Driving Tips

These are the general road rules used across Australia. This is not a complete list of the rules from each state and territory and is a guide only. If you wish to know more, consult the official driving guide for the appropriate state or territory.

Traffic Lights

(At intersections, roadworks, pedestrian crossings and other locations)

Red – Red means STOP. Stop as near as practicable to, but before reaching the stop line. Don't enter the intersection. A red arrow means you must not turn in the direction of the arrow.

Yellow – Yellow means STOP, if you can do so safely. A yellow arrow means stop travelling in the direction of the arrow, if you can do so safely. You may enter the intersection if you are so close that you will not stop safely before the stop line, but you must not block the intersection.

Green – Green means you may enter the intersection or turn in the direction of the arrow, but only if it is safe to do so, you are able to cross the entire intersection (including any marked foot crossings), and the road on the other side of the intersection is not blocked. Vehicles must give way to pedestrians when turning.

Bus and tram signals

These are extra signals specifically for buses and trams. (In Queensland bicycle riders can ride in bus lanes.) They are identified by a T or B set next to the other lights. Only buses and trams may move off when the T or B light shows. Other road users must wait for the normal green light.

Overhead lane lights

You must stay out of any lane with a red cross/light over it. Only drive in a lane which shows an illuminated arrow/light pointing downwards.

Stop Sign

Come to a complete halt before or at the stop line and give way to all traffic before proceeding. Give way to pedestrians on the road you are turning into.

Give Way Sign

You must slow down or stop your vehicle and give way to all traffic until it is safe to proceed. Give way to pedestrians when turning at an intersection.

Speed Limits

Speed limit signs

The number in the red circle tells you the maximum speed (km/h) at which you may travel. Drivers have a legal responsibility to select a speed that is appropriate for the prevailing conditions.

The black circle with a line through it or an End Limit sign mean the end of a set speed zone and the start of the open area speed limit (see State By State Comparison page xi).

Advisory speed signs

Advisory speed signs are yellow in colour and show the maximum speed that is safe in good conditions. Warning signs may be used in conjunction with advisory speed signs to advise how long you should look out for a particular hazard.

Eyre Highway, SA (68 K3) Photo: Rob Boegheim

Pacific Highway, NSW (23 G9) Photo: Viewfinder

Roundabouts

A roundabout is an intersection where all traffic moves in a clockwise direction around a central traffic island. You must give way to any vehicle in the roundabout. Move off when there is a safe distance between your vehicle and the vehicles on your right.

- Plan your route ahead and choose the correct lane when approaching the roundabout. Sometimes arrow markings are on the roadway to assist drivers in choosing the correct approach lane.
- Where there are lanes, use the left lane for a left turn, right lane for a right turn and either for straight ahead, unless there are lane arrows indicating differently.
- Look out for large vehicles displaying 'Do not overtake turning vehicle' signs. They may need more than one lane when turning on roundabouts so give them plenty of room.
- If you cannot leave the roundabout because it is unsafe, go around again.

Approach as you would if it was a normal intersection, using the indicator which you would normally use. Put on your left indicator after you pass the exit before the one you will take.
Turning left - approach with left indicator, keep it on throughout.
Turning right - approach with right indicator, indicate left to leave the roundabout if practicable.
Travelling straight ahead - approach with no indicator, indicate left to leave the roundabout if practicable.

Give way to all traffic on the roundabout

Roundabout ahead

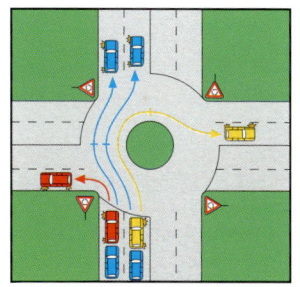

You should signal left prior to leaving a roundabout.

Intersections

Always give way if there is any risk of a collision with another vehicle or person. Slow down or stop and let that vehicle or person go first.

- At cross intersections where there are no traffic lights or signs:
  - Give way to vehicles approaching from your right
  - When turning right also give way to oncoming vehicles that are turning left or going straight ahead.
- Normal give way rules do not apply at terminating (T) intersections. Vehicles in the terminating road must give way to vehicles in the continuing road unless otherwise signed.
- Give way when facing a 'Turn left at any time with care' sign. Vehicles in a slip lane must give way to any pedestrian and to any vehicle approaching from the right, including an oncoming vehicle that is turning right at the intersection.
- Normal give way rules (see above) apply at intersections where the lights have failed.
- Normal give way rules apply when multiple vehicles are facing Stop or Give Way signs but only after they have given way to any other vehicle not facing a sign.

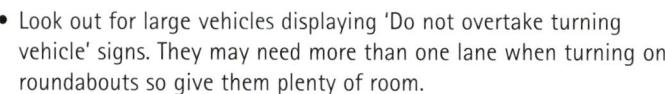

The red vehicles give way to the blue vehicles.

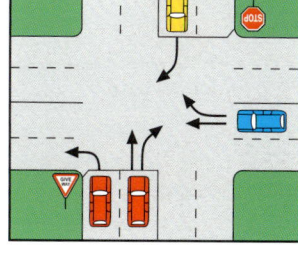

The red and yellow vehicles give way to the blue vehicle. Then, yellow gives way to red, but does not need to give way to the red vehicle which is turning right.

Touring North West Tasmania Photo: Rob Boegheim

x

Common Road Signs

 Beware kangaroos
 Turn 
 Narrow bridge
 Slippery road
 Give way to buses signalling their intention to pull out from the kerb (in a built up area)

 Side road intersection
 Curve
 Divided road ahead 
 End divided road 

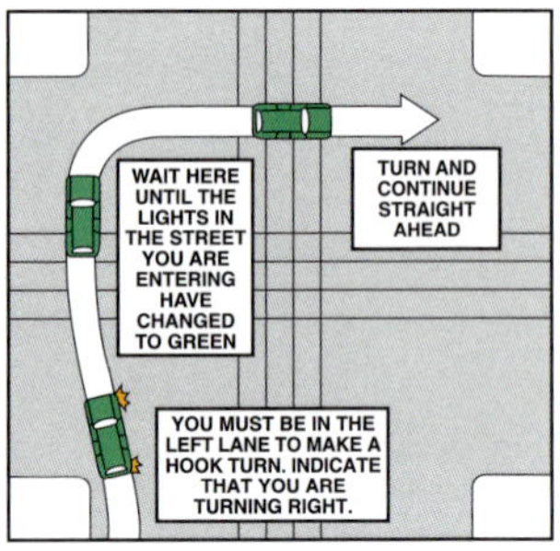

 T - intersection
 Winding road
 Road narrows  
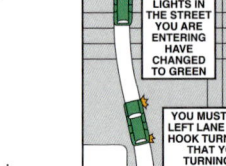 Do not overtake turning vehicle

 Crossroads
 Steep downgrade 
 Merging traffic 
 Lane indicated is closed

Right hook turns are necessary only at a number of intersections in Central Melbourne, and are indicated by a sign.

Remember these simple rules when driving in Australia:

- Keep left
- Obey the speed limit
- All drivers and passengers must wear a seatbelt where fitted, babies must travel in an approved restraint, and bicycle and motorcycle riders and their pillion passengers must wear a helmet
- The maximum legal limit for blood alcohol content is 0.05 (see page xi for info)
- It's illegal to use a hand-held mobile phone while driving

Pedestrian Crossings

- Always give way to pedestrians at crossings. Approach crossings at a speed which will enable you to stop safely before the crossing.
- Never overtake or pass a vehicle stopped at a pedestrian crossing.
- Give way to all pedestrians and cyclists when you are entering or leaving private property.

Western Explorer, Tas (54 F2) Photo: Rob Boegheim

Road Markings

Keep as close as practicable to the left edge of the road when there are no road markings or the road is marked with only a centre dividing line.

Broken single lines
You can cross them to overtake or turn.

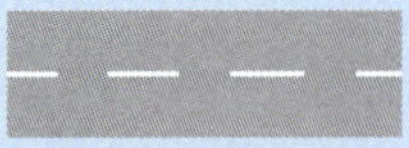

Continuous single lines or double lines with a continuous line closer to you
You cannot cross them to overtake, but may cross them when entering or leaving the road or to avoid an obstruction.

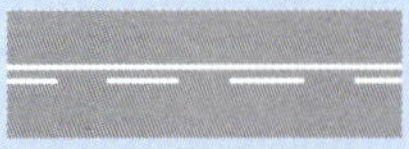

Double continuous white lines
You must keep left of double white lines except if you need to avoid an obstruction and it is safe to do so.

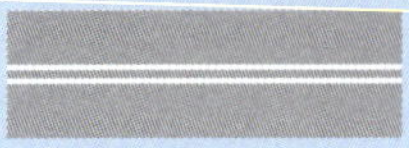

Double lines with a broken line closer to you
You may cross these lines to overtake or enter or leave a road if the road ahead is clear.

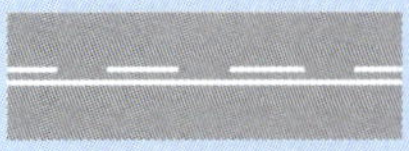

Lane markings
These are often used to separate lanes of traffic going in the same direction. Be sure to stay within a single marked lane. Signal before changing lanes and give way to traffic occupying the lane which you intend to enter.

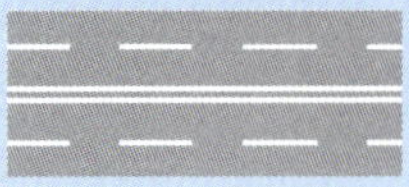

Lane arrows
Lane arrows indicate the correct lane for the direction you intend to take through an intersection. You must proceed only in the direction of the arrows in your lane.

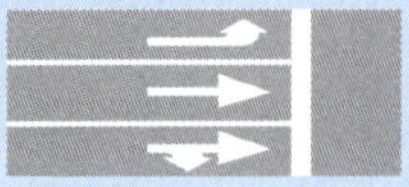

Traffic islands
Unless surrounded by a double line, a driver may cross over a painted traffic island to enter or leave a road, enter a turning lane (provided you give way to other vehicles entering the turning lane) or to avoid an obstruction.

The Hema 'Map Patrol' Photo: Splitimage

Night Driving
- Your headlights, taillights and number plate light must be on between sunset and sunrise and should be on at any other time when visibility is reduced by hazardous weather conditions.
- Dip your headlights when an approaching vehicle or the vehicle you are following is 200m away or as soon as the headlights of an approaching vehicle are dipped.
- Avoid driving at night in outback and remote areas.

Alcohol and Drugs

Blood and breath alcohol concentration (BAC) is measured in grams of alcohol per 100ml of blood. See the State by State Comparison for the legal limit for your licence category. Chewing gum, smoking a cigarette, drinking coffee, having a shower, exercising or using breath freshener will not reduce your BAC. It takes about one hour for the body to break down the alcohol content in one standard drink (but this varies from person to person).

Drugs can also affect your driving ability. Examples of prescription and over-the-counter drugs that can make you unfit to drive are:

- some pain killers,
- tranquillisers, sedatives and sleeping pills,
- medicines for blood pressure, nausea, allergies (antihistamines), inflammations and fungal infections, and
- some diet pills, travel sickness and cold and flu medicines.

Medicines are usually labelled with a warning if you shouldn't drive after taking them. Your doctor or pharmacist should advise you whether you can drive.

How many standard drinks to stay under .05?

This is a **guide** only. Some people can manage **less**.
The best option is to not drink at all before driving.

Men	Drinks	Women	Drinks
first hour	2	first hour	1
every hour after that	1	every hour after that	1

Standard drinks:
- 1 middy / pot / 285 ml of full strength beer (4.9% Alc./Vol)
- 1.6 middies / pots of light strength beer (2.7% Alc./Vol)
- 1 small glass / 100 ml of wine (12% Alc./Vol)
- 1 nip of spirits (40% Alc./Vol)
- 0.7 bottle of alcoholic soda

(A standard drink is any drink containing 10 gms of alcohol)

State by State Comparison	QLD	NSW	ACT	VIC	TAS	SA	WA	NT
Built up area speed limit	50[1]	50[1]	50[1]	50[1]	50[1]	50[1]	50[1]	60[5]
Open area speed limit[2]	100	100	100	100	100	100	110	N/A
Learner speed limit	POSTED LIMIT	80	POSTED LIMIT	POSTED LIMIT	80	80	100	80[3]
Provisional speed limit	POSTED LIMIT	90/100[4]	POSTED LIMIT	POSTED LIMIT	80[6]	100	110	100
Learner BAC limit*	0.00	0.00	0.02	0.00	0.00	0.00	0.02	0.00
Provisional BAC limit*	0.00	0.00	0.02	0.00	0.00	0.00	0.02	0.00
Open BAC limit*	0.05	0.05	0.05	0.05	0.05	0.05	0.05	0.05
Show L plate	YES	YES	YES	YES	YES	YES	YES	YES
Show P plate	NO	YES	YES	YES	YES[6]	YES	YES	YES
Report all accidents when:		•••		•	••			
Property damage exceeds	$2500	N/A	All	N/A	N/A	$1000	$1000	All
Injury/Death occurs	YES	YES	YES	YES	YES	YES	YES	YES

1. Unless signed otherwise.
2. Some states and territories have 110km/h limits in selected areas.
3. A learner must not drive at a speed greater than 80km/h unless permitted to do so by, and while under the direct supervision of, a person conducting a driving/riding course approved by the Registrar of Motor Vehicles.
4. First stage (P1) 90km/h. Second stage (P2) 100km/h.
5. Local Government authorities may apply to implement the national default urban speed limit of 50km/h.
6. Applies for first year only.
* Reading must be below the stated limit
• Property is damaged and the owner is not present or the police don't attend the scene.
•• A driver does not give his/her personal details in the prescribed manner.
••• A vehicle needs to be towed, there is damage to property or animals, a driver fails to stop or exchange information, or a driver may be under the influence of alcohol or drugs.

Preparing for Your Trip

Car Preparation

For a worry-free trip, ensure your car is serviced and thoroughly inspected by a mechanic at least one week before you plan to depart. As well as the normal servicing, inspect the following items for added safety and peace of mind:

- [ ] all tyres for signs of damage or wear. Check tread depth and tyre pressure,
- [ ] head and tail lights, park lights, brake lights and indicators,
- [ ] windscreen wipers, wiper blades and washers,
- [ ] horn,
- [ ] internal lights, gauges and warning lights,
- [ ] condition of seat belts, and
- [ ] clean lights, windows and mirrors.

Check and top up all fluid levels before you set off and again during your trip, especially if you are travelling considerable distances.

Avoiding a Breakdown

The RACQ suggests some basic precautions:

- Keep the car in good mechanical repair and always have plenty of fuel.
- Have a safety plan. Think now about what you would do if your vehicle breaks down.
- Plan your route. If travelling in an isolated area, tell someone which way you're going and your estimated time of arrival.
- Constantly be aware of where you are. Make mental notes of road names and landmarks.
- If the car is "playing up", stop at the first available safe area. Don't keep driving on the assumption you will reach your destination.

It is a good idea to have a mobile phone in your vehicle as it can shorten the time between breaking down and receiving assistance and you won't have to leave the safety of your vehicle to search for a public telephone.

Overnight campsite Photo: Henry Boegheim

Towing Trailers and Caravans

Before you plan your holiday, check your vehicle's specifications to find out the maximum load allowed by the vehicle and the towbar, and any other regulations and restrictions.

Towing takes more knowledge and skill and is more stressful than normal driving. It is more likely to cause tiredness so plan more rest stops and shorter travelling days. Allow for extra length, different braking technique, extra turning width and increased braking distance.

Check your trailer's –

- [ ] tyres and tyre pressures
- [ ] brakes, bearings and suspension
- [ ] lights and electrical connections compatibility
- [ ] couplings - towbar and towball
- [ ] load distribution, capacity and security.

Carry these in the car, but make sure there are no loose items that could prove dangerous under heavy braking:

Glove Box

- [ ] list of essential phone numbers
- [ ] phone card and coins
- [ ] motoring club membership card
- [ ] matches and/or lighter
- [ ] small torch & fresh batteries
- [ ] 12 volt light
- [ ] maps

Readily Accessible

- [ ] fire extinguisher
- [ ] reflective hazard signs
- [ ] first aid kit (including insect repellent)

In the Cargo Area – Essentials

- [ ] a comprehensive car tool kit
- [ ] jumper leads
- [ ] jack, solid block of wood, wheel brace and hubcap remover
- [ ] a canvas bucket or plastic decanter
- [ ] lubricating spray (eg. CRC or RP7)
- [ ] assorted nuts and bolts
- [ ] electrical wire and tape
- [ ] a light tarp for shade or groundsheet
- [ ] a strong, long rope for towing

In the Cargo Area – Replacements

- [ ] engine oil
- [ ] brake fluid, transmission or clutch fluid, etc.
- [ ] water for radiator and drinking
- [ ] replacement fuses (most newer cars have spare fuses stored in the fuse box)
- [ ] belts and hoses
- [ ] a spare fuel filter, especially if your car is fuel injected

Travelling with dad Photo: Splitimage

Driving with Children

Plan the trip

- Research where you're going and plan the route before you start. Show the children photos and brochures.
- Use the correct child restraints.
- Plan breaks every 1 to 2 hours and try to stop where there is a playground or other energy-burning opportunity. Take 30mins for the morning and afternoon tea breaks and around an hour for the lunch break. Sit back and relax while the children burn off excess energy.
- Don't travel too far – try to travel well within daylight hours.
- Remember it's a holiday for everyone and backseat travellers have a harder time enjoying long journeys.

Enjoy the trip

- Bring along plenty of good, nutritional snacks such as muesli bars and fruit and have a separate water bottle (with a straw) for each child. Don't feed children high energy, high sugar foods and drinks. Don't forget moist towelettes and car sickness remedies.
- Let each child bring a few favourite toys, games and books. Bring a stable table, colouring book and colouring pencils for each child. Older children could take their own photos with a disposable camera and write a journal about the trip.

Here are a few travel game suggestions:

- I Spy (Colour I Spy for younger children)
- Memory games, eg. I went shopping and I bought ...
- Car Bingo (make a selection of passing objects that the children have to spot and tick off as they go, for example, cars of a particular colour, wildlife, farm animals, road signs)
- Word games (play a word linking game where they have to spot something that starts with the last letter of the previous word, or use letters from registration plates to make up words or sentences).

Driver Fatigue

Stop driving and have a rest if you think you are experiencing any of these danger signs –

- you feel tired or can't keep your eyes open;
- lack of alertness;
- delayed reactions;
- your vision becomes fuzzy or dim or you start seeing things;
- droning or humming in your ears;
- unintentional changes in speed or fumbling gear changes;
- vehicle wandering across the road.

Camping with kids Photo: Rob Boegheim

xiv

Driving Tips:

- Eat a good meal well beforehand and be well rested before you start. Avoid alcohol and drugs (prescribed or illegal).
- Plan your trip to include regular rest breaks.
- Plan to drive when you would normally be awake. Try not to drive at night and avoid driving at dawn and dusk because of poor visibility. Plan to arrive at your destination relaxed and refreshed.
- Make sure the driver's seat is properly adjusted and that your seating position is high enough to get a clear view of the road. Adjust your mirrors after you have adjusted the seat.
- Stop and have a 15min rest after 2 hours of driving, or more often if you need it. Have a snack when you take your break and get out of your car and walk around. Maybe take photos or throw a ball around. If you find that nothing seems to help you stay awake, stop for a while. A short nap could be enough.
- If possible, share the driving with your passengers.
- Talk to your passengers or listen to music.
- Keep the air vents set to fresh air, not recirculated. Roll your window down and get some fresh air on your face.

Acknowledgments

We acknowledge the assistance and information provided by the following:

- Australian Red Cross
- Australian Transport Safety Bureau
- Department of Infrastructure, Energy and Resources, TAS
- Department of infrastructure, Planning and Environment, NT
- Department of Urban Services – Road Use Management, ACT
- National Road Transport Commission
- Queensland Police Service
- Queensland Transport
- Road User's Handbook. (2003) Roads and Traffic Authority, NSW
- Royal Automobile Club of Queensland
- Transport SA
- VicRoads
- Western Australia Police Service

Reproduced by permission. Details correct at February 2005.

Mitchell Falls, WA (81 C9) Photo: Henry Boegheim

Motoring Organisations

Australia's motoring clubs offer breakdown assistance, information and other services. They have reciprocal agreements so you only have to join one organisation to be covered Australia-wide.

If you belong to NRMA, AANT, RACQ, RAA, RACT, RACV or RAC and require assistance anywhere in Australia, call 13 11 11.

Route C171 near Mole Creek, Tas (54 G6) Photo Rob Boegheim

After an Accident

If you are involved in a crash that causes injury or death to any person or animal, damage to any property, or you are first at the scene of an accident, stop your vehicle as close as you can to the accident without causing more of a hazard than necessary.

You must stop if you are involved in an accident.

First:

- Note the position of your vehicle and then move it clear of traffic. If it can't be moved or there are other hazards, turn on the vehicle's hazard lights and/or use people or hazard signs to warn other drivers.
- Before helping anyone, check that your actions don't put yourself or others in danger. Don't stand on the roadway. Turn off all ignition switches, keep clear of fallen power lines and don't smoke or use naked flames.

See if anyone is injured:

- Look in and around all the vehicles. Count the number injured and what you think the injuries are. Render all reasonable assistance.
- If possible, send a bystander to get help. Dial 000 and ask for the Police and Ambulance if anyone is injured or killed. Ensure the location information that you give to the emergency operator is as accurate as possible to avoid delays. Tell the operator the number of injured and details of their injuries.
- Only remove injured people from vehicles if they are in further danger (danger of fire, explosion, traffic, etc.).
- If there is no further danger, ask people to stay in their cars.

If no one is injured:

- Call the police immediately if a person fails to stop or exchange information or a driver may be under the influence of alcohol or drugs.
- Report the accident to the police within 24 hours if you think the total damage exceeds the set limit in that state or territory (see State by State Comparison on page xi).

If the police are not in attendance:

- Don't admit to liability.
- Note the accident details, including:
  - The date, time and place of the accident and road and weather conditions at the time.
  - The estimated speed of vehicles.
  - A description of the damage and injuries sustained.
  - A diagram showing the positions of the vehicles before and after the collision.
  - The full name and address of the drivers and owners of the vehicles and the registration numbers. Give your details to any person involved in the accident or who has reasonable grounds for requiring such information (eg. injured person, witness acting on behalf of an injured person, person whose property has been damaged, etc.).
  - The names and addresses of as many witnesses as possible.
  - The state of any property involved and the owner's name.
- Remove all debris from the road.
- Remember, all accidents in some states and territories have to be reported.

Emergency Vehicles

On the approach of an emergency vehicle with its warning siren sounding (irrespective of whether the flashing lights are also operating), drivers and pedestrians are required to give way and ensure that the emergency vehicle is provided with a clear, uninterrupted passage.

Remember:
- Don't panic.
- Check where the emergency vehicle is coming from.
- Move to the left if you can.
- If you cannot move left, slow down or stop, even if you have a green light. Don't block off the emergency vehicle's route. Continue ahead until you can pull over to provide it with a clear passage.

Take it easy on the roads! Photo: Rob van Driesum

Insurance

Report to your insurance company as soon as possible. It is a good idea to ask the other drivers about their level of insurance coverage, however, an insurance policy may be voided if the vehicle is modified or the driver of the vehicle was driving under the influence of alcohol or drugs. Insurance coverage has four basic levels:

- all vehicles must have Compulsory Third Party, which covers death and injury claims for people other than the driver;
- Third Party Property covers other people's property;
- Third Party Property (Fire and Theft) covers other people's property and also covers your vehicle for fire damage or loss through theft; and
- Comprehensive covers other people's property and your property.

Animal Casualties

Take any action necessary to avoid an animal on the road but don't risk your own or another person's life for the sake of an animal. If you collide with an animal, try and lessen any suffering the animal may experience. If the animal has been killed, you should try to remove it from the road. Be careful as some native animals may have babies in their pouches. Contact the owner, Police or RSPCA if you hit a domestic animal. If any animal is hurt you should take it to the nearest vet or animal shelter.

Emergency First Aid

A rescuer should approach a road accident scene with caution to avoid personal risk.

Check for Danger
First, make a quick check for any danger to yourself, the accident victim, and any others in the area. Check for hazards such as fallen power lines, toxic fumes, leaking gas or traffic.

Make the area safe before attempting to assess the accident victim. If the victim is in a vehicle, turn off the engine and warn bystanders not to light cigarettes. Do not move any victim unless unconscious or it is essential to do so for safety. If moving the victim is essential, protect any obvious injuries.

Call for emergency personnel by dialling 000. If there is no mobile phone or bystander, stay with the victim and shout loudly to attract attention.

A motorcycle helmet should only be removed if absolutely necessary eg. if it is obstructing an unconscious person's breathing. A conscious person may be able to safely remove the helmet unaided.

Check the Victim's Response
When it is safe, quickly check the victim. First, check whether the victim is conscious. Speak loudly to the victim and give a gentle shake of the shoulder. Ask, "Can you hear me?" or "Squeeze my hand and let it go." If the victim does not respond to your voice or touch, assume unconsciousness and follow the **ABC** of resuscitation:

A – Clear and open the **Airway**.

B – Check for **Breathing** and be prepared to start resuscitation.

C – Check for **Circulation** and use heart-lung resuscitation if there are no signs of circulation.

Clear and Open the Airway
Open the victim's mouth and check for signs that the airway may be blocked. If there are signs that the airway might be blocked, turn the victim onto the side in the stable recovery position, clear the mouth of any food or fluids. Then, gently tilt back the head and support the jaw, keeping the face turned slightly downwards for drainage. If there are no signs that the airway might be blocked, leave the victim on their back.

Check for Breathing
Look, listen, and feel for signs of breathing. Look and feel over the lower ribs for any chest movement. Listen and feel for the escape of air from the mouth or nose. If there is no sign of breathing, resuscitation is needed. Begin mouth to mouth (or mouth to mask resuscitation if a mask is available) if you know how to do it. Otherwise, call for help from a trained bystander.

Give five initial breaths in about 10 seconds with the airway fully open, sealing the victim's nose with your cheek. Breathe into the victim until the chest is seen to rise. Allow the chest to empty whilst your mouth and nose are turned to the side to avoid the exhaled air.

- For an adult, give full breaths.
- For a baby, give five small puffs of air from your cheeks.
- For a child, give just enough breath to make the small chest rise.

Check for Signs of Circulation
After five breaths have been given, check:

- is the victim moving at all?
- is the victim breathing or gasping?
- is the victim's skin and face colour normal?
- does the victim have a pulse in the neck?

Campervan at Freycinet Peninsula, Tas (53 C14) Photo: Rob Boegheim

If there are signs of circulation, continue mouth to mouth resuscitation at the slower rate of 1 breath every 4 seconds for an adult, or 1 puff every 3 seconds for a baby. Recheck for signs of circulation every two minutes to be sure that the heart is still beating.

If there are no signs of circulation, begin cardiopulmonary resuscitation (CPR) if you have been trained. Recheck signs of circulation every 2 minutes to monitor progress.

Bleeding
Check for bleeding. Severe or continued bleeding may lead to collapse and death. Apply and maintain firm pressure over a sterile or clean bulky pad with your hand or fingers. A conscious victim can apply pressure to a wound if it can be reached. Use gloves if available.

- Assist the victim to lie down at total rest.
- If a limb is injured, raise the injured part and support as required.
- Loosen any tight clothing at neck and waist.
- Avoid all food, fluids, and stimulants in case an anaesthetic is needed.
- If bleeding shows through the bulky dressing, remove it and apply another sterile or clean bulky pad with more pressure. Do not cover up continuing bleeding with more padding.

Shock
An accident victim will always be shocked. In a serious injury, the shock will be severe.

Symptoms and signs of shock are:
- pale, cold and clammy skin
- extreme thirst
- giddy spells and/or fainting
- a weak, rapid pulse
- nausea or vomiting

Internal bleeding should be suspected if the victim's pulse is getting faster and weaker. Do not give any food, fluids, or stimulants. Where possible, the conscious victim should be assisted to lie down in the most comfortable position with all injured parts supported. If injuries permit, raise both legs to boost the circulation to the heart and brain. The unconscious victim should be placed in the Recovery Position. Protect the victim from heat or cold by placing a coat or blanket under and over the person.

If a limb or body part is out of alignment, do not try to replace it in its normal position but provide padding to support the injured part. Avoid any unnecessary movement and reassure the victim that an ambulance is coming.

Information supplied by Australian Red Cross. To know how to respond in a first aid emergency, Australian Red Cross recommends that you complete a first aid course. Call First Aid, Health & Safety Services on 1300 367 428.

Key map 1

Queensland

Lindeman Island (9 C8)

Distances are shown in kilometres and follow the most direct major sealed route

Bamaga	2712	2374	1000	2618	2712	2106	1743	2239	2077	2353	2702	1349	1926
Brisbane	361	1712	742	350	1172	969	1826	635	477	128	1363	1352
Bundaberg	1374	916	591	970	656	1624	297	651	412	1025	1150
Cairns	1618	1712	1111	743	1259	1077	1353	1702	349	931
Charleville	588	511	1039	1165	833	265	614	1269	691
Goondiwindi	1054	981	1708	647	359	222	1363	1234
Longreach	788	654	673	695	1044	762	180
Mackay	1289	334	774	971	394	968
Mount Isa	1327	1349	1694	895	474
Rockhampton	568	637	728	853
Roma	349	1004	875
Toowoomba	1353	1224
Townsville	582
Winton	

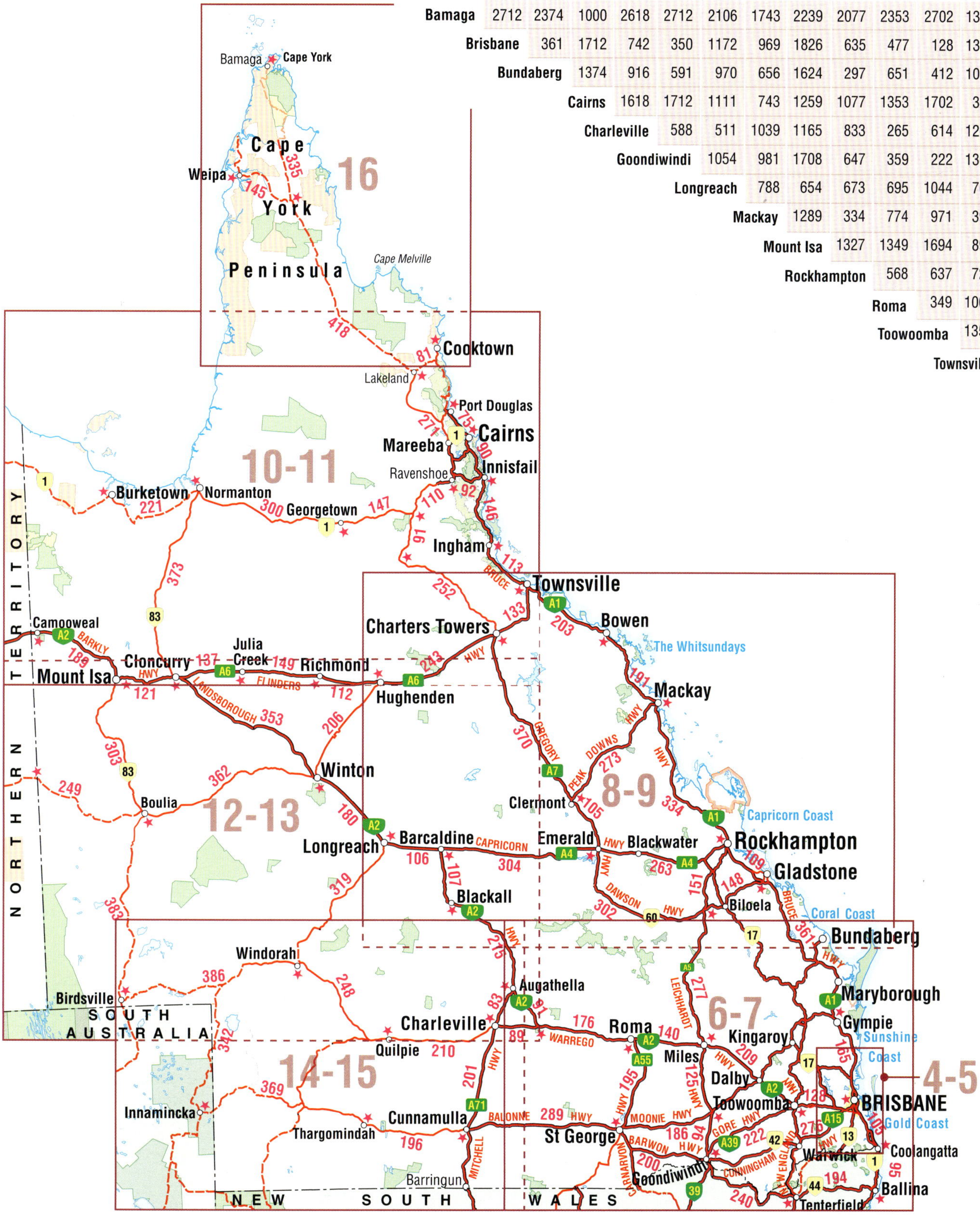

Brisbane CBD

Places of Interest
1. Anzac Memorial B3
2. Botanic Gardens C3
3. Brisbane Convention & Exhib Ctr C2
4. City Hall B2
5. Conrad Treasury Casino C2
6. Customs House B3
7. King George Square B2
8. Old Government House C3
9. Old Windmill Observatory B2
10. Performing Arts Complex C2
11. Queen Street Mall C2
12. Queensland Art Gallery C2
13. Queensland Cultural Centre C2
14. Queensland Museum C2
15. Queensland University of Tech C3
16. South Bank C2
17. St Johns Cathedral B3
18. St Stephens Cathedral B3
19. State Library of Queensland C2
20. Suncorp Entertainment Piazza C2
21. Victoria Army Barracks B1

Accommodation
30. Albert Park Hotel A2
31. Bridgewater Quest Apts B4
32. Brisbane Marriott B3
33. Carlton Crest Hotel B2
34. Centrepoint Apartments C2
35. City Backpackers B1
36. Dockside Apartment Hotel C4
37. Goodearth Hotel B2
38. Hilton Brisbane B3
39. Holiday Inn Hotel Brisbane B2
40. Hotel Conrad C2
41. Hotel George Williams Bris B2
42. Hotel Grand Chancellor B2
43. Hotel Ibis Brisbane B2
44. Medina Executive Brisbane B3
45. Mercure Hotel Brisbane C2
46. Metro Inn Tower Mill B2
47. Novotel Brisbane B3
48. Pacific International Apartments B3
49. Palace Embassy Backpackers B3
50. Quay West Suites Brisbane C3
51. Oaks North Quay B1
52. Rendezvous Hotel B2
53. Riverside Hotel C1
54. Rothbury on Ann Hotel B3
55. Royal Albert Hotel C3
56. Royal on the Park C3
57. Rydges South Bank Hotel C2
58. Sofitel Brisbane Hotel B3
59. Stamford Plaza Brisbane C3
60. Summit Central Apartments B2
61. The Astor Apartments B2
62. The Astor Metropole Motel B2
63. The Chifley on George C2
64. The Chifley on Lennons C2
65. The Manor Apartment Hotel B3
66. The Point Brisbane C4
67. The Sebel Suites Brisbane C3

LEGEND
- Freeway
- Metroad
- Highway
- Major Road
- Minor Road
- Lane / Path
- Railway, Station — Roma St
- Busway, Station — Underground
- Major Building
- Govt Building
- Accommodation
- Theatre/Cinema
- Shopping
- Church
- Hospital
- Ferry Route

© Hema Maps Pty Ltd

Brisbane Throughroads

4 Brisbane Region, Queensland

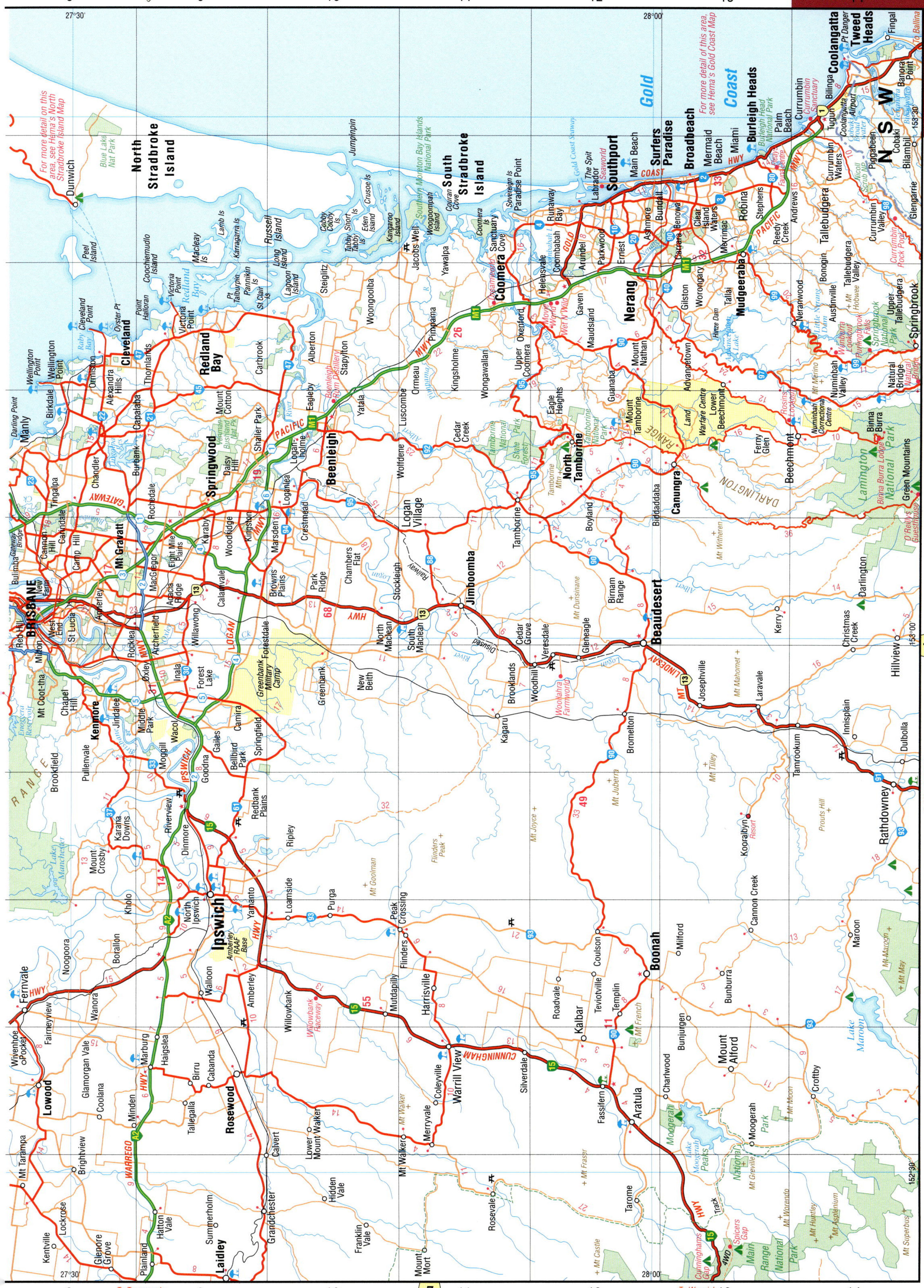

QLD
N S W
BRISBANE
Ipswich
Beenleigh
Beaudesert
Jimboomba
Logan Village
Springwood
Cleveland
Redland Bay
Coomera
Nerang
Mudgeeraba
Southport
Surfers Paradise
Broadbeach
Burleigh Heads
Coolangatta
Tweed Heads
Canungra
North Tamborine
Beechmont
Springbrook
Boonah
Kalbar
Aratula
Rosewood
Laidley
Lowood
Fernvale
Rathdowney
Warrill View
Harrisville
North Stradbroke Island
South Stradbroke Island
Gold Coast
For more detail on this area, see Hema's North Stradbroke Island Map
For more detail of this area, see Hema's Gold Coast Map
PACIFIC MWY
GATEWAY MWY
LOGAN MWY
IPSWICH MWY
CUNNINGHAM HWY
WARREGO HWY
MT LINDESAY HWY
To Toowoomba
To Warwick
To Woodenbong
To Murwillumbah
To Ballina

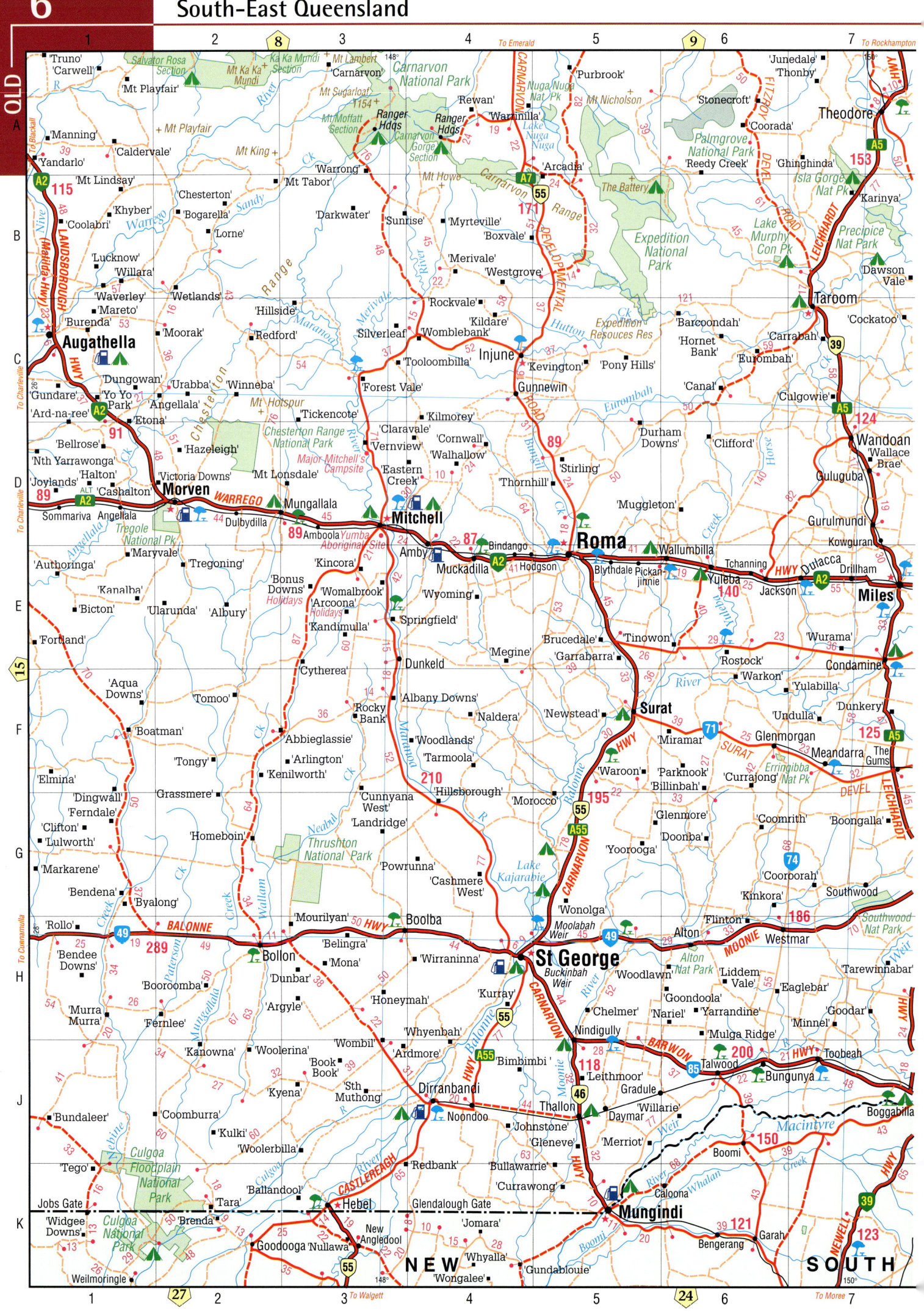

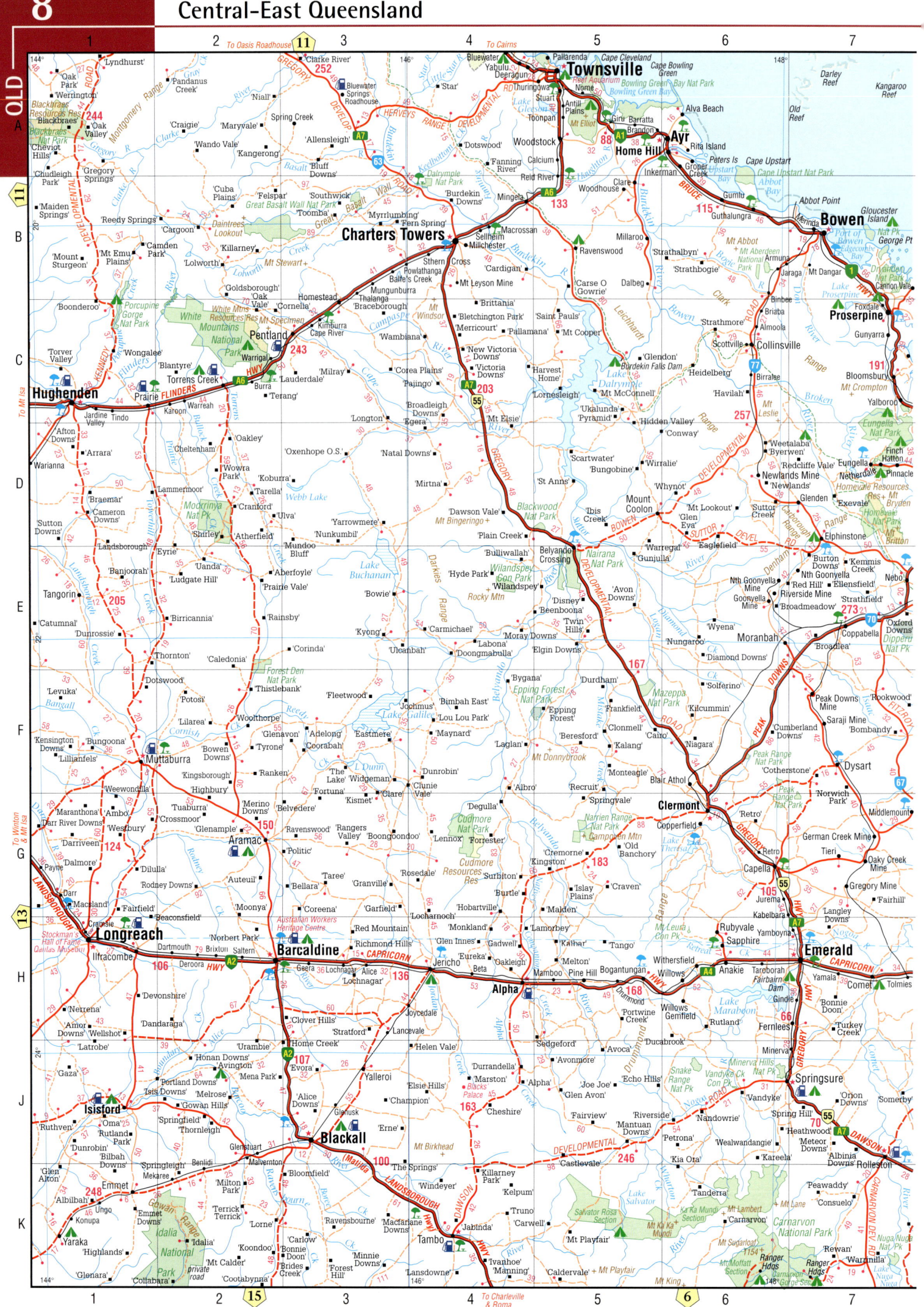

N
0
50
100km
© Hema Maps Pty Ltd
150°
152°
20°
22°
24°
Great Barrier Reef
CORAL SEA
SOUTH PACIFIC OCEAN
GREAT BARRIER REEF MARINE PARK
Mackay / Capricorn Section
TROPIC OF CAPRICORN
For more detail on this area, see Hema's Central Queensland Map
Wallaby Reef
Hardy Reef
Black Reef East
Hook Reef
Marion Reef
Hayman Island
Hook Island
WHITSUNDAY GROUP
Border Island
Whitsunday Island
The Whitsundays
Whitsunday Islands Nat Park
Airlie Beach
Shute Harbour
Hazelwood Island
Hamilton Island
Conway Nat Pk
Long Island
Lindeman Island
Lindeman Islands Nat Park
Conway Beach
Shaw Island
Repulse Bay
Laguna Quays
Midge Point
Blacksmith Is
Smith Islands Nat Park
Goldsmith Is
Linne Island
Wigton Island
Rabbit Is
Carlisle Is
Cockermouth Is
Calder Is
Newry Is
Brampton Is
Sth Cumberland Islands Nat Park
Calen
Seaforth
C Hillsborough NP
Scawfell Is
St Bees Is
Mt Ossa
Sand Bay
Bucasia
Eimeo
Kuttabul
Farleigh
Slade Point
Gargett
Marian
Mackay
Sandringham Bay
Mirani
Walkerston
Bakers Creek
Eton
Hay Point
Prudhoe Is
Homebush
Grasstree
Campwin Beach
NORTHUMBERLAND ISLANDS Nat Park
Hannaville
Knight Is
Digby Is
Hotspur Island
Shinfield
Sarina
Llewellyn Bay
Inco Bay
Pine Peak Island
Epsom
Coulston Park
Yukan
Cape Palmerston
Cape Palmerston Nat Park
'Strathdee'
Koumala
Temple Is
Curlew Is
Middle Island
Percy Isles NP
North East Island
PERCY ISLES
South Island
Greenhill
Koumala South
Ilbilbie
Yarrawonga Point
West Hill
West Hill Is
West Hill Nat Park
Poynter Island
Orkabie
Bamborough Is
Carmila
Carmila Beach
Aquila Is
Wild Duck Is
DUKE ISLANDS
Flaggy Rock
Broad Sound Is
'Collaroy'
Elalie
North Pt
Marble Is
High Peak Island
Long Island
Quail Is
Hexham Is
Cheviot Island
'Morpeth'
'Cardowan'
Clairview
Kalarka
Clairview Bluff
Arthur Pt
Broad Sound Channel
Stanage
Shoalwater Bay
Collins Is
Con Pk
Cape Townshend
Townshend Island
Leicester Is
Reef Point
Torilla
Broad Sound
St Lawrence
Rosewood Is
'Batheaston'
'Croydon'
Wumalgi
Shoalwater Bay
Peninsula
Warginburra Peninsula
Pearl Bay
Perforated Point
Port Clinton
Cape Clinton
Freshwater Bay
Cliff Point
Double Mtn
SHOALWATER BAY MILITARY TRAINING AREA
'May Downs'
Ogmore
Bowman
Kooltandra
Mt O'Connell NP
Cape Manifold
Tooloombah
Marlborough
Princhester
Stockyard Point
Byfield
Byfield National Park
Water Park Point
Junee Nat Park
'Junee'
'Eden Garry'
Kunawarara
'Barwon Park'
'Royles'
'Apis Creek'
Goodedulla Nat Park
Corio Bay
Capricorn
Capricorn Resort
North Keppel Island
Keppel Bay Islands Nat Park
'Kaiuroo'
Mt Etna Caves Nat Park
Yeppoon
Yaamba
The Caves
Roslyn Bay
Great Keppel Island
'Burkan'
Ridgelands
Cawarral
Capricorn Coast Nat Park
Emu Park
Coast
North Reef
Tryon Is
Wilson Is
Parkhurst
Mt Archer NP
Keppel Sands
North West Is
Wreck Island Scientific
CAPRICORN
Heron Island
Capricorn Cays
'Cooroorah'
Taunton Nat Park
Dalma
Bedford Weir
'Melmoth'
Foleyvale
Gracemere
Kabra
Rockhampton
Cape Keppel
Cape Capricorn
Erskine Is
GROUP
'Curragh'
Blackwater
Stanwell
Flat Top Resources Res
Keppel Bay
Broadmount
Curtis Is Nat Park
Curtis Island
Masthead Is
One Tree Island National Park
Bluff
Parnabal
Wycarbah
Westwood
Bouldercombe
Fitzroy Reef
Dingo
Duaringa
Mount Morgan
Port Alma
Black Head
Llewellyn Reef
Blackdown Tableland Nat Park
Gogango
Bajool
Baldercombe Gorge Resources Res
Marmor
Raglan
Port Curtis
Hoskyn Islands Scientific
'Eastbrook'
Ambrose
Southend
Facing Island
South Blackwater Mine
Wowan
Dululu
Mount Larcom
Yarwun
Gladstone
BUNKER GROUP
Fairfax Islands Scientific
Lady Musgrave Island
Mt Alma
'Lancefield'
Boyne Island
Tannum Sands
Benaraby
Richards Point
Bustard Point
'Woorona'
Deeford
Rodds Bay
Turkey Beach
'Perch Ck'
Rannes
Calliope
Taragoola
Barmundu
Rodds Bay
Avoondal
Eurimbula Nat Park
Bustard Bay
Woorabinda
Kokotungo
Goovigen
Iveragh
Round Hill Head
Joseph Banks (Round Hill Head) Con Park
Lady Elliot Island
Baralaba
Jambin
Callide
Boynedale
Boroorén
Seventeen Seventy
Agnes Water
'Mimosa Park'
Callide Coalfields
'Bindawalla'
Castle Tower Nat Park
'Goomally'
Weitalaba
Nagoorin
Miriam Vale
Deepwater Nat Park
Callide Dam
Ubobo
Mt Colosseum Nat Park
'Barranga'
Biloela
Thangool
Kroombit Tops National Park
'Planet Downs'
Banana
Littlemore
Bulyan
Makowata
Lowmead
Rules Beach
Wartburg
Bauhinia
Moura
Dawes Range
Many Peaks
Lake Cania
Winfield
Berajondo
Littabella Nat Park
'Bauhinia Downs'
Cania Gorge Nat Park
Mt Molangul
Kalpowar
Norval Park
Rosedale
Watalgan
Klanga
'Junedale'
'Thonby'
'Kurrajong'
Moonford
Mungungo
Kolan
Yandaran
Miara
Moore Park
'Purbrook'
Burnett Heads
Sandy Cape
Fraser Island
Monduran Dam
Avondale
Bancroft
Bargara
Coral Coast
HERVEY BAY MARINE PARK
Mt Nicholson
'Stonecroft'
'Glandore'
Three Moon
Monto
Mulgildie
South Kolan
Bundaberg
Rooney Pt
Rum Distillery
Marloo Bay
Palmgrove National Park
'Coorada'
Theodore
Camboon
Rawbelle
Bullyard
Elliott Heads
Orchid Beach
Platypus Bay
Waddy Point
Expedition Nat Park
Gin Gin
Elliott
To Miles
To Brisbane
To Brisbane
POMPEY COMPLEX
Ripetide Cay
Elusive Reef
Thomas Cay
SWAIN REEFS National Park
Gannet Cay
Capricorn Channel
Curtis Channel
Connors Range
Broadsound Range
Boomer Range
Dawson Range
Expedition Range
Shotover Range
Auburn Range
Burnett Range
Bruce Hwy
Developmental Road
Fitzroy Devel Road
Dawson Hwy
Leichhardt Hwy
Burnett Hwy
Capricorn Hwy
Goowarra
Tryphinia
Boolburra
Edungalba
A1
A3
A4
A5
16
17
39
60
7
229
263
105
109
145
102
166
162
97
46

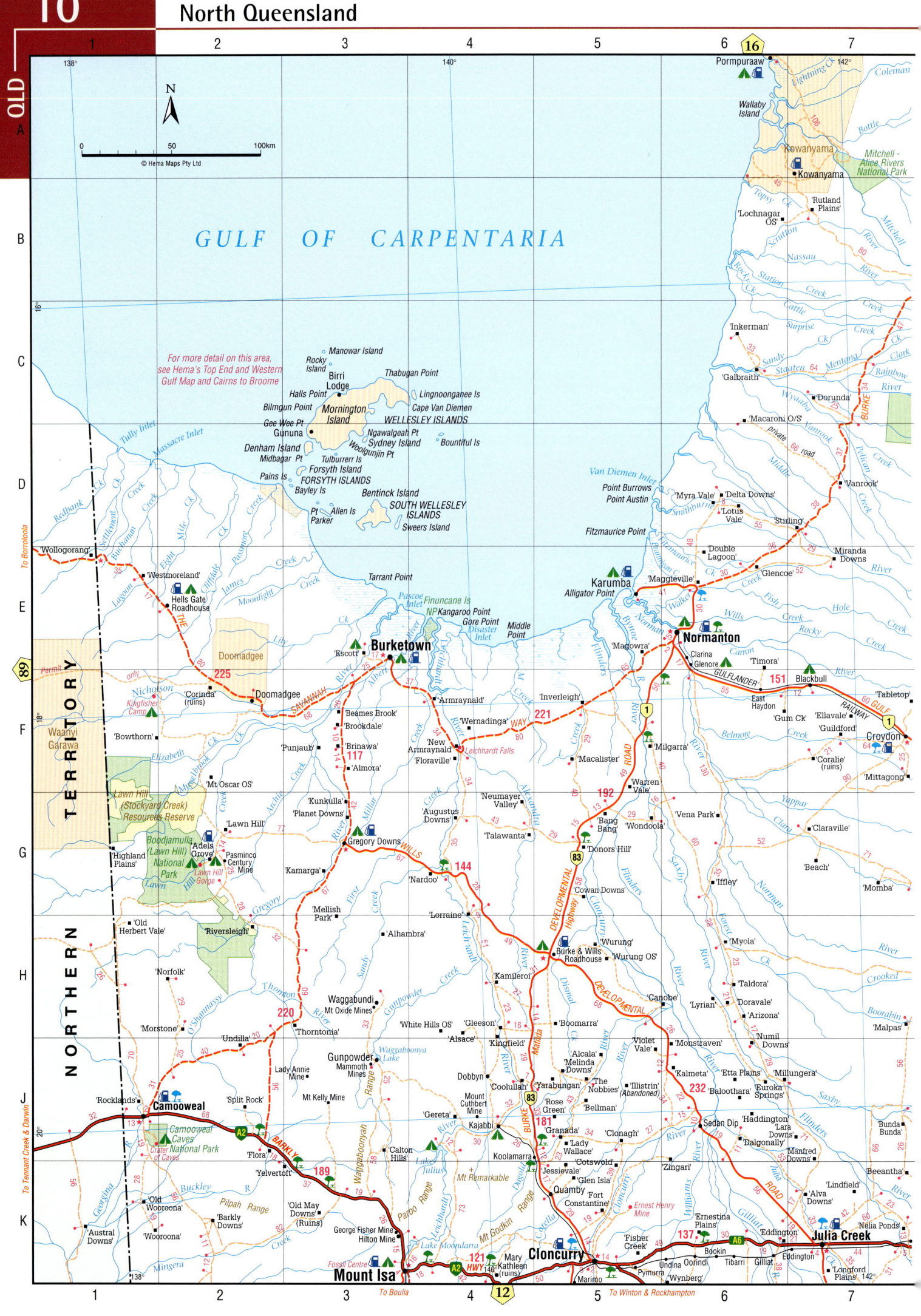

To Weipa & Cape York
CORAL SEA
GREAT BARRIER REEF MARINE PARK
Cairns Section
Great Barrier Reef
Ribbon Reef
For more detail on this area, see Hema's Townsville - Cairns - Cooktown, North Queensland, Cairns to Cooktown, Cairns to Broome and Atherton Tableland Maps
Cape Flattery
Starcke
Cape Bedford
Hope Vale
Cooktown
Lakefield National Park
Hann River Roadhouse
Laura
Old Laura
Agayna-Timara Ab Land Trust
Split Rock Art
Wulburjubur Aboriginal Land Trust
Palmer Goldfield Resources Res
Palmerville
Maytown (ruins)
Lakeland
Rossville
Helenvale
Archer Point
Walker Bay
Cruiser Pass
Papuan Pass
Obree Point
Cedar Bay Nat Park
Rattlesnake Point
Weary Bay
Bloomfield
Wujal Wujal
Daintree Nat Park
Cape Tribulation
Noah Beach
Thornton Beach
Alexandra Bay
Bailey Point
Cape Kimberley
Tongue Reef
Daintree
Wonga Beach
Low Isles
Mossman
Newell
Port Douglas
Trinity Opening
Michaelmas & Upolu Cays Nat Park
Arlington Reef
Mt Carbine
Maryfarms
Rumula
Craiglie
Oak Beach
Wangetti
Julatten
Mount Molloy
Palm Cove
Trinity Beach
Yorkeys Knob
Green Island Nat Park
Clifton Beach
Kuranda
Cairns
Cape Grafton
Yarrabah
Moore Reef
Fitzroy Island Nat Park
Sudbury Reef
Mareeba
Redlynch
Edmonton
Gordonvale
Grey Peaks Nat Park
Biboohra
Kingsborough
Dimbulah
Mutchilba
Walkamin
Atherton
Tolga
Yungaburra
Malanda
Herberton
High Island
Russell River Nat Park
Babinda
Bellenden Ker
Bramston Beach
Eubenangee Swamp Nat Park
Ella Bay Nat Park
Innisfail
Howie Reef
Etty Bay
Mourilyan Harbour
Mourilyan
Moresby
Cowley
Kurrimine Beach Nat Park
Kurrimine
Bingil Bay
Mission Beach
Dunk Island
Family Islands Nat Park
Bedarra Is
Hull Heads
Tully Heads
Tully
Silky Oak
Euramo
Murrigal
Edmund Kennedy Nat Park
Rockingham Bay
Kennedy
Cardwell
Goold Island Nat Park
Cape Richards
Cape Sandwich
Britomart Reef
Trunk Reef
Hinchinbrook Island Nat Park
Hillock Point
Abergowrie
Lucinda
Halifax
Pelorus Island
Orpheus Is Nat Park
Curacoa Island
Great Palm Island
Havannah Island
Halifax Bay Wetlands NP
Halifax Bay
Ingham
Trebonne
Toobanna
Forrest Beach
Bambaroo
Mutarnee
Moongobulla
Rollingstone
Magnetic Is Nat Park
Toomulla
Toolakea
Saunders Beach
Yabulu
Pallarenda
Deeragun
Thuringowa
Townsville
Stuart
Toonpan
Antill Plains
Woodstock
Calcium
Reid River
Mingela
Ravenswood
Charters Towers
Macrossan
Sellheim
Millchester
Fern Spring
Myrrlumbing
Dalrymple Nat Park
Burdekin Downs
Great Basalt Wall Nat Park
Pentland
Torrens Creek
Prairie
Hughenden
Richmond
Fossil Centre
Maxwelton
Gemoka
Nonda
Nelia
Warreah
Burra
Terang
Lauderdale
Kimburra
Cape River
White Mountains National Park
Porcupine Gorge Nat Park
Warrigal
Homestead
Mt Specimen
Mungunburra
Thalanga
Braceborough
Windsor
Pajingo
Powlathanga
Balfe's Creek
Sthern Cross
Mt Leyson Mine
Dotswood
Fanning River
Bluewater
Bluewater Springs Roadhouse
Spring Creek
Allensleigh
Clarke River
Greenvale
Christmas Creek
Camel Creek
Valley of Lagoons
Conjuboy
Spring Creek
The Lynd Junction
Oasis Roadhouse
The Lynd
Kidston
Einasleigh
Forsayth
Georgetown
Mt Surprise
Undara Volcanic Nat Pk
Mount Surprise
Forty Mile Scrub National Park
Mount Garnet
Innot Hot Springs
Ravenshoe
Millstream Falls Nat Pk
Tully Falls
Koombooloomba
Tumoulin
Kaban
Millaa Millaa
Ravenshoe
Chillagoe
Chillagoe-Mungana Caves Nat Park
Mungana
Almaden
Petford
Irvinebank
Emuford
Koorboora
Lappa
Mutchilba
Bulleringa National Park
Staaten River National Park
Tate River Tin Mine
Lyndbrook
Gilbert River
Mt Turner
Chadshunt
Durham
Einasleigh
Cobbold Gorge
Agate Creek Gemfields
Blackbraes Resources Res
Blackbraes Nat Park
Gregory Springs
Daintrees Lookout
Mt Stewart
Dunbar
Koolatah
Highbury
Gamboola
Wrotham Park
Bellevue
Sefton
Oroners OS
Kimba
Pinnacles
Fairlight
Jowalbinna
Ruth Creek Hut
Crocodile
Butchers Hill
Bonnyglen
Mt Mulgrave
St George O/S
Karma Waters
Hurricane
Nychum
Marble Creek
Mt Mulligan
Rookwood
Blackdown
Bolwarra
Torwood
Fischerton
Minnies OS
Abingdon Downs
Strathmore
Wallabadah OS
Inorunie
Lake Carlo
Ashvale
Esmeralda
Prospect
Glenora
Dumas
Agantra
Victoria Vale
Woodstock
Pelham (Abandoned)
Strathpark
Etheldale
Saxby Downs
Solway Downs
Somerville
Bylong
Runnymead
Rockvale
Molesworth
Cambridge Ruins
Burleigh
Olga Downs
Cambridge Downs
Silver Hills
Doncaster
Charlotte Plains
Dalkeith
Walkcege
Boonderoo
Torver Valley
Rokeby
Wongalee
Blantyre
Lolworth
Camden Park
Mt Emu Plains
Mount Sturgeon
Reedy Springs
Cargoon
Killarney
Kangerong
Wando Vale
Craigie
Cheviot Hills
Chudleigh Park
Gorge Ck
Oak Valley
Maiden Springs
Hampstead
Mount Norman
Middle Park
Elmore
Coalbrook
FLINDERS HWY
KENNEDY HWY
GREGORY DEVELOPMENTAL ROAD
PENINSULA DEVELOPMENTAL ROAD
BURKE DEVELOPMENTAL ROAD
HERVEYS RANGE DEVELOP RD
BRUCE HWY
To Winton
To Emerald
To Mackay
8 9 10 11 12 13 14
A B C D E F G H J K

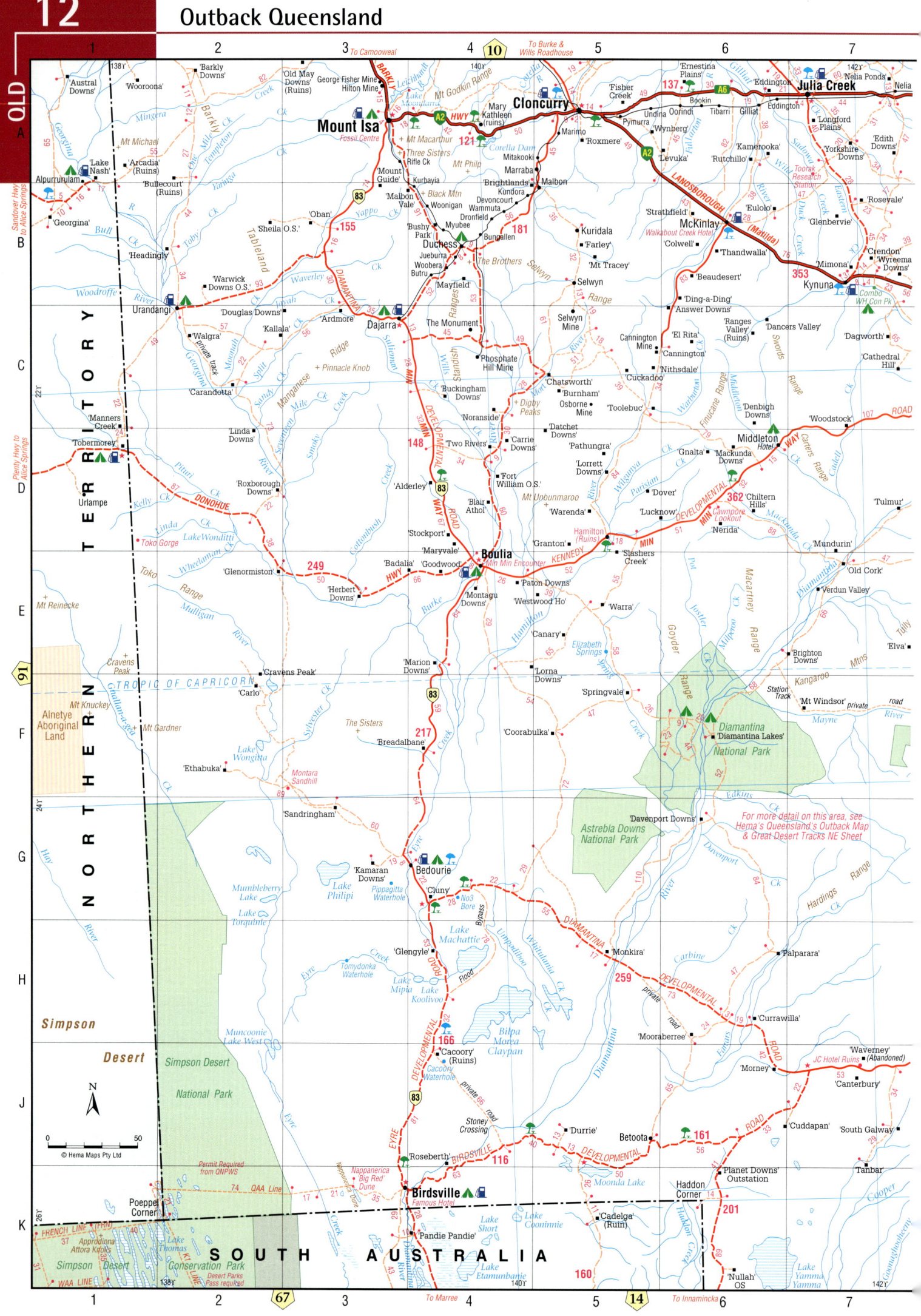

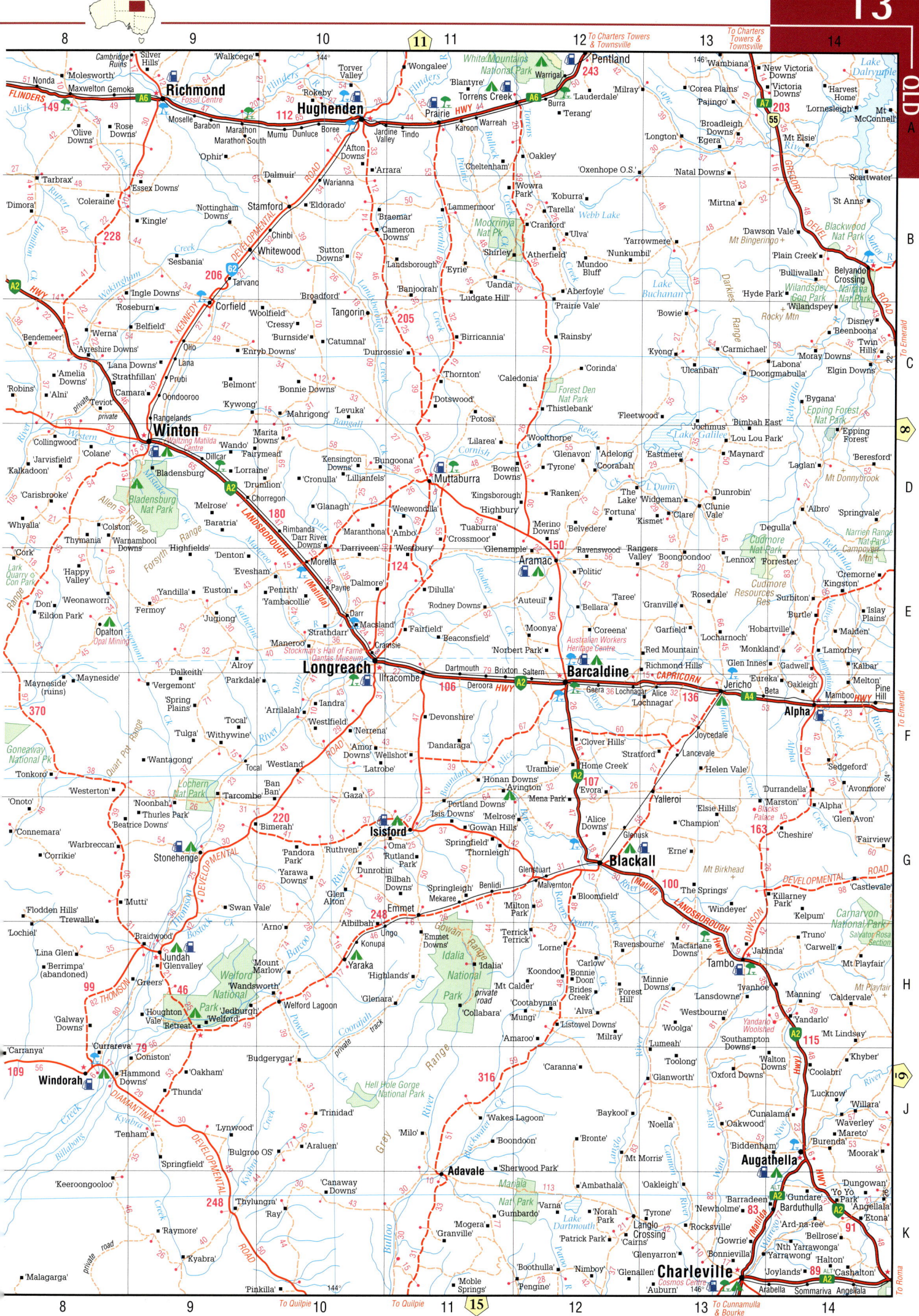

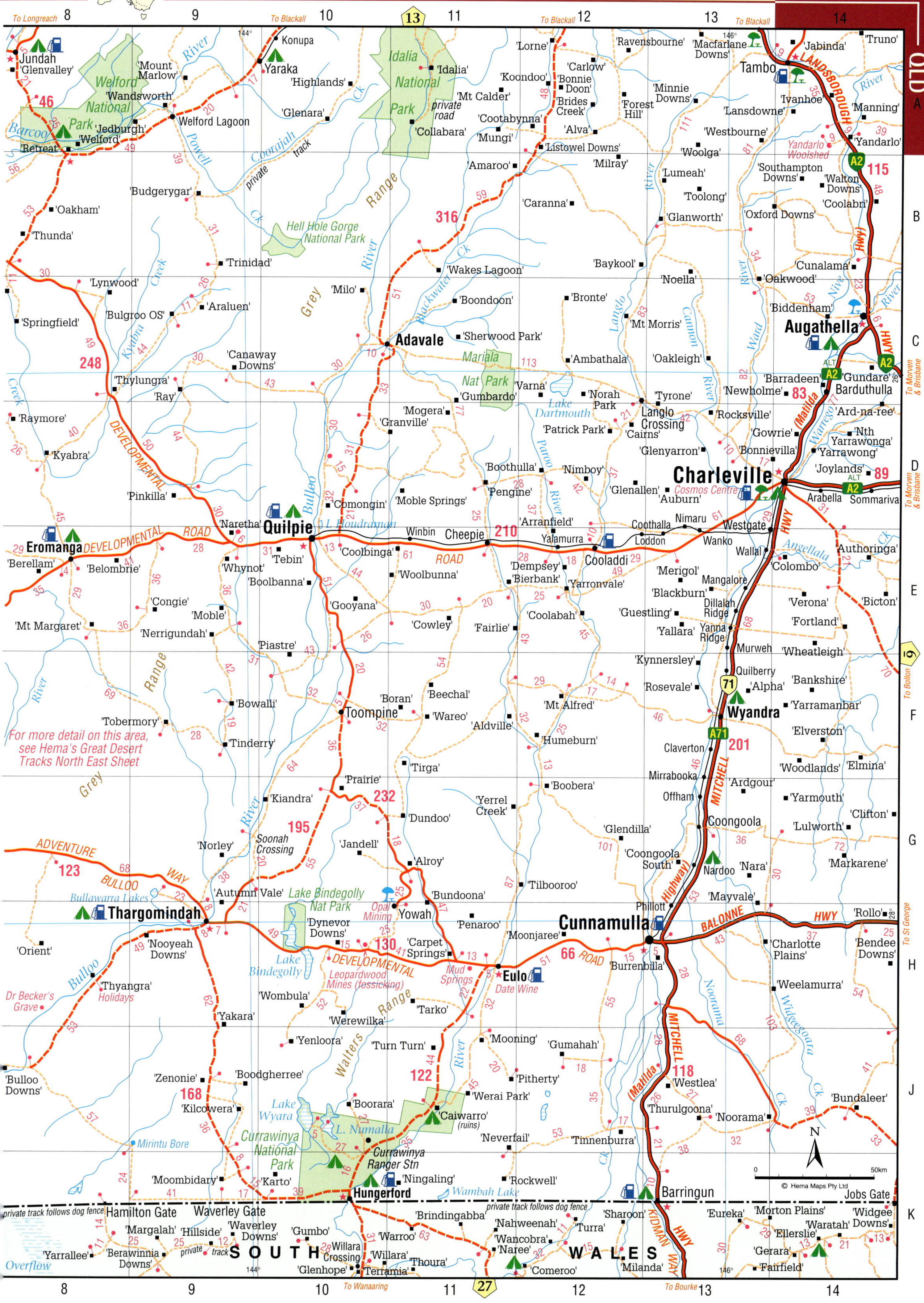
To Longreach
To Blackall
To Blackall
To Blackall
8
9
10
11
12
13
14
13
A
B
C
D
E
F
G
H
J
K
Jundah
'Glenvalley'
Welford National Park
'Mount Marlow'
'Wandsworth'
'Jedburgh'
'Welford'
'Retreat'
Barcoo
Welford Lagoon
Konupa
Yaraka
'Highlands'
'Glenara'
Idalia National Park
'Idalia'
'Mt Calder'
private road
'Collabara'
'Lorne'
'Koondoo'
'Carlow'
'Bonnie Doon'
'Brides Creek'
'Cootabynna'
'Mungi'
'Alva'
'Listowel Downs'
'Ravensbourne'
'Macfarlane Downs'
'Minnie Downs'
'Forest Hill'
'Milray'
Tambo
'Jabinda'
'Truno'
LANDSBOROUGH
'Ivanhoe'
'Lansdowne'
'Manning'
'Westbourne'
'Woolga'
Yandarlo Woolshed
'Yandarlo'
'Southampton Downs'
'Walton Downs'
'Coolabri'
'Oxford Downs'
A2
115
'Amaroo'
'Lumeah'
'Toolong'
'Glanworth'
'Caranna'
'Budgerygar'
Coorajah
private track
Powell
Range
'Oakham'
'Thunda'
Hell Hole Gorge National Park
316
'Trinidad'
'Wakes Lagoon'
Blackwater Ck
'Baykool'
'Noella'
'Cunalama'
'Oakwood'
'Lynwood'
'Springfield'
'Araluen'
'Bulgroo OS'
'Milo'
Grey
'Boondoon'
'Bronte'
'Mt Morris'
'Biddenham'
Augathella
248
'Canaway Downs'
Adavale
'Sherwood Park'
'Ambathala'
'Oakleigh'
Mariala Nat Park
'Varna'
'Gumbardo'
'Thylungra'
'Ray'
'Barradeen'
'Gundare'
'Newholme'
83
Barduthulla
To Morven & Brisbane
'Raymore'
'Mogera'
'Granville'
Lake Dartmouth
'Norah Park'
'Tyrone'
Langlo Crossing
'Cairns'
'Rocksville'
'Ard-na-ree'
'Patrick Park'
'Gowrie'
'Nth Yarrawonga'
'Yarrawong'
'Bonnievilla'
'Glenyarron'
'Kyabra'
DEVELOPMENTAL
'Boothulla'
'Nimboy'
Charleville
'Joylands'
89
Cosmos Centre
'Glenallen'
'Auburn'
Arabella
Sommariva
'Pinkilla'
'Comongin'
'Moble Springs'
'Pengine'
'Naretha'
Quilpie
L. Houdraman
'Arranfield'
Cootthalla
Nimaru
Westgate
Wanko
Winbin
Cheepie
210
Yalamurra
Loddon
Eromanga
DEVELOPMENTAL ROAD
'Berellam'
'Belombrie'
'Whynot'
'Tebin'
'Coolbinga'
ROAD
'Dempsey'
Cooladdi
'Merigol'
Wallal
'Colombo'
'Authoringa'
'Boolbanna'
'Woolbunna'
'Bierbank'
'Yarronvale'
'Blackburn'
Mangalore
'Verona'
'Bicton'
'Congie'
'Moble'
'Gooyana'
Dillalah Ridge
'Cowley'
'Coolabah'
'Guestling'
'Fortland'
'Mt Margaret'
'Nerrigundah'
'Fairlie'
'Yallara'
Yanna Ridge
'Piastre'
Murweh
'Wheatleigh'
'Kynnersley'
Quilberry
'Alpha'
'Bankshire'
'Beechal'
'Rosevale'
71
To Bollon
'Bowalli'
'Boran'
'Mt Alfred'
Wyandra
'Yarramanbar'
'Tobermory'
Toompine
'Wareo'
'Aldville'
'Elverston'
For more detail on this area, see Hema's Great Desert Tracks North East Sheet
'Tinderry'
'Humeburn'
Claverton
A71
201
'Woodlands'
'Elmina'
'Tirga'
Mirrabooka
'Prairie'
'Boobera'
'Ardgour'
'Kiandra'
232
'Yerrel Creek'
Offham
'Yarmouth'
MITCHELL
'Dundoo'
Coongoola
'Clifton'
195
'Glendilla'
'Lulworth'
Soonah Crossing
'Norley'
'Jandell'
'Coongoola South'
'Markarene'
ADVENTURE
123
BULLOO
WAY
'Alroy'
Nardoo
'Nara'
'Tilbooroo'
Highway
'Autumn Vale'
Lake Bindegolly Nat Park
'Bundoona'
'Mayvale'
Bullawarra Lakes
Thargomindah
Opal Mining
Yowah
Phillott
'Penaroo'
Cunnamulla
BALONNE
HWY
'Rollo'
To St George
'Dynevor Downs'
'Moonjaree'
'Orient'
'Nooyeah Downs'
130
'Carpet Springs'
DEVELOPMENTAL
66 ROAD
'Burrenbilla'
'Charlotte Plains'
'Bendee Downs'
Lake Bindegolly
Leopardwood Mines (fossicking)
Mud Springs
Eulo
Date Wine
'Thyangra' Holidays
'Weelamurra'
Dr Becker's Grave
'Wombula'
Range
'Tarko'
Nooraraa
Widgeegoara
'Yakara'
'Werewilka'
'Mooning'
'Gumahah'
'Yenloora'
Walters
'Turn Turn'
River
'Bulloo Downs'
'Zenonie'
'Boodgherree'
122
'Pitherty'
118
'Westlea'
168
'Werai Park'
'Bundaleer'
'Kilcowera'
Lake Wyara
'Boorara'
Caiwarro (ruins)
'Thurulgoona'
'Noorama'
Currawinya National Park
L. Numalla
'Neverfail'
'Tinnenburra'
Mirintu Bore
Currawinya Ranger Stn
N
0
50km
© Hema Maps Pty Ltd
'Moombidary'
'Karto'
'Ningaling'
'Rockwell'
Barringun
Jobs Gate
Hungerford
Wambah Lake
private track follows dog fence
Hamilton Gate
Waverley Gate
private track follows dog fence
'Brindingabba'
'Nahweenah'
'Sharoon'
'Turra'
'Eureka'
'Morton Plains'
'Widgee Downs'
'Waratah'
'Margalah'
'Hillside'
'Waverley Downs'
'Gumbo'
'Warroo'
'Wancobra'
KIDMAN
HWY
'Ellerslie'
'Yarrallee'
'Berawinnia Downs'
private track
SOUTH
Willara Crossing
'Willara'
'Naree'
WALES
'Gerara'
Overflow
'Glenhope'
'Terramia'
'Thoura'
'Comeroo'
'Milanda'
'Fairfield'
To Wanaaring
27
To Bourke
144°
146°

16 Cape York, Queensland

Katoomba Falls, Blue Mountains National Park (22 G7)

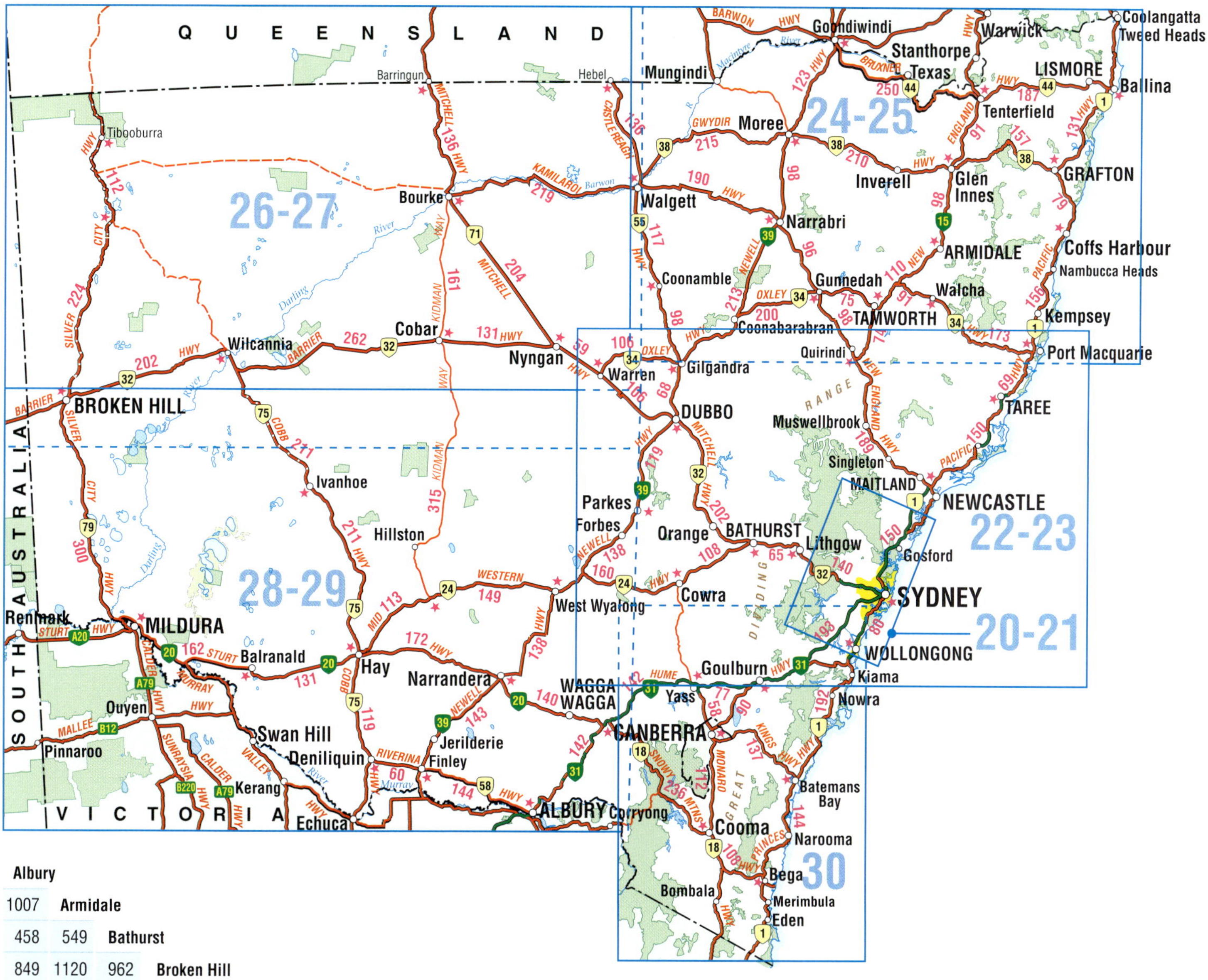

New South Wales

Key map **17**

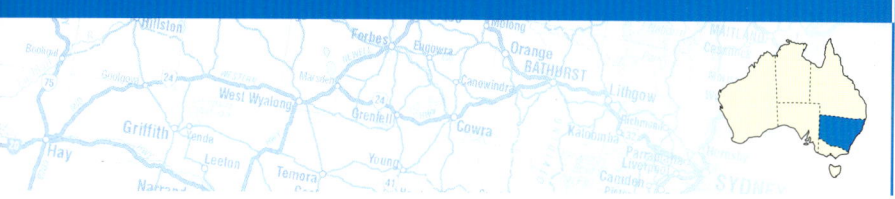

Albury													
1007	Armidale												
458	549	Bathurst											
849	1120	962	Broken Hill										
333	818	301	1096	Canberra									
548	432	202	760	403	Dubbo								
352	726	320	1115	92	422	Goulburn							
1184	194	743	1314	1044	626	797	Grafton						
1283	345	842	1413	1143	725	896	99	Lismore					
549	1244	823	300	882	812	901	1566	1665	Mildura				
709	329	322	1104	450	344	372	468	567	1192	Newcastle			
938	243	537	1313	665	547	572	237	336	1427	243	Port Macquarie		
545	465	205	1167	285	407	193	604	703	1028	164	379	Sydney	
902	105	444	1015	713	327	621	299	398	1139	277	276	413	Tamworth
136	871	322	860	236	412	255	1065	1164	560	644	859	448	766	Wagga Wagga
486	545	251	1218	226	458	134	684	783	949	244	473	80	440	389	Wollongong

Distances are shown in kilometres and assume the most direct major sealed route

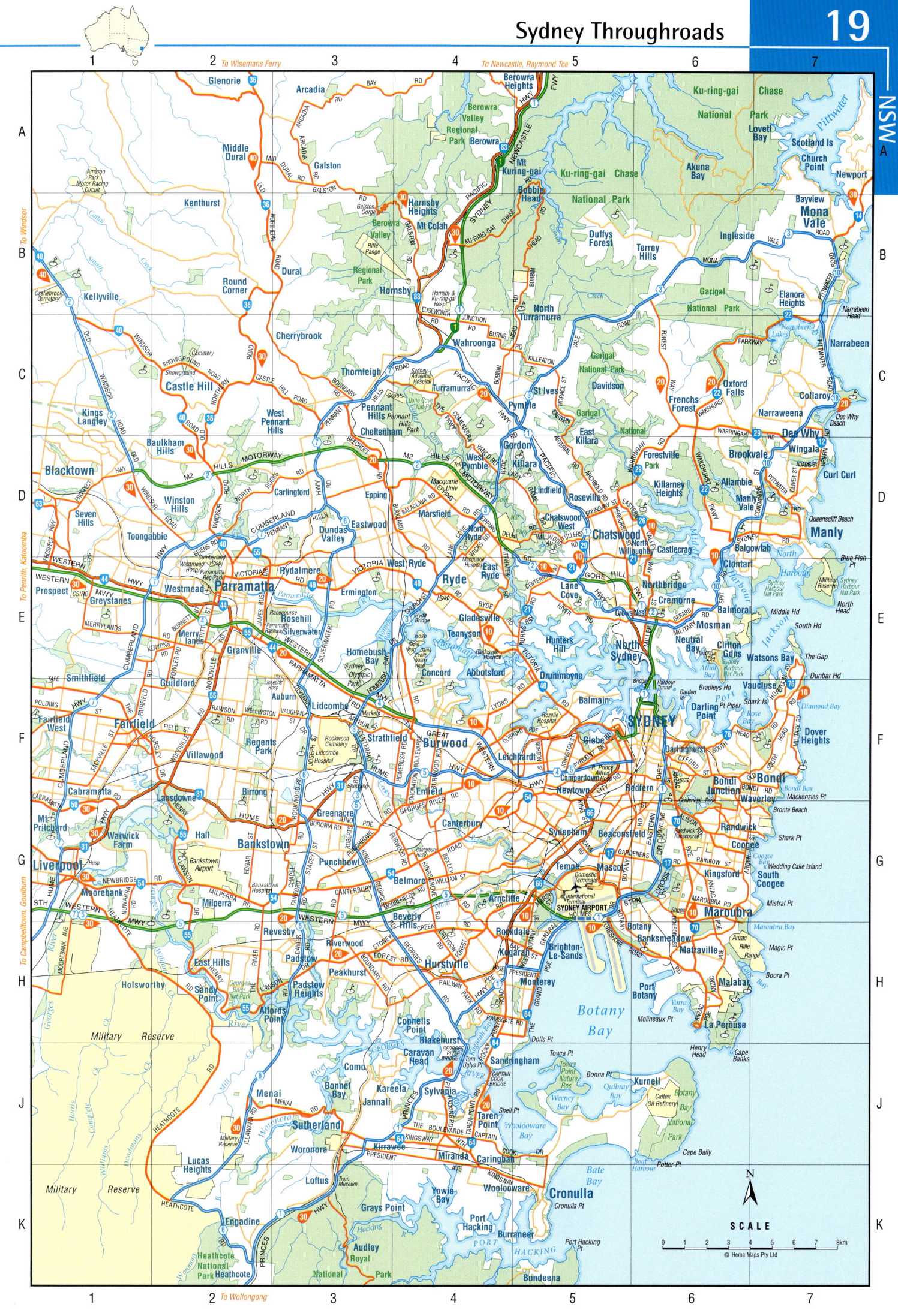

20 Sydney Region, New South Wales

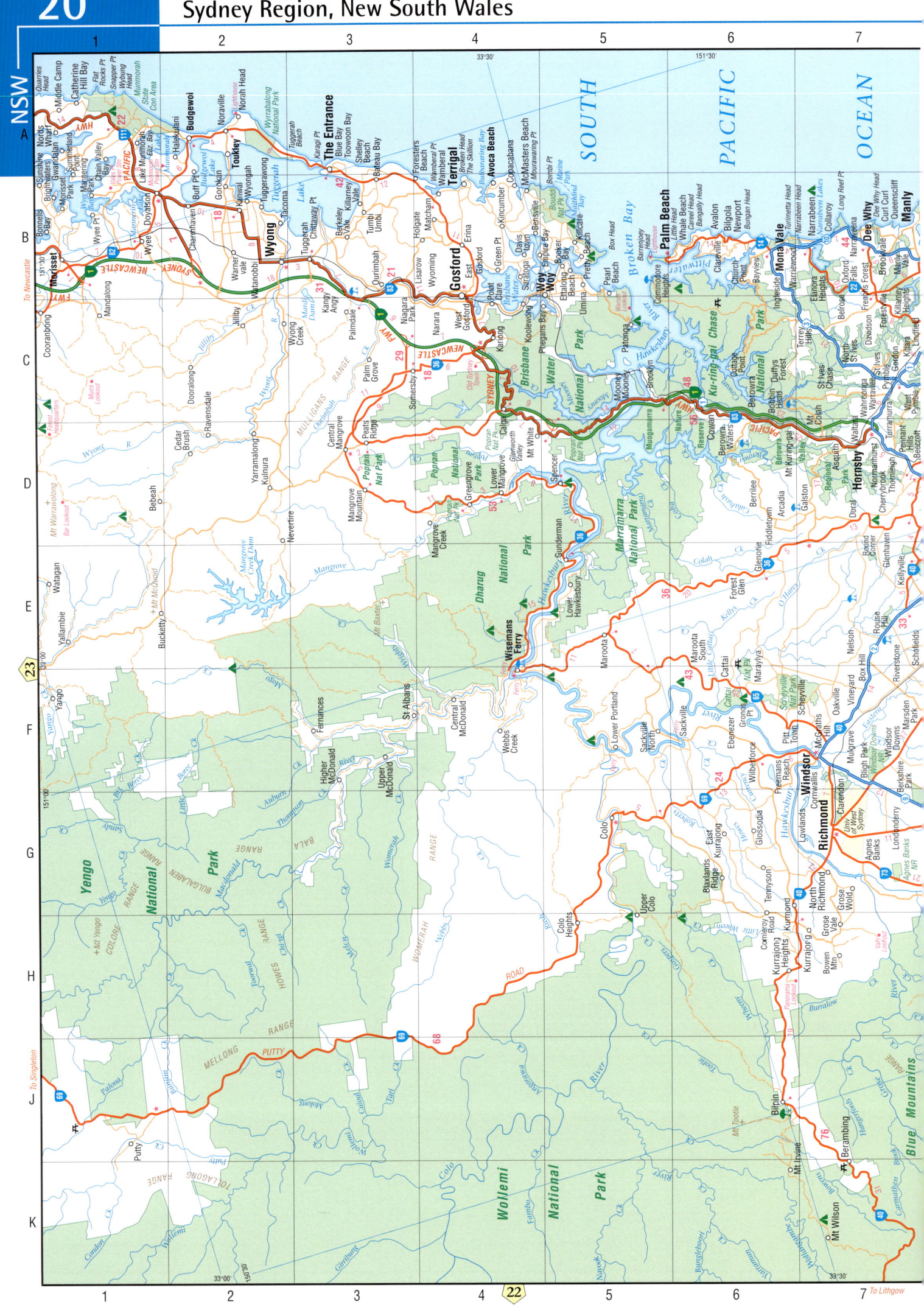

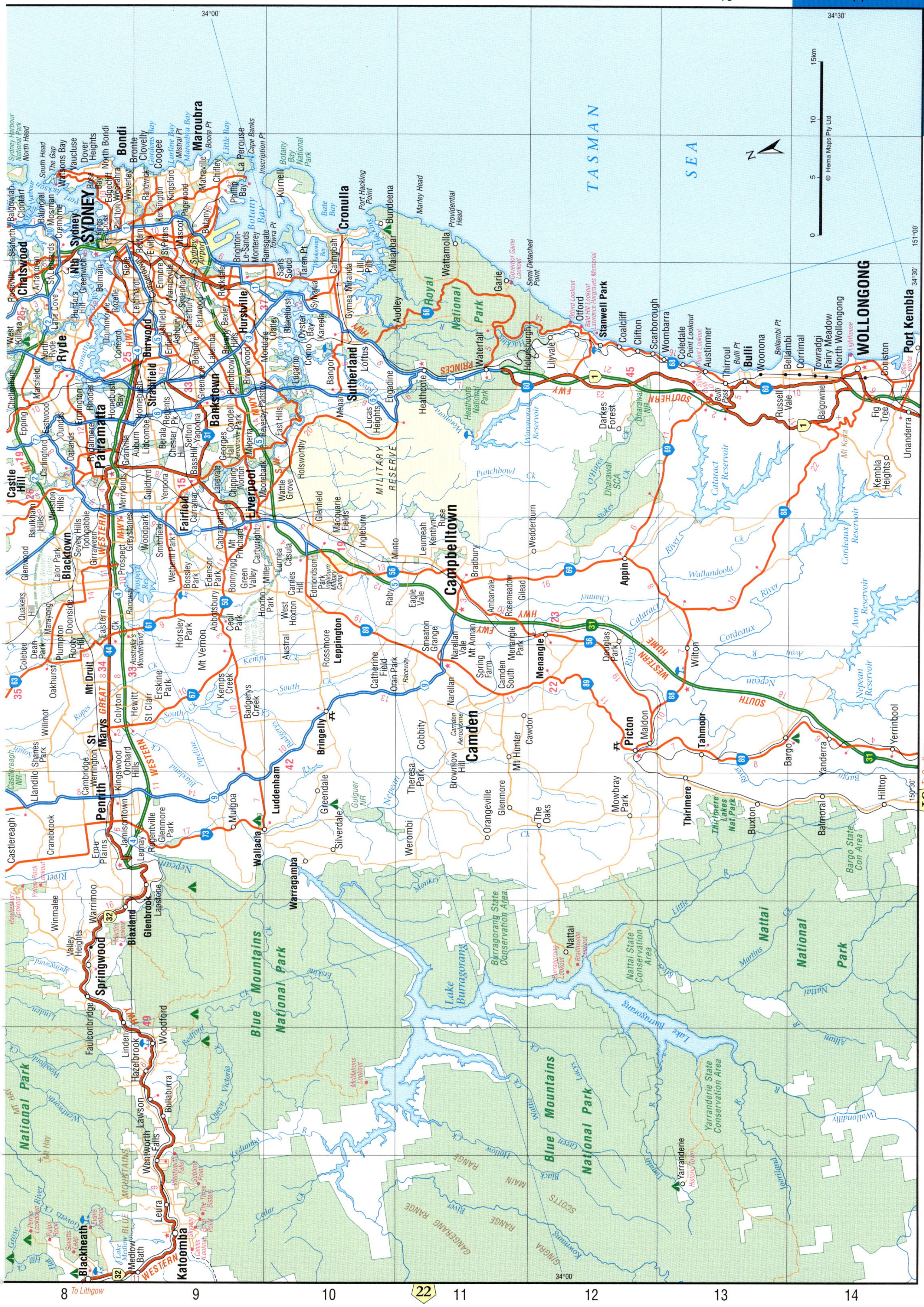
TASMAN
SEA
SYDNEY
Chatswood
Ryde
Parramatta
Bankstown
Hurstville
Cronulla
Sutherland
Liverpool
Campbelltown
Camden
Penrith
Blacktown
Castle Hill
Fairfield
Strathfield
Burwood
Bondi
Maroubra
La Perouse
Botany Bay
Royal National Park
Heathcote National Park
Stanwell Park
WOLLONGONG
Port Kembla
Bulli
Thirroul
Appin
Picton
Tahmoor
Thirlmere
Bargo
Wilton
Menangle
Leppington
Bringelly
Luddenham
Wallacia
Warragamba
Mulgoa
St Marys
Mt Druitt
Springwood
Blaxland
Glenbrook
Faulconbridge
Linden
Hazelbrook
Lawson
Wentworth Falls
Leura
Katoomba
Blackheath
Lake Burragorang
Blue Mountains National Park
Nattai National Park
Nattai
Yerranderie
Cataract Reservoir
Cordeaux Reservoir
Avon Reservoir
Nepean Reservoir
Dharawal SCA
MILITARY RESERVE
Thirlmere Lakes Nat Park
Bargo State Con Area
Nattai State Conservation Area
Burragorang State Conservation Area
Yarranderie State Conservation Area
To Lithgow
To Goulburn
To Nowra
© Hema Maps Pty Ltd
0 5 10 15km

22 Central-East New South Wales

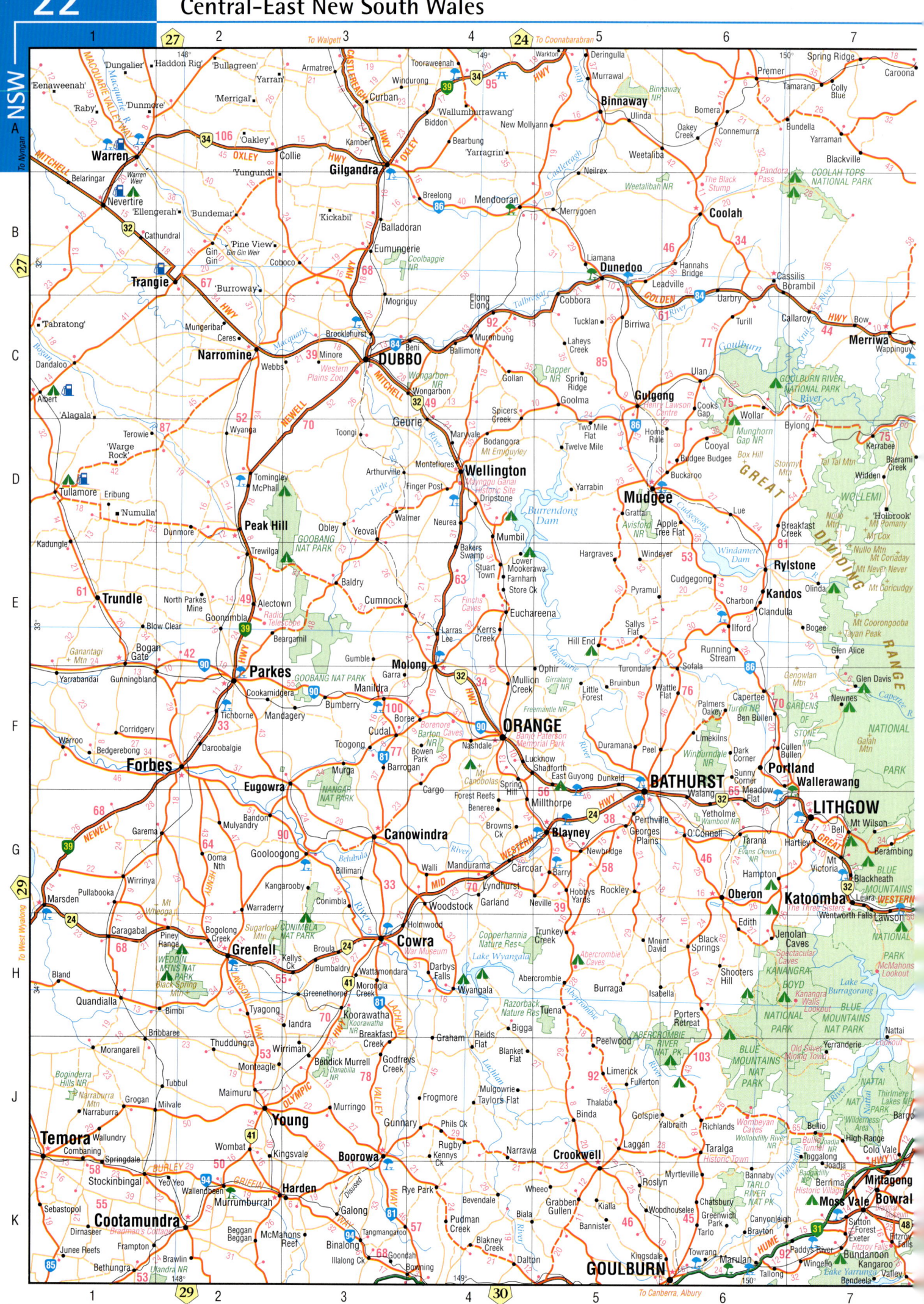

To Narrabri
To Tamworth
To Walcha
To Kempsey
To Nowra
Quirindi
Pine Ridge
Willow Tree
Murrurundi
Scone
Aberdeen
Muswellbrook
Denman
Singleton
Branxton
MAITLAND
Kurri Kurri
CESSNOCK
Raymond Terrace
NEWCASTLE
Nelson Bay
Belmont
Swansea
Morisset
Toronto
Wyong
The Entrance
Gosford
Terrigal
Palm Beach
Mona Vale
Hornsby
Manly
SYDNEY
Parramatta
Penrith
Richmond
Windsor
Springwood
Liverpool
Camden
Campbelltown
Picton
Sutherland
Helensburgh
Bulli
WOLLONGONG
Port Kembla
Shellharbour
Kiama
Gerringong
Gloucester
Dungog
Stroud
Bulahdelah
Wingham
TAREE
Forster
Tuncurry
Wauchope
Port Macquarie
Laurieton
Harrington
Pacific Palms
Seal Rocks
Tea Gardens
Hawks Nest
GREAT DIVIDING RANGE
LIVERPOOL RANGE
BARRINGTON TOPS NAT PARK
MYALL LAKES NATIONAL PARK
WOLLEMI NATIONAL PARK
YENGO NATIONAL PARK
ROYAL NATIONAL PARK
CROWDY BAY NATIONAL PARK
SOUTH PACIFIC OCEAN
TASMAN SEA
Illawarra Coast
For more details on this area, see Hema's Sydney to Brisbane Map
Opera House, Powerhouse Museum, Sydney Aquarium, Beautiful Harbour, Taronga Zoo, Sydney Tower, The Rocks, Australia's Wonderland, Darling Harbour
0 10 20 30 40 50 60km
© Hema Maps Pty Ltd

24 North-East New South Wales

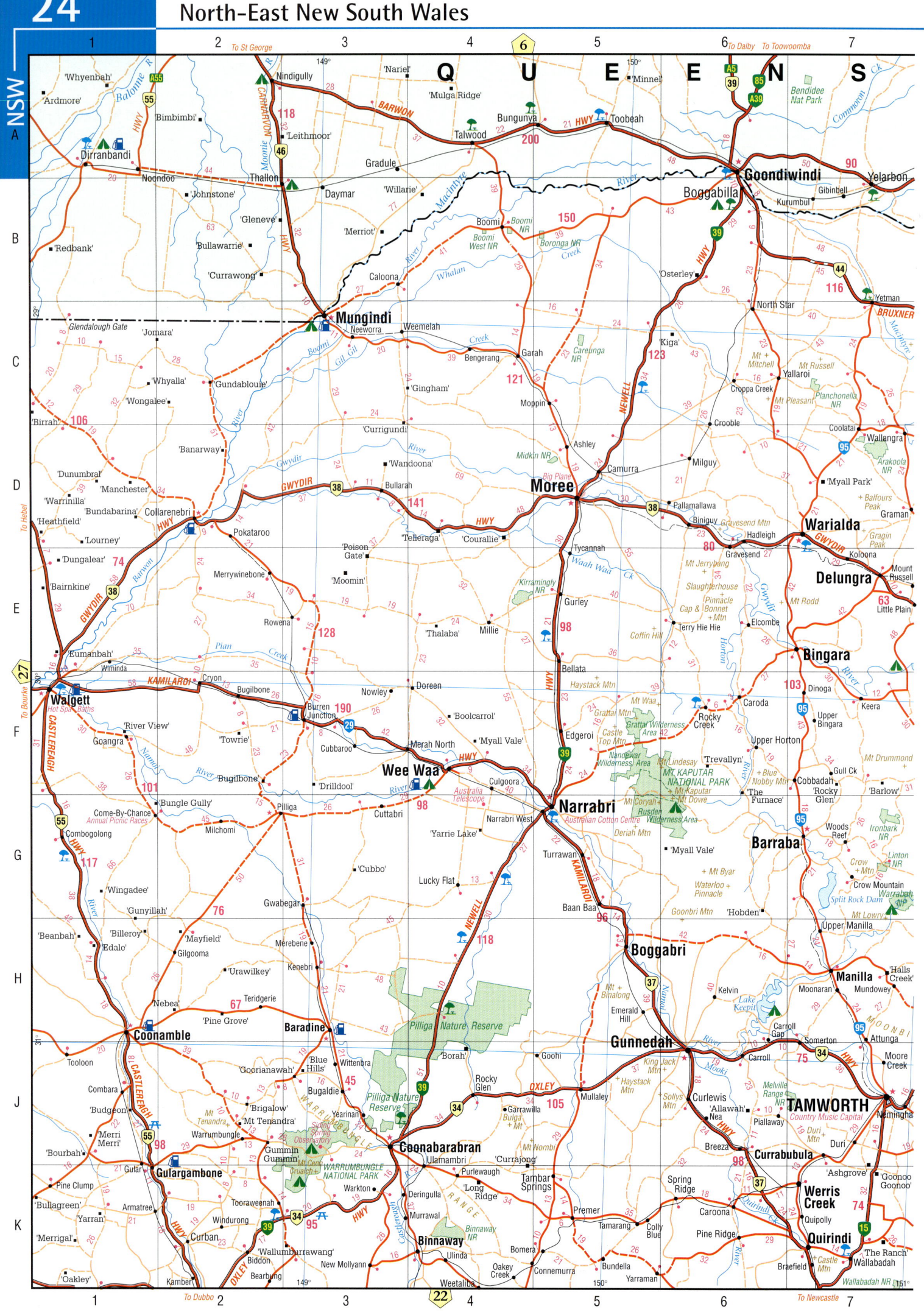

To Toowoomba, Brisbane
To Brisbane
To Brisbane, Surfers Paradise
L A N D
Warwick
Karara
Inglewood
Whetstone
Coolmunda Dam
CUNNINGHAM HWY
Killarney
Legume
Main Range Nat Park
Mt Barney Nat Park
Rathdowney
Lamington Nat Park
Binna Burra
O'Reillys
Springbrook
Coolangatta
Tweed Heads
Kingscliff
Murwillumbah
Pottsville
Woodenbong
Urbenville
Tooloom
Old Bonalbo
Bonalbo
Kyogle
Mullumbimby
Brunswick Heads
Byron Bay
Bangalow
Nimbin
Messines
Wylie Creek
Liston
Amosfield
Wilsons Downfall
Pikedale
Stanthorpe
Limevale
Texas
Silver Spur
Ballandean
Girraween NP
Sundown Nat Park
Boonoo Boonoo
Drake
Tabulam
Mummulgum
Casino
LISMORE
Ballina
Wardell
Lennox Head
Alstonville
Coraki
Woodburn
Evans Head
Broadwater
Mingoola
Bonshaw
Mole River
Wallangarra
Tenterfield
Sunnyside
Sandy Hill
Black Swamp
BRUXNER HWY
Alice
Busbys Flat
Wyan
Rappville
Bungulla
Baryulgil
Whiporie
Camira Ck
New Italy
BUNDJALUNG NATIONAL PARK
For more details on this area, see Hema's North East New South Wales Map
Ashford
'The Gulf'
Torrington
Stannum
Bolivia
ENGLAND
Deepwater
Tent Hill
Emmaville
Strathbogie
Bukkulla
Cherry Tree Hill
WASHPOOL NATIONAL PARK
157
Cangai
Fine Flower
Coaldale
Chatsworth
Harwood
Maclean
Iluka
Yamba
Angourie
Lawrence
Ulmarra
Cowper
Tyndale
Brooms Head
YURAYGIR NAT PARK
Dundee
Glen Elgin
Jackadgery
Copmanhurst
Oakwood
Nullamanna
Wellingrove
Sapphire
Kings Plains Nat Pk
Bald Knob
Shannon Vale
GWYDIR HWY
NYMBOIDA NAT PARK
Inverell
Elsmore
Matheson
Glen Innes
Red Range
Furracabad
Stonehenge
GRAFTON
South Grafton
Tucabia
Sandon
Pillar Valley
Minnie Water
Gilgai
Stannifer
Newton Boyd
Buccarumbi
Coutts Crossing
Dalmorton
Wooli
SOUTH
Halfway Creek
North Solitary Island NR
Stanborough
Tingha
Mayhole
Glencoe
Ben Lomond
Wandsworth
Llangothlin
Backwater
Oban
Wards Mistake
GUY FAWKES RIVER NAT PARK
Nymboida
Clouds Creek
Towallum
Kungala
Corindi Beach
Red Rock
Mullaway
Bundarra
Glenreagh
Nana Glen
Lower Bucca
Woolgoolga
Sandy Beach
Emerald Beach
Moonee Beach
'Laura'
'Baldersleigh'
Guyra
Black Mtn
Billys Creek
Dundurrabin
Tyringham
Ulong
Coramba
Korora
Coffs Harbour
Big Banana
Wongwibinda
Rockvale
Hernani
Bostobrick
Megan
Deer Vale
Dorrigo
Upper Orara
Boambee
Bonville
Sawtell
Kingstown
Yarrowyck
Tilbuster
Dumaresq
ARMIDALE
Wollomombi
Ebor
NEW ENGLAND NAT PARK
Thora
Bellingen
Raleigh
Urunga
Mylestom
PACIFIC
Uralla
Rocky River
'Balala'
'Retreat'
Dangarsleigh
Hillgrove
Jeogla
Kalang
Missabotti
Argents Hill
Bowraville
Nambucca Heads
Watsons Creek
'Longford'
Gostwyck
Kentucky
Enmore
Georges Junction
Lower Creek
Five Day Creek
Comara
Burrapine
Talarm
Macksville
Scotts Head
Bendemeer
Wollun
'East Lake'
OXLEY WILD RIVERS NATIONAL PARK
Bellbrook
Taylors Arm
Warrell Ck
Eungai
Grassy Head
Stuarts Point
South West Rocks
Arakoon
Smoky Cape
Moonbi
Woolbrook
Walcha Road
Walcha
Kootingal
Limbri
'Aberbaldie'
OXLEY
Moona Plains
Millbank
Willawarrin
Clybucca
Jerseyville
Kinchela Creek
Smithtown
Kookaburra
Gladstone
Sherwood
Kempsey
OCEAN
HAT HEAD NATIONAL PARK
Hat Head
Piallamore
Dungowan
Weabonga
Glen Morrison
Tia
Brackendale
Burnt Bridge
Crescent Head
Loomberah
'Carnegie'
Niangala
Woolomin
Yarrowitch
Upper Rollands Plains
Kundabung
Myrtle Scrub
WERRIKIMBE NAT PARK
Rollands Plains
Telegraph Point
Point Plomer
Limeburners Creek Nature Reserve
Bowling Alley Point
Nundle
Hanging Rock
Mt Seaview
Birdwood
Kindee
Pappinbarra
Pembroke
Yarras
Ellenborough
Long Flat
Beechwood
Port Macquarie
Tacking Point
Lake Innes Nature Res
Nowendoc
Wauchope
Lake Cathie
Byabarra
Barry
GREAT DIVIDING RANGE
To Gloucester
To Taree
0 10 20 30 40 50km
© Hema Maps Pty Ltd
N

26 North-West New South Wales

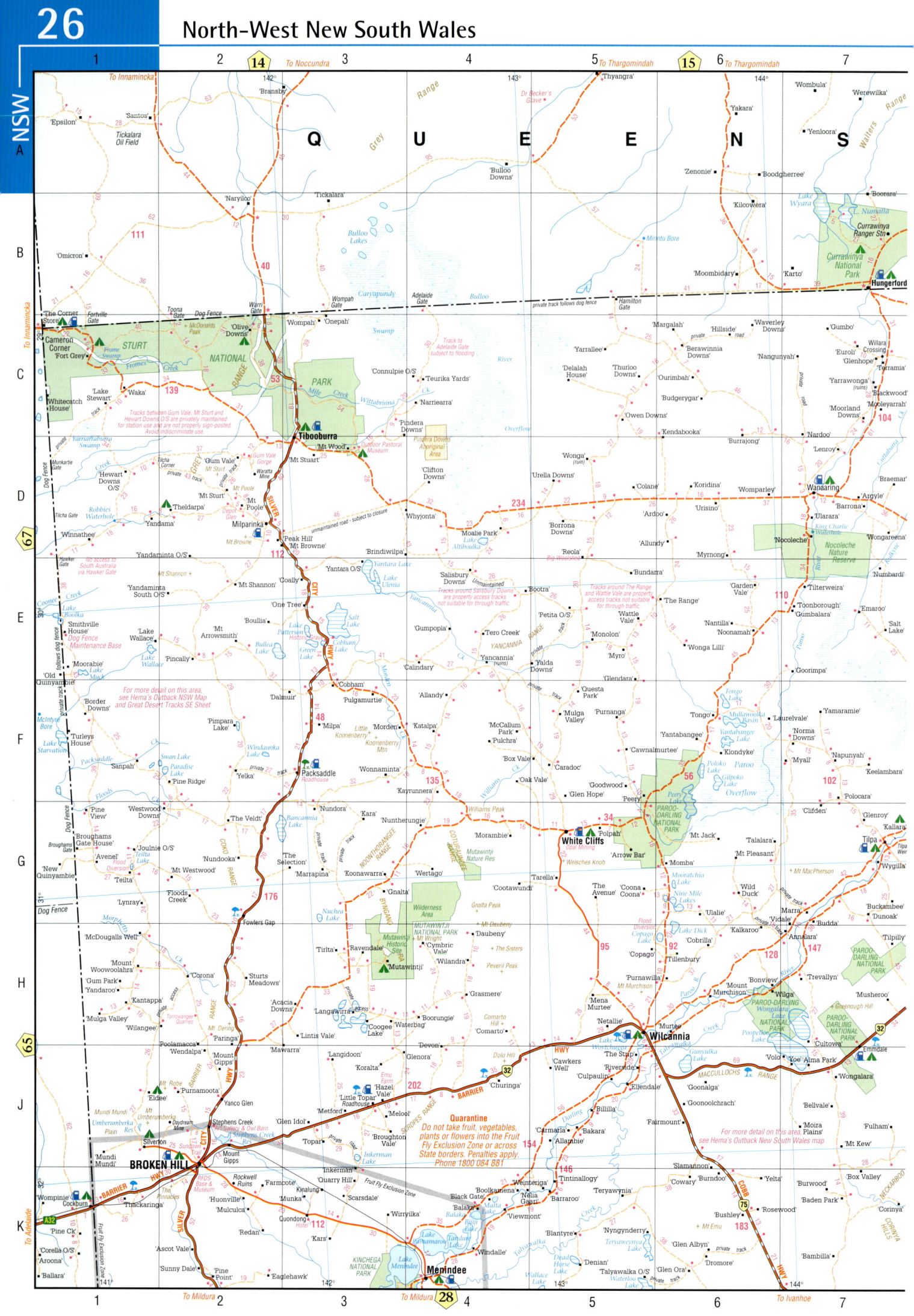

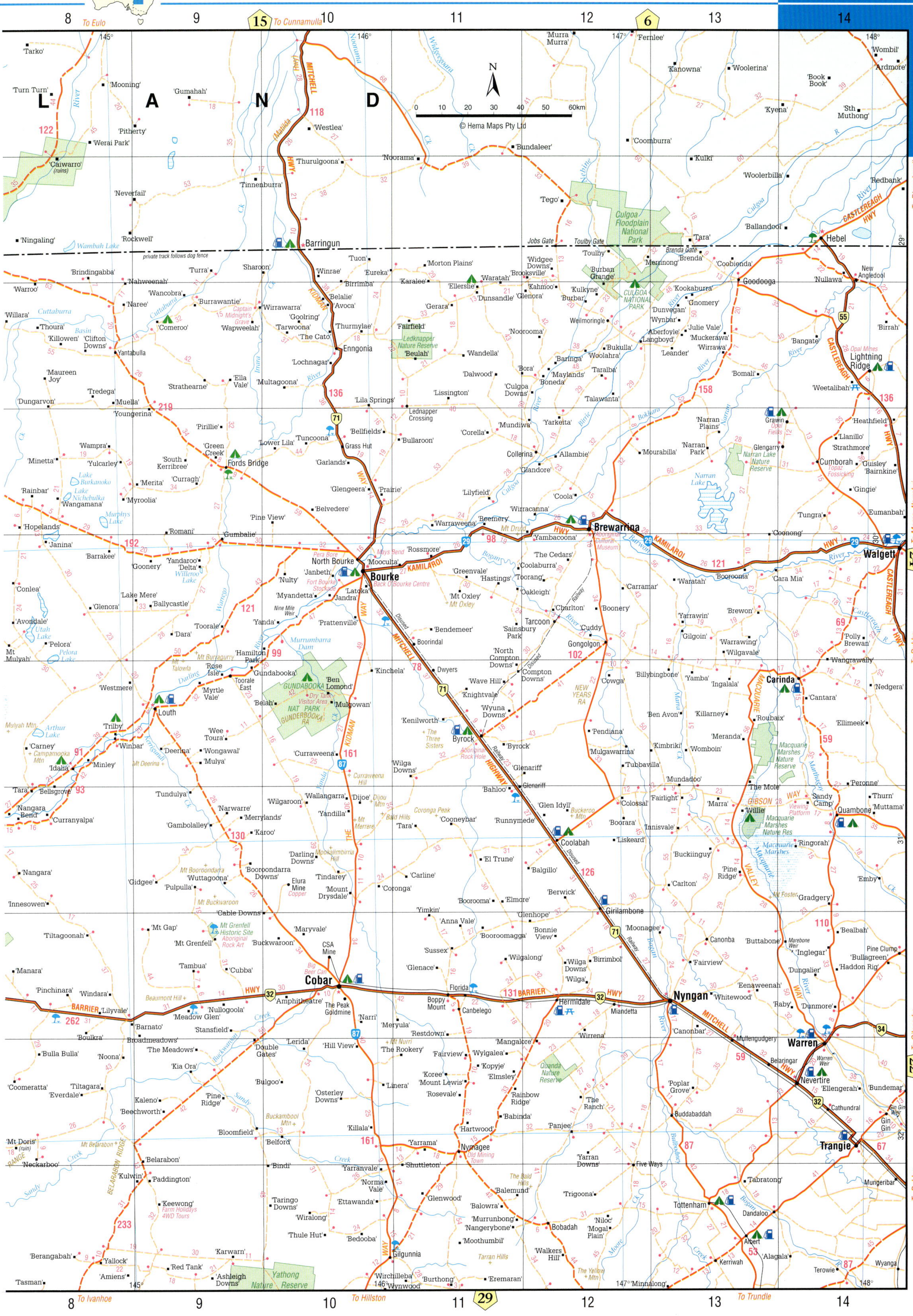

28 South-West New South Wales

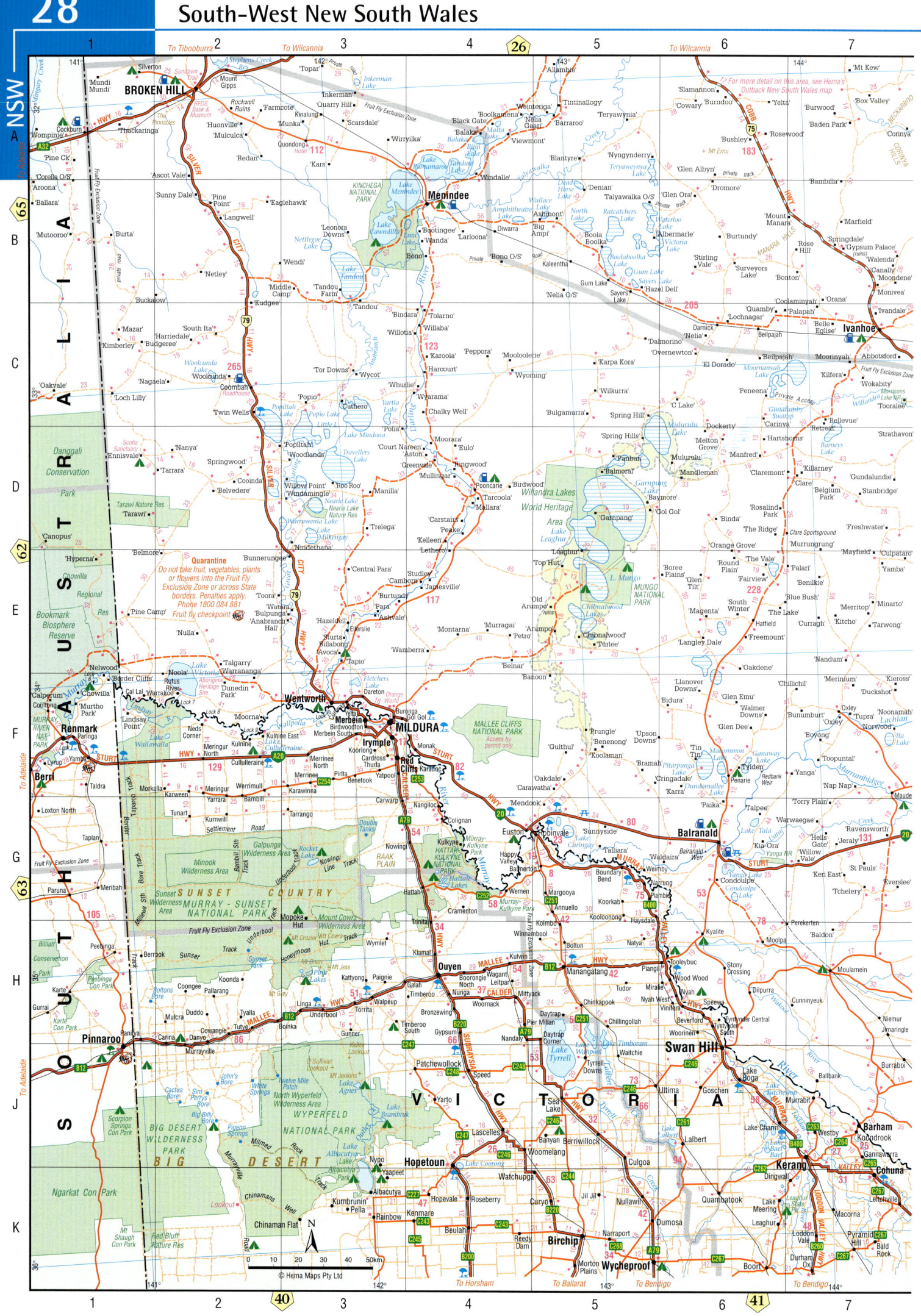

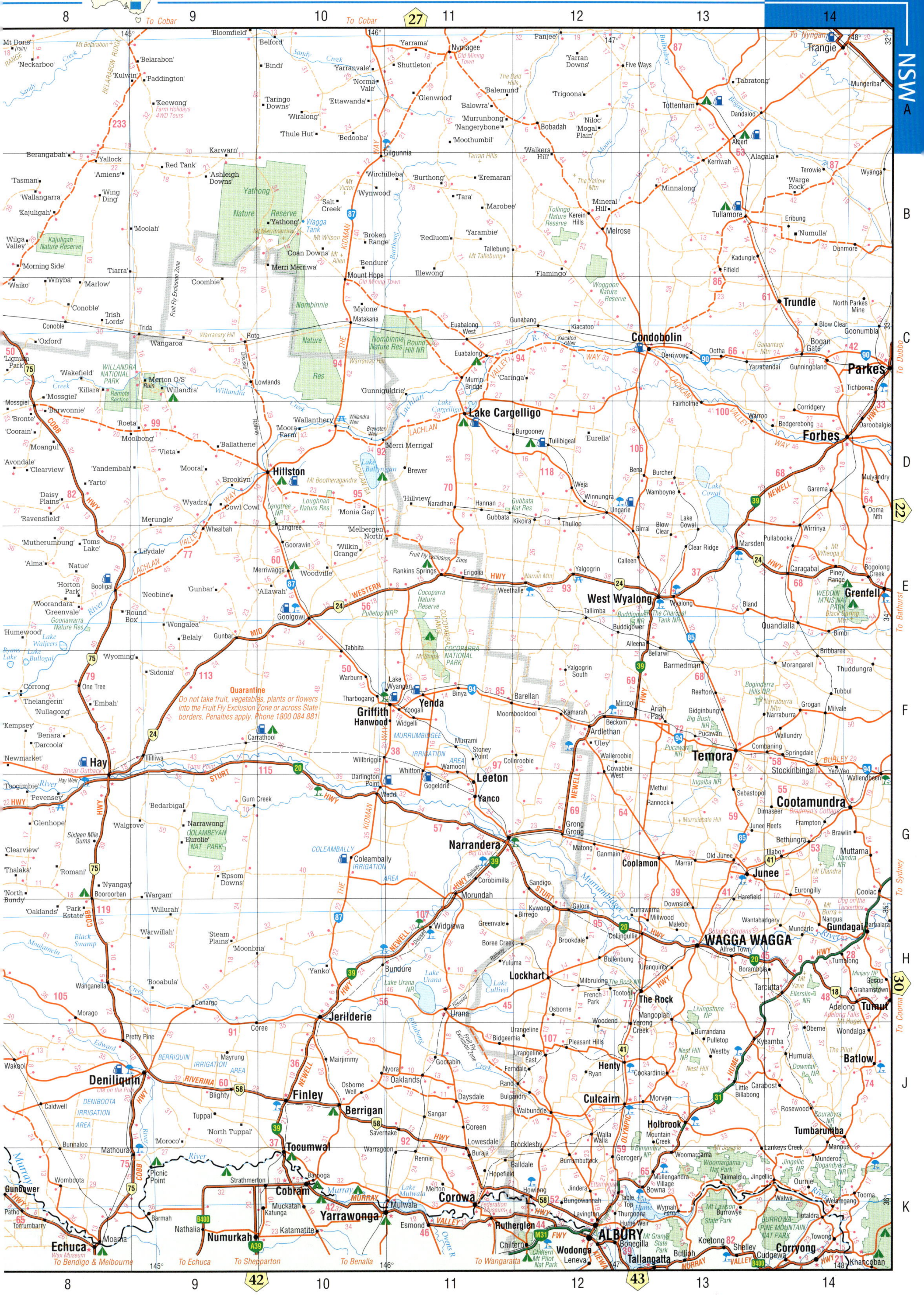
NSW
To Cobar
27
To Nyngan
Trangie
Nymagee
Tottenham
Dandaloo
Albert
Tullamore
Gilgunnia
Yathong Nature Reserve
Mount Hope
Trundle
Condobolin
Parkes
Lake Cargelligo
Forbes
Hillston
West Wyalong
Grenfell
Griffith
Hanwood
Yenda
Temora
Hay
Leeton
Yanco
Cootamundra
Narrandera
Coolamon
Junee
WAGGA WAGGA
Gundagai
Tumut
Lockhart
The Rock
Jerilderie
Deniliquin
Finley
Berrigan
Henty
Culcairn
Holbrook
Tumbarumba
Batlow
Tocumwal
Cobram
Corowa
Yarrawonga
Mulwala
Rutherglen
ALBURY
Wodonga
Tallangatta
Corryong
Khancoban
Echuca
Moama
Numurkah
Nathalia
To Bendigo & Melbourne
To Echuca
To Shepparton
To Benalla
To Wangaratta
To Bathurst
To Sydney
To Cooma
To Dubbo
Quarantine
Do not take fruit, vegetables, plants or flowers into the Fruit Fly Exclusion Zone or across State borders. Penalties apply. Phone 1800 084 881
42
43
22
30
8 9 10 11 12 13 14
A B C D E F G H J K

30 South-East New South Wales

Canberra CBD

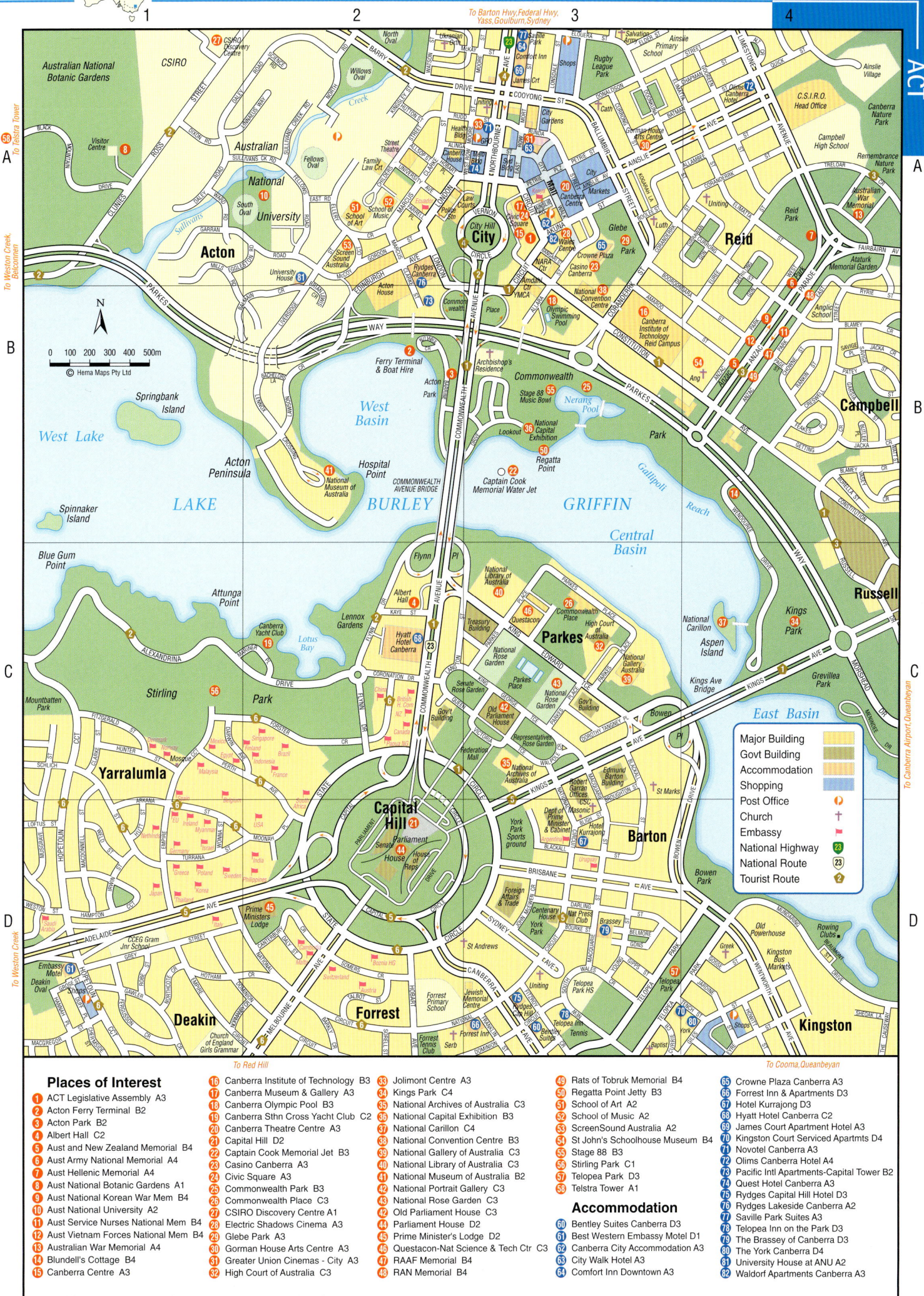

Places of Interest

1. ACT Legislative Assembly A3
2. Acton Ferry Terminal B2
3. Acton Park B2
4. Albert Hall C2
5. Aust and New Zealand Memorial B4
6. Aust Army National Memorial A4
7. Aust Hellenic Memorial A4
8. Aust National Botanic Gardens A1
9. Aust National Korean War Mem B4
10. Aust National University A2
11. Aust Service Nurses National Mem B4
12. Aust Vietnam Forces National Mem B4
13. Australian War Memorial A4
14. Blundell's Cottage B4
15. Canberra Centre A3
16. Canberra Institute of Technology B3
17. Canberra Museum & Gallery A3
18. Canberra Olympic Pool B3
19. Canberra Sthn Cross Yacht Club C2
20. Canberra Theatre Centre A3
21. Capital Hill D2
22. Captain Cook Memorial Jet B3
23. Casino Canberra A3
24. Civic Square A3
25. Commonwealth Park B3
26. Commonwealth Place C3
27. CSIRO Discovery Centre A1
28. Electric Shadows Cinema A3
29. Glebe Park A3
30. Gorman House Arts Centre A3
31. Greater Union Cinemas - City A3
32. High Court of Australia C3
33. Jolimont Centre A3
34. Kings Park C4
35. National Archives of Australia C3
36. National Capital Exhibition B3
37. National Carillon C4
38. National Convention Centre B3
39. National Gallery of Australia C3
40. National Library of Australia C3
41. National Museum of Australia B2
42. National Portrait Gallery C3
43. National Rose Garden C3
44. Old Parliament House C3
45. Prime Minister's Lodge D2
46. Questacon-Nat Science & Tech Ctr C3
47. RAAF Memorial B4
48. RAN Memorial B4
49. Rats of Tobruk Memorial B4
50. Regatta Point Jetty B3
51. School of Art A2
52. School of Music A2
53. ScreenSound Australia A2
54. St John's Schoolhouse Museum B4
55. Stage 88 B3
56. Stirling Park C1
57. Telopea Park D3
58. Telstra Tower A1

Accommodation

60. Bentley Suites Canberra D3
61. Best Western Embassy Motel D1
62. Canberra City Accommodation A3
63. City Walk Hotel A3
64. Comfort Inn Downtown A3
65. Crowne Plaza Canberra A3
66. Forrest Inn & Apartments D3
67. Hotel Kurrajong D3
68. Hyatt Hotel Canberra C2
69. James Court Apartment Hotel A3
70. Kingston Court Serviced Apartmts D4
71. Novotel Canberra A3
72. Olims Canberra Hotel A4
73. Pacific Intl Apartments-Capital Tower B2
74. Quest Hotel Canberra A3
75. Rydges Capital Hill Hotel D3
76. Rydges Lakeside Canberra A2
77. Saville Park Suites A3
78. Telopea Inn on the Park D3
79. The Brassey of Canberra D3
80. The York Canberra D4
81. University House at ANU A2
82. Waldorf Apartments Canberra A3

Legend

- Major Building
- Govt Building
- Accommodation
- Shopping
- Post Office
- Church
- Embassy
- National Highway
- National Route
- Tourist Route

32 Canberra Throughroads

Key map 33

Victoria

Sunrise, Port Phillip Bay (36 F6, 39 G13, 44 D1)

Distances are shown in kilometres and follow the most direct major sealed route

Albury	423	330	302	237	617	395	579	504	321	613	180	391	485	72	582
Ballarat		394	121	214	681	87	174	187	112	486	243	309	276	346	186
Bairnsdale			430	492	287	356	398	581	282	840	694	618	118	304	543
Bendigo				93	717	208	277	207	148	410	122	188	312	225	307
Echuca					751	284	370	300	210	376	71	154	374	160	400
Eden (NSW)						643	791	868	569	1127	694	905	405	591	830
Geelong							236	274	74	573	258	393	238	316	187
Hamilton								132	286	431	399	383	450	502	100
Horsham									299	299	329	251	463	432	232
Melbourne										558	184	336	164	242	261
Mildura											433	222	722	536	531
Shepparton												211	348	103	429
Swan Hill													500	314	385
Traralgon														406	425
Wangaratta															503
Warrnambool															

34 Melbourne CBD

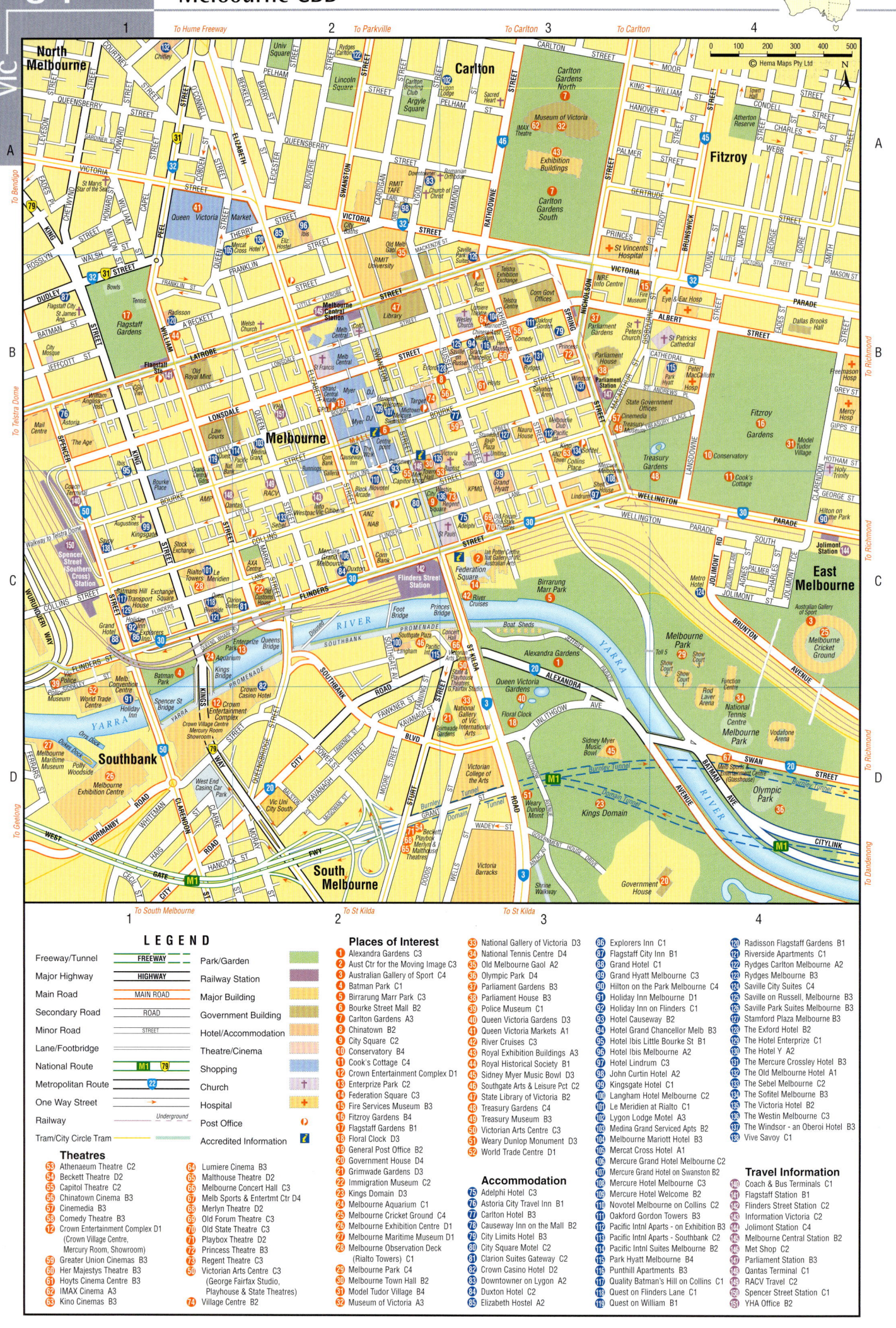

LEGEND

Freeway/Tunnel	FREEWAY
Major Highway	HIGHWAY
Main Road	MAIN ROAD
Secondary Road	ROAD
Minor Road	STREET
Lane/Footbridge	
National Route	M1 / 79
Metropolitan Route	22
One Way Street	→
Railway	Underground
Tram/City Circle Tram	
Park/Garden	
Railway Station	
Major Building	
Government Building	
Hotel/Accommodation	
Theatre/Cinema	
Shopping	
Church	✝
Hospital	✚
Post Office	
Accredited Information	i

Theatres
- 53 Athenaeum Theatre C2
- 54 Beckett Theatre D2
- 55 Capitol Theatre C2
- 56 Chinatown Cinema B3
- 57 Cinemedia B3
- 58 Comedy Theatre B3
- 12 Crown Entertainment Complex D1 (Crown Village Centre, Mercury Room, Showroom)
- 59 Greater Union Cinemas B2
- 60 Her Majestys Theatre B3
- 61 Hoyts Cinema Centre B3
- 62 IMAX Cinema A3
- 63 Kino Cinemas B3
- 64 Lumiere Cinema B3
- 65 Malthouse Theatre D2
- 66 Melbourne Concert Hall C3
- 67 Melb Sports & Entertmt Ctr D4
- 68 Merlyn Theatre D2
- 69 Old Forum Theatre C3
- 70 Old State Theatre C3
- 71 Playbox Theatre D2
- 72 Princess Theatre B3
- 73 Regent Theatre C3
- 50 Victorian Arts Centre C3 (George Fairfax Studio, Playhouse & State Theatres)
- 74 Village Centre B2

Places of Interest
- 1 Alexandra Gardens C3
- 2 Aust Ctr for the Moving Image C3
- 3 Australian Gallery of Sport C4
- 4 Batman Park C1
- 5 Birrarung Marr Park C3
- 6 Bourke Street Mall B2
- 7 Carlton Gardens A3
- 8 Chinatown B2
- 9 City Square C2
- 10 Conservatory B4
- 11 Cook's Cottage C4
- 12 Crown Entertainment Complex D1
- 13 Enterprize Park C2
- 14 Federation Square C3
- 15 Fire Services Museum B3
- 16 Fitzroy Gardens B4
- 17 Flagstaff Gardens B1
- 18 Floral Clock D3
- 19 General Post Office B2
- 20 Government House D4
- 21 Grimwade Gardens D3
- 22 Immigration Museum C2
- 23 Kings Domain D3
- 24 Melbourne Aquarium C1
- 25 Melbourne Cricket Ground C4
- 26 Melbourne Exhibition Centre D1
- 27 Melbourne Maritime Museum D1
- 28 Melbourne Observation Deck (Rialto Towers) C1
- 29 Melbourne Park C4
- 30 Melbourne Town Hall B2
- 31 Model Tudor Village B4
- 32 Museum of Victoria A3
- 33 National Gallery of Victoria D3
- 34 National Tennis Centre D4
- 35 Old Melbourne Gaol A2
- 36 Olympic Park D4
- 37 Parliament Gardens B3
- 38 Parliament House B3
- 39 Police Museum C1
- 40 Queen Victoria Gardens D3
- 41 Queen Victoria Markets A1
- 42 River Cruises C3
- 43 Royal Exhibition Buildings A3
- 44 Royal Historical Society B1
- 45 Sidney Myer Music Bowl D3
- 46 Southgate Arts & Leisure Pct C2
- 47 State Library of Victoria B2
- 48 Treasury Gardens C4
- 49 Treasury Museum B3
- 50 Victorian Arts Centre C3
- 51 Weary Dunlop Monument D3
- 52 World Trade Centre D1

Accommodation
- 75 Adelphi Hotel C3
- 76 Astoria City Travel Inn B1
- 77 Carlton Hotel B3
- 78 Causeway Inn on the Mall B2
- 79 City Limits Hotel B3
- 80 City Square Motel C2
- 81 Clarion Suites Gateway C2
- 82 Crown Casino Hotel D2
- 83 Downtowner on Lygon A2
- 84 Duxton Hotel C2
- 85 Elizabeth Hostel A2
- 86 Explorers Inn C1
- 87 Flagstaff City Inn B1
- 88 Grand Hotel C1
- 89 Grand Hyatt Melbourne C3
- 90 Hilton on the Park Melbourne C4
- 91 Holiday Inn Melbourne D1
- 92 Holiday Inn on Flinders C1
- 93 Hotel Causeway B2
- 94 Hotel Grand Chancellor Melb B3
- 95 Hotel Ibis Little Bourke St B1
- 96 Hotel Ibis Melbourne A2
- 97 Hotel Lindrum C3
- 98 John Curtin Hotel A2
- 99 Kingsgate Hotel C1
- 100 Langham Hotel Melbourne C3
- 101 Le Meridien at Rialto C1
- 102 Lygon Lodge Motel A3
- 103 Medina Grand Serviced Apts B2
- 104 Melbourne Mariott Hotel B3
- 105 Mercat Cross Hotel A1
- 106 Mercure Grand Hotel Melbourne C2
- 107 Mercure Grand Hotel on Swanston B2
- 108 Mercure Hotel Melbourne B3
- 109 Mercure Hotel Welcome B2
- 110 Novotel Melbourne on Collins B2
- 111 Oakford Gordon Towers B3
- 112 Pacific Intnl Aparts - on Exhibition B3
- 113 Pacific Intnl Aparts - Southbank D2
- 114 Pacific Intnl Suites Melbourne B3
- 115 Park Hyatt Melbourne B4
- 116 Punthill Apartments B3
- 117 Quality Batman's Hill on Collins C1
- 118 Quest on Flinders Lane C1
- 119 Quest on William B1
- 120 Radisson Flagstaff Gardens B1
- 121 Riverside Apartments C1
- 122 Rydges Carlton Melbourne A2
- 123 Rydges Melbourne B3
- 124 Saville City Suites C4
- 125 Saville on Russell, Melbourne B3
- 126 Saville Park Suites Melbourne B3
- 127 Stamford Plaza Melbourne B3
- 128 The Exford Hotel B2
- 129 The Hotel Enterprize C1
- 130 The Hotel Y A2
- 131 The Mercure Crossley Hotel B3
- 132 The Old Melbourne Hotel A1
- 133 The Sebel Melbourne C1
- 134 The Sofitel Melbourne B3
- 135 The Victoria Hotel B2
- 136 The Westin Melbourne B2
- 137 The Windsor - an Oberoi Hotel B3
- 138 Vive Savoy C1

Travel Information
- 140 Coach & Bus Terminals C1
- 141 Flagstaff Station B1
- 142 Flinders Street Station C2
- 143 Information Victoria C2
- 144 Jolimont Station C4
- 145 Melbourne Central Station B2
- 146 Met Shop C2
- 147 Parliament Station B3
- 148 Qantas Terminal C1
- 149 RACV Travel C2
- 150 Spencer Street Station C1
- 151 YHA Office B2

Melbourne Throughroads

36 Melbourne Region, Victoria

To Yea
To Alexandria
To Mt Baw Baw
To Traralgon
To Morwell
To Cowes, Wonthaggi
To Wonthaggi
To Wonthaggi To Yarram
Whittlesea
Humevale
Kinglake Central
Kinglake
Kinglake East
Kinglake National Park
Castella
Toolangi
Marysville
Narbethong
St Fillans
Cambarville
Woodstock
Yan Yean
Yan Yean Res
Wollert
Mernda
Doreen
Arthurs Creek
Strathewen
Nutfield
Cottles Bridge
St Andrews
Steels Creek
Dixons Creek
Long Gully
Chum Creek
Fernshaw
Maroondah Res
Yarra Ranges National Park
Upper Yarra Dam
Reefton
McMahons Creek
Epping
Hurstbridge
Yarrambat
Panton Hill
Christmas Hills
Yarra Glen
Tarrawarra
Healesville
South Morang
Diamond Creek
Plenty
Kangaroo Ground
Watsons Creek
Sugarloaf Res
Yering
Bundoora
Greensborough
Kingsbury
Watsonia
Eltham
Macleod
Rosanna
Heidelberg
Warrandyte
Wonga Park
Coldstream
Gruyere
Lilydale
Killara
Templestowe
Northcote
Bulleen
Doncaster
Warrandyte State Park
Seville
Wandin North
Woori Yallock
Launching Place
Don Valley
Wesburn
Millgrove
Warburton
Warburton East
Cement Creek
Big Pats Ck
Old Warburton
Britannia Creek
Yarra Junction
Collingwood
Balwyn
Richmond
Box Hill
Ringwood
Croydon
Camberwell
Vermont
Bayswater
Kalorama
Mt Dandenong
Olinda
Silvan
Yellingbo
Gladysdale
Hoddles Creek
Three Bridges
Powelltown
Burwood
Boronia
Ferntree Gully
The Basin
Sassafras
Burleigh
Monbulk
Kallista
Macclesfield
Nangana
Kurth Kiln Park
Beenak
Caulfield
Glen Waverly
Knoxfield
Scoresby
Oakleigh
Upper Ferntree Gully
Belgrave
Menzies Ck
Clematis
Avonsleigh
Emerald
Lakeside
Cockatoo
Gembrook
Clayton
Moorabbin
Springvale
Mulgrave
Rowville
Lysterfield Lake Park
Narre Warren East
Bunyip State Park
Cheltenham
Mentone
Dingley Village
Noble Park
Dandenong
Narre Warren North
Mt Burnett
Mordialloc
Braeside
Keysborough
Narre Warren
Berwick
Beaconsfield Upper
Pakenham Upper
Nar Nar Goon North
Cornucopia
Tonimbuk
Garfield North
Jindivick North
Jindivick
Aspendale
Edithvale
Chelsea
Bonbeach
Carrum
Patterson Lakes
Lyndhurst
Beaconsfield
Officer
Pakenham
Maryknoll
Tynong North
Labertouche
Jindivick West
Tarago
Nar Nar Goon
Tynong
Garfield
Bunyip
Longwarry North
Robin Hood
Drouin West
Rokeby
Buln Buln
Seaford
Carrum Downs
Skye
Cranbourne
Clyde
Longwarry
Brandy Creek
Drouin
Frankston
Cardinia
Pakenham South
Cora Lynn
Vervale
Iona
Davey Pt
Mt Eliza
Langwarrin
Devon Meadows
Fiveways
Koo-Wee-Rup North
Bayles
Catani
Modella
Drouin Sth
Warragul
Baxter
Pearcedale
Dalmore
Koo-wee-rup
Yallock
Ripplebrook
Lardner
Bull Swamp
Schnapper Point
Somerville
Cannons Ck
Warneet
Tooradin
Monomeith
Yannathan
Moorooduc
Tyabb
Chinaman Island
Pelican Point
Caldermeade
Heath Hill
Athlone
Hallora
Ellinbank
Tetoora Road
Lang Lang
Western Port
Old Tyabb
Scrub Pt
Mountain View
Sea View
Hastings
Lang Lang Beach
Poowong North
Ferndale
Mornington
Bittern
Fairhaven
Jam Jerrup
Poowong East
French Island National Park
French Island
Nyora
Poowong
Strzelecki
Merricks North
Red Hill
Crib Point
Red Hill South
Balnarring
HMAS Cerberus
Stony Point
Tankerton
The Gurdies
Loch
Ranceby
Merricks
Somers
Pioneer Bay
St Helier
Arawata
Merricks Beach
Balnarring Beach
Tenby Pt
Grantville
Woodleigh
Jeetho
Shoreham
Pt Leo
Corinella
Bena
Kardella
Fairbank
Queensferry
Kernot
Krowera
Korumburra
Cowes
Coronet Bay
Almurta
Kilcunda Road
Jumbunna
Kardella South
Ruby
Flinders
Ventnor
Phillip Island
Rhyll
Glen Forbes
Korumburra South
Leongatha
West Head
Summerland
Bass
Bass Landing
Blackwood Forest
Glen Alvie
Burndale
Moyarra

38 South-West Victoria

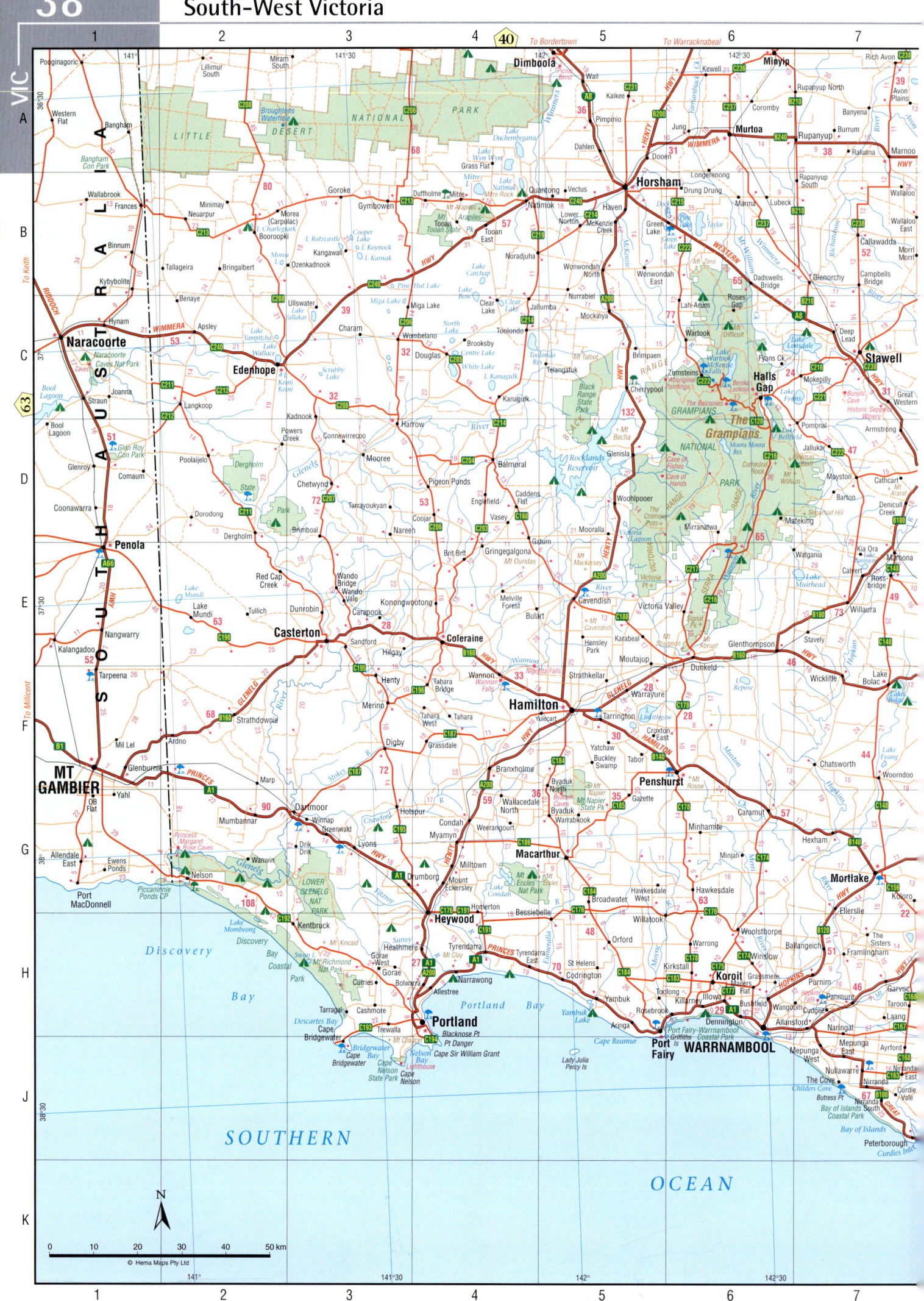

39

40 North-West Victoria

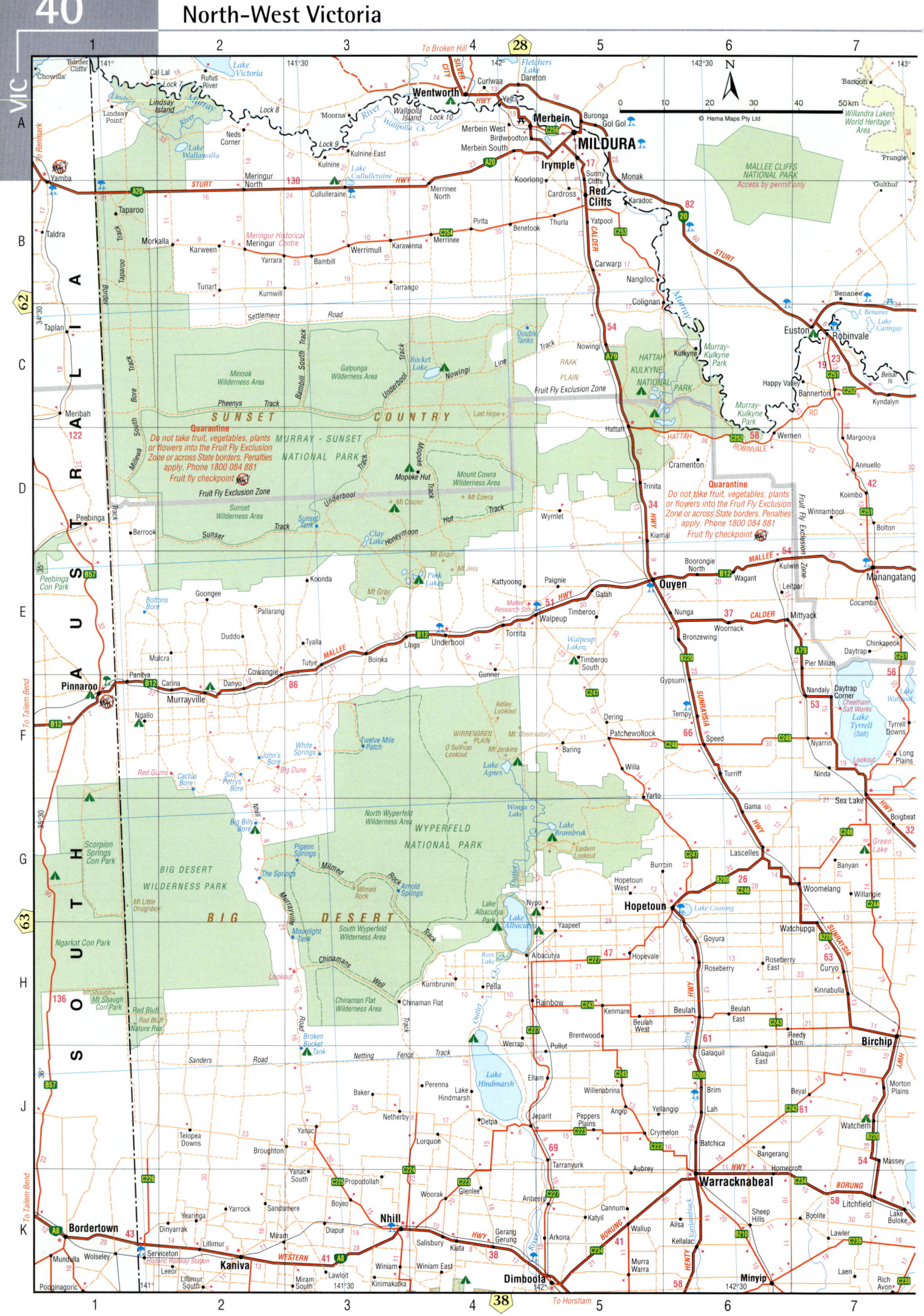

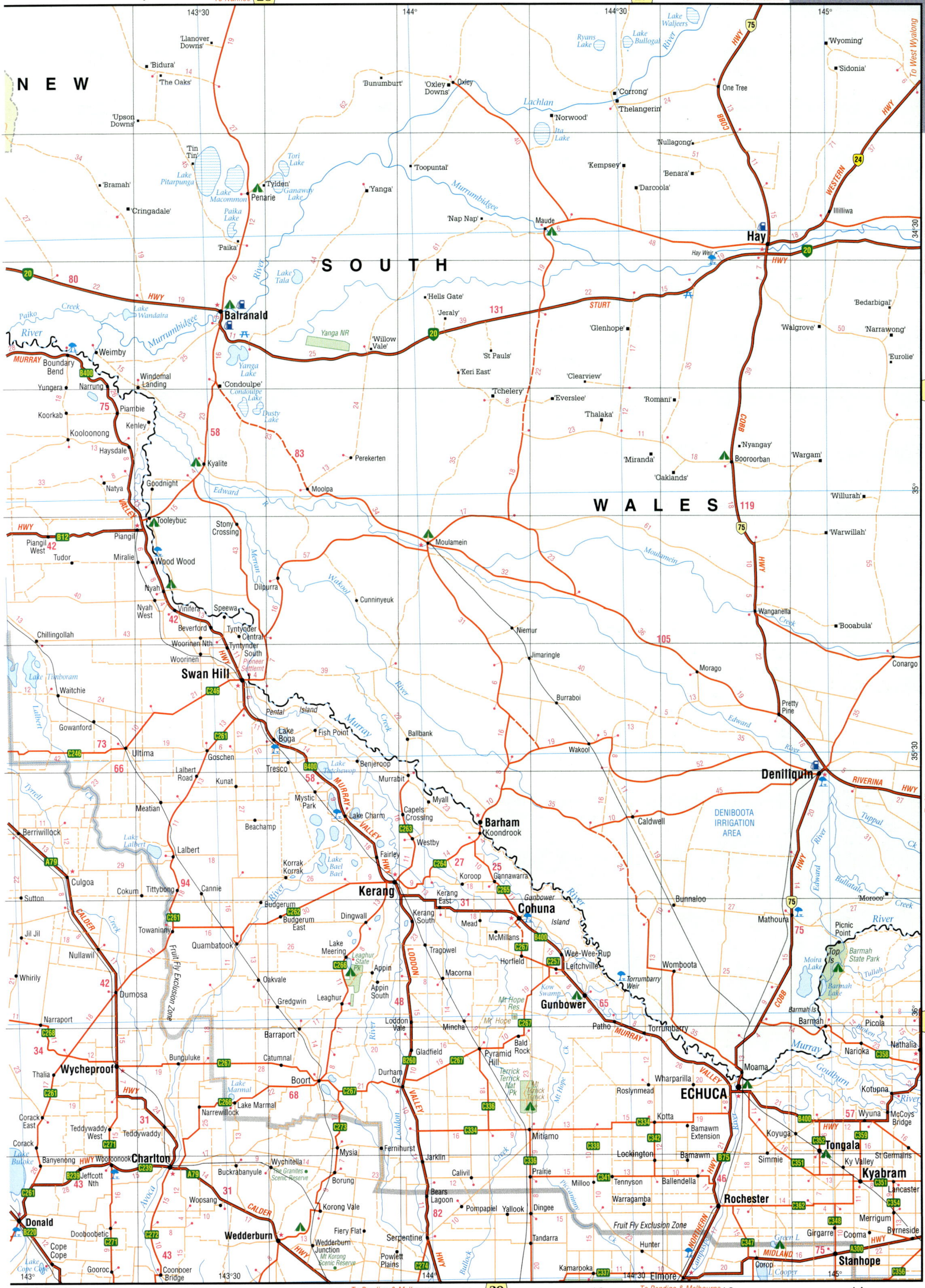

VIC
To Ivanhoe 28
29
To Wilcannia
NEW SOUTH WALES
Lake Waljeers
Ryans Lake
Lake Bullogal
'Llanover Downs'
'Bidura'
'The Oaks'
'Upson Downs'
'Bunumburt'
'Oxley Downs'
Oxley
'Corrong'
'Thelangerin'
One Tree
'Wyoming'
'Sidonia'
To West Wyalong
Lachlan
'Norwood'
Ita Lake
'Nullagong'
'Benara'
'Kempsey'
'Darcoola'
Tin Tin
Tori Lake
Lake Pitarpunga
Lake Macommon
Tyldem
Penarie
Ganaway Lake
'Bramah'
'Toopuntal'
'Yanga'
Murrumbidgee
'Cringadale'
Paika Lake
'Paika'
'Nap Nap'
Maude
Hay
Hay Weir
Illilliwa
To Wagga Wagga
Lake Tala
'Hells Gate'
'Jeraly'
STURT HWY
'Glenhope'
'Bedarbigal'
'Walgrove'
'Narrawong'
'Eurolie'
Paiko Creek
Lake Wandaira
Balranald
River
MURRAY
Boundary Bend
Weimby
Yanga NR
'Willow Vale'
'St Pauls'
'Keri East'
'Clearview'
Yanga Lake
Windomal Landing
Yungera
Narrung
'Condoulpe'
Condoulpe Lake
'Tchelery'
'Everslee'
'Romani'
'Thalaka'
Piambie
Koorkab
Kenley
Dusty Lake
Kooloonong
Haysdale
Kyalite
Perekerten
'Miranda'
'Nyangay'
Booroorban
'Wargam'
'Oaklands'
Natya
Goodnight
Edward
Moolpa
'Willurah'
Tooleybuc
Stony Crossing
Piangil West
Piangil
Moulamein
'Warwillah'
Tudor
Miralie
Wood Wood
Merran
Moulamein
Nyah
Dilpurra
Wakool
Cunninyeuk
Nyah West
Vinifera
Speewa
Wanganella Creek
'Booabula'
Chillingollah
Beverford
Tyntynder Central
Niemur
Woorinen Nth
Tyntynder South
Jimaringle
Conargo
Woorinen
Pioneer Settlement
Lake Timboram
Swan Hill
Waitchie
Morago
Burraboi
Pental Island
Pretty Pine
Lalbert
Gowanford
Fish Point
Lake Boga
Ballbank
Edward River
Ultima
Goschen
Wakool
Tresco
Lake Tutchewop
Benjeroop
Deniliquin
RIVERINA HWY
Lalbert Road
Kunat
Murrabit
To Albury
Tyrrell
Mystic Park
Myall
Meatian
Lake Charm
Capels Crossing
Barham
Koondrook
Caldwell
DENIBOOTA IRRIGATION AREA
Tuppal
Berriwillock
Beachamp
Lake Lalbert
Lalbert
Westby
Korrak Korrak
Lake Bael Bael
Fairley
Koroop
Gannawarra
Culgoa
Sutton
Cokum
Tittybong
Cannie
Budgerum
Kerang
Kerang East
Gunbower
Cohuna
Bunnaloo
Moroco
Budgerum East
Dingwall
Kerang South
Mead
Island
Mathoura
Picnic Point
Jil Jil
Towaninny
McMillans
Wee-Wee-Rup
Barmah State Park
Top Is
Nullawil
Quambatook
Lake Meering
Leaghur State Pk
Tragowel
Horfield
Leitchville
Womboota
Moira Lake
Whirily
Fruit Fly Exclusion Zone
Appin
Appin South
Macorna
Torrumbarry Weir
Barmah Lake
Dumosa
Oakvale
Gredgwin
Leaghur
Kow Swamp
Gunbower
Narraport
Loddon Vale
Mincha
Mt Hope
Patho
Torrumbarry
Barmah
Picola
Barraport
Gladfield
Pyramid Hill
Bald Rock
Nathalia
Narioka
Wycheproof
Bunguluke
Catumnal
Durham Ox
Moama
Thalia
Boort
Terrick Terrick Nat Pk
Wharparilla
Kotupna
Lake Marmal
ECHUCA
Roslynmead
Goulburn
Corack East
Teddywaddy West
Teddywaddy
Narrewillock
Kotta
Bamawm Extension
Wyuna
McCoys Bridge
Corack
Lake Buloke
Banyenong
Wooroonook
Charlton
Mysia
Fernihurst
Jarklin
Mitiamo
Lockington
Bamawm
Koyuga
Simmie
Tongala
St Germains
Ky Valley
Jeffcott Nth
Buckrabanyule
Wychitella
The Granites Scenic Reserve
Calivil
Prairie
Milloo
Tennyson
Ballendella
Kyabram
Lancaster
Avoca
Woosang
Borung
Bears Lagoon
Warragamba
Rochester
Korong Vale
Pompapiel
Yallook
Dingee
Donald
Doboobetic
Wedderburn
Fiery Flat
Wedderburn Junction
Mt Korong Scenic Reserve
Serpentine
Tandarra
Fruit Fly Exclusion Zone
Merrigum
Girgarre
Cooma
Byrneside
Cope Cope
Hunter
Green L
MIDLAND HWY
Gooroc
Coonooer Bridge
Powlett Plains
Bullock
Kamarooka
Elmore
Corop
Cooper
Stanhope
To Shepparton
To Cobram
To St Arnaud
To Bendigo & Melbourne
39
42

42 North-East Victoria

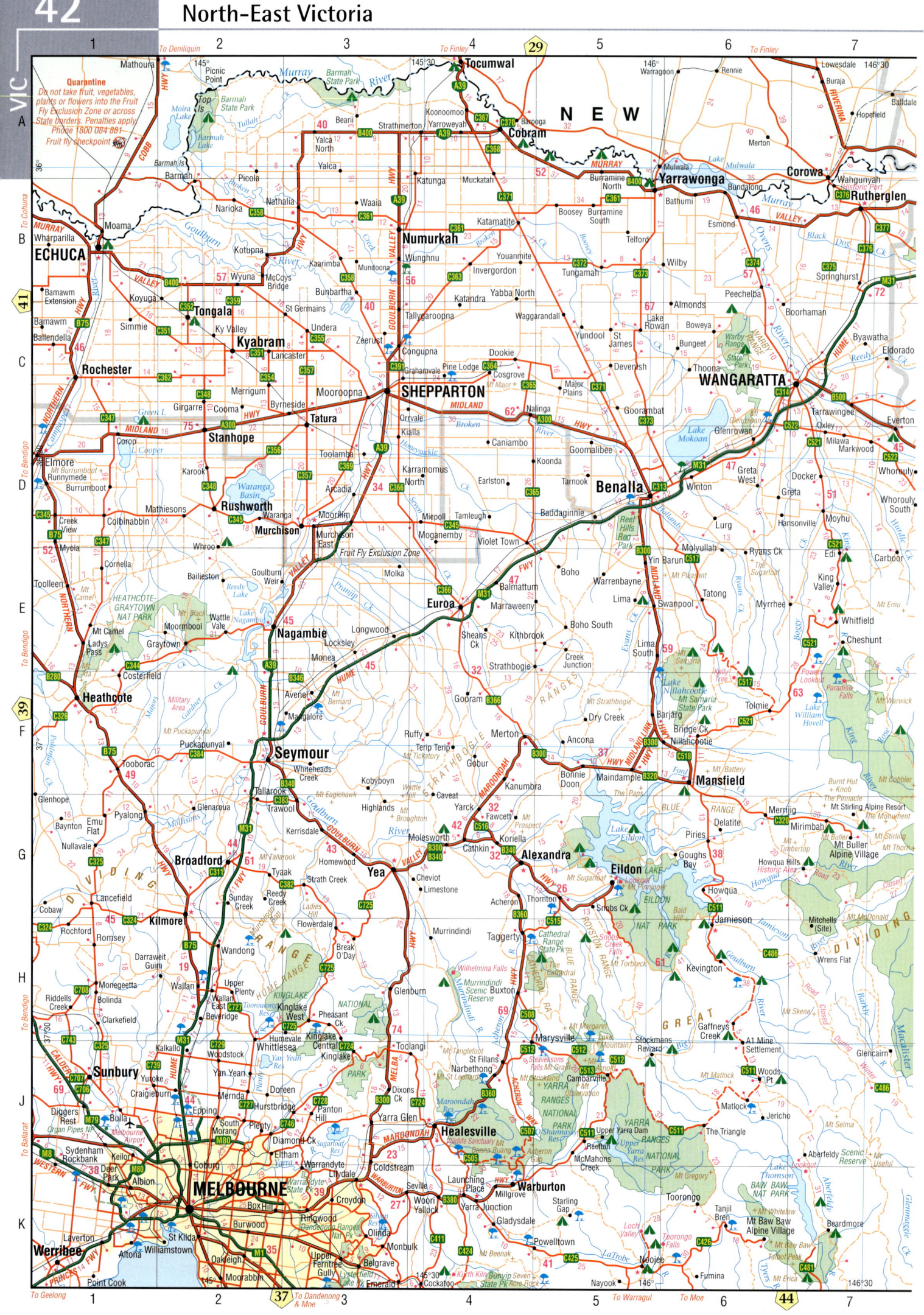

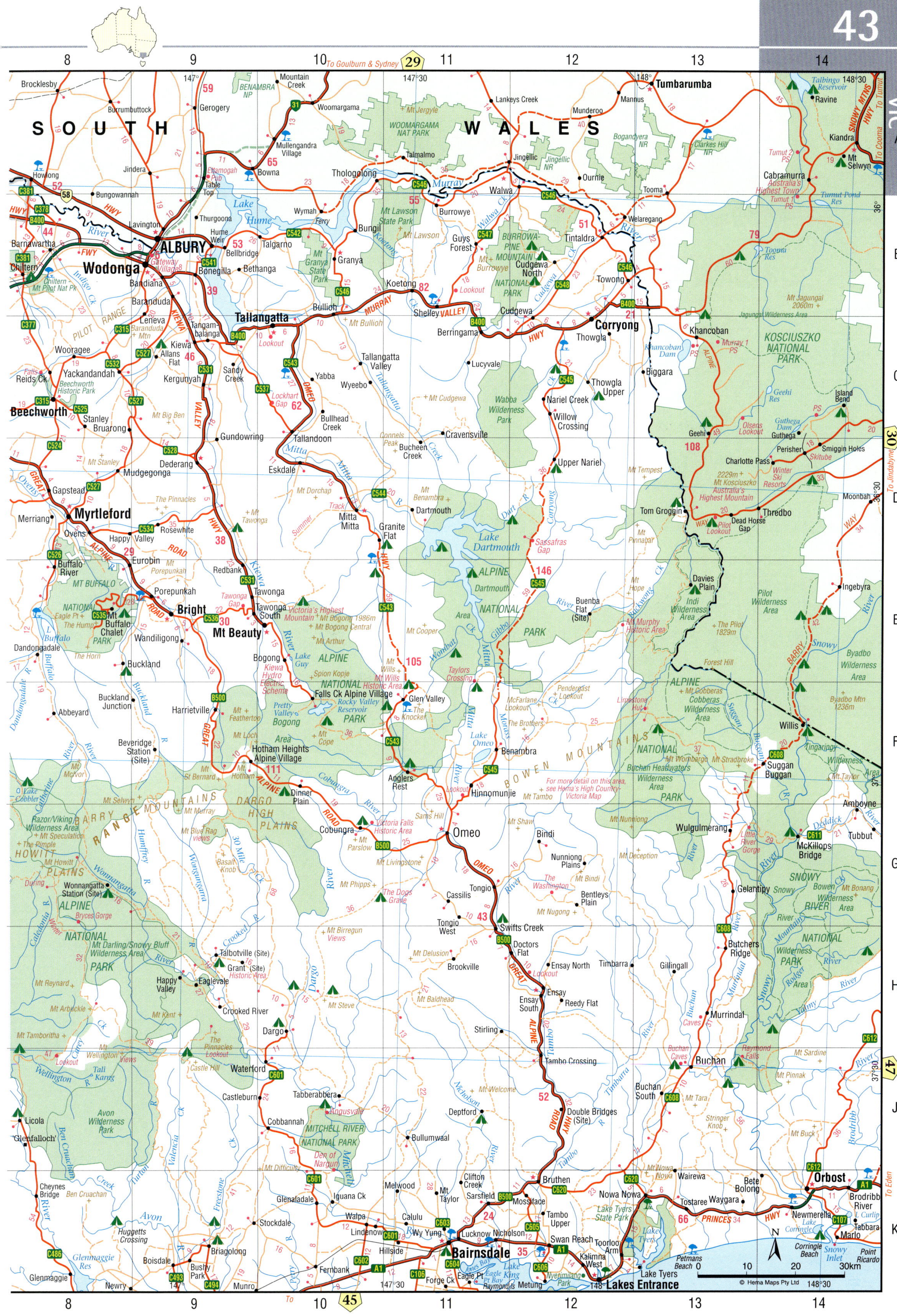
SOUTH WALES
To Goulburn & Sydney 29
Tumbarumba
Brocklesby
Burrumbuttock
Gerogery
Mountain Creek
BENAMBRA NP
Woomargama
WOOMARGAMA NAT PARK
Mt Jergyle
Lankeys Creek
Munderoo
Mannus
Bogandyera NR
Clarkes Hill NR
Talbingo Reservoir
Ravine
Kiandra
Mt Selwyn
Tumut 2 PS
Cabramurra
Australia's Highest Town
Tumut 1 PS
Tumut Pond Res
Jindera
Mullengandra Village
Bowna
Talmalmo
Jingellic
Jingellic NR
Ournie
Tooma
Howlong
Bungowannah
Table Top
Thologolong
Murray
Walwa
Welaregang
Lake Hume
Wymah
Ferry
Burrowye
Tintaldra
Lavington
Thurgoona
Hume Weir
Bungil
Mt Lawson State Park
Guys Forest
BURROWA-PINE MOUNTAIN NATIONAL PARK
Cudgewa North
Tooma Res
Barnawartha
ALBURY
Wodonga
Bellbridge
Talgarno
Bethanga
Bonegilla
Granya
Mt Granya State Park
Chiltern
Chiltern-Mt Pilot Nat Pk
Bandiana
Baranduda
Leneva
Tallangatta
Bullioh
Koetong
Shelley
Cudgewa
Towong
Corryong
Khancoban
Thowgla
Berringama
Mt Jagungal 2060m
Jagungal Wilderness Area
KOSCIUSZKO NATIONAL PARK
Murray 1 PS
Khancoban Dam
Pilot Range
Tangambalanga
Kiewa
Allans Flat
Woorage
Yackandandah
Reids Ck
Beechworth Historic Park
Kergunyah
Sandy Creek
Lockhart Gap
Yabba
Tallangatta Valley
Wyeebo
Lucyvale
Biggara
Thowgla Upper
Nariel Creek
Willow Crossing
Geehi Res
Island Bend
Guthega Dam
Guthega
Beechworth
Stanley
Bruarong
Mt Big Ben
Bullhead Creek
Mt Cudgewa
Wabba Wilderness Park
Olsens Lookout
Geehi
Perisher
Smiggin Holes
Skitube
Charlotte Pass
Gundowring
Tallandoon
Cravensville
Connels Peak
Bucheen Creek
Dederang
Mudgegonga
Mt Stanley
Eskdale
Upper Nariel
Mt Tempest
2229m Mt Kosciuszko Australia's Highest Mountain
Winter Ski Resorts
Gapstead
Merriang
Myrtleford
Ovens
The Pinnacles
Mt Tawonga
Mt Dorchap
Mitta Mitta
Granite Flat
Mt Benambra
Dartmouth
Tom Groggin
Pilot Lookout
Dead Horse Gap
Thredbo
Moonbah
To Jindabyne 30
Happy Valley
Rosewhite
Eurobin
Buffalo River
MT BUFFALO
Mt Porepunkah
Porepunkah
Redbank
Lake Dartmouth
ALPINE NATIONAL PARK
Dartmouth
Sassafras Gap
Davies Plain
Indi Wilderness Area
Pilot Wilderness Area
Ingebyra
Bright
Mt Buffalo Chalet
Tawonga Gap
Tawonga
Tawonga South
Mt Beauty
Victoria's Highest Mountain Mt Bogong 1986m
Mt Bogong Central
Mt Arthur
Buenba Flat (Site)
Mt Murphy Historic Area
The Pilot 1829m
Dandongadale
Wandiligong
Buckland
Bogong
Kiewa Hydro Electric Scheme
Lake Guy
Spion Kopje
ALPINE
Mt Wills
Mt Wills Historic Area
Taylors Crossing
Forest Hill
Byadbo Wilderness Area
Snowy
Buckland Junction
Abbeyard
Harrietville
Mt Feathertop
Falls Ck Alpine Village
Pretty Valley
Rocky Valley Reservoir
Bogong
PARK
Glen Valley
The Knocker
McFarlane Lookout
Pendergast Lookout
Limestone Hut
Mt Cobberas
Cobberas Wilderness Area
Byadbo Mtn 1236m
Beveridge Station (Site)
Mt Loch
Mt Cope
The Brothers
Lake Omeo
Benambra
BOWEN MOUNTAINS
For more detail on this area, see Hema's High Country Victoria Map
Willis
Tingaringy
Suggan Buggan
Mt Stradbroke
Mt Wombargo
Buchan Headwaters Wilderness Area
Mt McIvor
Hotham Heights Alpine Village
Mt Hotham
Mt St Bernard
Anglers Rest
Hinnomunjie
Mt Tambo
Amboyne
Lake Cobbler
Mt Selwyn
BARRY MOUNTAINS
Mt Murray
DARGO HIGH PLAINS
Dinner Plain
Cobungra
Sams Hill
Victoria Falls Historic Area
Mt Shaw
Bindi
Mt Nunniong
Wulgulmerang
Little River Gorge
McKillops Bridge
Tubbut
Razor/Viking Wilderness Area
Mt Speculation
The Pimple
HOWITT PLAINS
Mt Howitt
Mt Blue Rag Views
30 Mile Ck
Mt Parslow
Omeo
Mt Livingstone
Nunniong Plains
Mt Deception
SNOWY RIVER NATIONAL PARK
Bowen Ck Wilderness Area
Mt Bonang
Wonnangatta Station (Site)
Basalt Knob
Mt Phipps
The Dogs Grave
Cassilis
Tongio
The Washington
Mt Bindi
Bentleys Plain
Gelantipy
Bryces Gorge
Mt Birregun Views
Tongio West
Swifts Creek
Mt Nugong
Mt Darling/Snowy Bluff Wilderness Area
Talbotville (Site)
Grant (Site) Historic Area
Mt Delusion
Brookville
Doctors Flat
Ensay North
Timbarra
Gillingall
Butchers Ridge
Snowy Wilderness Area
Mt Reynard
Happy Valley
Eaglevale
Lookout
Ensay
Reedy Flat
Ensay South
Murrindal
Buchan Caves
Mt Arbuckle
Crooked River
Mt Steve
Mt Baldhead
Mt Kent
Mt Tamboritha
Dargo
The Pinnacles Lookout
Stirling
Raymond Falls
Mt Wellington Views
Castle Hill
Tali Karng
Waterford
Tambo Crossing
Buchan
Mt Sardine
Mt Pinnak
Wellington
To 47
Castleburn
Tabberabbera
Mt Welcome
Buchan South
Mt Tara
Licola
Avon Wilderness Park
Angusvale
Deptford
Double Bridges (Site)
Stringer Knob
Glenfalloch
Cobbannah
MITCHELL RIVER NATIONAL PARK
Mt Buck
Den of Nargun
Bullumwaal
Mt Difficulty
Cheynes Bridge
Ben Cruachan
Melwood
Mt Taylor
Clifton Creek
Sarsfield
Bruthen
Mossiface
Wairewa
Nowa Nowa
Bete Bolong
Orbost
Glenaladale
Iguana Ck
Tostaree
Waygara
Brodribb River
Avon
Huggetts Crossing
Stockdale
Walpa
Lindenow
Calulu
Wy Yung
Lucknow
Nicholson
Tambo Upper
Lake Tyers State Park
Newmerella
Curlip
Marlo
Tabbara
Briagolong
Hillside
Bairnsdale
Swan Reach
Toorloo Arm
Kalimna West
Lake Tyers
Petmans Beach
Corringle Beach
Snowy Inlet
Point Ricardo
Glenmaggie Res
Boisdale
Bushy Park
Glenmaggie
Newry
Munro
Fernbank
Eagle Pt
Forge Ck
Raymond Is
Eagle Point Bay
Lake King
Metung
Nyerimilang Park
Lakes Entrance
Lake Tyers
To Eden
0 10 20 30km
© Hema Maps Pty Ltd
To 45
148°30
147°30
148°
147°
36°
36°30
37°
37°30
8 9 10 11 12 13 14
A B C D E F G H J K

44 Gippsland Region, Victoria

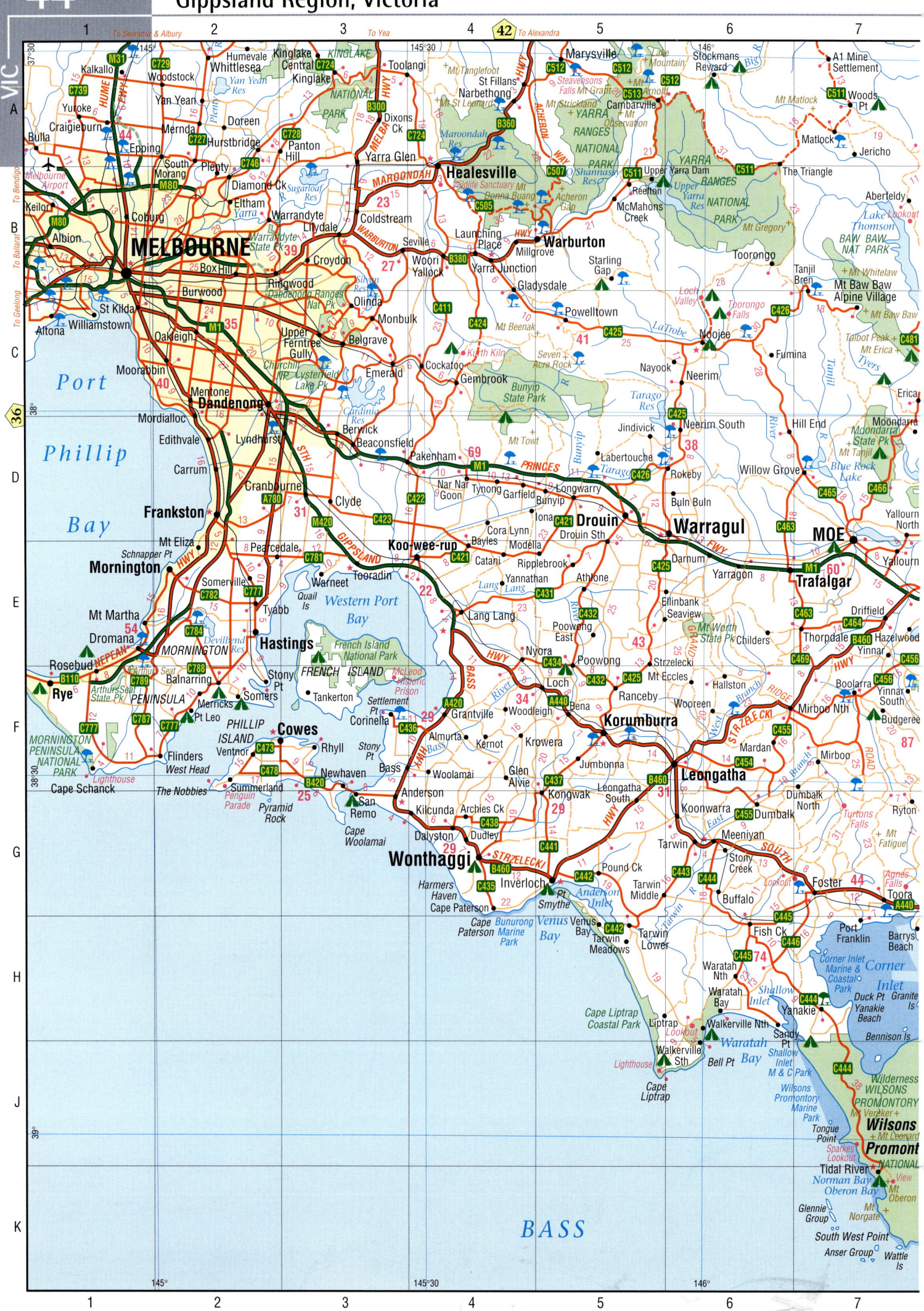

Glencairn
Road Closed During Winter
C486
Mt Tamboritha Lookout
Macalister
Wellington R
Mt Wellington Views
Tali Karng
Carey Ck
Avon Wilderness Park
Licola
Mt Selma
'Glenfalloch'
Scenic Reserve
Mt Useful
Ben Cruachan
Ben Cruachan Creek
Turton
Valencia Ck
Freestone Ck
The Pinnacles Lookout
Castle Hill
Waterford
C601
Castleburn
Cobbannah
Tabberabbera
Angusvale
MITCHELL RIVER NATIONAL PARK
Den of Nargun
Mitchell
Mt Difficulty
Glenaladale
Iguana Ck
Deptford
Mt Welcome
Nicholson
Bullumwaal
Tambo Crossing
To Omeo
To Dargo
OMEO
ALPINE
HWY
GREAT
ROAD
Double Bridges (Site)
Tambo
Bruthen
C620
Clifton Creek
Melwood
Mt Taylor
Sarsfield
B500
Mossiface
Tambo Upper
Calulu
C603
Wy Yung
Walpa
Lindenow
C601
Hillside
Lucknow
Nicholson
Bairnsdale
C605
Swan Reach
A1
Kalimna West
To Orbost
Lakes Entrance
Nyerimilang Park
C606
Metung
Eagle Pt
Eagle Point Bay
Lake King
Jones Bay
Raymond Is
Paynesville
Bunga Arm
Beach
C604
Forge Ck
C106
Goon Nure
Wattle Pt
Lake Victoria
THE LAKES NATIONAL PARK
Mile
Aberfeldy
Beardmore
Cheynes Bridge
River
Glenmaggie
Glenmaggie Res
Glenmaggie Ck
Huggetts Crossing
Avon
Stockdale
Briagolong
Boisdale
Bushy Park
C493
C494
Munro
HWY
A1
Fernbank
C602
Perry
Walhalla
Walhalla Historic Area
Rawson
C461
Coopers Creek
Seaton
Thomson
Heyfield
Tinamba
C105
Newry
Maffra
Stratford
C495
Cowwarr
River
Airlie
Clydebank
C106
Bengworden
Meerlieu
Moondarra Res
Toongabbie
C488
Nambrok
C487
Bundalaguah
C491
C106
Cobains
Marlay Point
Lake Wellington
Holland Landing
Loch Sport
C481
Tyers River
Tyers Park
C105
Glengarry
Tyers
Kilmany
Wurruk
Sale
The Heart
Seacombe
La Trobe River
TRARALGON
PRINCES
A1
Rosedale
C485
Longford
Lake Coleman
Lake Reeve
Ninety
Gippsland Lakes Coastal Park
MORWELL
HYLAND
Holey Plains State Park
C485
Paradise Beach
Golden Beach
Loy Yang
Traralgon Sth
C482
Merriman
Willung
Stradbroke West
The
Churchill
Gormandale
Powers Hill Lookout
Little
Monkey
Ck
Creek
C496
Stradbroke
C483
RD
MORWELL NAT PARK
Mt Tassie Lookout
Carrajung
Seaspray
RIDGE
C484
Balook
TARRA-BULGA NAT PARK
HWY
C453
Giffard
Lake Denison
GRAND
Tarra
C484
Won Wron
Bruthen
Darriman
A440
C482
Jack Smith Lake
Hiawatha Falls
Jack River
Devon
Greenmount
Woodside
C453
Woodside Beach
Wonyip
Yarram
Albert R
C459
Reeves Beach
Binginwarri
GIPPSLAND
Alberton
C452
Tarraville
St Margaret Is
Manns Beach
McLaughlins Beach
Welshpool
Port Welshpool
Sunday Is
Port Albert
Clonmel Is
Nooramunga Marine & Coastal Park
Little Snake Is
Snake Is
Mt Hunter
Mt Margaret
Mt Roundback
Area
Johnny Souey Pt
Wilsons Promontory Marine Park
ory
PARK
Sealers Cove
Horn Pt
Mt Wilson
Brown Head
Cape Wellington
Waterloo Bay
Mt Boulder
South Peak
Lighthouse
South Point
STRAIT
N
0 10 20 30km
© Hema Maps Pty Ltd
146°30
147°
147°30
148°
37°30
38°
38°30
39°
43
47
8 9 10 11 12 13 14
A B C D E F G H J K

46 South-East Victoria

VIC
To Willis
To Cooma & Canberra
43
30
NEW SOUTH WALES
TASMAN SEA
Wilderness Coast
Headwaters Area
NATIONAL PARK
Wulgulmerang
Mt Taylor
Mt Tingaringy
Amboyne
Tubbut
Deddick
McKillops Bridge
Delegate River
Delegate
Dellicknora
Haydens Bog
Mt Delegate
Bendoc North
Bendoc
Lower Bendoc
Craigie
Mila
Bondi Gulf NR
Maharatta
Coolumbooka NR
Platts
Rockton
SOUTH EAST FORESTS NAT PK
Burragate
Egan Peaks NR
MT IMLAY NAT PK
Towamba
Pericoe
Lochiel
Greigs Flat
Nethercote
Pambula
Pambula Beach
Haycock Point
Eden
Twofold Bay
Boyds Tower
Boydtown
Edrom
BEN BOYD NATIONAL PARK
Kiah
Mt Imlay
Saltwater Creek
Wonboyn Lake
Bittangabee Bay
Lighthouse
Disaster Bay
Green Cape
Cabanandra
Gelantipy
Bonang
Mt Bonang
SNOWY RIVER NATIONAL PARK
Bowen Ck
Snowy River Wilderness Area
Butchers Ridge
Gillingall
Mountain River
Wilderness PARK
Rodger Area
Goongerah
Mt Jersey
ERRINUNDRA NATIONAL PARK
Errinundra
Mt Ellery
Combienbar
Buldah
Chandlers Creek
Nungatta
Nungatta South
Genoa
Mt Merragunegin
COOPRACAMBRA NATIONAL PARK
Wilderness Area
Wroxham
Wangarabell
Mt Buckle
Narrabarba
Timbillica
Newtons Beach
Ranger Station
NADGEE NATURE RESERVE
Maramingo Hill
Mallacoota Lookout
Murrindal
Buchan Caves
Buchan
Raymond Falls
Buchan South
Mt Tara
Mt Sardine
Mt Pinnak
Mt Jack
Mt Kuark
Noorinbee North
Noorinbee
Tonghi Ck
Club Terrace
LIND NATIONAL PARK
Cann River
Rainforest Walk
ALFRED NATIONAL PARK
Genoa
Gipsy Pt
Fairhaven
Cape Howe
Cape Howe Wilderness Area
Lake Barracoota
Genoa Peak Lookout
Mallacoota
Mallacoota Inlet
Bastion Point
Gabo Island
Lighthouse
Stringer Knob
Mt Buck
Murrungowar
Bemm River Rainforest
Mt Bemm
Bellbird Creek
Manorina
Wairewa
Bete Bolong
Tostaree
Waygara
Orbost
Brodribb River
Newmerella
Cabbage Tree Creek
Cabbage Tree Palms Reserve
PRINCES HWY
MONARO (CANN VALLEY) HWY
Lake Curlip
Corringle
Tabbara
Marlo
Corringle Beach
Snowy Inlet
Point Ricardo
Cape Conran
Cape Conran Coastal Park
Pearl Point
Bemm River
Lake Furnell
Swan Lake
Sydenham Inlet
Tamboon
Tamboon Inlet
Point Hicks
Lighthouse
Mt Everard
CROAJINGOLONG NATIONAL PARK
Petrel Pt
Rame Head
Wingan Inlet
Sandpatch Wilderness Area
Sandpatch Pt
Little Rame Head
Petmans Beach
148°30
149°
149°30
150°
37°
37°30
38°
38°30
39°
0 10 20 30 40 50 km
N
© Hema Maps Pty Ltd

48 Key map

Tasmania

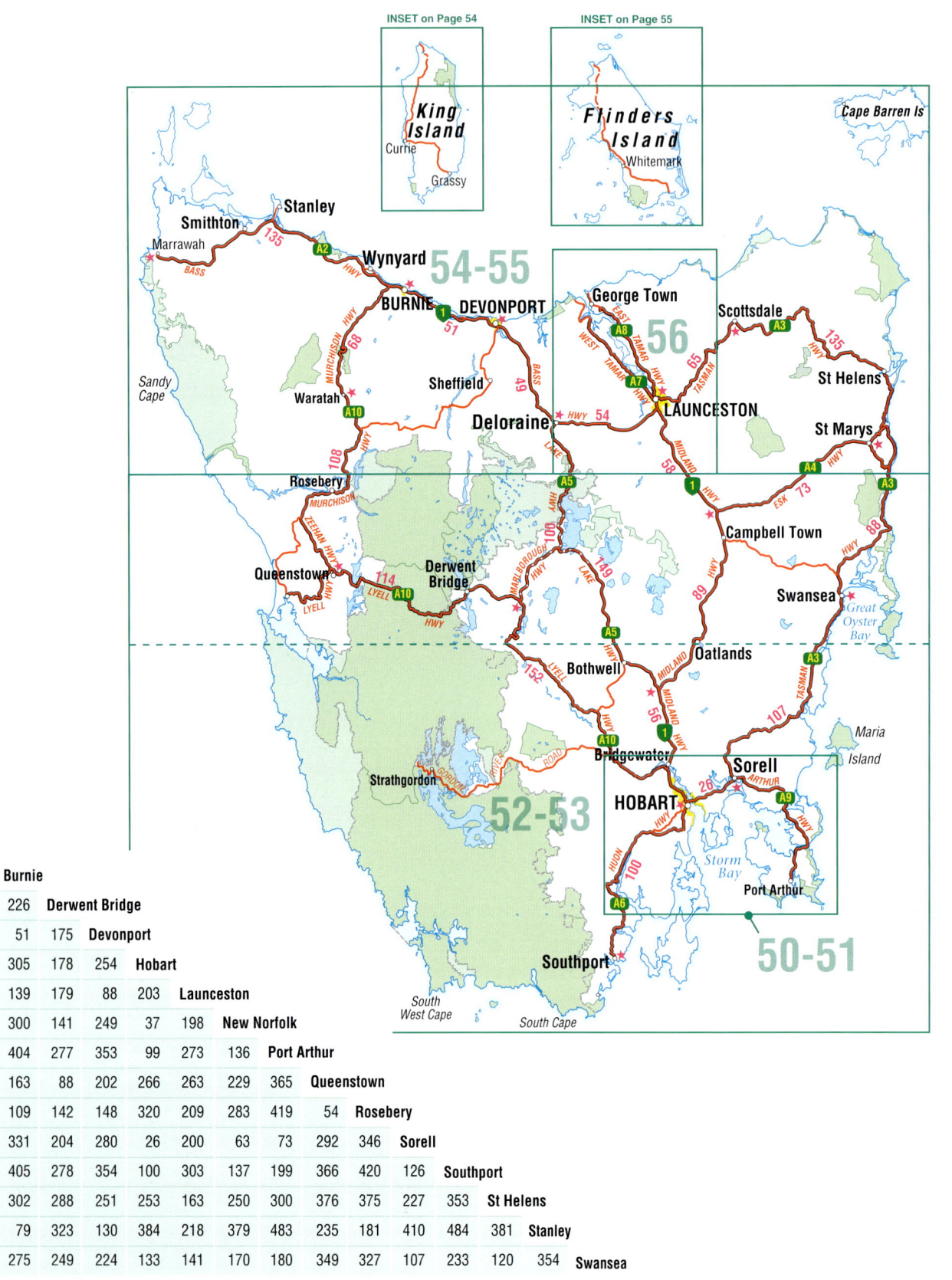

Wineglass Bay (53 C14)

INSET on Page 54 — King Island (Currie, Grassy)
INSET on Page 55 — Flinders Island (Whitemark)

Cape Barren Is

54-55
56
52-53
50-51

Burnie											
226	**Derwent Bridge**										
51	175	**Devonport**									
305	178	254	**Hobart**								
139	179	88	203	**Launceston**							
300	141	249	37	198	**New Norfolk**						
404	277	353	99	273	136	**Port Arthur**					
163	88	202	266	263	229	365	**Queenstown**				
109	142	148	320	209	283	419	54	**Rosebery**			
331	204	280	26	200	63	73	292	346	**Sorell**		
405	278	354	100	303	137	199	366	420	126	**Southport**	
302	288	251	253	163	250	300	376	375	227	353	**St Helens**
79	323	130	384	218	379	483	235	181	410	484	381	**Stanley**
275	249	224	133	141	170	180	349	327	107	233	120	354	**Swansea**

Distances are shown in kilometres and follow the most direct major sealed route

Hobart CBD

49
TAS

Legend

Major Road	DAVEY STREET	Shopping Area	
Route Number	1 A3	Church	+
Street	DUKE STREET	Hospital	+
Lane/Walkway		Park / Reserve	
One Way Street	→	Accredited Information	i
Railway		Post Office	

SCALE: 0 200m 400m 600m 800m 1km
© Hema Maps Pty Ltd

Places of Interest

1. Anglesea Barracks C2
2. Battery Point Area D2
3. Bellerive Oval C4
4. Cat & Fiddle Arcade C2
5. Designer Makers at Design Object Tas B1
6. Federation Concert Hall C2
7. Franklin Square C2
8. Gasworks Shopping Village C2
9. Hobart Cruises C2
10. Hobart Town Hall C2
11. Kelly Steps C2
12. Maritime Museum C2
13. Narryna Heritage Museum C2
14. Parliament House C2
15. Penitentiary Chapel & Courts C2
16. Royal Tasmanian Botanic Gardens B2
17. Royal Tennis Centre C2
18. Salamanca Market (Saturday) C2
19. Tasmanian Museum & Art Gallery C2
20. Theatre Royal C2
21. Village Cinema Centre C2
22. Wrest Point Casino D2

Accommodation

25. Blue Hills Motel & Apartments D2
26. Chancellor Inn C2
27. City View Motel A4
28. Corus Hotel Hobart C2
29. Customs House Waterfront Hotel C2
30. Davey Place Holiday Town Houses D1
31. Doherty's Hotel C2
32. Fountainside Motor Inn C2
33. Graham Court Apartments A1
34. Grosvenor Court Apartments D2
35. Hobart Macquarie Motor Inn C2
36. Hobart Tower Motel A1
37. Hotel Grand Chancellor C2
38. Lenna of Hobart C2
39. Macquarie Manor C2
40. Mayfair Plaza Motel C1
41. Montgomery's Private Hotel & YHA C2
42. Portsea Terrace C2
43. Quest Waterfront C2
44. Rydges Hobart B1
45. Salamanca Inn C2
46. Somerset on the Pier C2
47. St Ives Motel Apartments D2
48. The Lodge on Elizabeth B1
49. The Old Woolstore C2
50. Waratah Motor Hotel C1
51. Woolmers Inn D2
52. Wrest Point Hotel Casino D2

Services

55. Allport Library & Museum C2
56. Jewish Synagogue C2
56. Police Headquarters C2
 . Post Office C2
57. Qantas C2
58. RACT C2
59. Royal Hobart Hospital C2
60. St Davids Cathedral C2
61. St Helens Hospital C2
62. Tasmanian Visitor Information Centre C2
63. YHA Head Office C2

50 Hobart Region, Tasmania

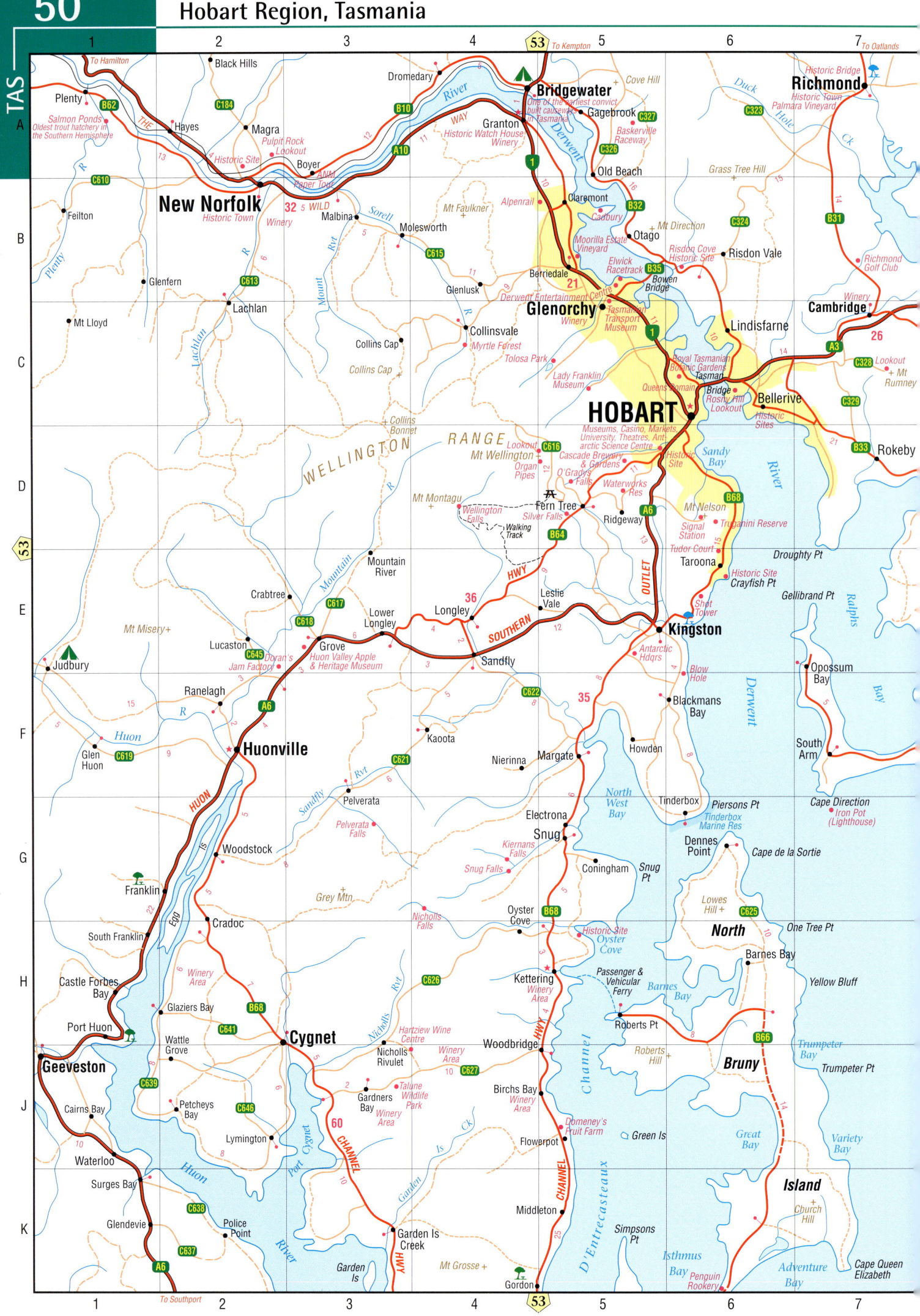

TAS
To Triabunna
53
8
9
10
11
12
13
14
A
B
C
D
E
F
G
H
J
K
Nugent
Orielton
Pawleena
Orielton Rt
Sorell Rt
Rvt
A3
C332
C331
C335
C349
C330
C334
B33
B37
C341
C343
C344
C347
C338
A9
Mt Lord
Penna
Wattle Hill
Gordon SL
Corbetts Lookout
Kellevie
Ragged Tier
Bream Ck
Marion Bay
Cape Bernier
Point du Ressac
Winery
Sorell
Midway Pt
Orani Vineyard
Forcett
Pitt Water
Tasmania Golf Club
Oyster Farm
Bream Creek
Museum
Copping
ARTHUR
HWY
Convict & Colonial Collection
Seven Mile Beach Equestrian Centre
Lewisham
Hobart Airport
Llanherne Golf Club
Royal Hobart Golf Club
Seven Mile Beach
Sandy Pt
Tiger Head
Dodges Ferry
Carlton
Carlton Bluff
Cape Paul Lamanon
Blackman Bay
North Bay
Cape Frederick Hendrick
Tasman Monument
Roches Beach
Primrose Sands
Primrose Pt
Dunalley
Denison Canal
Lauderdale
Fulham Is
Dunalley Bay
Mt Forestier
Frederick Henry Bay
Green Head
Wellard Bridge
73
Forestier
Sandford
Sloping Is
Lime Bay Nature Res
Smooth Is
King George Is
Murdunna
Cape Surville
Tasman National Park
Cremorne
Whitehouse Pt
Mt Augustus
Pipe Clay Lagoon
Mt Stewart
Chronicle Pt
Peninsula
Coal Mines Historic Site
Macgregor Peak
Cape Deslacs
Clifton Beach
Mutton Bird Viewing (Summer)
Convict Settlement Ruins
Flinders Bay
Flinders Ck
North West Head
Norfolk Bay
Gwandalan
Garnetts Bridge
Deer Pt
Lookout
Sandford Equestrian Centre
Tessellated Pavement
Cape Contrariety
Saltwater River
Eaglehawk Bay
Eaglehawk Neck
Officers Quarters & Dogline
Historic Site
Pirates Bay
Iron Pot Lookout
Hurdle Bridge
Halfway Bluff
Cashs Lookout
Penzance
Tasman Blowhole
Tasman Arch
Devils Kitchen
Betsey Is
Doo Town
Premaydena
Taranna
Tasmanian Devil Centre
Mt Communication
Koonya
Waterfall Bay
Camp Falls
Outer North Head
O'Hara Bluff
Auk Pt
Sand Dunes
Nubeena
Tasman
Peninsula
Storm Bay
Parsons Bridge
Oakwood
Thumb Pt
Wedge Bay
Mimosa Falls
White Beach
Wedge Is
Bush Mill Railway
Isle of the Dead Historic Site
Cape Hauy
Fortescue Bay
The Lanterns
Highcroft
Port Arthur
Convict Ruins
Historic Ghost Tours
Ocean Kayaking Tours
Two Island Bay
Port Arthur
Palmers Lookout
Stormlea
Curio Bay
Remarkable Cave
Maingon Blowhole
Munro Bight
West Arthur Head
Raoul Bay
Black Head
Cape Pillar
Chasm Lookout
Maingon Bay
Cape Raoul
Tasman Is
Lighthouse
N
SCALE
0
5
10 km
© Hema Maps Pty Ltd

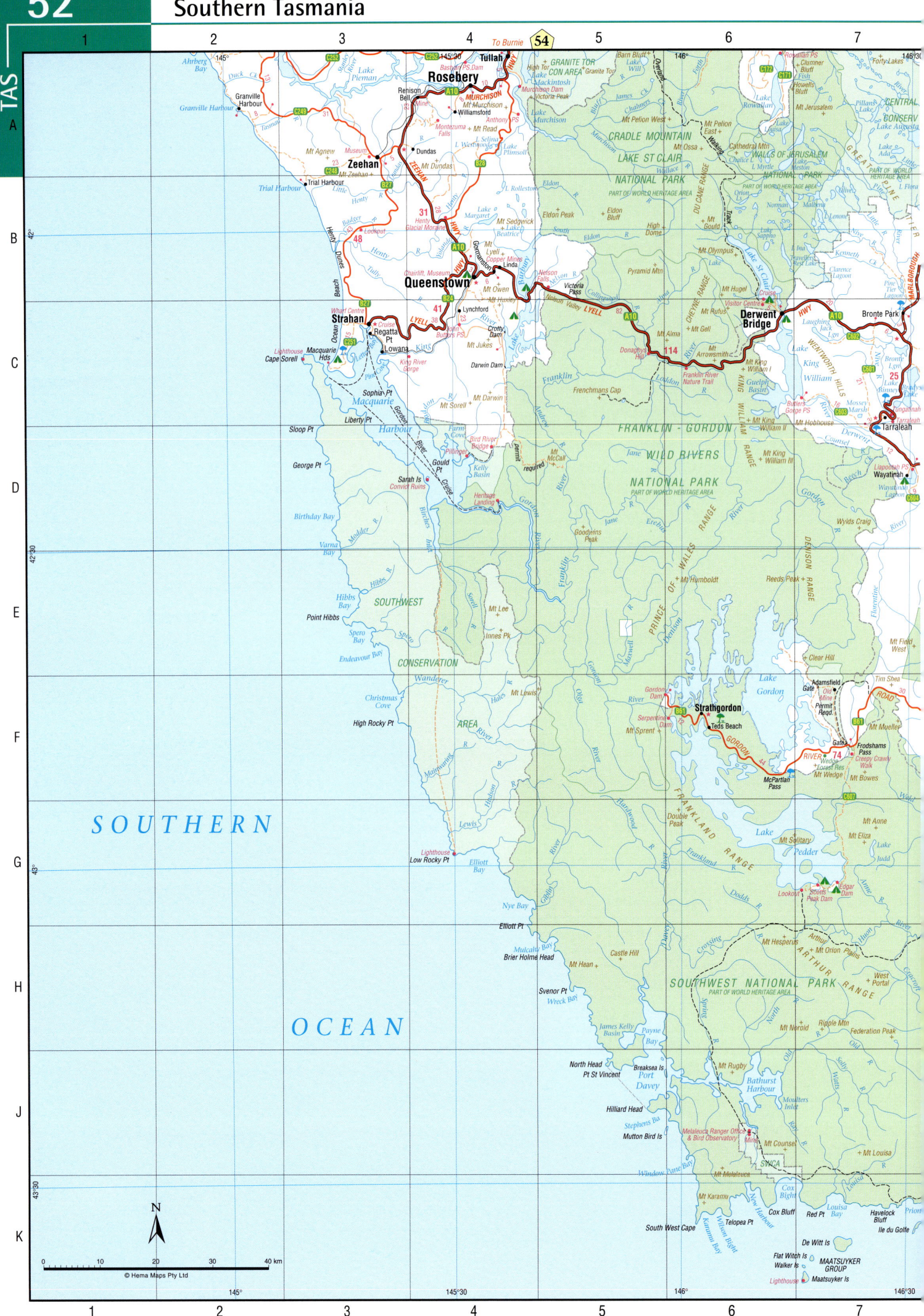

52 Southern Tasmania

To Devonport, Launceston
To Launceston
55
To St Marys
To St Marys St Helens
8
9
10
11
12
13
14
A
B
C
D
E
F
G
H
J
K
147°
147°30
148°
148°30
42°
42°30
43°
43°30
HOBART
New Norfolk
Bridgewater
Brighton
Glenorchy
Lindisfarne
Bellerive
Rokeby
Lauderdale
Kingston
Huonville
Cygnet
Geeveston
Dover
Southport
Sorell
Richmond
Midway Pt
Campbell Town
Ross
Oatlands
Bothwell
Hamilton
Kempton
Swansea
Bicheno
Triabunna
Orford
Dunalley
Nubeena
Port Arthur
Eaglehawk Neck
Poatina
Avoca
Conara
Cleveland
Epping Forest
Tunbridge
Mona Vale
York Plains
Parattah
Jericho
Apsley
Melton Mowbray
Colebrook
Campania
Dysart
Bagdad
Mangalore
Pontville
Gretna
Hayes
Magra
Plenty
Lachlan
Maydena
Westerway
National Park
Ouse
Miena
Tods
Steppes
Wilburville
Waddamana
Interlaken
Little Swanport
Buckland
Copping
Forcett
Lewisham
Carlton
Primrose Sands
Taranna
Koonya
Premaydena
Saltwater River
Snug
Margate
Woodbridge
Middleton
Franklin
Cradoc
Judbury
Lonnavale
Alonnah
Lunawanna
Adventure Bay
Cockle Creek
Catamaran
Ida Bay
Lune River
Hastings
Strathblane
Raminea
Great Western Tiers Conservation Area
Central Plateau Conservation Area
Douglas-Apsley National Park
Freycinet National Park
Freycinet Peninsula
Schouten Island
Maria Island National Park
Maria Island
Forestier Peninsula
Tasman Peninsula
Tasman Nat Park
Bruny Island
South Bruny National Park
Hartz Mtns Nat Park
Mount Field Nat Park
Buckland Military Training Area
Great Oyster Bay
Frederick Henry Bay
Norfolk Bay
Storm Bay
Marion Bay
D'Entrecasteaux Channel
TASMAN SEA
Great Lake
Lake Sorell
Lake Crescent
Lake Echo
Arthurs Lake
Meadowbank Lake
Midland Hwy
Lake Hwy
Lyell Hwy
Tasman Hwy
Arthur Hwy
Huon Hwy
Channel Hwy
Heritage Hwy
Esk Hwy
A1
A3
A4
A5
A6
A9
A10

54 Northern Tasmania

INSET
FURNEAUX GROUP
Flinders Island
Whitemark
Lady Barron
Killiecrankie
Emita
Memana
Cape Barren Island
Clarke Island
Banks Strait
BASS STRAIT
Swan Is
Waterhouse Is
Ninth Is
Noland Bay
Anderson Bay
Ringarooma Bay
Cape Portland
Great Musselroe Bay
Poole
Cape Naturaliste
MOUNT WILLIAM NAT PARK
Eddystone Pt
Gladstone
Bridport
Waterhouse
Tomahawk
Stony Head
Low Head
George Town
Bell Bay
Port Sorell
Beaconsfield
Exeter
Lilydale
Scottsdale
Derby
Branxholm
Ringarooma
Weldborough
Pyengana
St Helens
Binalong Bay
Scamander
Falmouth
St Marys
Fingal
Mathinna
Avoca
Rossarden
LAUNCESTON
St Leonards
Deloraine
Westbury
Perth
Longford
Evandale
Cressy
Poatina
Conara
Campbell Town
Ross
Tunbridge
Oatlands
Bicheno
Swansea
Great Oyster Bay
Freycinet Peninsula
FREYCINET NATIONAL PARK
DOUGLAS-APSLEY NATIONAL PARK
BEN LOMOND NATIONAL PARK
Great Lake
Arthurs Lake
Lake Sorell
Lake Crescent
Miena
Bothwell
GREAT WESTERN TIERS CONSERVATION AREA
CENTRAL PLATEAU CONSERVATION AREA
WESTERN TIERS
MIDLAND HWY
TASMAN HWY
To Hobart
53

56 Launceston Region, Tasmania

Key map 57

South Australia

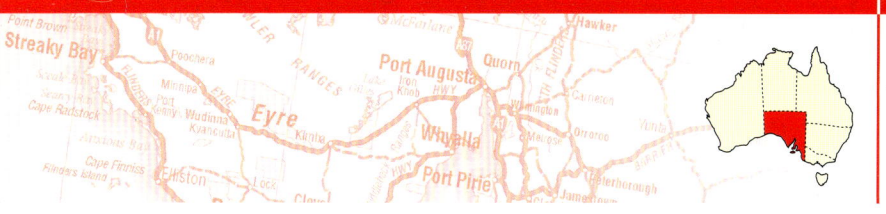

Paddle Steamer Murraylands, Murray River (62 C5, 65 H13)

Adelaide													
272	Bordertown												
1185	1457	Birdsville											
511	783	1219	Broken Hill										
771	1043	1358	882	Ceduna									
843	1115	886	954	1002	Coober Pedy								
1065	1337	417	1099	1238	926	Innamincka							
1262	1534	1305	1373	1421	419	1345	Kulgera						
671	943	514	705	844	372	554	971	Marree					
454	184	1639	965	1225	1297	1519	1716	1125	Mt Gambier				
1050	1312	920	1151	1199	197	960	391	406	1494	Oodnadatta			
243	148	1428	754	1014	1086	1308	1505	914	332	1283	Pinnaroo		
306	578	893	417	465	537	773	956	379	760	734	549	Port Augusta	
646	918	1233	757	404	877	1113	1296	719	1100	1074	889	340	Port Lincoln
252	298	1234	560	897	969	1114	1388	720	368	1166	150	432	772	Renmark
1257	1529	1844	1368	486	1488	1724	1970	1330	1711	1685	1500	951	890	1383	WA-SA Border Village

Distances are shown in kilometres and follow the most direct major sealed route where possible

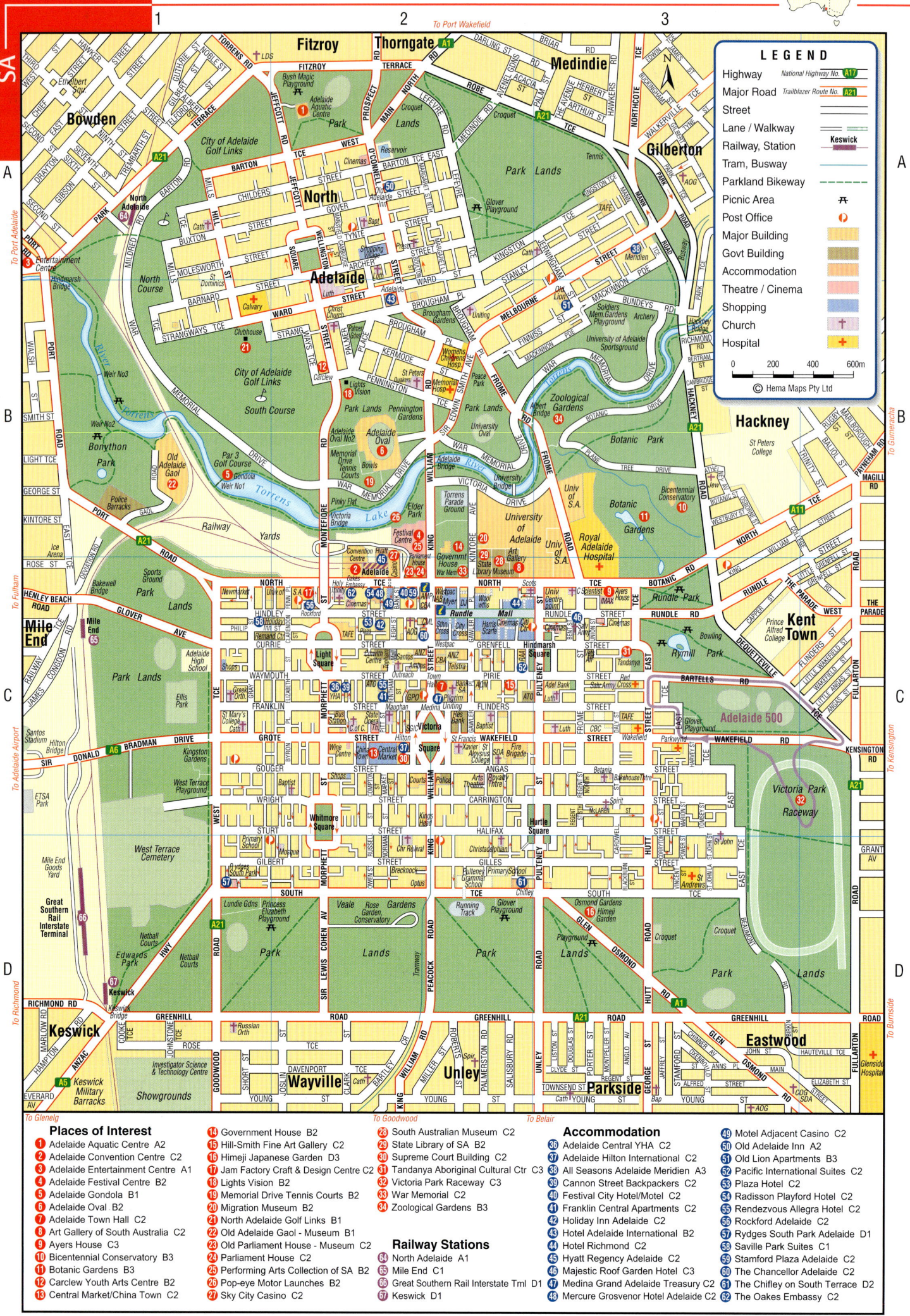

58 Adelaide CBD

Places of Interest
1. Adelaide Aquatic Centre A2
2. Adelaide Convention Centre C2
3. Adelaide Entertainment Centre A1
4. Adelaide Festival Centre B2
5. Adelaide Gondola B1
6. Adelaide Oval B2
7. Adelaide Town Hall C2
8. Art Gallery of South Australia C2
9. Ayers House C3
10. Bicentennial Conservatory B3
11. Botanic Gardens B3
12. Carclew Youth Arts Centre B2
13. Central Market/China Town C2
14. Government House B2
15. Hill-Smith Fine Art Gallery C2
16. Himeji Japanese Garden D3
17. Jam Factory Craft & Design Centre C2
18. Lights Vision B2
19. Memorial Drive Tennis Courts B2
20. Migration Museum B2
21. North Adelaide Golf Links B1
22. Old Adelaide Gaol - Museum B1
23. Old Parliament House - Museum C2
24. Parliament House C2
25. Performing Arts Collection of SA C2
26. Pop-eye Motor Launches B2
27. Sky City Casino C2
28. South Australian Museum C2
29. State Library of SA B2
30. Supreme Court Building C2
31. Tandanya Aboriginal Cultural Ctr C3
32. Victoria Park Raceway C3
33. War Memorial C2
34. Zoological Gardens B3

Railway Stations
63. North Adelaide A1
64. Mile End C1
65. Great Southern Rail Interstate Tml D1
66. Keswick D1

Accommodation
36. Adelaide Central YHA C2
37. Adelaide Hilton International C2
38. All Seasons Adelaide Meridien A3
39. Cannon Street Backpackers C2
40. Festival City Hotel/Motel B2
41. Franklin Central Apartments C2
42. Holiday Inn Adelaide C2
43. Hotel Adelaide International B2
44. Hotel Richmond C2
45. Hyatt Regency Adelaide C2
46. Majestic Roof Garden Hotel C3
47. Medina Grand Adelaide Treasury C2
48. Mercure Grosvenor Hotel Adelaide C2
49. Motel Adjacent Casino C2
50. Old Adelaide Inn A2
51. Old Lion Apartments B3
52. Pacific International Suites C2
53. Plaza Hotel C2
54. Radisson Playford Hotel C2
55. Rendezvous Allegra Hotel C2
56. Rockford Adelaide C2
57. Rydges South Park Adelaide D1
58. Saville Park Suites C1
59. Stamford Plaza Adelaide C2
60. The Chancellor Adelaide C2
61. The Chifley on South Terrace D2
62. The Oakes Embassy C2

Adelaide Throughroads

Adelaide Region, South Australia

Fleurieu Peninsula, South Australia

62 South-East South Australia

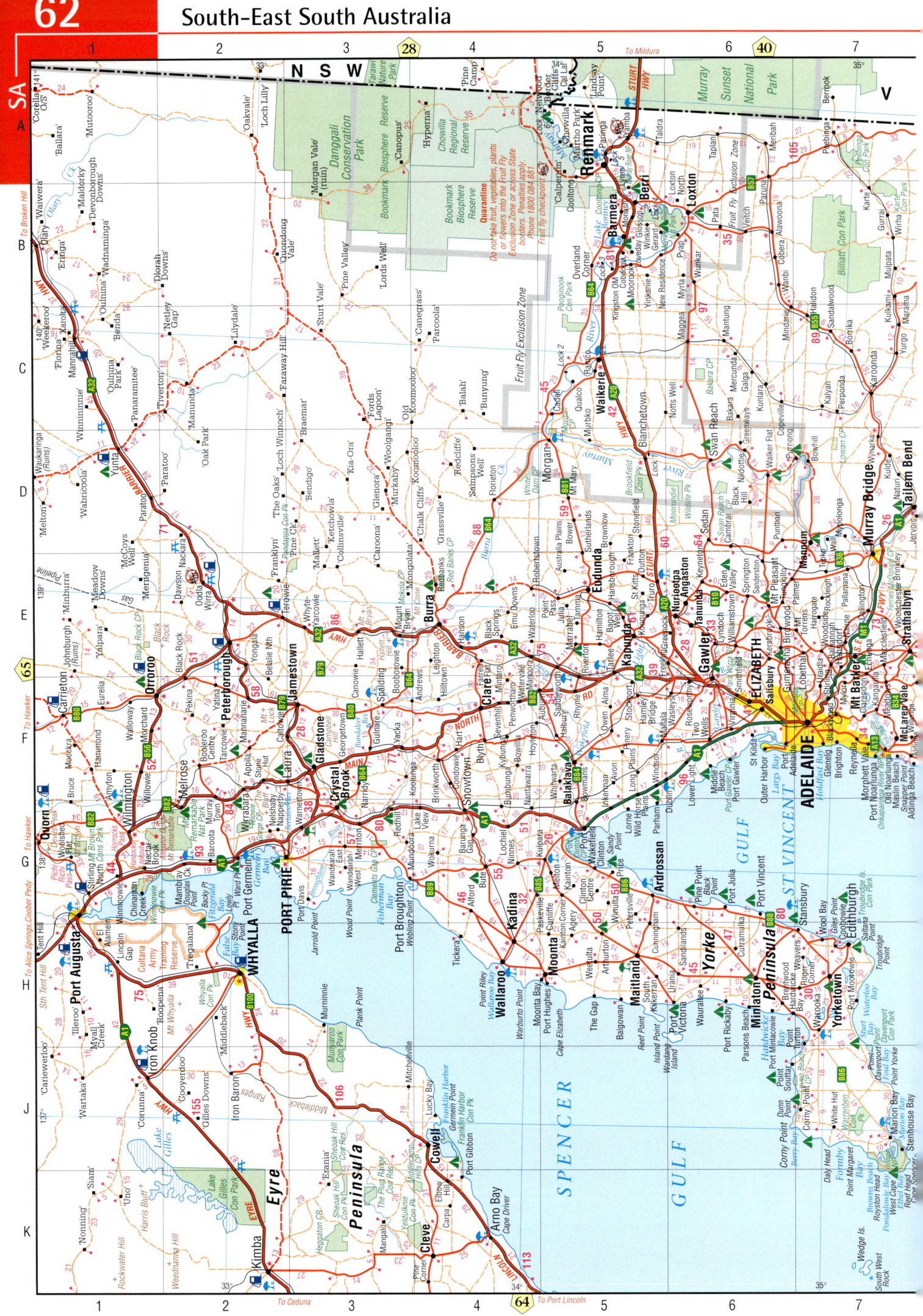

SA
VICTORIA
SOUTHERN
OCEAN
Encounter Bay
Investigator
Strait
To Ouyen
To Horsham
To Hamilton
Pinnaroo
Lameroo
Bordertown
Kaniva
Keith
Naracoorte
Edenhope
Casterton
Penola
MT GAMBIER
Millicent
Port MacDonnell
Beachport
Robe
Kingston SE
Meningie
Tintinara
Coonalpyn
Goolwa
Victor Harbor
Kingscote
Kangaroo Island
Fleurieu Peninsula
Penneshaw
Parndana
American River
Lake Alexandrina
Lake Albert
Coorong
Lacepede Bay
Rivoli Bay
Cape Jaffa
Ngarkat Con Park
Big Desert Wilderness Park
Little Desert National Park
Flinders Chase National Park
PRINCES HWY
DUKES HWY
RIDDOCH HWY
MALLEE HWY
PLAYFORD HWY
WEST END HWY
GLENELG HWY
8
9
10
11
12
13
14
A
B
C
D
E
F
G
H
J
K
40
38
© Hema Maps Pty Ltd

64 Central-East South Australia

To Marree & Birdsville
To Innamincka
67
Leigh Creek
Copley
Lake Torrens
LAKE TORRENS National Park
Lake Frome Regional Reserve
LAKE FROME
NORTH FLINDERS RANGES
Blinman
Parachilna
Wilpena
Flinders Ranges National Park
For more detail on this area see Hema's Map of The Flinders Ranges and Great Desert Tracks SE Sheet
Hawker
Cradock
Quorn
Port Augusta
Carrieton
Orroroo
Iron Knob
Wilmington
Melrose
WHYALLA
Port Germein
PORT PIRIE
Peterborough
Jamestown
Laura
Gladstone
Crystal Brook
Port Broughton
Burra
Clare
Wallaroo
Kadina
Moonta
Yorke Peninsula
Maitland
Ardrossan
Balaklava
Port Wakefield
Kapunda
Eudunda
Morgan
Waikerie
Barmera
Renmark
Berri
Loxton
Gawler
ELIZABETH
ADELAIDE
Mt Barker
Murray Bridge
Tailem Bend
McLaren Vale
Strathalbyn
Goolwa
Victor Harbor
Kingscote
Minlaton
Yorketown
Edithburgh
Fleurieu Peninsula
GULF ST VINCENT
Lake Alexandrina
Meningie
Pinnaroo
Lameroo
Karoonda
Mannum
Blanchetown
Nuriootpa
Tanunda
Angaston
Yunta
Olary
Cockburn
BROKEN HILL
NEW SOUTH WALES
VICTORIA
Danggali Conservation Park
Bookmark Biosphere Reserve
Murray Sunset National Park
SUNSET COUNTRY
Ngarkat Con Park
Fruit Fly Exclusion Zone
Quarantine
Do not take fruit, vegetables, plants or flowers into the Fruit Fly Exclusion Zone or across State borders. Penalties apply. Phone 1800 084 881
Fruit fly checkpoint
To Kingston SE
63
To Keith
To Cobar
To Tibooburra
To Wentworth
To Mildura
To Ouyen
8
9
10
11
12
13
14
A
B
C
D
E
F
G
H
J
K

66 North-East South Australia

QUEENSLAND
SA
Birdsville
'Roseberth'
BIRDSVILLE DEVELOPMENTAL ROAD
116
'Durrie'
Betoota
'Planet Downs' Outstation
Haddon Corner
Shallow Lake
Moonda Lake
Permit Required from QNPWS
Simpson Desert National Park
QAA Line
Lake Poeppel
Poeppel Corner
French Line (FRN)
Approdinna Attara Knolls
Lake Thomas
Simpson Desert Conservation Park
Desert Parks Pass required
WAA Line
Erabena Track
Knolls Track
K1 Line
Rig Road
Poolawanna No1 Oil Well
Poolawanna Lake
Nappanerica 'Big Red' Dune
EYRE DEVELOPMENTAL ROAD
'Pandie Pandie'
Diamantina River
Lake Short
Lake Etamunbanie
Lake Uloowaranie
Lake Cooninnie
'Cadelga' (Ruin)
'Nullah' OS
160
'Alton Downs'
Andrewilla Waterhole
Goyder Lagoon
Inside Track often closed due to flooding
INSIDE TRACK
Strzelecki Desert
Providence Creek
'Cordillo Downs' Australia's Largest Merting Shed
Arrabury
Peera Peera Poolanna Lake
Simpson Desert Regional Reserve
Desert Parks Pass required
Lake Griselda
Lake Umaroona
WARBURTON TRACK
public access route (WAB)
Yelpawaralina Track (YLP)
Warburton Crossing
'Clifton Hills'
BIRDSVILLE TRACK
315
Lake Marradnoranie
Lake Apanburra
Lake Goyder
Lake Toontoowaranie
Coongie Lake
Leap Year Bore
Mulga Bore
Montecollina
Willawilaninna Lake
Kallakoopah Creek
Lake Warrandirinna
Pantoowarinna Lake
Mt Gason Bore
Sturt Stony Desert
Lake Koodnanie
For more detail on this area, see Hema's Great Desert Tracks South East Sheet and Hema's Central Australia Map
Cooper Creek
Walkers Crossing
Innamincka Regional Reserve
Desert Parks Pass required
141 DOWNS
Patchawarra Bore
Innamincka No 2 Bore
Innamincka No 1 Bore
Burke & Wills Dig Tree
Nappa Merrie
To Eromanga
Lake Peera Mudla Yeppa
Warburton River
'Cowarie'
'Kalamurina'
Lake Howitt
Mirra Mitta Bore
Tirrawarra Oil & Gas Field
'Gidgealpa'
Durrantie
Bunyeroo WH
Cullyamurra Waterhole
'Innamincka'
Innamincka
The Warburton Groove
Koolkootinnie Lake
Kalamurra Lake
Lake Perigundi
Lake Andree
'Mungeranie'
Mungerannie Roadhouse
Lake Kittakittaooloo
(STR) TRACK
Moomba Oil & Gas Field
Della Gas Field
Dullingari Oil & Gas Field
Innamincka No 3 Bore
Lake Eyre National Park
Desert Parks Pass required
LAKE EYRE NORTH
Tirari Desert
Lake Ngapakaldi
Lake Mulapula
Lake Puntawolona
'Mulka'
Lake Warrakalanna
Lake Hope
Big Lake Moonba
Lake Moonba
STRZELECKI CREEK
'Epsilon'
Strzelecki Desert
Lake Killalpaninna
Cooper Ck Ferry
Lake Killamperpunna
Flood Bypass
'Etadunna'
Lake Merteree
'Merty Merty'
Elliot Price Con Park
Madigan Gulf
Lake Florence
Cannuwaukaninna Bore
Lake Kopperamanna
Lake Gregory
206
Belt Bay
Jackboot Bay
'Dulkaninna'
Strzelecki Regional Reserve
Strzelecki Crossing
123
STRZELECKI TRACK
Emergency BORE TRACK
'Omicron'
To Noccundra
Bollards Lagoon
'Bollards Lagoon'
'The Corner Store'
Dog Fence
Cameron Corner
Sturt National Park
'Fort Grey'
'Lindon'
Lake Ellen
public access route
'Muloorina'
Lake Eyre National Park
LAKE EYRE SOUTH
'Clayton'
Clayton River
Cooranna Creek
Mirrawilkanna Creek
Lake Blanche
Montecollina Bore
'Whitecatch House'
'Lake Stewart'
To Tibooburra
Curdimurka
Finniss Springs
OODNADATTA TRACK
Lake Phillipson
Bopeechee
Alberrie Creek
'Finniss Springs'
'Stuart Creek'
Wongianna
Callanna
'Callanna'
Marree
Lake Harry
'Lake Harry' (Ruin)
Frome Creek
'Mundowdna'
OLD GHAN RAIL ROUTE
Lake Arthur
'Murnpeowie'
'Blanchewater' (Ruin)
'Mount Hopeless'
Lake Callabonna
'Old Tilcha' (ruins)
Munkartie Gate
Tilcha Gate
'Hewart Downs'
'Winnathee'
Mt Distance
Mt Freeling
196
Fossil Reserve S.A. Museum Entry Permit required
Dog Fence
'Moolawatana'
Mt Babbage
Mt Fitton
'Mt Fitton'
No access to South Australia via Hawkers Gate
Hawkers Gate
'Mt Freeling'
Mt Livingston
Mt Neil
'Wilpoolinna'
'Witchelina'
Farina (Ruins)
'Farina'
80
'Mulgaria'
Stuart Creek Opal Deposit
STRZELECKI TRACK
151
Lake Yannirpi
'Smithville House'
Lake Arthur
'Mt Lyndhurst'
'Avondale'
NORTH
'Umberatana'
Yudnamutana
Freeling Heights
Paralana Hot Springs
'North Mulga'
Paralana
Lake Cootabarlow
Coonee
'Moorabie'
Lyndhurst
Mt Painter
Arkaroola
'Arkaroola'
Andamooka
Opal Fields
'Myrtle Springs'
Telford
Leigh Creek Coalfield
'Depot Springs'
FLINDERS
'Owieandana'
Mt Serle
'Mt Serle'
Yankaninna
Bentonyah Hill
Vulkathuna - Gammon Ranges Nat Park
'Wooltana'
Rotten Swamp
McIntyre Bore
'Border Downs'
Lake Torrens
Leigh Creek
Copley
Aroona Dam
'North Moolooloo'
Angepena
'Maynards Well'
Iga Warta
Nepabunna
Mt McKinley
Italowie Gorge
Balcanoona
103
RANGES
'Wertaloona'
Lake Coontayunta
Lake Bumbarlow
Lake Starvation
'Turleys House'
LAKE TORRENS National Park
'Andamooka'
The Knob
Ediacara Con Res
Beltana Roadhouse
Beltana
'Beltana'
'Puttapa'
Sliding Rock Mine
'Warraweena'
Nantawarrina
'Nantawarrina'
Lake Frome Regional Reserve
LAKE FROME
Lake Elder
Lake Maljanapa
'Pine View'
'Westwood Downs'
To Silver City Hwy
To Hawker
To Bedourie
NSW
137° 138° 139° 140° 141°
26° 27° 28° 29° 30°
91 12 14 26 65 B83
8 9 10 11 12 13 14
A B C D E F G H J K

68 Western South Australia

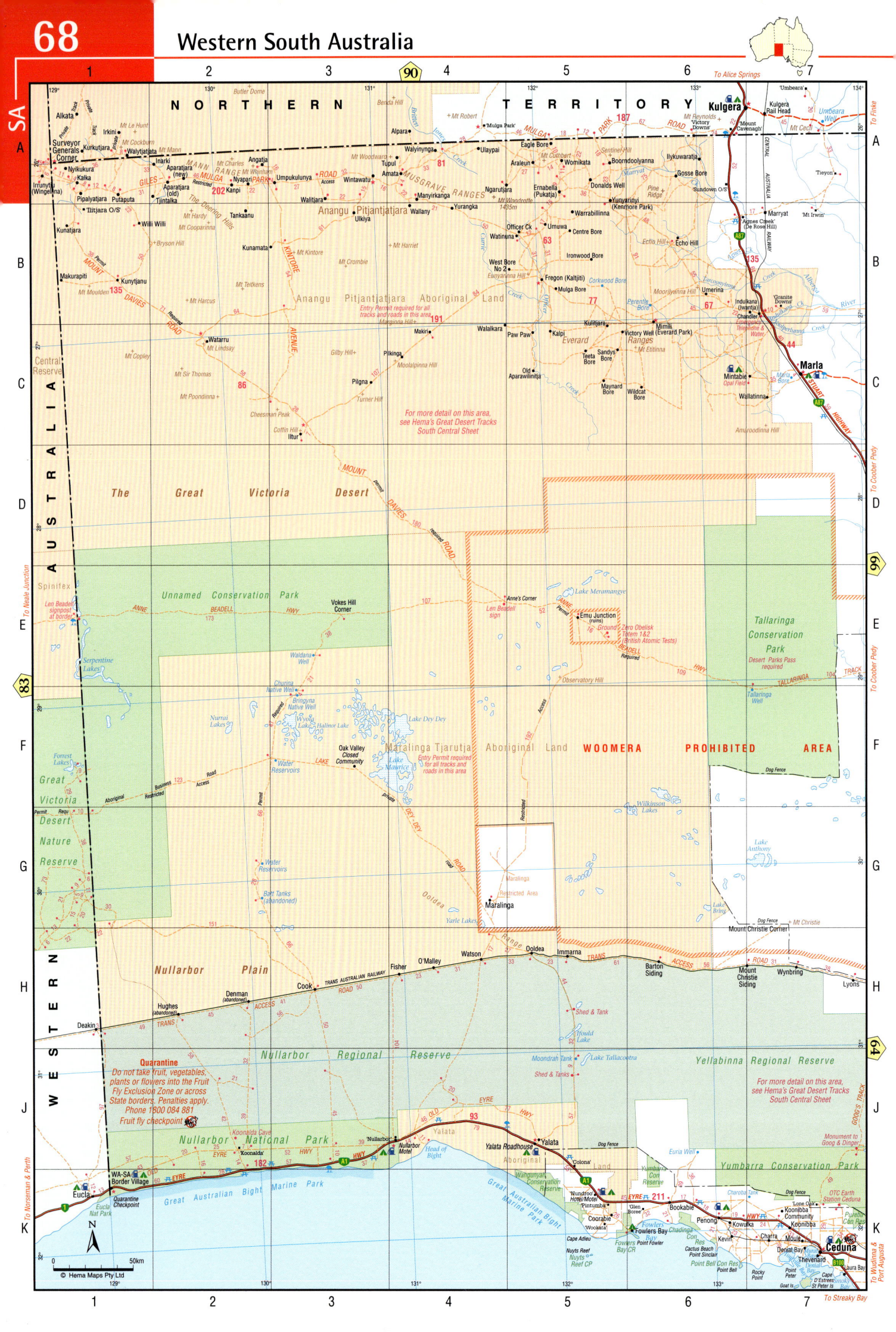

Key map 69

Western Australia

Sunrise, Geographe Bay, Dunsborough (73 J11, 74 G1)

Distances are shown in kilometres and follow the most direct major sealed route where possible

1401	2020	411	1564	939	3610	1977	805	835	483	1315	342	2618	**Albany**
3101	615	2245	1051	1676	1063	845	2197	1942	2589	1462	2427	**Broome**
1585	1832	182	1376	751	3422	1748	774	606	667	1086	**Bunbury**
2338	867	904	985	819	2457	662	1460	480	1625	**Carnarvon**
918	1994	721	1538	1069	3584	2169	392	1145	**Esperance**
1822	1347	424	964	339	2937	1142	980	**Geraldton**
904	1602	592	1146	677	3192	1786	**Kalgoorlie**
2690	259	1566	631	1256	1849	**Karratha**
4096	1610	3240	2046	2671	**Kununurra**
1597	1081	569	625	**Mt Magnet**
2050	456	1194	**Newman**
1434	1650	**Perth**
2506	**Port Hedland**
WA-SA Border Village

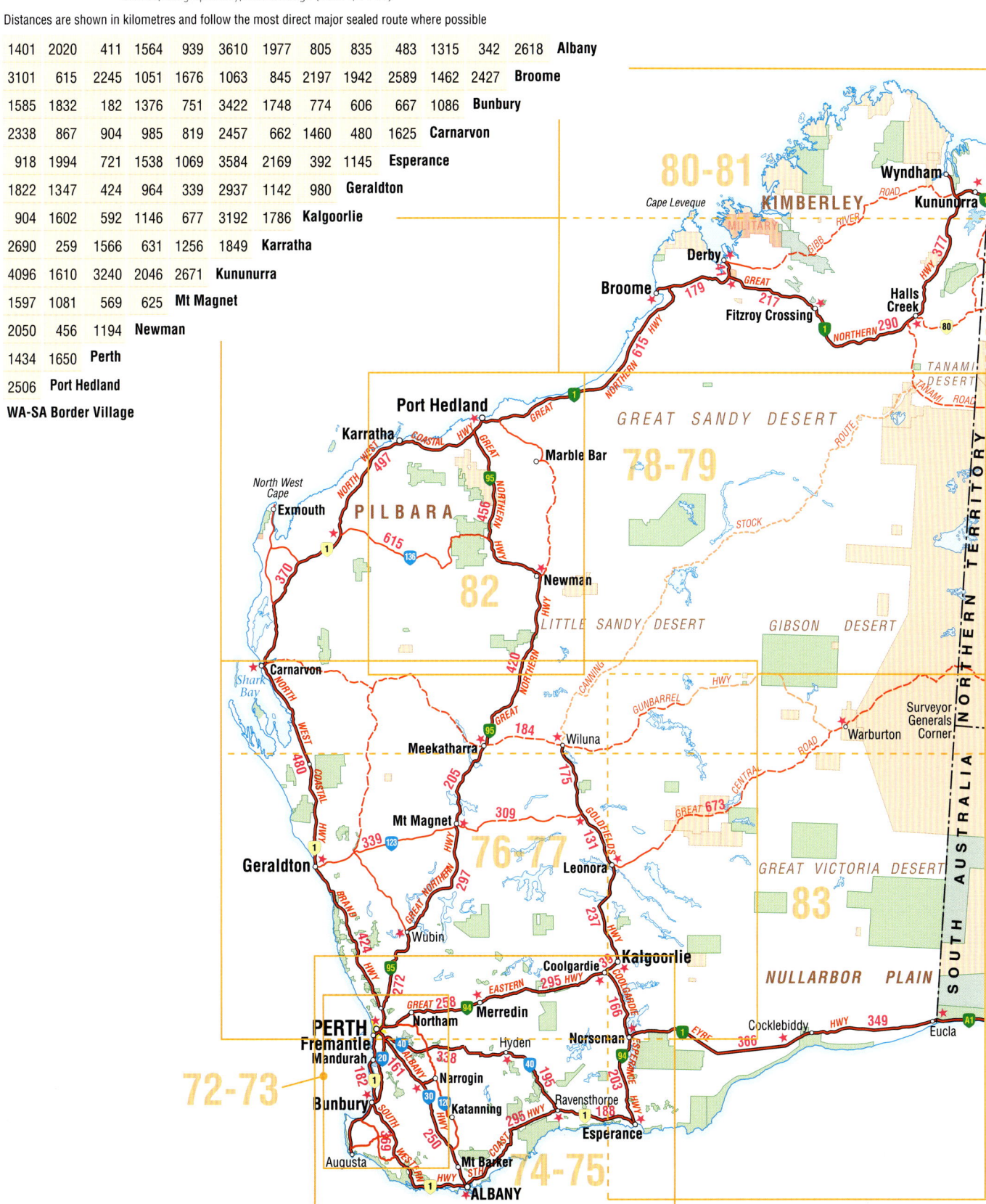

Perth CBD

Points of Interest
1. Allan Green Plant Conservatory B2
2. Art Gallery of Western Australia A3
3. Barracks Archway B1
4. Forrest Chase B3
5. Government House B3
6. Hay Street Mall B2
7. His Majesty's Theatre B2
8. Horizon Planetarium A1
9. Horseshoe Bridge B2
10. King Street Arts Centre B2
11. Kings Park B1
12. Kings Park Lookout C1
13. Langley Park C3
14. Members Equity Stadium A4
15. Murray Street Mall B2
16. Old Council House B3
17. Old Court House B3
18. Old Mill C1
19. Old Perth Boys School B2
20. Old Perth Observatory B1
21. Parliament House B1
22. Perth concert Hall B3
23. Perth Convention Exhibition Ctr B2
24. Perth Entertainment Centre A2
25. Perth Inst of Contemporary Arts A3
26. Perth Mint B4
27. Perth Town Hall B3
28. Scitech Discovery Centre A1
29. St George's Cathedral B3
30. St Mary's RC Cathedral B3
31. State Library of Western Aust A3
32. State War Memorial C1
33. Swan Bells C2
34. The Cloisters B2
35. The Deanery B3
36. Wellington Square B4
37. Western Australia Museum A3

Accommodation
38. Aarons All Suites B3
39. Aarons Hotel Perth B3
40. Acacia Hotel A3
41. Best Western Emerald Hotel B1
42. Comfort Hotel Perth City C4
43. Comfort Inn Wentworth Plaza B2
44. Criterion Hotel B3
45. Crowne Plaza Perth C4
46. Globe Hotel and Backpackers B2
47. Goodearth Hotel C4
48. Grand Central Backpackers B3
49. Holiday Inn City Centre Perth B3
50. Hotel Grand Chancellor A2
51. Hotel Ibis Perth B3
52. Hyatt Regency Perth C4
53. Kings Perth Hotel B3
54. Medina Grand Hotel B2
55. Mounts Bay Waters Apartments B1
56. Novotel Langley Hotel Perth C3
57. Pacific International Suites Perth B2
58. Parmelia Hilton Hotel Perth B2
59. Perth Ambassador Hotel C4
60. Quest West End Apart Hotel B2
61. River View on Mount Street B1
62. Rydges Perth B2
63. Saville Park Suites Perth C4
64. Sheraton Perth Hotel C3
65. Sullivans Hotel C1
66. The Chifley on the Terrace B2
67. The Commodore Hotel B3
68. The Duxton Hotel Perth B3
69. The Melbourne Hotel B2
70. The Mercure Hotel B3
71. The New Esplanade Hotel Perth B2
72. The Sebel Perth B3

Travel Information
73. City West Train Station A1
74. Claisebrook Train Station A4
75. East Perth Train Station A4
76. McIver Train Station B3
77. Perth Train Station B3
78. Perth Visitor Centre B2
79. RAV Office B3
80. Wellington Street Bus Station (Day Tour Bus Departure Point) A2
81. Westrail Centre (Interstate Bus and Rail Departure Point) A4
82. YHA Office A3

Legend
- Freeway
- Major Road
- State Route No.
- Street
- Lane/Walkway
- Railway, Station
- Post Office
- Major Building
- Govt Building
- Accommodation
- Theatre/Cinema
- Shopping
- Church
- Hospital

Scale: 0 – 800m

© Hema Maps Pty Ltd

Perth Throughroads

Perth Region, Western Australia

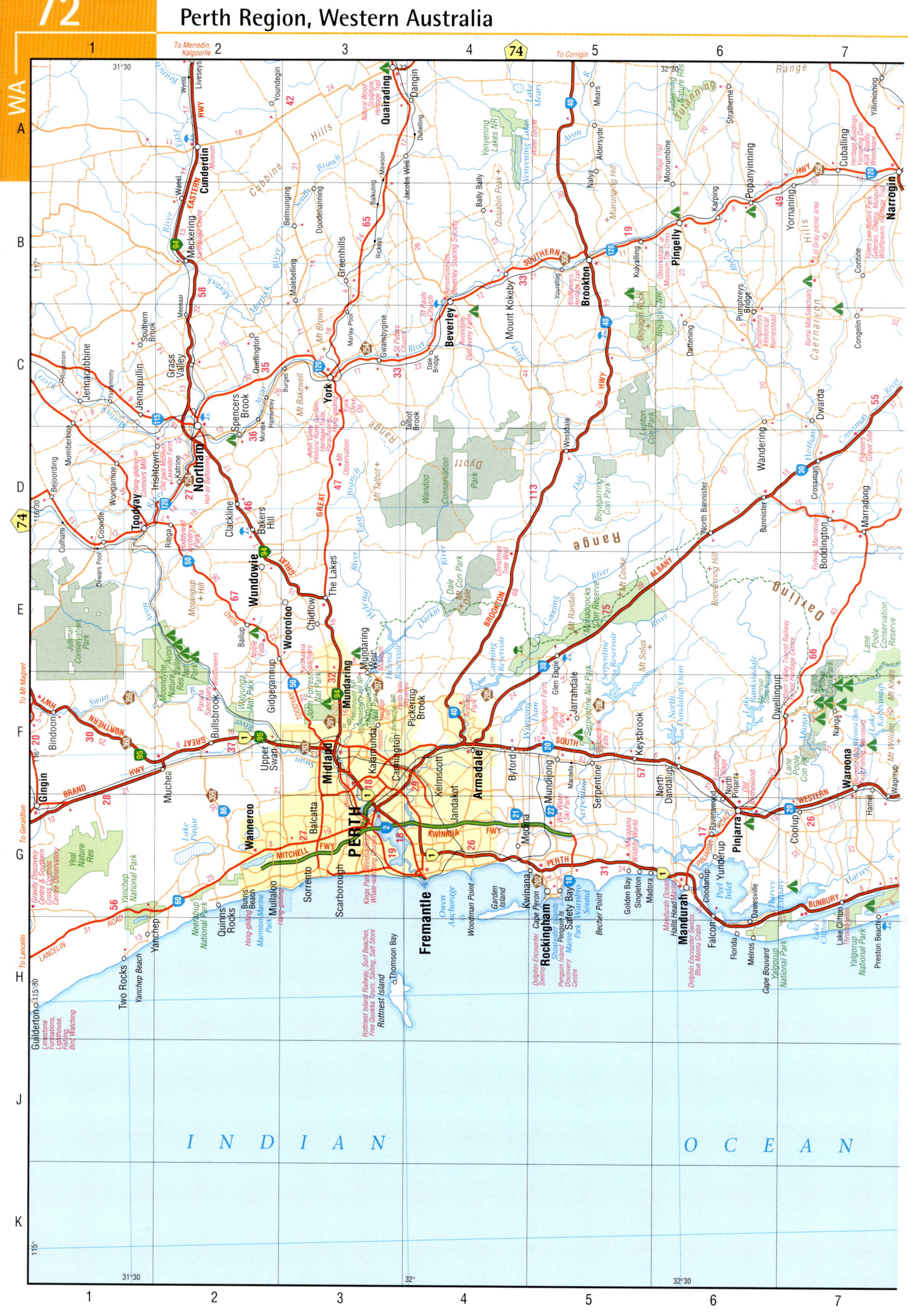

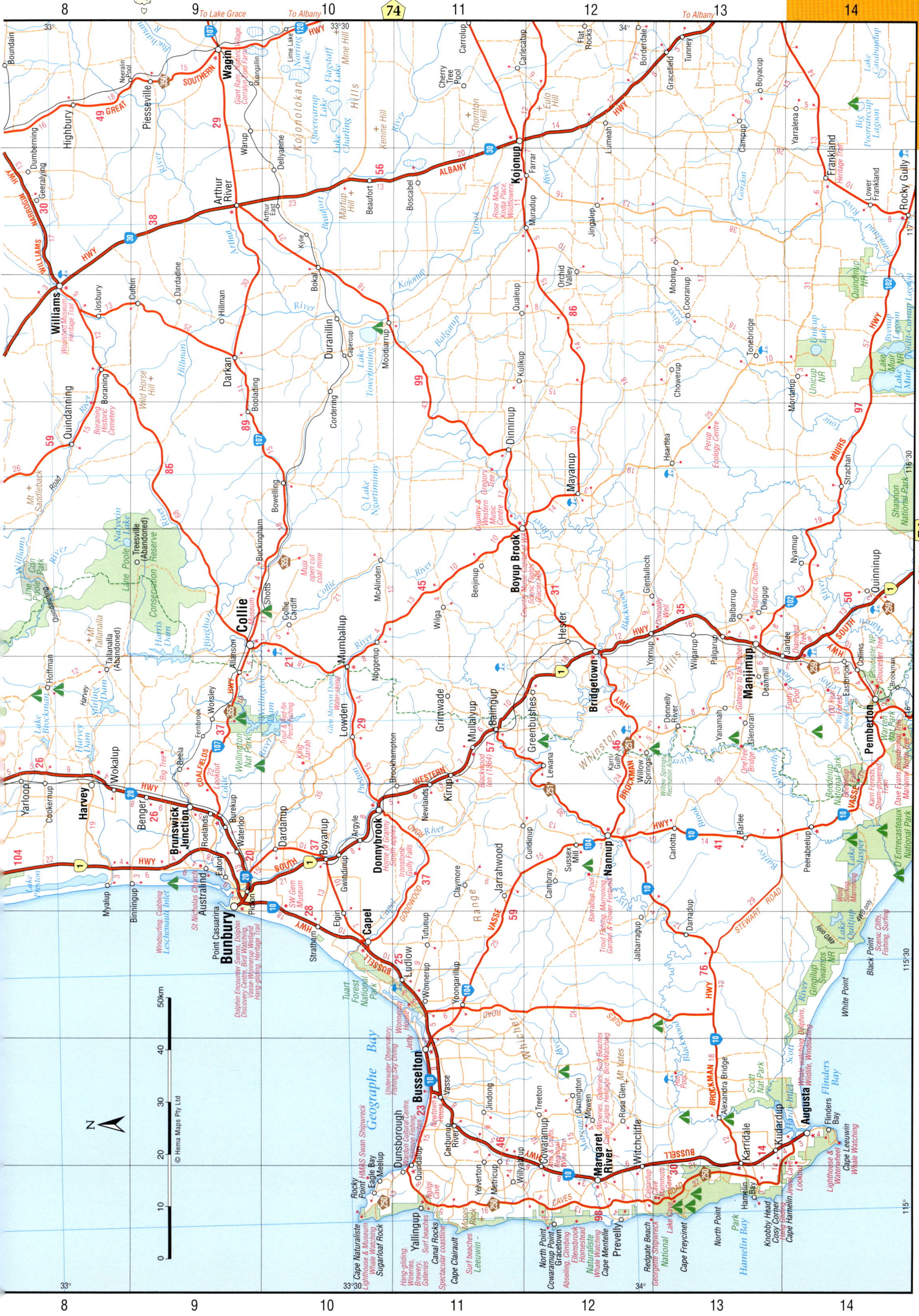

74 South-West Western Australia

Kalgoorlie
Boulder
Coolgardie
Kurrawang
Bonnie Vale
Bulong
'Hampton Hill'
Golden Ridge
Curtin
Randell
Karonie
'Avoca Downs'
'Cowarna Downs'
Karonie Mine
Lake Yindarlgooda
Lake Roe
To Leonora
Mt Burgess
'Mt Burgess'
Bullabulling
Brown Lake
Hannan Lake
Mt Marion
Kambalda NR
'Woolubar'
'Mt Monger'
Randalls Mine
Kambalda
Kambalda West
Private Road Restricted Access
Lake Lefroy
St Ives Mine
Yalca Hill
'Madoonia Downs'
'Mandilla'
Roysalt Siding
Widgiemooltha
Burra Rock
Nepean
Nickel Mine
Victoria Rock Nature Res
Victoria Rock
Goldfields Woodlands Cons Pk
Goldfields Woodlands Nat Park
Boorabbin Nat Park
Boorabbin
Koorarawalyee
Weowanie Rock
Yellowdine Nature Res
Yellowdine
Southern Cross
Moorine Rock
Bodallin
Bullfinch
Koolyanobbing
'Jaurdi'
Lake Deborah West
Lake Deborah East
Lake Seabrook
Kangaroo Rock
Lake Baladjie
Baladjie Lake NR
Strawberry Rocks
Marvel Loch
Cockatoo Tank
Toomey Hills
JILBADJI NATURE RESERVE
Noombenberry Rock
Mt Hampton
Skeleton Rocks
Glenelg Rock
Welcome Hill
Anderson Rocks
King Rocks
Wave Rock
Hyden
Karlgarin
Lake Carmody
Marble Rock
Modesty Rock
Lake Hurlstone
L Hurlstone NR
Lake Varley
L Varley NR
Holt Rock
Kerrigan Rocks
Dragon Rocks NR
Dragon Rocks
L Gulson
Varley
Mt Vernon
Mt Sheridan
Harris NR
Lake Fox
Lake Camm
Lake Biddy
NEWDEGATE
Newdegate
Lake King NR
Lake King
Lake Ace NR
Breakaway Ridge NR
Lakeland NR
Lake Lockhart
Pallarup NR
Dunn Rock NR
Lake Pallarup
One Mile Rocks NR
Lake Chidnup
Lake Magenta
Lake Magenta Nature Res
Ravensthorpe
Fitzgerald
Jerramungup
Gairdner
Boxwood Hill
Bremer Bay
'Minarup'
'Cape Riche'
Cape Riche
Pt Irby
Cheyne Bay
Beaufort Inlet
Cape Knob
Dillon Bay
Pt Henry
Haul Off Rock
Nat Park Point
Island Nature Res
FITZGERALD RIVER NATIONAL PARK
Mt Drummond
Annie Peak
West Mt Barren
Pt Charles
Pt Charles Bay
Pt Ann
Gordon Inlet
Doubtful Islands Bay
Hood Pt
Culham Inlet
Hopetoun
Mason Bay
Powell Pt
Lake Shaster NR
Lake Shaster
Jerdacuttup Lakes NR
Jerdacuttup Lakes
'Maydon'
Kundip NR
'Nurragi'
Munglinup
'Clare Downs'
Cascade
Cheadanup Nature Res
Stokes Nat Park
Stokes Inlet
Shoal Cape
'Fairfield'
'Dalyup'
Lake Gore
Pink Lake
Butty Head
Observatory Pt
Esperance
Esperance Bay
WEST GROUP
Cape Le Grand
Mondrain Island
Mississippi Pt
Rossiter Bay
Hammer Head
Recherche Archipelago Nature Reserve
Cape Le Grand Nat Park
'Gerbryn'
'Peak Downs'
Condingup
'Veperey'
'Warrawoona'
'Zeehan'
'Lauriana'
'Wittenoom Hill'
Muntz NR
Beaumont NR
Kau Rock NR
Burdett South NR
Mt Ridley
Truslove Townsite NR
Scaddan
Grass Patch
Bishops Nature Res
Griffiths Nature Res
'Kappi Ki'
Pyramid Lake
Lake Mends
Salmon Gums
Nature Res
Peak Charles National Park
Peak Charles
Lake Sharpe
Lake Tay
Kumarl
Ninety Mile Tank
Frank Hann National Park
Lillian Stoke Rock
Mt Gibbs
Hatter Hill
Diggers Rock
'Karak Park'
Swallow Rock
Lake Hope
Mt Gordon
BREMER RANGE
Lake Johnston
Mt Day
McDermid Rock
Sandalwood Rocks
Mt Holland
HOLLAND TRACK
Lake Barker
Diamond Rock
Thursday Rock
Cave Hill Nature Res
Cave Hill
Higginsville
Binaronca Nature Res
Higginsville Mine
Lake Cowan
Wingarnie
Pioneer
'Buldania'
Mt Thirsty
NORSEMAN
Norseman
Mt Norcott
Bromus
Woolyeenyer Hill
Lake Dundas
DUNDAS NATURE RESERVE
Lake Gilmore
'Mareil'
Private Mining Road
COOLGARDIE ESPERANCE HWY
HWY
Young
Oldfield
Lort
West
Phillips
Hamersley
Fitzgerald
Gairdner
Bremer
To Adelaide
To Cape Arid Nat Park
SOUTHERN OCEAN
N
0 50 100km
© Hema Maps Pty Ltd
120°
122°
32°
34°
8 9 10 11 12 13 14
A B C D E F G H J K

76 Central West Western Australia

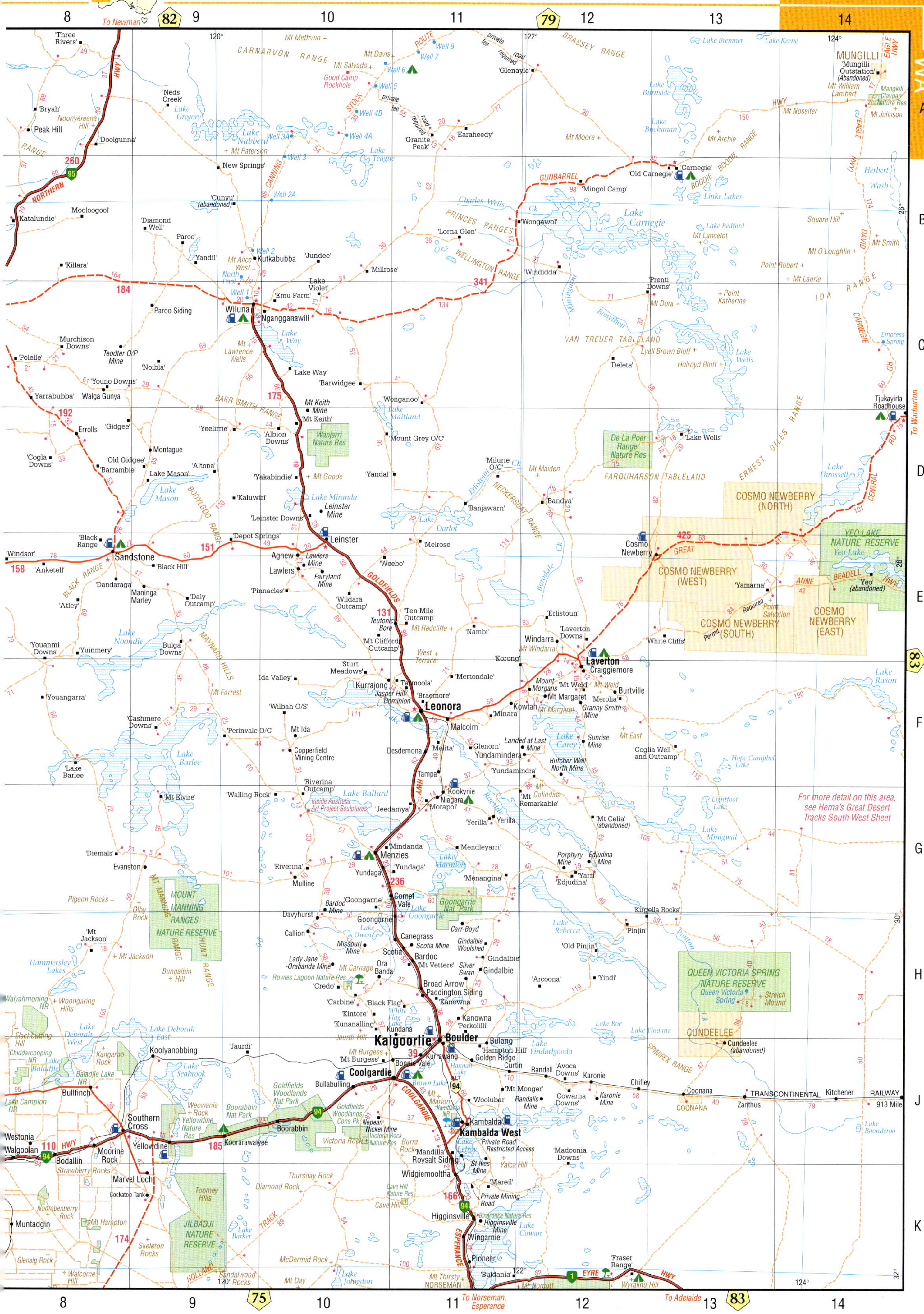
To Newman
To Warburton
To Norseman, Esperance
To Adelaide
For more detail on this area, see Hema's Great Desert Tracks South West Sheet
CARNARVON RANGE
BRASSEY RANGE
MUNGILLI
Wiluna
Ngangganawili
Lake Way
Sandstone
Leinster
Agnew
Lawlers
Leonora
Malcolm
Laverton
Craiggiemore
Burtville
Cosmo Newberry
COSMO NEWBERRY (NORTH)
COSMO NEWBERRY (WEST)
COSMO NEWBERRY (SOUTH)
COSMO NEWBERRY (EAST)
YEO LAKE NATURE RESERVE
Yeo Lake
Tjukayirla Roadhouse
Lake Carnegie
Carnegie
Old Carnegie
Mingol Camp
Wongawol
Windidda
Prenti Downs
VAN TREUER TABLELAND
FARQUHARSON TABLELAND
De La Poer Range Nature Res
Lake Wells
Wanjarri Nature Res
Kutkabubba
Menzies
Kookynie
Niagara
Yundamindera
Mount Morgans
Mt Margaret
Kurrajong
Lake Ballard
Davyhurst
Goongarrie
Goongarrie Nat Park
Comet Vale
Kalgoorlie
Boulder
Coolgardie
Kambalda
Kambalda West
Widgiemooltha
Higginsville
Norseman
Southern Cross
Bullfinch
Westonia
Walgoolan
Bodallin
Moorine Rock
Marvel Loch
Yellowdine
Koolyanobbing
Boorabbin
Boorabbin Nat Park
Goldfields Woodlands Nat Park
MOUNT MANNING RANGES NATURE RESERVE
JILBADJI NATURE RESERVE
Toomey Hills
Muntadgin
QUEEN VICTORIA SPRING NATURE RESERVE
CUNDEELEE
Cundeelee
Coonana
Zanthus
Kitchener
TRANSCONTINENTAL RAILWAY
913 Mile
Karonie
Chifley
Randell
Bulong
Kanowna
Broad Arrow
Ora Banda
Menangina
Lake Rebecca
Lake Carey
Lake Minigwal
Lake Barlee
Lake Noondie
Lake Mason
Lake Darlot
Lake Maitland
Lake Miranda
Lake Cowan
GOLDFIELDS HWY
GREAT CENTRAL RD
GUNBARREL HWY
NORTHERN HWY
EYRE HWY
COOLGARDIE ESPERANCE HWY
CANNING STOCK ROUTE

78 North Western Australia

8
9
10
11
12
13
14
80
81
77
83
88
90
A
B
C
D
E
F
G
H
J
K
To Kununurra
To Katherine
To Alice Springs
To Yulara
To Kalgoorlie
Broome
Derby
Fitzroy Crossing
Halls Creek
KIMBERLEY
Lacepede Islands
BEAGLE BAY
KING SOUND
Curtin Air Base
Mowanjum
Looma
Camballin
Noonkanbah
Yungngora
Bayulu
Ngumpan
Wangkatjungka
Djugerari
Bidyadanga
Bililuna (Mindibungu)
Balgo
Yagga Yagga
Warmun (Turkey Creek)
PURNULULU NAT PARK
Wolfe Creek Meteorite Crater
Wolfe Creek Crater NP
BILLILUNA
LAKE GREGORY
BALGO
Mangkururrpa (Tanami Downs)
Yiningarra
TANAMI
DESERT
G R E A T   S A N D Y   D E S E R T
Telfer Mine
Woodie Woodie Mine
RUDALL RIVER NATIONAL PARK
Punmu
Parnngurr (Cotton Creek) (Diesel only)
Kunawarritji
Gary Junction
Windy Corner
KIWIRRKURRA
Kiwirrkurra
MARUWA
CENTRAL AUSTRALIA
Lake Mackay
NGAANYATJARRA LAND COUNCIL
KURLKUTA
Haasts Bluff
Walungurru (Kintore)
G I B S O N   D E S E R T
GIBSON DESERT NATURE RESERVE
MUNGILLI
Mungilli Outstation (Abandoned)
Everard Junction
CLUTTER BUCK HILL
Tjukurla
Kulail
Docker River (Kaltukatjara)
Warakurna
Warakurna Roadhouse
Wannarn
CENTRAL RESERVE
Warburton
WARBURTON
Tjirrkarli
TJIRRKARLI
Lake Carnegie
Carnegie
Blackstone (Papulankutja)
Jameson (Mantamaru)
Kanpa
Warning to travellers
Travelling in Australia's arid regions can be extremely hazardous, especially during the summer months (October-March). Always seek local advice as to road conditions and notify the police of your intended destination and ETA. Always carry plenty of fuel and water. In the event of a breakdown, remain near your vehicle.
For more detail on this area, see Hema's Great Desert Tracks North West Sheet
For more detail on this area, see Hema's map of the Kimberley
The Tablelands Track between Yulumbu (Tablelands) and Bedford Downs homesteads has been closed until further notice

80 The Kimberley, Western Australia

8 9 10 11 12 13 14

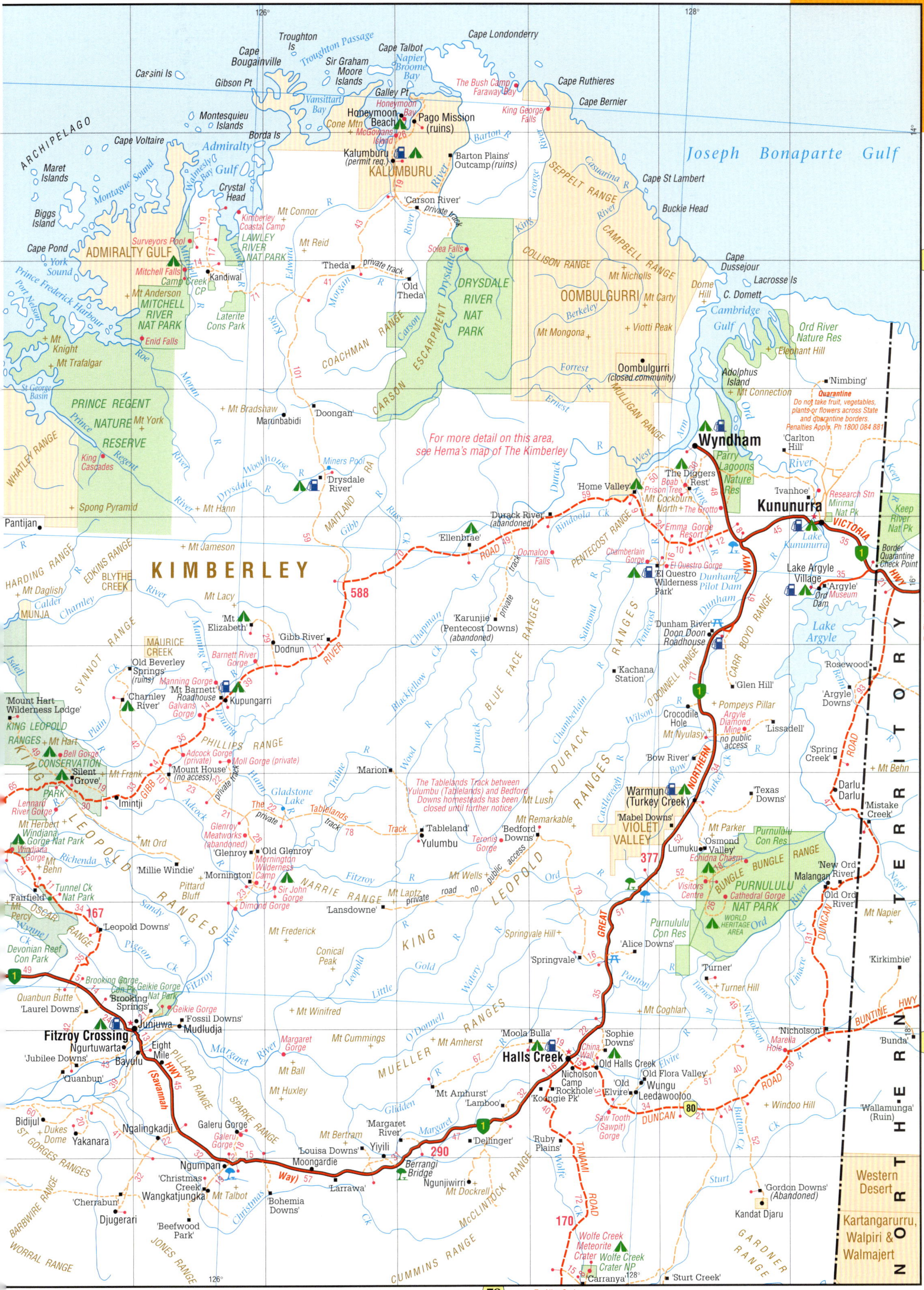

8 9 10 11 12 13 14

The Pilbara, Western Australia

Fuel Warning
Unleaded and leaded fuel is not available between Tjukayirla Roadhouse (WA) and Yulara (NT). Carry enough fuel for the 815km journey.
For more detail on this area, see Hema's Great Desert Tracks South West Sheet
Warning to Travellers
Travelling in Australia's arid regions can be extremely hazardous, especially during the summer months (October-March). Always seek local advice as to road conditions and notify the police of your intended destination and ETA. Always carry plenty of fuel and water. In the event of a breakdown, remain near your vehicle.
For more detail on this area, see Hema's Great Desert Tracks North West Sheet
Permit required from Ngaanyatjarra Land Council to travel Old Gunbarrel Highway
Quarantine
Do not take fruit, vegetables, plants or flowers across State borders.
Penalties Apply. Ph 1800 084 881
GIBSON DESERT NATURE RESERVE
CENTRAL RESERVE
GREAT VICTORIA DESERT
NULLARBOR PLAIN
GREAT VICTORIA DESERT NATURE RESERVE
NEALE JUNCTION NATURE RESERVE
PLUMRIDGE LAKES NATURE RESERVE
QUEEN VICTORIA SPRING NATURE RESERVE
UNNAMED CONSERVATION PARK
NULLARBOR REGIONAL RESERVE
NULLARBOR NATIONAL PARK
DUNDAS NATURE RESERVE
CAPE ARID NAT PARK
NUYTSLAND NATURE RESERVE
GREAT AUSTRALIAN BIGHT
SOUTHERN OCEAN
SOUTH AUSTRALIA
Anangu Pitjantjatjara
Maralinga - Tjarutja
Warburton
Laverton
Leonora
Kalgoorlie
Boulder
Kambalda West
Norseman
Esperance
Balladonia
Caiguna
Cocklebiddy
Madura
Eucla
Border Village
Tjukayirla Roadhouse
Cosmo Newberry
Tjuntjuntjara
Longest straight stretch in Australia (146.6km)
TRANSCONTINENTAL RAILWAY
0 50 100km
© Hema Maps Pty Ltd

84 Key map
Northern Territory

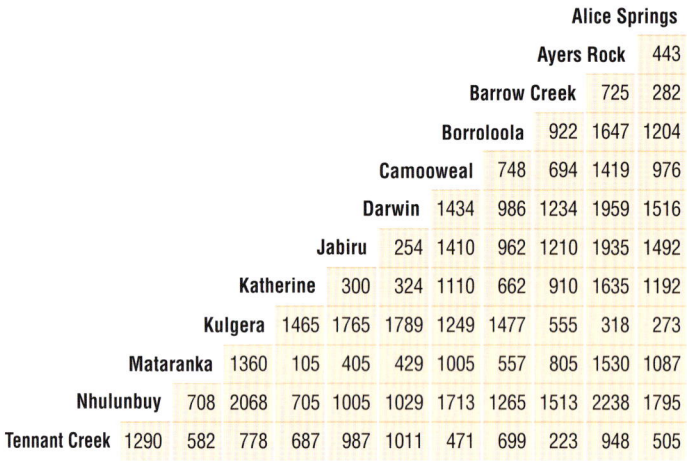

Chambers Pillar (91 H8)

Distance Table (km)

	Alice Springs	Ayers Rock	Barrow Creek	Borroloola	Camooweal	Darwin	Jabiru	Katherine	Kulgera	Mataranka	Nhulunbuy
Ayers Rock	443										
Barrow Creek	725	282									
Borroloola	922	1647	1204								
Camooweal	748	694	1419	976							
Darwin	1434	986	1234	1959	1516						
Jabiru	254	1410	962	1210	1935	1492					
Katherine	300	324	1110	662	910	1635	1192				
Kulgera	1465	1765	1789	1249	1477	555	318	273			
Mataranka	1360	105	405	429	1005	557	805	1530	1087		
Nhulunbuy	708	2068	705	1005	1029	1713	1265	1513	2238	1795	
Tennant Creek	1290	582	778	687	987	1011	471	699	223	948	505

Distances are shown in kilometres and follow the most direct major sealed route where possible

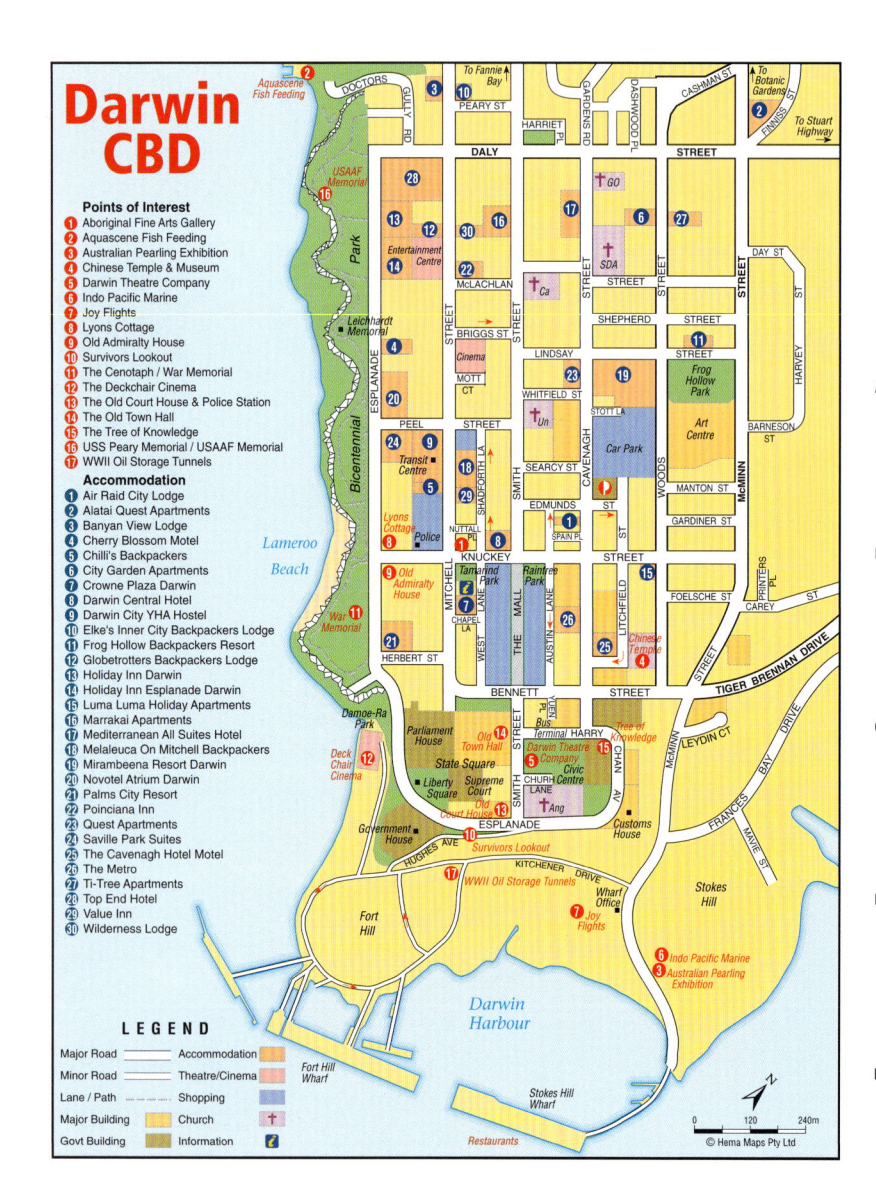

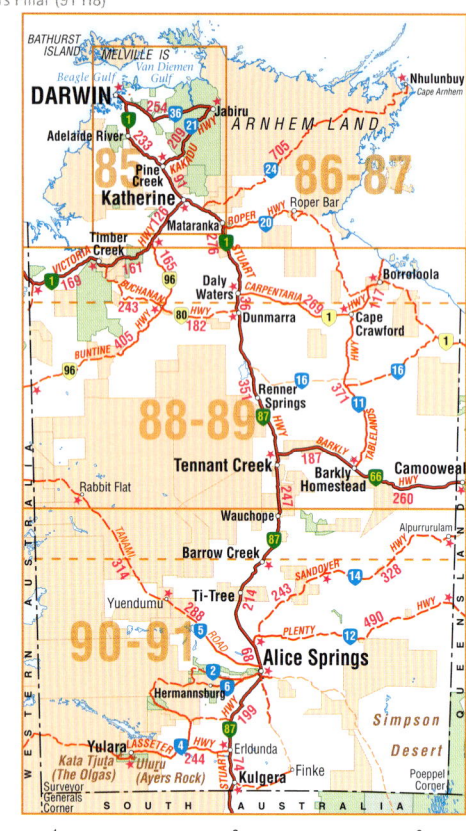

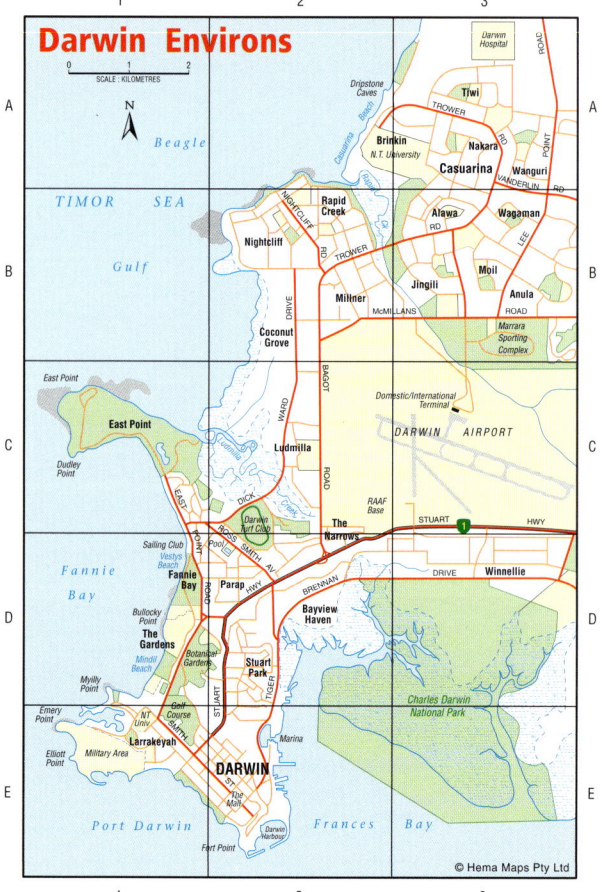

Darwin CBD

Points of Interest
1. Aboriginal Fine Arts Gallery
2. Aquascene Fish Feeding
3. Australian Pearling Exhibition
4. Chinese Temple & Museum
5. Darwin Theatre Company
6. Indo Pacific Marine
7. Joy Flights
8. Lyons Cottage
9. Old Admiralty House
10. Survivors Lookout
11. The Cenotaph / War Memorial
12. The Deckchair Cinema
13. The Old Court House & Police Station
14. The Old Town Hall
15. The Tree of Knowledge
16. USS Peary Memorial / USAAF Memorial
17. WWII Oil Storage Tunnels

Accommodation
1. Air Raid City Lodge
2. Alatai Quest Apartments
3. Banyan View Lodge
4. Cherry Blossom Motel
5. Chilli's Backpackers
6. City Garden Apartments
7. Crowne Plaza Darwin
8. Darwin Central Hotel
9. Darwin City YHA Hostel
10. Elke's Inner City Backpackers Lodge
11. Frog Hollow Backpackers Resort
12. Globetrotters Backpackers Lodge
13. Holiday Inn Darwin
14. Holiday Inn Esplanade Darwin
15. Luma Luma Holiday Apartments
16. Marrakai Apartments
17. Mediterranean All Suites Hotel
18. Melaleuca On Mitchell Backpackers
19. Mirambeena Resort Darwin
20. Novotel Atrium Darwin
21. Palms City Resort
22. Poinciana Inn
23. Quest Apartments
24. Saville Park Suites
25. The Cavenagh Hotel Motel
26. The Metro
27. Ti-Tree Apartments
28. Top End Hotel
29. Value Inn
30. Wilderness Lodge

Legend
- Major Road
- Minor Road
- Lane / Path
- Major Building
- Govt Building
- Accommodation
- Theatre/Cinema
- Shopping
- Church
- Information

Darwin Environs

Darwin Region, Northern Territory

The Top End, Northern Territory

ARAFURA SEA
ARNHEM LAND
Arnhem Land
GULF OF CARPENTARIA
Wessel Islands
Cape Wessel
Rimbija Is
Marchinbar Is
Cumberland Strait
Guluwuru Is
Stevens Is
Raragala Is
Truant Is
Drysdale Is
Wigram Is
The English Company's Islands
Cunningham Islands
Bromby Islands
Cape Wilberforce
Elcho Is
Alger Is
Pt Napier
Inglis Is
Galiwinku
Flinders Pt
Buckingham Bay
Probable Is
Mallison Is
Everett Is
Rorruwuy
Bremer Is
Nhulunbuy
Yirrkala
Cape Arnhem
GOVE PENINSULA
Dhalinybuy
Arnhem Bay
Port Bradshaw
Gapuwiyak
Lake Evella
Gurrumuru
'Mt Alexander' (ruins)
Garrthalala
Birany Birany
Pt Alexander
Caledon Bay
Mt Caledon
Cape Grey
Trial Bay
Bald Pt
Gan Gan
Baniyala
Pt Arrowsmith
Cape Shield
Round Hill Is
Isle Woodah
Nicol Is
Morgan Is
Blue Mud Bay
Burney Is
Hawknest Is
North Point Is
Chasm Is
Bustard Is
North East Isles
Cape Barrow
Bickerton Is
Winchelsea Is
Milyakburra
Alyangula
Umbakumba
GROOTE EYLANDT
Angurugu
Ilyungmadja Pt
Tasman Pt
South Pt
Cape Beatrice
Numbulwar
Sandy Is
Edward Is
Turner Pt
Cuthbert Pt
Braithwaite Pt
Junction Bay
Rolling Bay
Hawkesbury Pt
Nth East Pt
Skirmish Pt
False Pt
Cape Stewart
North West Crocodile Is
Mooroongga Is
Rabuma Is
Howard Is
Boucaut Bay
Maningrida
Ji-Marda
Milingimbi
Castlereagh Bay
Banyan Is
Mapurru
Goomadeer
Gochin Jiny Jirra
Yathalamarra
Nangalala
Ramingining
Closed to all non-local traffic
'Old Arafura' (ruins)
Mirrnatja
Manmoyi
FREDERICK HILLS
CENTRAL ARNHEM ROAD
MITCHELL RANGE
Koolatong
Goyder
Emu Springs
Mt Flemming
PARSONS RANGE
BATH RANGE
Mt Ranken
Walker
Permit Required
705
Mt Marumba
Black Mountain
Weemol
Bulman
Mt Catt
Mt Stretton
Mainoru Store
Mt Bridges
'Mountain Valley'
'Mainoru'
Mt Bray
Mt Lunee
Mt Throsby
'Wongolara'
Whamelk Bluff
Three Graces
'Conways'
Mt Furner
Mt Bagster
Mt Phillip
Mt Favenc
Mt Karmain
Mt Chapman
HIGH BLACK RANGE
DOWNERS RANGE
COLLERA MTNS
Mt Warrington
Buddawarka
Urapunga
Ngukurr
Roper Bar
'Moroak'
Mt Eleanor
Yutpundji-Djindiwirritj
'St Vidgeon' (ruins)
Mt Boxall
Port Roper
Limmen Bight
Maria Is
Bringung
'Roper Valley'
Mt Price
ROPER HWY
176
Mt Eclipse
Mt St Vidgeon
Marra
Beatrice Is
For more detail on this area, see Hema's Top End & Western Gulf map and Cairns to Broome map
Mt Forrest
Mt Hughes
Mt Davidson
Hodgson Downs
Mt Kelly
Miniyeri
'Hodgson Downs'
Mason Bluff
Proposed Limmen National Park
Limmen River Fishing Camp
Maria Lagoon
Rosie Creek Fishing Camp
The Four Archers
372
'Nathan River'
'Hodgson River'
Alawa
'Lorella Springs'
'Nutwood Downs'
'Minamia' (Cox River)
TAWALLAH RANGE
Wurralibi
Sir Edward Pellew Group
Barranyi (North Island) Nat Park
Port McArthur River Mine
West Island
Watson Is
North Is
Cape Vanderlin
'Bing Bong'
Bing Bong Loading Facility
Centre Is
South West Is
Vanderlin Is
Port McArthur
King Ash Bay
Borroloola
Narwinbi
Mt Feathertop
McARTHUR RIVER
'Manangoora'
'Warby'
'Greenbank'
'Seven Emu'
Jandanku
'Bauhinia Downs'
'Tawallah'
'Billengarrah'
117
Caranbirini Con Res
Bukalara Rock
McArthur River Mine (HYC)
McLEOD RANGE
Scarlet Hill
CARPENTARIA HWY
Mt Jee
'Tanumbirini'
'Broadmere'
To Cape Crawford
To Burketown
89
N
0 50 100km
© Hema Maps Pty Ltd

88 Central Northern Territory

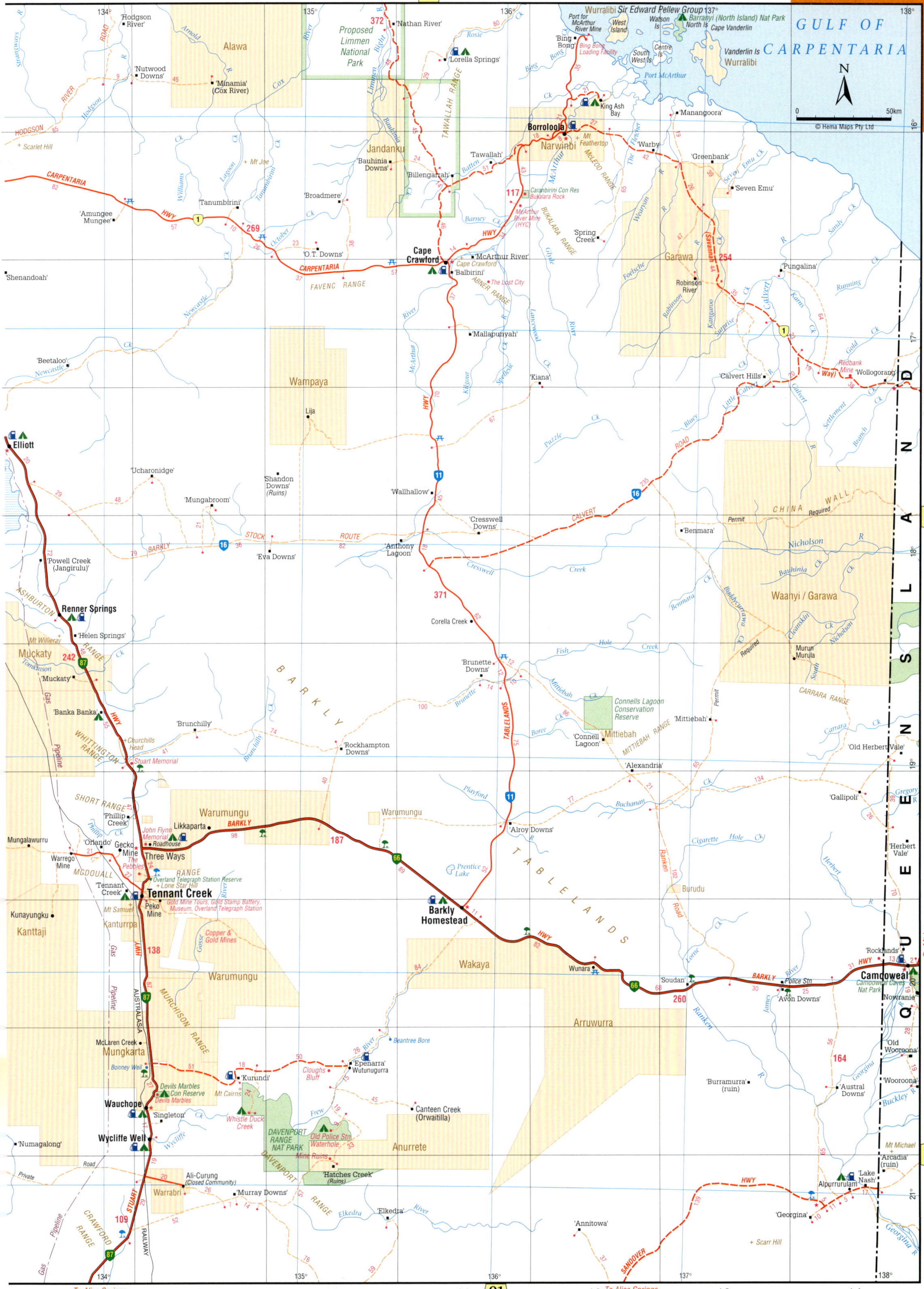
GULF OF CARPENTARIA
Sir Edward Pellew Group
Wurralibi
Port for McArthur River Mine
West Island
Watson Is
Barranyi (North Island) Nat Park
North Is
Cape Vanderlin
Vanderlin Is
Wurralibi
South West Is
Centre Is
Port McArthur
Bing Bong Loading Facility
'Bing Bong'
King Ash Bay
'Manangoora'
Borroloola
Narwinbi
Mt Feathertop
'Warby'
'Greenbank'
'Seven Emu'
'Tawallah'
'Billengarrah'
TAWALLAH RANGE
Proposed Limmen National Park
'Nathan River'
'Lorella Springs'
Jandanku
'Bauhinia Downs'
'Broadmere'
'O.T. Downs'
Carambirini Con Res
Bukalara Rock
McArthur River Mine (HYC)
BUKALARA RANGE
McLEOD RANGE
'Spring Creek'
Garawa
Robinson River
'Pungalina'
Cape Crawford
'McArthur River'
Cape Crawford
'Balbirini'
ABNER RANGE
The Lost City
FAVENC RANGE
CARPENTARIA HWY
Alawa
'Minamia' (Cox River)
'Hodgson River'
'Nutwood Downs'
HODGSON RIVER
Scarlet Hill
'Amungee Mungee'
'Tanumbirini'
Mt Joe
'Shenandoah'
'Mallapunyah'
'Kiana'
'Calvert Hills'
Redbank Mine
'Wollogorang'
Wampaya
Lija
'Beetaloo'
Elliott
'Ucharonidge'
'Shandon Downs' (Ruins)
'Mungabroom'
'Wallhallow'
'Cresswell Downs'
CALVERT ROAD
'Benmara'
CHINA WALL
Permit Required
'Eva Downs'
BARKLY STOCK ROUTE
'Anthony Lagoon'
'Powell Creek' (Jangirulu)
ASHBURTON RANGE
Renner Springs
'Helen Springs'
Mt Willieray
Muckaty
'Muckaty'
'Banka Banka'
WHITTINGTON RANGE
Churchills Head
Stuart Memorial
Corella Creek
'Brunette Downs'
BARKLY
TABLELANDS
Connells Lagoon Conservation Reserve
'Connell Lagoon'
Mittiebah
MITTIEBAH RANGE
'Mittiebah'
Waanyi / Garawa
Murrun Murula
CARRARA RANGE
'Old Herbert Vale'
'Brunchilly'
'Rockhampton Downs'
'Alexandria'
'Gallipoli'
'Herbert Vale'
SHORT RANGE
'Phillip Creek'
Warumungu
Likkaparta
John Flynn Memorial
Roadhouse
'Orlando'
Gecko Mine
The Pebbles
Three Ways
Mungalawurru
Warrego Mine
McDOUALL RANGE
Overland Telegraph Station Reserve
Lone Star Hill
'Tennant Creek'
Tennant Creek
Mt Samuel
Peko Mine
Gold Mine Tours, Gold Stamp Battery, Museum, Overland Telegraph Station
Kunayungku
Kanttaji
Kanturrpa
Copper & Gold Mines
Warumungu
'Alroy Downs'
Prentice Lake
Burudu
Barkly Homestead
Wakaya
Wunara
'Soudan'
Camooweal
Camooweal Caves Nat Park
'Rocklands'
'Avon Downs'
Police Stn
'Nowranie'
Arruwurra
MURCHISON RANGE
McLaren Creek
Mungkarta
Bonney Well
Beantree Bore
'Epenarra' Wutunugurra
Cloughs Bluff
'Kurundi'
Devils Marbles Con Reserve
Devils Marbles
Mt Cairns
Wauchope
'Singleton'
Whistle Duck Creek
Canteen Creek (Orwaitilla)
DAVENPORT RANGE NAT PARK
Old Police Stn Waterhole
Mine Ruins
Anurrete
Wycliffe Well
'Numagalong'
Ali-Curung (Closed Community)
'Hatches Creek' (Ruins)
DAVENPORT RANGE
Warrabri
'Murray Downs'
'Elkedra'
'Annitowa'
'Burramurra' (ruin)
'Old Wooroona'
'Wooroona'
'Austral Downs'
Mt Michael
'Arcadia' (ruin)
'Lake Nash'
Alpurrurulam
'Georgina'
Scarr Hill
SANDOVER HWY
CRAWFORD RANGE
STUART HWY
AUSTRALASIA RAILWAY
To Roper Bar
To Burketown
To Mt Isa
To Alice Springs
To Alice Springs
QUEENSLAND
© Hema Maps Pty Ltd

90 Southern Northern Territory

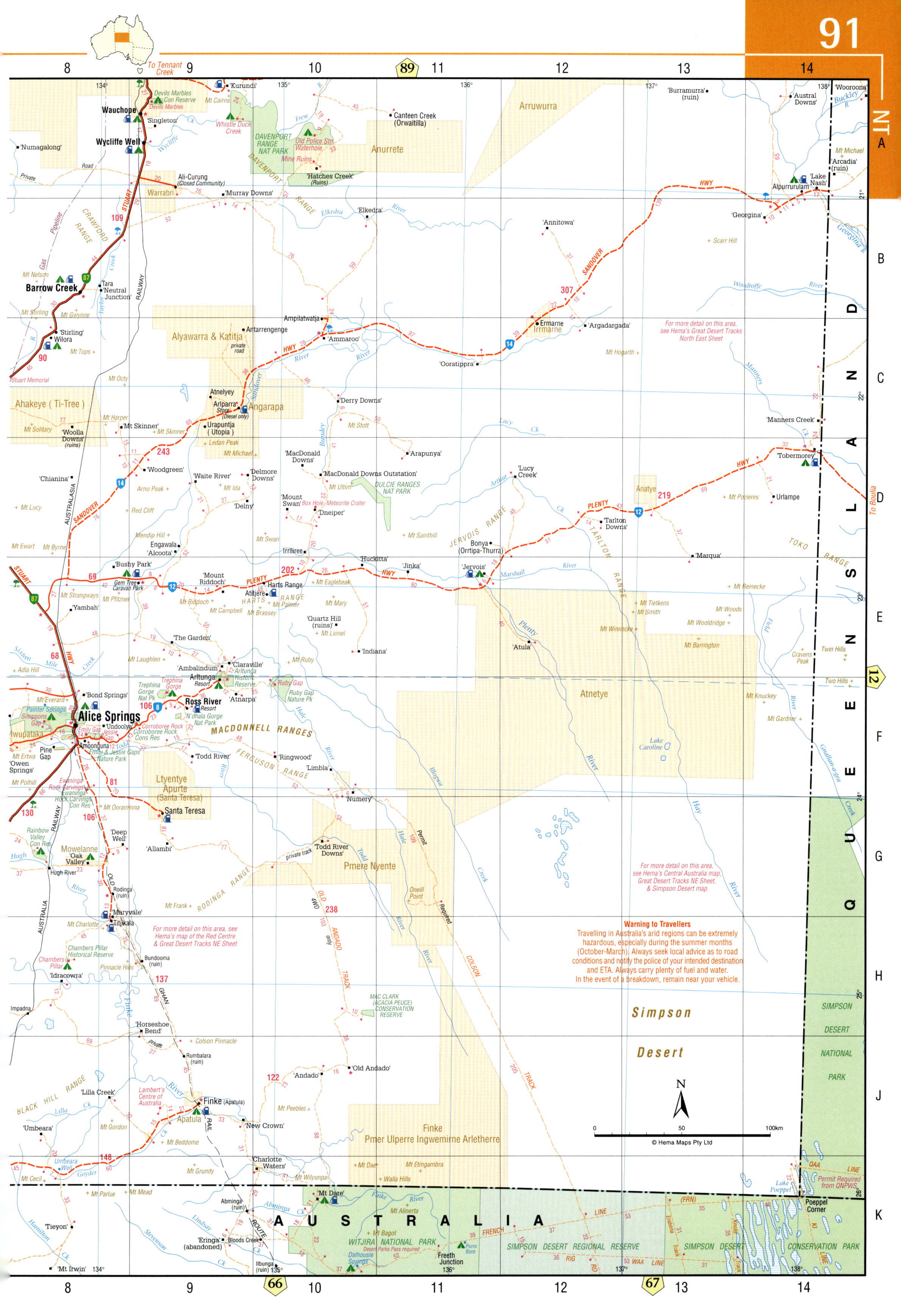
To Tennant Creek
8
9
10
89
11
12
13
14
NT
A
B
C
D
E
F
G
H
J
K
'Kurundi'
Devils Marbles Con Reserve
Devils Marbles
Mt Cairns
Wauchope
'Singleton'
Whistle Duck Creek
Canteen Creek (Orwaitilla)
Arruwurra
'Burramurra' (ruin)
'Austral Downs'
'Wooroona'
Buckley
Wycliffe Well
DAVENPORT RANGE NAT PARK
Old Police Stn Waterhole
Mine Ruins
Anurrete
'Hatches Creek' (Ruins)
'Numagalong'
Road
Private
Ali-Curung (Closed Community)
Warrabri
'Murray Downs'
STUART
109
Pipeline
Gas
CRAWFORD RANGE
DAVENPORT RANGE
Elkedra
'Elkedra'
River
'Annitowa'
HWY
Mt Michael
'Arcadia'
'Lake Nash'
Alpurrurulam
'Georgina'
Scarr Hill
Georgina R
Mt Nelson
Barrow Creek
Tara
'Neutral Junction'
RAILWAY
SANDOVER
307
Woodroffe
River
Mt Stirling
Mt Gwynne
Ampilatwatja
Antarrengene
Alyawarra & Katitja
private road
'Ammaroo'
'Stirling'
Wilora
Mt Tops
90
Ermarne
Irrmarne
'Argadargada'
For more detail on this area, see Hema's Great Desert Tracks North East Sheet
Mt Hogarth
'Ooratippra'
Stuart Memorial
Mt Octy
Atnelyey
Arlparra Store (Diesel only)
Angarapa
'Derry Downs'
Ahakeye (Ti-Tree)
Mt Harper
'Mt Skinner'
Mt Skinner
Urapuntja (Utopia)
Mt Stott
Lucy
Ck
Manners
'Manners Creek'
Mt Solitary
'Woolla Downs' (ruins)
Ledan Peak
Mt Michael
243
'Arapunya'
'MacDonald Downs'
'Tobermorey'
'Lucy Creek'
'MacDonald Downs Outstation'
'Chianina'
'Woodgreen'
'Waite River'
'Delmore Downs'
Mt Ultim
DULCIE RANGES NAT PARK
Arthur
HWY
Anatye
219
Mt Ida
Arno Peak
Mt Lucy
'Mount Swan'
Box Hole Meteorite Crater
'Dneiper'
Mt Porteres
Urlampe
To Boulia
PLENTY
'Delny'
Red Cliff
AUSTRALASIA
SANDOVER
JERVOIS RANGE
'Tarlton Downs'
TARLTON RANGE
Mt Sainthill
Mendip Hill
Engawala
'Alcoota'
Mt Swan
Irrilirree
Bonya (Orrtpia-Thurra)
'Marqua'
TOKO RANGE
Mt Ewart
Mt Byrne
'Bushy Park'
'Mount Riddoch'
'Huckitta'
'Jinka'
'Jervois'
Marshall
River
STUART
69
Gem Tree Caravan Park
PLENTY
202
Mt Eaglebeak
HWY
Harts Range
Atitjere
HARTS RANGE
Mt Palmer
Mt Reinecke
Mt Strangways
Mt Ritzner
Mt Riddoch
Mt Campbell
Mt Brassey
Mt Mary
Mt Tietkens
Mt Smith
Mt Woods
Mt Wooldridge
'Yambah'
'Quartz Hill (ruins)'
Mt Lionel
Plenty
Mt Winnecke
Mt Barrington
'The Garden'
'Indiana'
'Atula'
Twin Hills
Cravens Peak
Sixteen Mile Creek
68
HWY
Mt Laughlen
Mt Ruby
'Ambalindum'
'Claraville'
Arltunga Resort
Arltunga Historic Reserve
Adla Hill
Two Hills
12
'Bond Springs'
Trephina Gorge
Trephina Gorge Nat Pk
Ruby Gap
Ruby Gap Nature Pk
Atnetye
Mt Knuckey
Mt Everard
Painter Springs
Simpsons Gap
106
Ross River
Resort
N'dhala Gorge Nat Park
'Atnarpa'
Alice Springs
'Undoolya'
Corroboree Rock
Corroboree Rock Cons Res
Emily Gap
Jessie Gap
MACDONNELL RANGES
Mt Gardner
Iwupataka
Amoonguna
Emily & Jessie Gaps Nature Park
Pine Gap
'Todd River'
'Ringwood'
FERGUSON RANGE
Hale
River
Lake Caroline
Mt Ertwa
'Owen Springs'
'Limbla'
Illogwa
Ltyentye Apurte (Santa Teresa)
Mt Polhill
Ewaninga Rock Carvings
Ewaninga Rock Carvings Con Res
81
'Numery'
Hay
River
130
106
Mt Ooraminna
Santa Teresa
'Deep Well'
Rainbow Valley Con Res
Mowelanne
'Oak Valley'
Hugh
'Allambi'
'Todd River Downs'
Pmere Nyente
Permit
For more detail on this area, see Hema's Central Australia map, Great Desert Tracks NE Sheet, & Simpson Desert map
Hugh River
private track
RODINGA RANGE
Rodinga (ruin)
OLD
238
4WD
ANDADO
only
TRACK
Oneill Point
Required
Creek
'Maryvale'
Titjikala
Mt Frank
Mt Charlotte
For more detail on this area, see Hema's map of the Red Centre & Great Desert Tracks NE Sheet
Warning to Travellers
Travelling in Australia's arid regions can be extremely hazardous, especially during the summer months (October-March). Always seek local advice as to road conditions and notify the police of your intended destination and ETA. Always carry plenty of fuel and water. In the event of a breakdown, remain near your vehicle.
Chambers Pillar Historical Reserve
Chambers Pillar
Pinnacle Hills
Bundooma (ruin)
COLSON
'Idracowra'
137
GHAN
Impadna
Finke
MAC CLARK (ACACIA PEUCE) CONSERVATION RESERVE
Simpson
Desert
SIMPSON DESERT NATIONAL PARK
'Horseshoe Bend'
Colson Pinnacle
private
Rumbalara (ruin)
'Old Andado'
'Andado'
TRACK
122
BLACK HILL RANGE
'Lilla Creek'
Lambert's Centre of Australia
Finke (Aparatjara)
Apatula
Mt Peebles
Lilla
N
0
50
100km
© Hema Maps Pty Ltd
'Umbeara'
Mt Gordon
'New Crown'
Mt Beddome
Finke Pmer Ulperre Ingwemirne Arletherre
148
Umbeara Well
Goyder
Mt Grundy
'Charlotte Waters'
Mt Dare
Mt Etingambra
Walla Hills
Mt Wilyunpa
QAA
LINE
Permit Required from ONPWS
Lake Poeppel
Mt Cecil
Mt Parlue
Mt Mead
Abminga (ruin)
'Mt Dare'
Abminga
Ck
Finke
River
Mt Alinerta
Poeppel Corner
'Tieyon'
Lindsay
AUSTRALIA
ROUTE
Mt Bagot
WITJIRA NATIONAL PARK
Desert Parks Pass required
Dalhousie Springs
Purni Bore
FRENCH
LINE
(FRN)
Erabena
Track
Knolls
Track
SIMPSON DESERT REGIONAL RESERVE
SIMPSON DESERT CONSERVATION PARK
Hamilton
Stevenson
'Eringa' (abandoned)
Bloods Creek
Freeth Junction
RIG
RD
WAA
LINE
K1
'Mt Irwin'
Ilbunga (ruin)
134°
135°
136°
137°
138°
21°
22°
23°
24°
25°
26°
66
67
TRACK

92 913 Mile – Bathurst

A

913 Mile WA 77 J14 83 F3
A1 Mine Settlement VIC 42 H6 44 A7 46 C1
Abbeyard VIC 43 F8
Abbotsbury NSW 21 E9
Abbotsford NSW 19 E4
Abbotsham TAS 54 E6
Aberbaldie Nature Res NSW 25 J8
Abercorn QLD 7 A9
Abercrombie NSW 22 H5
Abercrombie River Nat Park NSW 22 J6 30 A5
Aberdeen NSW 23 C8
Aberfeldy VIC 42 J7 44 B7 46 D1
Aberfoyle Park SA 60 J2 61 C6
Abergowrie QLD 11 F13
Abminga SA 66 A4 91 K9
Acacia Ridge QLD 3 H4 5 E9
Acacia Store NT 85 D2 86 D4
Acheron VIC 42 G4
Acland QLD 7 F10
Acraman Creek Con Park SA 64 D3
Actaeon Island TAS 53 K9
Acton ACT 31 A1 32 D4
Adaminaby NSW 30 F2
Adamsfield TAS 52 F7
Adavale QLD 13 K11 15 C11
Addington VIC 39 D10
Adelaide SA 59 G4 60 G2 61 A6 62 F7 65 J10
Adelaide CBD SA 58
Adelaide River NT 85 E2 86 E4
Adelong NSW 29 H14 30 D1
Adjungbilly NSW 30 D1
Admiral Bay WA 79 C8 80 J2
Adolphus Island WA 81 C13
Advancetown QLD 5 C13
Adventure Bay TAS 53 J10
Afterlee NSW 25 B12
Agery SA 62 H5 65 G9
Agnes Banks NSW 20 G7
Agnes Banks Nature Res NSW 20 G7 23 G8
Agnes Water QLD 9 J12
Agnew WA 77 E10
Ahrberg Bay TAS 54 H2
Aileron NT 90 D7
Ailsa VIC 40 K6
Ainslie ACT 32 D5
Aireys Inlet VIC 36 K1 39 J11
Airlie VIC 45 D11 46 E4
Airlie Beach QLD 9 B8
Akuna Bay NSW 19 A6
Alawa NT 84 B3
Alawoona SA 62 B6 65 J13
Albacutya VIC 28 K3 40 H4
Albany WA 74 K6
Albany Creek QLD 3 B2 4 F7
Albany Island QLD 16 B2
Albatross Bay QLD 16 F1
Alberrie Creek SA 67 H8
Albert NSW 22 C1 27 K13 29 A13
Albert Park VIC 36 D7
Alberton QLD 5 C10
Alberton SA 59 E2 60 F1
Alberton TAS 55 E12
Alberton VIC 45 G9 46 H2
Albion QLD 3 D4
Albion VIC 36 C6 39 F13 42 K1 44 B1
Albury NSW 29 K12 43 B9
Alcomie TAS 54 C3
Alderley QLD 3 D3
Aldersyde WA 72 A5
Aldgate SA 59 J7 60 H4 61 B7
Aldinga SA 61 E5 62 F7 65 K10
Aldinga Beach SA 61 E4 62 F7 65 K9
Aldinga Scrub Con Park SA 61 E4 65 K9
Alectown NSW 22 E2
Alexander Heights WA 71 C4
Alexander Morrison Nat Park WA 76 H4
Alexandra VIC 42 G4
Alexandra Bridge WA 73 J13
Alexandra Headland QLD 4 D1 7 E13
Alexandra Hills QLD 5 D8
Alford SA 62 G4 65 G9
Alfords Point NSW 19 H3
Alfred Cove WA 71 H3
Alfred Nat Park VIC 47 C12
Alfred Town NSW 29 H13
Algebuckina Bridge SA 66 E5
Alger Island NT 87 C11
Algester QLD 3 J4
Alice NSW 7 K12 25 C12
Alice QLD 8 H3 13 F13
Alice Springs NT 91 F8
Ali-Curung NT 89 K9 91 A9
Alkata NT 68 A1 79 K14 83 A7 90 J1
Allambie NSW 19 D6
Allans Flat VIC 43 C9
Allansford VIC 38 H7
Allanson WA 73 F9
Alleena NSW 29 E13
Allen Island QLD 10 D3
Allenby Gardens SA 59 F3
Allendale East SA 38 G1 63 B14
Allestree VIC 38 H4
Allies Creek QLD 7 D9
Allora QLD 7 H11
Allworth NSW 23 D11
Alma SA 62 F5 65 H10
Almaden QLD 11 E11
Almonds VIC 42 C6
Almoola QLD 8 C6
Almurta VIC 37 K12 44 F4
Alonnah TAS 53 J10
Aloomba QLD 11 D13
Alpara NT 68 A4 90 K4
Alpha QLD 8 H4 13 F14
Alpine Nat Park VIC 30 J1 43 F10 46 B3
Alpurrurulam NT 12 A1 89 K14 91 A14
Alstonville NSW 7 K13 25 C14
Althorpe Islands SA 63 J8 64 K7
Alton QLD 6 H6
Alton Nat Park QLD 6 H6
Altona VIC 35 E1 36 D6 39 F13 42 K1 44 C1
Altona Meadows VIC 35 E1
Alum Cliffs State Res TAS 54 F7
Alva Beach QLD 8 A6
Alvie VIC 39 H9
Alyangula NT 87 F12
Amamoor QLD 7 D12
Amanbidji NT 86 K2 88 B2
Amaroo ACT 32 A5
Amata SA 68 A4 90 K4
Ambarvale NSW 21 E11
Amberley QLD 5 H9
Ambleside SA 60 H4
Amboola QLD 6 D3
Amboyne VIC 43 G14 47 A9
Ambrose QLD 9 H11
Amby QLD 6 E4
Amelup WA 74 H7
Amen Corner SA 63 J8 65 K8
American River SA 63 H9
Amherst VIC 39 C10
Amity QLD 4 B7 7 G13
Amoonguna NT 91 F8
Amosfield NSW 25 B10
Amphitheatre VIC 39 C9
Ampilatwatja NT 91 C10
Amyton SA 62 F1 65 D9
Anakie QLD 8 H6
Anakie VIC 36 E2 39 F12
Anakie East VIC 36 E2
Anakie Junction VIC 36 D2 39 F12
Ancona VIC 42 F5
Andamooka SA 67 K8
Anderson VIC 44 G3
Anderson Island TAS 55 C9
Ando NSW 30 H3
Andover TAS 53 D11
Andrews QLD 5 B14
Andrews SA 62 F4 65 F10
Anembo NSW 30 F4
Angahook Lorne State Park VIC 39 J11
Angaston SA 60 A7 62 E6 65 H10
Angatja SA 68 A2 90 K3
Angellala QLD 6 D1 13 K14
Angip VIC 40 J5
Angle Vale SA 60 C3
Anglers Rest VIC 43 F11 46 A5
Anglesea VIC 36 K2 39 H11
Angorichina Village SA 65 B10
Angourie NSW 25 E13
Angove Con Park SA 60 E3
Angurugu NT 87 F12
Anna Bay NSW 23 E11
Anne's Corner SA 68 E5
Annerley QLD 3 F4 5 E8
Annuello VIC 28 G5 40 D7
Anser Group VIC 44 K7 46 K1
Anson Bay NT 86 E2
Ansons Bay TAS 55 D14
Antarrengene NT 91 C9
Antill Plains QLD 8 A5 11 H14
Antill Ponds TAS 53 C11 55 K11
Antwerp VIC 40 K5
Anula NT 84 B3
Anxious Bay SA 64 F4
Aparatjara (new) SA 68 A2 90 K2
Aparatjara (old) SA 68 A2 90 K2
Apollo Bay VIC 39 K10
Appila SA 62 F2 65 E10
Appin NSW 21 E12 23 J8 30 A7
Appin VIC 41 H10
Appin South VIC 41 H10
Apple Tree Flat NSW 22 D6
Applecross WA 71 H3
Apslawn TAS 53 B13 55 J13
Apsley TAS 53 D10
Apsley VIC 38 C2
Aquila Island QLD 9 E9
Arabella QLD 13 K14 15 D14
Arakoola Nature Res NSW 24 D7
Arakoon NSW 25 J12
Arakwal Nat Park NSW 25 B14
Araleun SA 68 A5 90 K5
Araluen NSW 30 E5
Araluen Nature Res NSW 30 E5
Aramac QLD 8 G2 13 E12
Aramara QLD 7 C11
Arana Hills QLD 3 C2
Aranda ACT 32 D4
Ararat VIC 39 D8
Aratula QLD 5 J12 7 H12
Arawata VIC 37 J14
Arcadia NSW 19 A3 20 D6
Arcadia VIC 42 D3
Archdale VIC 39 B9
Archer River Roadhouse QLD 16 G3
Archerfield QLD 3 G3 5 E9
Archies Creek VIC 44 G4
Ardeer VIC 35 D1
Ardglen NSW 23 B8
Ardlethan NSW 29 F12
Ardno VIC 38 F2
Ardrossan SA 62 G5 65 H9
Areyonga NT 90 G6
Argents Hill NSW 25 H12
Argyle WA 73 G10 74 G3
Ariah Park NSW 29 F13
Aringa VIC 38 H5
Arkaroola SA 67 J11
Arkona VIC 40 K5
Arlparra NT 91 C9
Arltunga NT 91 F9
Arltunga Historic Res NT 91 F9
Armadale VIC 35 E4
Armadale WA 72 F4 74 D3
Armatree NSW 22 A3 24 K1
Armidale NSW 25 G9
Armstrong VIC 38 D7
Armuna QLD 8 B6
Armytage VIC 39 H10
Arncliffe NSW 19 G4
Arno Bay SA 62 K4 64 G7
Arnold VIC 39 A10
Arrino WA 76 G4
Artarmon NSW 21 C8
Arthur East WA 73 B10
Arthur Pieman Con Area TAS 54 F2
Arthur Point QLD 9 F9
Arthur River TAS 54 D1
Arthur River WA 73 B9 74 F5
Arthurs Creek VIC 37 A9
Arthurs Lake TAS 53 B9 55 J9
Arthurs Seat State Park VIC 36 J7 39 H14 44 F1
Arthurton SA 62 H5 65 H8
Arthurville NSW 22 D3
Arundel QLD 5 B12
Ascot QLD 3 D4 4 E7
Ascot VIC 39 D10
Ascot WA 71 F5
Ashbourne SA 63 F8 65 K10
Ashbury NSW 21 C9
Ashfield NSW 21 C9
Ashfield WA 71 E5
Ashford NSW 25 D8
Ashgrove QLD 3 D3
Ashley NSW 24 D5
Ashmore QLD 5 B12
Ashton SA 59 G7 60 G4 61 A7
Ashville SA 63 D8 65 K11
Aspen Island ACT 31 C4
Aspendale VIC 37 F8
Aspley QLD 3 B4 4 E7
Aspley VIC 63 A12
Asquith NSW 20 D7
Astrebla Downs Nat Park QLD 12 G5
Athelstone SA 59 E7 60 F3
Atherton QLD 11 D12
Athlone VIC 37 H13 44 E5
Athol Park SA 59 E3
Atitjere NT 91 E10
Atnelyey NT 91 C9
Attadale WA 71 H2
Attunga NSW 24 H7
Aubigny QLD 7 G10
Aubrey VIC 40 K5
Auburn NSW 19 F3 21 D9
Auburn SA 62 F5 65 G10
Auburn River Nat Park QLD 7 C9
Audley NSW 19 K3 21 C10
Augathella QLD 6 C1 13 J14 15 C14
Augusta WA 73 J14 74 H2
Augustus Island WA 80 D7
Auldana SA 59 G6
Aurora Kakadu NT 85 D6 86 D6
Aurukun Community QLD 16 G1
Austinmer NSW 21 C13
Austinville QLD 5 C14
Austral NSW 21 F10
Australia Plains SA 62 E5 65 G11
Australind WA 73 G9
Avalon NSW 20 B6
Avalon Beach VIC 36 F3
Avenel VIC 42 F3
Avenue SA 63 C12
Avisford Nature Res NSW 22 D5
Avoca TAS 53 A12 55 H12
Avoca VIC 39 C9
Avoca Beach NSW 20 B4
Avoid Bay SA 64 H5
Avon SA 62 F5 65 H9
Avon Plains VIC 38 A7
Avon Valley Nat Park WA 72 E2 74 C3 76 K5
Avondale QLD 7 A11 9 K12
Avonsleigh VIC 37 E11
Awabakal Nature Res NSW 23 E10
Axedale VIC 39 B12
Ayr QLD 8 A6
Ayrford VIC 38 J7
Ayton QLD 11 B12

B

Baalijin Nature Res NSW 25 G11
Baan Baa NSW 24 G5
Babel Island TAS 55 B10
Babinda QLD 11 E13
Bacchus Marsh VIC 36 B3 39 E12
Back River Nature Res NSW 23 A9 25 K8
Backstairs Passage SA 61 K1 63 G8
Backwater NSW 25 F10
Baddaginnie VIC 42 D5
Baden TAS 53 D11
Badgebup WA 74 G6
Badger Island TAS 55 C8
Badgerys Creek NSW 21 F9
Badgingarra WA 76 H4
Badgingarra Nat Park WA 76 H4
Badja NSW 30 F4
Badja Swamps Nature Res NSW 30 F4
Badu Island QLD 16 A1
Baerami NSW 23 D8
Baerami Creek NSW 22 D7
Bagdad TAS 53 E10
Bago Bluff Nat Park NSW 23 A13 25 K11
Bagot Well SA 62 E5 65 H10
Bailieston VIC 39 A14 42 E2
Bailup WA 72 E2
Baird Bay SA 64 E3
Bairnsdale VIC 43 K11 45 C13 46 D6
Bajool QLD 9 H10
Bakara SA 62 C6 65 J12
Bakara Con Park SA 62 C6 65 H12
Baker VIC 40 J3
Baker Gully SA 60 J2 61 C6
Baker Lake WA 83 B5
Bakers Creek QLD 9 D8
Bakers Hill WA 72 D2
Bakers Swamp NSW 22 E4
Baking Board QLD 7 E8
Baladjie Lake Nature Res WA 75 A8 77 J8
Balaklava SA 62 F5 65 G9
Balbarrup WA 73 E13
Balcatta WA 71 D3 72 G3
Bald Hills QLD 3 A3
Bald Island WA 74 K7
Bald Knob NSW 25 E10
Bald Knob QLD 4 F2
Bald Rock VIC 28 K7 41 J11
Bald Rock Nat Park NSW 7 K11 25 C10
Baldry NSW 22 E3
Balfe's Creek QLD 8 B3 11 J13
Balfour TAS 54 E2
Balga WA 71 D3
Balgo WA 79 D13
Balgowan SA 62 H5 65 H8
Balgowlah NSW 19 D6 21 B8
Balgownie NSW 21 D14
Balhannah SA 60 G5 62 E7 65 J10
Balingup WA 73 F11 74 G3
Balkuling WA 72 B3
Balladonia WA 83 H2
Balladoran NSW 22 B3
Ballajura WA 71 C5
Ballalaba NSW 30 E4
Ballan VIC 36 B2 39 E11
Ballan North VIC 36 A2
Ballandean QLD 25 B10
Ballangeich VIC 38 H7
Ballarat VIC 39 E10
Ballark VIC 36 C1
Ballbank NSW 28 J7 41 F11
Balldale NSW 29 K11 42 A7
Ballendella VIC 41 K13 42 C1
Balliang VIC 36 D3 39 F12
Balliang East VIC 36 D3 39 F12
Ballidu WA 76 H6
Ballimore NSW 22 C4
Ballina NSW 7 K14 25 C14
Ballina Nature Res NSW 25 C14
Bally Bally WA 72 B4
Balmain NSW 19 F5 21 C8
Balmattum VIC 42 E4
Balmoral NSW 19 E6 21 B8 21 G14
Balmoral QLD 3 E5
Balmoral VIC 38 D4
Balnarring VIC 37 J8 39 H14 44 F2
Balnarring Beach VIC 37 J8
Balook VIC 45 F8 46 G2
Balranald NSW 28 G6 41 C9
Balwyn VIC 35 D5 37 D8
Bamaga QLD 16 B2
Bamarang Nature Res NSW 30 C5
Bamawm VIC 41 K13 42 C1
Bamawm Extension VIC 41 J13 42 B1
Bambaroo QLD 11 G13
Bambill VIC 28 G2 40 B3
Bamboo WA 78 E7 82 C7
Bamboo Spring NT 88 C1
Bamborough Island QLD 9 E10
Bambra VIC 39 H11
Ban Ban Springs QLD 7 C10
Banana QLD 9 K10
Bancroft QLD 7 A9 9 K11
Bandiana VIC 43 B9
Bandon NSW 22 G2
Bandon Grove NSW 23 C10
Banealla SA 63 B9
Bangadilly Nat Park NSW 22 K7 30 B6
Bangalow NSW 7 K13 25 B14
Bangerang VIC 40 J6
Bangham SA 38 A1
Bangham Con Park SA 38 A1 63 A11
Bangholme VIC 35 H6
Bangor NSW 21 C10
Bangor TAS 55 E10 56 D5
Baniyala NT 87 E12
Banks ACT 32 K4
Banks Strait TAS 55 B13
Banksia Beach QLD 4 D4
Banksia Park SA 59 D7
Banksmeadow NSW 19 H6
Bankstown NSW 19 G2 21 D9
Bannaby NSW 22 K6 30 B5
Bannerton VIC 28 G5 40 C7
Bannister NSW 22 K5 30 B4
Bannister WA 72 D6 74 E4
Bannockburn VIC 36 F1 39 G11
Banora Point NSW 5 A14
Banyabba Nature Res NSW 25 D12
Banyan VIC 28 J5 40 G7
Banyan Island NT 87 C10
Banyena VIC 38 A7
Banyenong VIC 41 K8
Banyo QLD 3 C5
Barabon QLD 13 A9
Baradine NSW 24 H3
Barakee Nat Park NSW 23 A11
Barakula QLD 7 D8
Baralaba QLD 9 J9
Baranduda VIC 43 B9
Barcaldine QLD 8 H2 13 F12
Bardoc WA 77 H11 83 F1
Bardoc Mine WA 77 G10
Bardon QLD 3 E3
Barduthulla QLD 13 K14 15 C14
Barellan NSW 29 F12
Barfold VIC 39 C12
Bargara QLD 7 A12 9 K13
Bargo NSW 21 F13 22 J7 30 A7
Bargo State Con Area NSW 21 G14
Barham NSW 28 J7 41 G11
Baring VIC 40 F5
Baringhup VIC 39 C11
Barjarg VIC 42 F5
Bark Hut Inn NT 85 D4 86 E5
Barkly Homestead NT 89 H11
Barkstead VIC 39 E11
Barlee WA 73 G13
Barlee Range Nature Res WA 78 G3 82 G1
Barmah VIC 29 K9 41 H14 42 A2
Barmah Island VIC 41 H14 42 A2
Barmah State Park VIC 41 H14 42 A2
Barmedman NSW 29 F13
Barmera SA 62 B5 65 H13
Barmundu QLD 9 J11
Barnawartha VIC 43 B8
Barnes Bay TAS 50 H6 53 H10
Barneys Lake NSW 28 D7
Barongarook VIC 39 J10
Barooga NSW 29 K10 42 A4
Barool Nat Park NSW 25 E11
Baroota SA 62 G2 65 E9
Barossa Valley SA 60 A6
Barpinba VIC 39 G10
Barraba NSW 24 G7
Barrabool VIC 36 G2 39 G11
Barradale WA 78 G2
Barramunga VIC 39 J10
Barranyi (North Island) Nat Park NT 87 J13 89 A13
Barraport VIC 41 J10
Barratta QLD 8 A5
Barren Grounds Nature Res NSW 23 K8 30 C7
Barrington NSW 23 B11
Barrington TAS 54 F7
Barrington Tops Nat Park NSW 23 C10
Barringun NSW 15 K13 27 B10
Barrogan NSW 22 F3
Barron Gorge Nat Park QLD 11 D12
Barron Island NT 85 B5 86 C6
Barrow Creek NT 91 B8
Barrow Island WA 78 E2
Barrow Island Nature Res WA 78 E3
Barry NSW 22 G5 23 A10 25 K8
Barrys Beach VIC 44 H7 46 H1
Barrys Reef VIC 39 E12
Barton ACT 31 D3 32 E5
Barton SA 68 H6
Barton VIC 38 D7
Barton Nature Res NSW 22 F4
Barton Siding SA 66 K1
Barunga NT 85 J7 86 G7
Barunga Gap SA 62 G4 65 G9
Barwell Con Park SA 64 F5
Barwell Con Res SA 64 F5
Barwon Downs VIC 39 J10
Barwon Heads VIC 36 H4 39 H12
Baryulgil NSW 25 D12
Bascombe Well Con Park SA 64 F5
Bascombe Well Con Res SA 64 G5
Basket Range SA 60 G4
Basket Swamp Nat Park NSW 7 K11 25 C11
Bass VIC 37 K11 44 F3
Bass Hill NSW 21 D9
Bass Landing VIC 37 K11
Bass Strait 39 K12 44 K5 54 B3 56 A3
Bassendean WA 71 E6
Batchelor NT 85 E2 86 E4
Batchica VIC 40 J6
Bateau Bay NSW 20 B3
Batehaven NSW 30 F6
Batemans Bay NSW 30 F5
Batesford VIC 39 G12
Bathumi VIC 42 B6
Bathurst NSW 22 F5

Bathurst Bay – Boucaut Bay 93

Bathurst Bay QLD 16 H5
Bathurst Island NT 86 B2
Batlow NSW 29 J14 30 E1
Battery Point TAS 49 C2
Bauhinia QLD 9 K8
Baulkham Hills NSW 19 D2 21 E8
Bauple QLD 7 C12
Baw Baw Nat Park VIC 42 K6 44 B7 46 D1
Bawley Point NSW 30 E6
Baxter VIC 37 G9
Bay of Fires Con Res TAS 55 E14
Bay of Islands Coastal Park VIC 38 J7
Bayles VIC 37 G12 44 E4
Bayley Island QLD 10 D3
Baynton VIC 39 C13 42 G1
Bayswater VIC 35 E7 37 D9
Bayswater WA 71 E5
Bayulu WA 79 B11 81 J9
Bayview NSW 19 B7 20 B6
Bayview Haven NT 84 D2
Beachamp VIC 41 G9
Beachmere QLD 4 E5
Beachport SA 63 C13
Beachport Con Park SA 63 C13
Beacon WA 76 H7
Beaconsfield NSW 19 G5
Beaconsfield TAS 55 E8 56 D2
Beaconsfield VIC 37 F10 44 D3
Beaconsfield Upper VIC 37 F11
Beagle Bay WA 79 A9 80 F4
Beagle Gulf NT 85 B1 86 C3
Bealiba VIC 39 B9
Bearbung NSW 22 A4 24 K2
Beardmore VIC 42 K7 45 C8 46 D2
Beargamil NSW 22 E2
Bearii VIC 42 A3
Bears Lagoon VIC 41 K11
Beatrice Island NT 87 H11
Beaudesert QLD 5 E12 7 H13
Beaufort VIC 39 E9
Beaufort WA 73 B10
Beaumaris TAS 55 F14
Beaumont SA 59 H5
Beaumont Nature Res WA 75 F14 83 J2
Beauty Point TAS 55 E9 56 D2
Beazleys Bridge VIC 39 A8
Bebeah NSW 20 D1
Beckenham WA 71 H6
Beckom NSW 29 F12
Bedarra Island QLD 11 F13
Bedford WA 71 E4
Bedford Park SA 59 K3
Bedgerebong NSW 22 F1 29 D14
Bedourie QLD 12 G4
Bedunburra WA 79 B9 80 H5
Beeac VIC 39 H10
Beech Forest VIC 39 J10
Beechboro WA 71 D5
Beechford TAS 55 D9 56 B3
Beechmont QLD 5 D14
Beechwood NSW 23 A13 25 K11
Beechworth VIC 43 C8
Beechworth Historic Park VIC 43 C8
Beecroft NSW 20 D7
Beecroft Head NSW 30 D7
Beedelup Nat Park WA 73 F14 74 J3
Beekeepers Nature Res WA 76 G3
Beela WA 73 F9
Beenak VIC 37 D12
Beenleigh QLD 5 D10 7 G13
Beerburrum QLD 4 F3 7 F13
Beerwah QLD 4 F2 7 E12
Bees Nest Nature Res NSW 30 C5
Bega NSW 30 H5
Beggan Beggan NSW 22 K2 30 B1
Beilpajah NSW 28 C6
Bejoording WA 72 D1
Belair SA 59 J4 60 H2 61 B6
Belair Nat Park SA 59 J5 60 H3 61 B7
Belalie North SA 62 E2 65 E10
Belaringar NSW 22 B1 27 J13
Belbora NSW 23 C12
Belconnen ACT 30 D3 32 C3
Belconnen Town Centre ACT 32 C3
Beldon WA 71 A1
Belford Nat Park NSW 23 D9
Belgrave VIC 37 E10 42 K3 44 C3
Bell NSW 22 G7
Bell QLD 7 E10
Bell Bay TAS 55 D9 56 C2
Bellambi NSW 21 C13
Bellara QLD 4 D4
Bellarine VIC 36 G5 39 G13
Bellarwi NSW 29 F13
Bellata NSW 24 E5
Bellbird NSW 23 E9
Bellbird Creek VIC 47 D10
Bellbird Park QLD 5 F9
Bellbrae VIC 36 J2 39 H12
Bellbridge VIC 43 B9
Bellbrook NSW 25 H11
Bellenden Ker QLD 11 D13
Bellerive TAS 50 C6 53 F11
Bellevue WA 71 E7
Bellevue Heights SA 59 K4 60 H2 61 B6
Bellingen NSW 25 G12
Bellinger River Nat Park NSW 25 G12
Bellingham TAS 55 D10 56 B5
Bellmere QLD 4 F4
Bellmount Forest NSW 30 C3
Belltrees NSW 23 B9
Belmont NSW 23 F10
Belmont QLD 3 F6
Belmont VIC 36 G2
Belmont WA 71 F5
Belmore NSW 19 G4 21 C9
Belmunging WA 72 B3
Beloka NSW 30 H2
Belowra NSW 30 G4
Belrose NSW 20 B7
Belsar Island VIC 40 C7
Beltana SA 65 A10 67 K10
Beltana Roadhouse SA 65 A10 67 K10
Belton SA 65 D10
Belyando Crossing QLD 8 E5 13 B14
Belyuen NT 85 C1 86 D3
Bemboka NSW 30 H4
Bemm River VIC 47 D10
Ben Boyd Nat Park NSW 30 J5 47 A14
Ben Bullen NSW 22 F6
Ben Halls Gap Nat Park NSW 23 A9
Ben Lomond NSW 25 F9
Ben Lomond Nat Park TAS 55 G12
Bena NSW 29 D13
Bena VIC 37 K13 44 F5
Benalla VIC 42 D5
Benambra VIC 43 F11
Benambra Nat Park NSW 29 K13 43 A9
Benandarah NSW 30 E6
Benaraby QLD 9 J11
Benaye VIC 38 C2
Bencubbin WA 74 A6 76 J7
Bendalong NSW 30 D6
Bendeela NSW 22 K7 30 C6
Bendemeer NSW 25 H8
Bendick Murrell NSW 22 J3 30 A2
Bendidee Nat Park QLD 7 H8 24 A7
Bendigo VIC 39 B12
Bendoc VIC 30 K3 47 A10
Bendoc North VIC 47 A11
Bendoc Upper VIC 30 K3
Bendolba NSW 23 D10
Beneree NSW 22 G4
Benetook VIC 28 F3 40 B4
Benger WA 73 G9
Bengerang NSW 6 K6 24 C4
Bengworden VIC 45 C12 46 E5
Beni NSW 22 C4
Benjeroop VIC 41 F10
Benjinup WA 73 E11
Benlidi QLD 8 K2 13 G11
Bennison Island VIC 44 H7 46 J1
Benowa QLD 5 B13
Bensville NSW 20 B4
Bentinck Island QLD 10 D3
Bentley NSW 25 B13
Bentley WA 71 H5
Bentleys Plain VIC 43 G12 46 B7
Benwerrin VIC 39 J11
Berajondo QLD 9 K12
Berala NSW 21 D9
Berambing NSW 20 J7 22 G7
Beremboke VIC 36 C2
Beresfield NSW 23 E10
Beresford SA 66 G7
Bergalia NSW 30 F5
Berkeley Vale NSW 20 B3
Berkshire Park NSW 20 F7
Bermaguee Nature Res NSW 30 H5
Bermagui NSW 30 H5
Bermagui South NSW 30 H5
Bernacchi TAS 53 A8 55 H8
Bernier and Dorre Island Nature Res WA 76 A1 78 J1
Bernier Island WA 76 A1 78 J1
Berowra NSW 19 A4 20 C6
Berowra Heights NSW 19 A5
Berowra Valley Regional Park NSW 19 A4 20 D7
Berowra Waters NSW 20 D6
Berri SA 28 F1 62 B5 65 H13
Berridale NSW 30 G2
Berriedale TAS 50 B5
Berrigan NSW 29 J10
Berrilee NSW 20 D6
Berrima NSW 22 K7 30 B6
Berringa VIC 39 F10
Berringama VIC 43 C11
Berriwillock VIC 28 J5 41 G8
Berrook VIC 28 H1 40 D1 62 A7 65 J13
Berry NSW 30 C7
Berry Springs NT 85 D2 86 D4
Berrybank VIC 39 G9
Berwick VIC 37 F10 44 D3
Bessiebelle VIC 38 H5
Bet Bet VIC 39 B10
Beta QLD 8 H4 13 F13
Bete Bolong VIC 43 K14 47 D8
Bethanga VIC 43 B9
Bethania QLD 3 K6
Bethany SA 60 B6
Bethungra NSW 22 K1 29 G14
Betoota QLD 12 J5 14 C3 67 A14
Betsey Island TAS 51 G8 53 G11
Beulah TAS 54 F7
Beulah VIC 28 K4 40 H6
Beulah East VIC 40 H6
Beulah Park SA 59 G5
Beulah West VIC 40 H5
Bevendale NSW 22 K4 30 B3
Beverford VIC 28 H6 41 E9
Beveridge VIC 39 E14 42 H2
Beveridge Station (site) VIC 43 F9
Beverley WA 72 C4 74 D4
Beverly Hills NSW 19 G4 21 C9
Bewong NSW 30 D6
Bews SA 63 B8 65 K12
Bexhill NSW 25 B13
Bexley NSW 21 C9
Beyal VIC 40 J7
BHP 10 Yandicoogina Mine WA 78 F6 82 F5
Biala NSW 22 K4 30 B3
Biamanga Nat Park NSW 30 H5
Bibbenluke NSW 30 J3
Biboohra QLD 11 D12
Bibra Lake WA 71 K3
Bicheno TAS 53 A14 55 H14
Bickerton Island NT 87 F12
Bicton WA 71 H2
Biddaddaba QLD 5 D12
Biddon NSW 22 A4 24 K2
Bidgeemia NSW 29 J11
Bidijul WA 79 C11 81 J8
Bidyadanga (Lagrange) WA 79 C8 80 J2
Big Bush Nature Res NSW 29 F13
Big Desert Wilderness Park VIC 28 J2 40 G2 63 A9 65 K14
Big Green Island TAS 55 C9
Big Heath Con Park SA 63 B12
Big Pats Creek VIC 37 C13
Bigga NSW 22 H4 30 A3
Biggara VIC 43 C13
Biggenden QLD 7 B11
Biggs Flat SA 60 H4
Biggs Island WA 81 B8
Bilambil NSW 5 B14 25 A14
Bilbaringa SA 60 C4
Bilgola NSW 20 B6
Billiatt Con Park SA 28 H1 62 B7 65 J13
Billiluna (Mindibungu) WA 79 D13
Billimari NSW 22 G3
Billinga QLD 5 A14
Billinooka WA 78 G7
Billinudgel Nature Res NSW 25 B14
Billinudgell NSW 25 B14
Billys Creek NSW 25 F11
Biloela QLD 9 J10
Bilpin NSW 20 J6 23 G8
Bilyana QLD 11 F13
Bimberamala Nat Park NSW 30 E6
Bimbi NSW 22 H2 29 E14
Binalong NSW 22 K3 30 B2
Binalong Bay TAS 55 E14
Binaronca Nature Res WA 75 C13 77 K11 83 G1
Binbee QLD 8 B6
Binda NSW 22 J5 30 A4
Bindango QLD 6 E4
Bindarri Nat Park NSW 25 G12
Bindi VIC 43 G12 46 A7
Bindi Bindi WA 76 H5
Bindoon WA 72 F1 74 B3 76 K5
Bingara NSW 24 E7
Bingil Bay QLD 11 E13
Binginwarri VIC 45 G8 46 H2
Biniguy NSW 24 D6
Binjour QLD 7 B10
Binjura Nature Res NSW 30 G3
Binna Burra QLD 5 D14 7 H13 25 A13
Binnaway NSW 22 A5 24 K4
Binnaway Nature Res NSW 22 A5 24 K4
Binningup WA 73 G9 74 F2
Binnu WA 76 E3
Binnum SA 38 B1 63 A11
Binya NSW 29 F11
Birany Birany NT 87 D12
Birchip VIC 28 K5 40 H7
Birchs Bay TAS 50 J4 53 H10
Bird Island TAS 54 B1
Birdsville QLD 12 K3 14 C1 67 A11
Birdwood NSW 23 A12 25 K11
Birdwood SA 60 E6 62 E6 65 J10
Birdwoodton VIC 28 F3 40 A4
Biriwal Bulga Nat Park NSW 23 A12 25 K10
Birkdale QLD 3 F7 5 D8
Birkenhead SA 59 D1
Birnam Range QLD 5 E12
Birralee QLD 8 C6
Birralee TAS 55 F8 56 G2
Birrego NSW 29 H12
Birregurra VIC 39 H10
Birri Lodge QLD 10 C3
Birriwa NSW 22 C5
Birrong NSW 19 F2
Birru QLD 5 J9
Bishops Nature Res WA 75 F12 83 J1
Bishopsbourne TAS 55 G9 56 J3
Bittern VIC 37 J9
Black Andrew Nature Res NSW 30 C2
Black Forest SA 59 H3
Black Hill SA 62 D6 65 J11
Black Hill Con Park SA 59 E7 60 F3
Black Hills TAS 50 A2 53 F9
Black Jungle Con Res NT 85 C2 86 D4
Black Mountain NSW 25 G9
Black Mountain Nat Park QLD 11 B12 16 K6
Black Point NT 86 B5
Black Range State Park VIC 38 C5
Black River TAS 54 C3
Black Rock SA 62 E2 65 E10
Black Rock VIC 35 G4 36 E7
Black Rock Con Park SA 62 E1 65 E10
Black Springs NSW 22 H6
Black Springs SA 62 E4 65 G10
Black Swamp NSW 25 C11
Blackall QLD 8 J3 13 G12
Blackbraes Nat Park QLD 8 A1 11 H10
Blackbull QLD 10 F7
Blackburn VIC 35 D6
Blackbutt QLD 7 E11
Blackdown Tableland Nat Park QLD 9 H8
Blackfellows Caves SA 63 B14
Blackheath NSW 21 K8 22 G7
Blackmans Bay TAS 50 F6 53 G10
Blacksmith Island QLD 9 C8
Blackstone (Papulankutja) WA 79 K13 83 B7
Blacktown NSW 19 D1 21 E8
Blackville NSW 22 A7
Blackwater QLD 9 H8
Blackwood SA 59 K4 60 H3 61 B6 62 F7 65 J10
Blackwood VIC 39 E12
Blackwood Creek TAS 53 A9 55 H9
Blackwood Forest VIC 37 K12
Blackwood Nat Park QLD 8 D5 13 B14
Bladensburg Nat Park QLD 13 D9
Blair Athol QLD 8 F6
Blair Athol SA 59 E4
Blairgowrie VIC 36 J6
Blakehurst NSW 19 H4 21 C10
Blakeview SA 60 C3
Blakeville VIC 36 A2 39 E11
Blakney Creek NSW 22 K4 30 B3
Blanchetown SA 62 D5 65 H11
Bland NSW 22 H1 29 E13
Blandford NSW 23 B9
Blanket Flat NSW 22 J4 30 A3
Blaxland NSW 21 H8 23 G8
Blaxlands Ridge NSW 20 G6
Blayney NSW 22 G5
Blessington TAS 55 G11
Blewitt Springs SA 60 K2 61 D6
Bligh Park NSW 20 F7
Blighty NSW 29 J9
Blinman SA 65 B10
Bloods Creek SA 66 A4 91 K9
Bloods Range (Puntitjata) NT 79 J14 90 H1
Bloomfield QLD 11 B12
Bloomsbury QLD 8 C7
Blow Clear NSW 22 E1 29 C14 29 E13
Blue Bay NSW 20 A3
Blue Lake Nat Park QLD 5 B8 7 G14
Blue Mountains Nat Park NSW 21 H9 22 H7 30 A5
Blue Mud Bay NT 87 F11
Blue Rocks TAS 55 B9
Bluewater QLD 8 A4 11 H14
Bluewater Springs Roadhouse QLD 8 A3 11 H13
Bluff QLD 9 H8
Bluff River Nature Res NSW 25 C10
Blyth SA 62 F4 65 G10
Blythdale QLD 6 E5
Boambee NSW 25 G13
Boat Harbour TAS 54 D4
Boat Harbour Beach TAS 54 C4
Boatswain Point SA 63 D12
Bobadah NSW 27 K12 29 A12
Bobbin Head NSW 19 A5 20 C6
Bobin NSW 23 B12
Bobundara Nature Res NSW 30 H3
Bodalla NSW 30 G5
Bodallin WA 75 B8 77 J8
Bodangora NSW 22 D4
Boddington WA 72 D7 74 E4
Bogan Gate NSW 22 E1 29 C14
Bogandyera Nature Res NSW 29 K14 30 F1 43 A12
Bogangar NSW 25 A14
Bogantungan QLD 8 H5
Bogee NSW 22 E7
Boggabilla NSW 6 J7 24 B6
Boggabri NSW 24 H5
Boginderra Hills Nature Res NSW 22 J1 29 F13
Bogolong Creek NSW 22 H2 29 E14
Bogong VIC 43 E10
Boho VIC 42 E5
Boho South VIC 42 E5
Boigbeat VIC 40 G7
Boinka VIC 28 H2 40 E3
Boisdale VIC 43 K9 45 C10 46 E4
Bokal WA 73 C10
Bokarina QLD 4 D1
Bolgart WA 74 B4 76 J5
Bolinda VIC 39 D13 42 H1
Bolivar SA 59 A2 60 D2
Bolivia NSW 25 D10
Bolivia Hill Nature Res NSW 25 D10
Bollanolla Nature Res NSW 25 H12
Bollon QLD 6 H2
Bolton VIC 28 H5 40 D7
Boltons Beach Con Area TAS 53 D13
Bolwarra VIC 38 H4
Bolwarrah VIC 36 A1 39 E11
Bomaderry NSW 30 C7
Bombala NSW 30 J3
Bombo NSW 23 K8 30 B7
Bomera NSW 22 A6 24 K5
Bonalbo NSW 7 K12 25 B12
Bonang VIC 30 K2 47 A10
Bonbeach VIC 37 F8
Bondi NSW 19 F7 21 B8
Bondi Gulf Nature Res NSW 30 K3 47 A11
Bondi Junction NSW 19 F6
Bonegilla VIC 29 K12 43 B9
Boneo VIC 36 K7
Bongaree QLD 4 D4 7 F13
Bongil Bongil Nat Park NSW 25 G13
Bonnells Bay NSW 20 B1
Bonnet Bay NSW 19 J3
Bonnie Doon VIC 42 F5
Bonnie Rock WA 76 H7
Bonnie Vale WA 75 A12 77 J11
Bonny Hills NSW 23 A13
Bonnyrigg NSW 21 E9
Bonogin QLD 5 C14
Bonshaw NSW 7 K9 25 C8
Bonville NSW 25 G12
Bonya (Orrtipa-Thurra) NT 91 D12
Bonython ACT 32 J3
Booborowie SA 62 E3 65 F10
Boobyalla TAS 55 C12
Booderee Nat Park ACT 30 D7
Boodie Island WA 78 E2
Boodjamulla (Lawn Hill) Nat Park QLD 10 G2
Bookabie SA 64 C1 68 K6
Bookaloo SA 65 C8
Bookar VIC 39 G8
Booker Bay NSW 20 B5
Bookham NSW 30 C2
Bookin QLD 10 K6 12 A6
Bool Lagoon SA 38 D1 63 B12
Boolading WA 73 D9
Boolarra VIC 44 F7 46 G1
Boolba QLD 6 H3
Boolburra QLD 9 H9
Boolcunda SA 65 D9
Booleroo Centre SA 62 F2 65 E10
Booligal NSW 29 E8
Boolite VIC 40 K7
Boomi NSW 6 J6 24 B4
Boomi Nature Res NSW 24 B4
Boomi West Nature Res NSW 24 B4
Boonah QLD 5 H12 7 H12
Boonanarring Nature Res WA 74 B3 76 J5
Boonanghi Nature Res NSW 25 J11
Boonarga QLD 7 E8
Boondall QLD 3 B5 4 E7
Boondooma QLD 7 D9
Boonmoo QLD 11 D12
Boonoo Boonoo NSW 25 C10
Boonoo Boonoo Nat Park NSW 7 K11 25 B11
Boonooroo QLD 7 C13
Boorabbin WA 75 B10 77 J10
Boorabbin Nat Park WA 75 A10 77 J9
Booragoon WA 71 J3
Booral NSW 23 D11
Boorcan VIC 39 H8
Boorganna Nature Res NSW 23 A12
Boorhaman VIC 42 C6
Boorindal NSW 27 E11
Boorndoolyanna SA 68 A5 90 K6
Boorongie North VIC 28 H4 40 E6
Booroolong Nature Res NSW 25 G9
Booroopki VIC 38 B2
Booroorban NSW 29 G8 41 D13
Boorowa NSW 22 J3 30 B2
Boort VIC 28 K6 41 J10
Boosey VIC 42 B5
Booti Booti Nat Park NSW 23 C13
Booyal QLD 7 B11
Bopeechee SA 67 H8
Boppy Mount NSW 27 H11
Borallon QLD 5 H8
Borambil NSW 22 B6
Borambola NSW 29 H14
Boraning WA 73 C8
Borda Island WA 81 B9
Borden WA 74 H7
Border Island QLD 9 B8
Border Ranges Nat Park NSW 7 J12 25 A12
Border Store NT 85 C7 86 D7
Borderdale WA 73 A12
Bordertown SA 40 K1 63 B10
Boree NSW 22 F4
Boree QLD 13 A10
Boree Creek NSW 29 H12
Boreen Point QLD 7 D13
Boro NSW 30 D4
Boronga Nature Res NSW 24 B5
Boronia VIC 37 D9
Boronia Heights QLD 3 K4
Boroobin QLD 4 G2
Bororen QLD 9 J11
Borrika SA 62 C7 65 J12
Borroloola NT 87 K12 89 B12
Borung VIC 41 K10
Boscabel WA 73 B11
Bossley Park NSW 21 E9
Bostobrick NSW 25 G11
Boston Island SA 64 H6
Botany NSW 19 H6 21 B9
Botany Bay NSW 19 H5 21 B9
Botany Bay Nat Park NSW 19 J6 21 B10 23 H9
Bothwell TAS 53 D9
Boucaut Bay NT 87 C9

94 Bouddi NP – Campbells Forest

Bouddi Nat Park NSW 20 B5 23 G10
Boulder WA 75 A12 77 J11 83 F1
Bouldercombe QLD 9 H10
Boulia QLD 12 E4
Boundain WA 73 A8
Boundary Bend VIC 28 G5 41 C8
Bountiful Island QLD 10 D4
Bourke NSW 27 E10
Bournda Nat Park NSW 30 J5
Bow NSW 22 C7
Bowden SA 58 A1
Bowelling WA 73 D10 74 F4
Bowen QLD 8 B7
Bowen Mountain NSW 20 H7
Bowen Park NSW 22 F4
Bowenvale VIC 39 C10
Bowenville QLD 7 F10
Bower SA 62 D5 65 G11
Boweya VIC 42 C6
Bowhill SA 62 D7 65 J11
Bowillia SA 62 F4 65 G9
Bowling Alley Point NSW 23 A9 25 K8
Bowling Green Bay QLD 8 A5
Bowling Green Bay Nat Park QLD 8 A6
Bowman QLD 9 F9
Bowmans SA 62 F5 65 H9
Bowna NSW 29 K13 43 A10
Bowning NSW 22 K4 30 C2
Bowral NSW 22 K7 30 B6
Bowraville NSW 25 H12
Box Hill NSW 20 F7
Box Hill VIC 35 D6 37 D9 39 F14 42 K2 44 B2
Boxwood Hill WA 75 H8
Boyacup WA 73 A13
Boyagarring Con Park WA 72 D5
Boyagin Nature Res WA 72 C6 74 D4
Boyanup WA 73 G10 74 G3
Boydtown NSW 30 K5 47 A14
Boyeo VIC 40 K3
Boyer TAS 50 A3 53 F10
Boyland QLD 5 D12
Boyne Island QLD 9 J11
Boynedale QLD 9 J11
Boyup Brook WA 73 E11 74 G4
Bracalba QLD 4 G4
Brachina SA 65 B10
Bracken Ridge QLD 3 A4 4 E6
Brackendale NSW 25 J9
Bracknell TAS 55 G9 56 K3
Bradbury NSW 21 E11
Bradbury SA 60 H4 61 B7
Braddon ACT 32 D5
Bradvale VIC 39 F9
Braefield NSW 23 A8 24 K7
Braeside VIC 35 H5 37 F8
Brahma Lodge SA 59 B5
Braidwood NSW 30 E5
Bramfield SA 64 F4
Brampton Island QLD 9 C8
Brampton Islands Nat Park QLD 9 C8
Bramston Beach QLD 11 E13
Bramwell Junction QLD 16 D2
Brandon QLD 8 A5
Brandy Creek VIC 37 G14
Branxholm TAS 55 E12
Branxholme VIC 38 F4
Branxton NSW 23 D10
Brawlin NSW 22 K2 29 G14 30 B1
Bray Junction SA 63 C12
Braybrook VIC 35 C1
Brayfield SA 64 G6
Brayton NSW 22 K6 30 B5
Brazendale Island TAS 53 B9 55 J9
Breadalbane NSW 30 C4
Breadalbane TAS 55 G10 56 H5
Break O'Day VIC 42 H3
Breakaway Ridge Nature Res WA 75 F8
Breakfast Creek NSW 22 D6 22 J3 30 A2
Breaksea Island TAS 52 J5
Bream Creek TAS 51 B12 53 F12
Breamlea VIC 36 H3
Bredbo NSW 30 F3
Breelong NSW 22 B4
Breeza NSW 24 J6
Bremer Bay WA 75 H9
Bremer Island NT 87 C13
Brendale QLD 3 A3
Brentwood SA 62 H6 65 J8
Brentwood VIC 40 H5
Breona TAS 53 A8 55 H8
Bretti NSW 23 B11
Bretti Nature Res NSW 23 B11
Brewarrina NSW 27 D12
Brewer NSW 29 D11
Brewster VIC 39 E9
Briaba QLD 8 C6
Briagolong VIC 43 K9 45 C11 46 D4
Bribbaree NSW 22 H1 29 F14
Bribie Island QLD 4 D3 7 F13
Bribie Island Nat Park QLD 4 E3 7 F13
Bridge Creek VIC 42 F6
Bridgeman Downs QLD 3 B3
Bridgenorth TAS 55 F9 56 F4
Bridgetown WA 73 F12 74 H3
Bridgewater SA 60 H4
Bridgewater TAS 50 A5 53 F10
Bridgewater VIC 39 A11
Bridport TAS 55 D11 56 B7
Brigalow QLD 7 E9
Bright VIC 43 E9
Brighton QLD 3 A4 4 E6
Brighton SA 59 K2 60 H1 61 B5 62 F7 65 J10
Brighton TAS 53 F10
Brighton VIC 35 F3 36 E7
Brighton-Le-Sands NSW 19 H5 21 B9
Brightview QLD 5 K8
Brightwaters NSW 20 B1
Brim VIC 40 J6
Brimbago SA 63 B10
Brimboal VIC 38 D3
Brimpaen VIC 38 C5
Brindabella NSW 30 D2
Brindabella Nat Park NSW 30 D2
Brinerville NSW 25 G11
Bringalbert VIC 38 B2
Bringelly NSW 21 F10
Bringung NT 87 H8
Brinkin NT 84 A2
Brinkley SA 62 E7 65 K11
Brinkworth SA 62 F4 65 G9
Brisbane QLD 3 E4 5 E8 7 G13
Brisbane CBD QLD 2
Brisbane Forest Park QLD 3 D1 4 G7
Brisbane Ranges Nat Park VIC 36 D2 39 F12
Brisbane Water Nat Park NSW 20 C5 23 G9
Brit Brit VIC 38 E4
Britannia Creek VIC 37 C12
Brittons Swamp TAS 54 C2
Brixton QLD 8 H2 13 E11
Broad Arrow WA 77 H11 83 F1
Broad Sound QLD 9 F9
Broad Sound Island Nat Park QLD 9 E9
Broadbeach QLD 5 B13 7 H13
Broadford VIC 39 C14 42 G2
Broadmarsh TAS 53 E10
Broadmeadows SA 60 D3
Broadmeadows VIC 35 B3 36 B7
Broadmont QLD 9 H10
Broadwater NSW 7 K13 25 C14
Broadwater VIC 38 G5
Broadwater Nat Park NSW 7 K13 25 C14
Brocklehurst NSW 22 C3
Brocklesby NSW 29 J12 43 A8
Brockman WA 73 F14
Brockman Mine WA 78 F4 82 F2
Brockman Nat Park WA 74 J3
Brodribb River VIC 43 K14 47 D9
Brogo NSW 30 H5
Broke NSW 23 E9
Broken Bay NSW 20 B5 23 G9
Broken Hill NSW 26 J2 28 A2 65 C14
Bromby Islands NT 87 C12
Bromelton QLD 5 F12
Brompton SA 59 F3
Bromus WA 75 D13 83 H1
Bronte NSW 21 B9
Bronte Park TAS 52 C7 54 K7
Bronzewing VIC 28 H4 40 E6
Brookdale NSW 29 H12
Brooker SA 64 G6
Brookfield NSW 23 D11
Brookfield QLD 3 E1 5 G8
Brookfield Con Park SA 62 D5 65 H11
Brookhampton WA 73 F11
Brooking Gorge Con Park WA 79 B11 81 H8
Brooklands QLD 5 F11
Brooklyn NSW 20 C5
Brooklyn VIC 35 D1
Brooklyn Park SA 59 G3
Brooks Creek NT 85 F3 86 E4
Brooksby VIC 38 C4
Brookstead QLD 7 G10
Brookton WA 72 B5 74 D5
Brookvale NSW 19 D6 20 B7
Brookville VIC 43 H11 46 B6
Brooloo QLD 7 E12
Brooman NSW 30 E6
Broome WA 79 B8 80 H3
Broomehill WA 74 G6
Brooms Head NSW 25 E13
Brooweena QLD 7 C11
Broughton VIC 40 J2
Broughton Island NSW 23 D12
Broula NSW 22 H3
Broulee NSW 30 F6
Brovinia QLD 7 C9
Brownlow SA 62 D5 65 H11
Brownlow Hill NSW 21 F11
Browns Creek NSW 22 G4
Browns Plains QLD 3 K4 5 E10
Bruarong VIC 43 C8
Bruce ACT 32 C4
Bruce SA 62 F1 65 D9
Bruce Rock WA 74 C7 76 K7
Brucknell VIC 39 J8
Bruinbun NSW 22 F5
Brukunga SA 60 H6
Brungle NSW 30 D1
Brunswick VIC 35 C3 36 C7
Brunswick Bay WA 80 C7
Brunswick Heads NSW 7 J14 25 B14
Brunswick Junction WA 73 G9 74 F3
Bruthen VIC 43 K12 45 B14 46 D7
Bryden QLD 4 J6
Buangor VIC 39 D8
Bucasia QLD 9 D8
Buccarumbi NSW 25 E11
Buccleuch SA 63 C8 65 K12
Buchan VIC 43 J13 47 C8
Buchan South VIC 43 J13 47 C8
Bucheen Creek VIC 43 D11
Buchfelde SA 60 B3
Buckaroo NSW 22 D6
Buckenderra NSW 30 G2
Bucketty NSW 20 E1 23 F9
Buckingham SA 63 B10
Buckingham WA 73 E10
Buckland TAS 53 E12
Buckland VIC 43 E8
Buckland Junction VIC 43 F8
Buckleboo SA 64 E6
Buckley VIC 36 H1 39 H11
Buckley Swamp VIC 38 F5
Buckrabanyule VIC 41 K9
Budawang Nat Park NSW 30 E5
Buddabaddah NSW 27 J13
Buddawarka NT 87 G3
Budderoo Nat Park NSW 23 K8 30 B7
Buddigower NSW 29 E12
Buddigower Nature Res NSW 29 E12
Buddina QLD 4 D1
Buderim QLD 4 E1 7 E13
Budgee Budgee NSW 22 D6
Budgeree VIC 44 F7 46 G1
Budgerum VIC 41 H9
Budgerum East VIC 41 H10
Budgewoi NSW 20 A2 23 F10
Buenba Flat (site) VIC 43 E12
Buff Point NSW 20 A2
Buffalo VIC 44 G6
Buffalo River VIC 43 E8
Bugaldie NSW 24 J3
Bugan Nature Res NSW 23 A11
Bugilbone NSW 24 F2
Bugong Nat Park NSW 30 C6
Builyan QLD 9 K11
Bukalong NSW 30 J3
Bukkulla NSW 25 D8
Bulahdelah NSW 23 D12
Bulanjarr (Mowla Bluff) WA 79 C10 80 J5
Bulart VIC 38 E4
Buldah VIC 47 B11
Bulga NSW 23 D9
Bulgandry NSW 29 J12
Bulimba QLD 3 D4 5 E8
Bull Creek WA 71 J4
Bull Swamp VIC 37 H14
Bulla NT 86 J2 88 A2
Bulla VIC 35 A1 36 B6 39 E13 42 J1 44 A1
Bullabulling WA 75 A11 77 J10
Bullaburra NSW 21 J9
Bullagreen NSW 22 A2 24 K1 27 H14
Bullarah NSW 24 D3
Bullarook VIC 39 E11
Bullarto VIC 39 D11
Bullea Lake NSW 26 E2
Bulleen VIC 37 C8
Bullen Range Nature Res ACT 32 H1
Bullenbung NSW 29 H12
Bullengarook VIC 36 A4
Bulleringa Nat Park QLD 11 E10
Bullfinch WA 75 A8 77 J8
Bullhead Creek VIC 43 C10
Bulli NSW 21 C13 23 J8 30 B7
Bullio NSW 22 J7 30 A6
Bullioh VIC 29 K13 43 B10
Bullock Creek QLD 11 E11
Bullsbrook WA 72 F2
Bullumwaal VIC 43 J11 45 B12 46 D6
Bullyard QLD 7 A11 9 K12
Bulman NT 87 F9
Buln Buln VIC 37 F14 44 D6
Bulong WA 75 A13 77 J11 83 F1
Bulwer QLD 4 B4
Bulwer Island QLD 3 C6
Bulyee WA 74 D6
Bumbaldry NSW 22 H3
Bumberry NSW 22 F3
Bumbunga SA 62 G4 65 G9
Bunbartha VIC 42 B3
Bunburra QLD 5 H13
Bunbury WA 73 G9 74 F2
Bunbury Con Res SA 63 C10
Bundaberg QLD 7 A12 9 K13
Bundalaguah VIC 45 D10 46 E4
Bundall QLD 5 B12
Bundalong VIC 42 B6
Bundanoon NSW 22 K7 30 B6
Bundarra NSW 25 F8
Bundeena NSW 19 K5 21 B10 23 J9
Bundella NSW 22 A6 24 K5
Bunding VIC 36 A1
Bundjalung Nat Park NSW 25 D13
Bundook NSW 23 B11
Bundooma NT 91 H9
Bundoora VIC 35 B5 37 B8
Bundure NSW 29 H11
Bung Bong VIC 39 C9
Bunga NSW 30 H5
Bungabbee Nature Res NSW 25 B13
Bungador VIC 39 H9
Bungal VIC 36 C1 39 F11
Bungallen QLD 12 B4
Bungarby NSW 30 H3
Bungaree VIC 39 E11
Bungawalbin Nat Park NSW 7 K13 25 C13
Bungawalbin Nature Res NSW 25 D13
Bungeet VIC 42 C6
Bungendore NSW 30 D4
Bungil VIC 43 B10
Bungonia NSW 30 C5
Bungowannah NSW 29 K12 43 A8
Bungulla NSW 25 C10
Bunguluke VIC 41 J9
Bungunya QLD 6 J6 24 A4
Bungwahl NSW 23 D12
Buninyong VIC 39 E10
Bunjurgen QLD 5 H13
Bunker Group QLD 9 J13
Bunkers Con Res SA 65 B10
Bunnaloo NSW 29 J8 41 H13
Bunnan NSW 23 C8
Buntine WA 76 H5
Bunya NSW 23 C12
Bunya QLD 3 C2
Bunya Mountains Nat Park QLD 7 E10
Bunyan NSW 30 G3
Bunyaville State Forest Park QLD 3 C2
Bunyip VIC 37 F13 44 D5
Bunyip State Park VIC 37 E13 42 K4 44 C4
Buraja NSW 29 K11 42 A7
Burakin WA 76 H6
Burbank QLD 3 G6 5 D8
Burcher NSW 29 D13
Burdett South Nature Res WA 75 F13 83 J1
Burekup WA 73 G9
Burford Island NT 86 B5
Burges WA 72 C3
Burgooney NSW 29 D12
Burke and Wills Roadhouse QLD 10 H5
Burketown QLD 10 E3
Burleigh VIC 37 D11
Burleigh Head Nat Park QLD 5 B13
Burleigh Heads QLD 5 B13 7 H13
Burma Road Nature Res WA 76 F4
Burnbank VIC 39 D10
Burndale VIC 37 K12
Burney Island NT 87 F12
Burnie TAS 54 D5
Burning Mountain Nature Res NSW 23 B9
Burns Beach WA 72 G2
Burns Creek TAS 55 F11
Burnside SA 59 G6 60 G3 61 A6
Burnt Bridge NSW 25 J12
Burnt School Nature Res NSW 30 F4
Burnt-Down Scrub Nature Res NSW 25 D11
Buronga NSW 28 F3 40 A5
Burpengary QLD 4 F5
Burra NSW 30 E3
Burra QLD 8 C2 11 K12 13 A12
Burra SA 62 E4 65 G10
Burraboi NSW 28 J7 41 F12
Burracoppin WA 74 B7 76 J7
Burraga NSW 22 H5
Burragate NSW 30 J4 47 A13
Burragorang State Con Area NSW 21 H11
Burramine North VIC 42 A5
Burramine South VIC 42 B5
Burrandana NSW 29 J13
Burraneer NSW 19 K4
Burrapine NSW 25 H11
Burrell Creek NSW 23 B12
Burren Junction NSW 24 F3
Burrendong Dam NSW 22 D5
Burrill Lake NSW 30 E6
Burringbar NSW 25 A14
Burringurrah WA 78 J4 82 K2
Burrinjuck NSW 30 C2
Burrinjuck Dam NSW 30 C2
Burrinjuck Nature Res NSW 30 C2
Burroin VIC 40 G5
Burrowa-Pine Mountain Nat Park VIC 29 K14 43 B12
Burrowye VIC 29 K13 43 B11
Burrum VIC 38 A7
Burrum Coast Nat Park QLD 7 A12
Burrum Heads QLD 7 B12
Burrumbeet VIC 39 E10
Burrumboot VIC 39 A13 42 D1
Burrumbuttock NSW 29 K12 43 A8
Burrup Peninsula WA 78 D4 82 C1
Burswood WA 71 F4
Burton SA 59 A4 60 D2
Burtville WA 77 F12 83 D2
Burwood NSW 19 F4 21 C9
Burwood VIC 35 E5 37 D8 39 F14 42 K2 44 C2
Burwood East VIC 35 E6
Busbys Flat NSW 25 C12
Bushfield VIC 38 H6
Bushy Park TAS 53 F9
Bushy Park VIC 43 K9 45 C10 46 E4
Busselton WA 73 J11 74 G2
Bustard Bay QLD 9 J12
Bustard Island NT 87 F12
Butcher Well North Mine WA 77 F12 83 E1
Butchers Ridge VIC 43 H13 47 B8
Bute SA 62 G4 65 G9
Butler Tanks SA 64 G6
Butru QLD 12 B4
Butterfly Gorge Nature Park NT 85 G3 86 F5
Butterleaf Nat Park NSW 25 D10
Buxton NSW 21 G13
Buxton VIC 42 H4
Buxtonville QLD 7 B12
Byabarra NSW 23 A13 25 K11
Byaduk VIC 38 G5
Byaduk North VIC 38 F5
Byawatha VIC 42 C7
Byee QLD 7 D10
Byfield QLD 9 G10
Byfield Nat Park QLD 9 G11
Byford WA 72 F4 74 D3
Bygnunn WA 79 A9 80 E5
Bylong NSW 22 D7
Byrnes Scrub Nature Res NSW 25 F12
Byrneside VIC 41 K14 42 C3
Byrnestown QLD 7 B10
Byrock NSW 27 F11
Byron Bay NSW 7 K14 25 B14
Bywong NSW 30 D4

C

Cabanandra NSW 47 A9
Cabanda QLD 5 J9
Cabawin QLD 7 F8
Cabbage Tree Creek VIC 47 D10
Cabbage Tree Palms Res VIC 47 D9
Caboolture QLD 4 F4 7 F12
Caboonbah QLD 4 K5
Cabramatta NSW 19 F1 21 E9
Cabramurra NSW 30 F1 43 A14
Caddens Flat VIC 38 D4
Cadell SA 62 C5 65 G12
Cadney Homestead SA 66 E3
Cadney Park SA 66 E3
Cadoux WA 74 A5 76 J6
Caiguna WA 83 H4
Cairns QLD 11 D13
Cairns Bay TAS 50 J1 53 H9
Cal Lal NSW 28 F1 40 A1 62 A5 65 G14
Calamvale QLD 3 J4 5 E9
Calca SA 64 E3
Calcifer QLD 11 D11
Calcium QLD 8 A5 11 H14
Calder TAS 54 D4
Calder Island QLD 9 C9
Caldermeade VIC 37 H12
Caldwell NSW 29 J8 41 G12
Calen QLD 9 C8
Calga NSW 20 C4
Calingiri WA 74 A4 76 J5
Calivil VIC 41 K11
Callanna SA 67 H9
Callaroy NSW 22 C7
Callawadda VIC 38 B7
Calleen NSW 29 E12
Callide QLD 9 J10
Callide Coalfields QLD 9 J10
Callington SA 60 J7 62 E7 65 J10
Callion WA 77 H10
Calliope QLD 9 J11
Caloona NSW 6 K6 24 B3
Caloundra QLD 4 D2 7 E13
Calpatanna Waterhole Con Park SA 64 E3
Caltowie SA 62 F2 65 F10
Calulu VIC 43 K11 45 B12 46 D5
Calvert QLD 5 J10
Calvert VIC 38 E7
Calwell ACT 32 J4
Camballin WA 79 B10 80 H6
Cambalong NSW 30 J3
Cambarville VIC 37 A14 42 J5 44 A5
Camberwell NSW 23 D9
Camberwell VIC 35 D5 37 D8
Cambewarra Range Nature Res NSW 30 C6
Camboon QLD 7 A8 9 K10
Cambooya QLD 7 G10
Cambrai SA 62 D6 65 H11
Cambray WA 73 G12
Cambrian Hill VIC 39 E10
Cambridge NSW 21 G8
Cambridge TAS 50 C7 53 F11
Cambridge Gulf WA 81 C13
Cambridge Ruins QLD 11 K9
Camden NSW 21 F11 23 H8 30 A7
Camden South NSW 21 F11
Camel Lake Nature Res WA 74 H6
Camels Hump Nature Res NSW 23 B11
Camena TAS 54 E6
Cameron Corner NSW QLD SA 14 K4 26 C1 67 G14
Camerons Gorge Nature Res NSW 23 B9
Camira QLD 3 J1 5 F9
Camira Creek NSW 25 D12
Camooweal QLD 10 J1 89 H14
Camooweal Caves Nat Park QLD 10 J2 89 H14
Camp Creek Con Park WA 81 C9
Camp Hill QLD 3 F5 5 E8
Camp Mountain QLD 3 C1 4 G7
Campania TAS 53 E11
Campbell ACT 31 B4 32 E5
Campbell Town TAS 53 B11 55 J11
Campbellfield VIC 35 B3 36 B7
Campbells Bridge VIC 38 B7
Campbells Creek VIC 39 C11
Campbells Forest VIC 39 A11

Campbelltown – Cockle Creek 95

Campbelltown NSW 21 E11 23 J8 30 A7
Campbelltown SA 59 F6 60 F3
Campbelltown VIC 39 C11
Campbellville QLD 4 E2
Camperdown NSW 19 F5 21 C9
Camperdown VIC 39 H8
Campup WA 73 A13
Campwin Beach QLD 9 D8
Camurra NSW 24 D5
Canaga QLD 7 E9
Canbelego NSW 27 H11
Canberra ACT 30 D3
Canberra CBD ACT 31
Canberra City ACT 31 A3 32 D5
Candelo NSW 30 J4
Cane River Con Park WA 78 F3
Canegrass WA 77 H11
Cangai NSW 25 D11
Cania Gorge Nat Park QLD 7 A9 9 K11
Caniambo VIC 42 D4
Cann River VIC 47 C11
Canna WA 76 F4
Cannawigara SA 63 B10
Cannie VIC 41 G9
Canning Vale WA 71 J5
Cannington WA 71 H5 72 F3
Cannington Mine QLD 12 C5
Cannon Creek QLD 5 H13
Cannon Hill QLD 3 E5 5 E8
Cannon Vale QLD 8 B7
Cannons Creek VIC 37 H10
Cannum VIC 40 K5
Canonba NSW 27 H13
Canowie SA 62 E3 65 F10
Canowindra NSW 22 G3
Canteen Creek (Orwaitilla) NT 89 J11 91 A11
Canterbury NSW 19 G4 21 C9
Canunda Nat Park SA 63 C13
Canungra QLD 5 D13 7 H13
Canyonleigh NSW 22 K6 30 B5
Cap Island Con Park SA 64 G4
Capalaba QLD 3 G7 5 D8 7 G13
Capalaba West QLD 3 F7
Capamauro Nature Res WA 76 G4
Caparra NSW 23 B12
Cape Adieu SA 68 K5
Cape Arid WA 83 J2
Cape Arid Nat Park WA 83 J2
Cape Arnhem NT 87 D13
Cape Barren Island TAS 55 A14
Cape Barrow NT 87 F11
Cape Baskerville WA 79 A8 80 F3
Cape Bauer SA 64 E3
Cape Beatrice NT 87 G13
Cape Bedford QLD 11 A12 16 K7
Cape Bernier WA 81 A12
Cape Borda WA 79 A9 80 F4
Cape Bossut WA 79 C8 80 J2
Cape Bougainville WA 81 A10
Cape Bouvard WA 72 H6 74 E2
Cape Bowling Green QLD 8 A6
Cape Brewster WA 80 C7
Cape Bridgewater VIC 38 J3
Cape Byron NSW 7 J14 25 B14
Cape Carnot SA 64 J5
Cape Clear VIC 39 F10
Cape Cleveland QLD 8 A5
Cape Clinton QLD 9 F11
Cape Cockburn NT 86 B6
Cape Conran Coastal Park VIC 47 D10
Cape Cossigny WA 78 D5 82 B3
Cape Crawford NT 89 C11
Cape Croker NT 86 A6
Cape Cuvier WA 78 H1
Cape De Couedic SA 63 K9
Cape Degerando TAS 55 K14
Cape Direction QLD 16 F4
Cape Dombey NT 86 F2
Cape Don NT 86 B5
Cape Dussejour WA 81 C13
Cape Farewell TAS 54 A6
Cape Farquhar WA 78 H1
Cape Flattery QLD 11 A12 16 J7
Cape Ford NT 86 E2
Cape Fourcroy NT 86 C2
Cape Freycinet WA 73 K13 74 H1
Cape Gambier NT 85 B2 86 C4
Cape Gantheaume SA 63 H9
Cape Gantheaume Con Park SA 63 H9
Cape Grafton QLD 11 D13
Cape Grenville QLD 16 D3
Cape Grey NT 87 E12
Cape Grim TAS 54 B1
Cape Hamelin WA 73 K14
Cape Helvetius NT 86 C2
Cape Hillsborough Nat Park QLD 9 C8
Cape Hotham NT 85 B3 86 C4
Cape Hotham Forestry Res NT 86 C4
Cape Howe NSW VIC 30 K5 47 C14
Cape Jaubert WA 79 C8 80 K2
Cape Jervis SA 61 K1 63 G8 65 K9
Cape Keer-weer QLD 16 G1
Cape Keith NT 85 A3 86 B4
Cape Keraudren TAS 54 A1
Cape Keraudren WA 78 D6 82 A6
Cape Kimberly QLD 11 C12
Cape Knob WA 75 J9
Cape Lambert WA 78 D4 82 C2
Cape Latouche Treville WA 79 B8 80 J2
Cape Le Grand WA 75 H13 83 J1
Cape Le Grand Nat Park WA 75 G14 83 J1
Cape Leeuwin WA 73 J14 74 J2
Cape Leseur WA 76 B1 78 K1
Cape Leveque WA 80 E4
Cape Liptrap VIC 44 H5
Cape Liptrap Coastal Park VIC 44 H5
Cape Londonderry WA 81 A11
Cape Manifold QLD 9 G11
Cape Melville QLD 16 H6
Cape Melville Nat Park QLD 16 H6
Cape Missiessy WA 79 C8 80 K2
Cape Naturaliste TAS 55 C14
Cape Naturaliste WA 73 K10 74 G1
Cape Nelson VIC 38 J3
Cape Nelson State Park VIC 38 J3
Cape Otway VIC 39 K9
Cape Palmerston QLD 9 E9
Cape Palmerston Nat Park QLD 9 E9
Cape Pasley WA 83 J2
Cape Paterson VIC 44 G4
Cape Peron North WA 76 A1 78 J1
Cape Pillar TAS 51 K14 53 H13
Cape Pond WA 81 B8
Cape Portland TAS 55 C13
Cape Range Nat Park WA 78 F1
Cape Richards QLD 11 F13
Cape Riche WA 75 J8
Cape River QLD 8 C3 11 K12
Cape Rodstock SA 64 F3
Cape Ronsard WA 78 J1
Cape Ruthieres WA 81 A12
Cape Schanck VIC 36 K7 39 J13 44 F1
Cape Scott NT 86 F2
Cape Shield NT 87 E12
Cape Sidmouth QLD 16 G4
Cape Sorell TAS 54 K3
Cape St Cricq WA 76 A1 78 J1
Cape St Lambert WA 81 B12
Cape Stewart NT 87 C10
Cape Talbot WA 81 A11
Cape Thouin WA 78 D5 82 B4
Cape Torrens Con Park SA 63 K8
Cape Tribulation QLD 11 B12
Cape Upstart QLD 8 A6
Cape Upstart Nat Park QLD 8 A6
Cape Van Diemen NT 86 B3
Cape Van Diemen QLD 10 C4
Cape Vancouver WA 74 K7
Cape Vanderlin NT 87 J13 89 A13
Cape Voltaire WA 81 B9
Cape Wellington VIC 45 K8 46 K2
Cape Wessel NT 87 A13
Cape Weymouth QLD 16 E4
Cape Wickham TAS 54 A6
Cape Wilberforce NT 87 C12
Cape York QLD 16 B2
Cape York Peninsula QLD 16 F2
Capel WA 73 H10 74 G2
Capella QLD 8 G6
Capels Crossing VIC 41 G11
Capercup WA 73 C10
Capertee NSW 22 F6
Capital Hill ACT 31 D2 32 E5
Capoompeta Nat Park NSW 25 D10
Capricorn Coast Nat Park QLD 9 G11
Capricorn Group QLD 9 H12
Capricorn Roadhouse WA 78 G6 82 H6
Capricornia Cays Nat Park QLD 9 H13
Captain Billy Landing QLD 16 D3
Captains Creek Nature Res NSW 25 B11
Captains Flat NSW 30 E4
Carabost NSW 29 J14
Caragabal NSW 22 H1 29 E14
Caralue SA 64 F6
Caralue Bluff Con Park SA 64 F6
Caramut VIC 38 G6
Caranbirini Con Res NT 87 K11 89 B12
Carapooee VIC 39 B9
Carapook VIC 38 E3
Carappee Hill Con Park SA 64 F6
Caravan Head NSW 19 J4
Carawa SA 64 D3
Carboor VIC 42 E7
Carbrook QLD 5 C9
Carbunup River WA 73 J11
Carcoar NSW 22 G4
Carcuma Con Park SA 63 C8 65 K12
Cardinia VIC 37 G11
Cardross VIC 28 F3 40 B5
Cardwell QLD 11 F13
Careunga Nature Res NSW 24 C5
Carey Gully SA 60 G4
Cargerie VIC 39 F11
Cargo NSW 22 F4
Carina QLD 3 F5
Carina VIC 28 H2 40 F2
Carina Heights QLD 3 F5
Carinda NSW 27 F14
Carindale QLD 3 F6 5 E8
Carine WA 71 D2
Caringbah NSW 19 J4 21 B10
Carisbrook VIC 39 C10
Carlecatup WA 73 A11
Carlingford NSW 19 D3 21 D8
Carlisle WA 71 G5
Carlisle Island Nat Park QLD 9 C8
Carlisle River VIC 39 J9
Carlisle State Park VIC 39 J9
Carlotta WA 73 G13
Carlsruhe VIC 39 D12
Carlton TAS 51 C10 53 F11
Carlton VIC 34 A3 35 D3
Carlyam Nature Res WA 76 H6
Carmila QLD 9 E9
Carmila Beach QLD 9 E9
Carnamah WA 76 G5
Carnarvon WA 76 A2 78 J1
Carnarvon Nat Park QLD 6 A4 8 K6 13 H14
Carnes SA 66 J4
Carnes Hill NSW 21 E10
Carngham VIC 39 E10
Caroda NSW 24 F6
Caroona NSW 22 A7 24 K6
Carpa SA 62 K4 64 G7
Carpendeit VIC 39 H9
Carpenter Rocks SA 63 C14
Carrai Nat Park NSW 25 H10
Carrajung VIC 45 F9 46 G3
Carramar NSW 21 D9
Carranballac VIC 39 F8
Carrara QLD 5 B13
Carrathool NSW 29 F9
Carr-Boyd WA 77 H11 83 E1
Carrick TAS 55 G9 56 H4
Carrickalinga SA 61 G3 63 G8 65 K9
Carrieton SA 62 F1 65 D10
Carroll NSW 24 J6
Carroll Gap NSW 24 H6
Carrolup WA 73 A11
Carrow Brook NSW 23 C9
Carrum VIC 35 J5 37 F8 39 G14 44 D2
Carrum Downs VIC 35 J6 37 F9
Carseldine QLD 3 B4 4 E7
Cartwright NSW 21 E9
Carwarp VIC 28 G3 40 B5
Cascade WA 75 F12
Cascade Nat Park NSW 25 G12
Casey ACT 32 A4
Cashmere QLD 3 A1 4 F6
Cashmore VIC 38 H3
Casino NSW 7 K12 25 C13
Cassilis NSW 22 B6
Cassilis VIC 43 G11 46 B6
Cassini Island WA 81 A9
Castambul SA 60 F4
Castella VIC 37 A11
Casterton VIC 38 E3 63 A13
Castle Forbes Bay TAS 50 H1 53 H9
Castle Hill NSW 19 C2 21 D8
Castle Rock NSW 23 C8
Castle Tower Nat Park QLD 9 J11
Castleburn VIC 43 J9 45 A11 46 C4
Castlecrag NSW 19 D6
Castlemaine VIC 39 C11
Castlereagh NSW 21 G8
Castlereagh Bay NT 87 C10
Castlereagh Nature Res NSW 21 G8 23 G8
Castleton QLD 11 G10
Casuarina NT 84 A3
Casula NSW 21 E10
Cataby WA 74 A2 76 J4
Catamaran TAS 53 K9
Catani VIC 37 G12 44 E4
Cataract Nat Park NSW 25 B11
Cathcart NSW 30 J4
Cathcart VIC 38 D7
Cathedral Beach QLD 7 B13
Cathedral Range State Park VIC 42 H5
Cathedral Rock Nat Park NSW 25 G10
Catherine Field NSW 21 F10
Catherine Hill Bay NSW 20 A1
Cathkin VIC 42 G4
Cathundral NSW 22 B1 27 J14
Cattai NSW 20 F6
Cattai Nat Park NSW 20 F6 23 G9
Catumnal VIC 41 J10
Caulfield VIC 35 E5 37 D8
Cavan NSW 30 C3
Cavan SA 59 D4 60 E2
Cave Hill Nature Res WA 75 B12 77 K11
Caveat VIC 42 F4
Cavendish VIC 38 E5
Caversham WA 71 D6
Caveside TAS 54 G7
Cawarral QLD 9 G10
Cawcowing Lakes WA 74 A5 76 J6
Cawdor NSW 21 F11
Cawongla NSW 25 B13
Cecil Park NSW 21 E9
Cecil Plains QLD 7 G9
Cedar Bay Nat Park QLD 11 B12
Cedar Brush NSW 20 D2
Cedar Creek QLD 4 G6 5 D11
Cedar Grove QLD 5 E11
Cedar Point NSW 25 B13
Cedarton QLD 4 G2
Ceduna SA 64 C2 68 K7
Cement Creek VIC 37 C13
Central Castra TAS 54 E6
Central Mangrove NSW 20 D3
Central McDonald NSW 20 F4
Central Mount Wedge NT 90 D5
Central Plateau Con Area TAS 52 A7 53 A9 54 H7 56 K2
Central Tilba NSW 30 G5
Centre Bore SA 68 B5
Centre Island NT 87 J13 89 A13
Ceratodus QLD 7 B9
Ceres NSW 22 C2
Ceres VIC 36 G2 39 G12
Cervantes WA 76 H4
Cessnock NSW 23 E10
Chadinga Con Res SA 64 C1 68 K6
Chadstone VIC 35 E5
Chaelundi Nat Park NSW 25 F11
Chain of Lagoons TAS 55 G14
Chain of Ponds SA 60 E5
Chain Valley Bay NSW 20 A1
Chakola NSW 30 G3
Chalky Island TAS 55 B8
Chambers Bay NT 85 B4 86 C5
Chambers Flat QLD 5 E10
Chambers Pillar Historical Res NT 91 H8
Chambigne Nature Res NSW 25 E12
Champagny Island WA 80 C6
Chandada SA 64 E4
Chandler QLD 3 F7 5 D8
Chandler SA 66 C2 68 B7
Chandlers Creek VIC 30 K3 47 B11
Channar Mine WA 78 G5 82 G3
Channel Island NT 85 C2
Chapel Hill QLD 3 F2 5 F8
Chapman ACT 32 G2
Chappell Islands TAS 55 C8
Chapple Vale VIC 39 J9
Charam VIC 38 C3
Charbon NSW 22 E6
Charles Darwin Nat Park NT 84 D3
Charleston SA 60 G5
Charleston Con Park SA 60 G6
Charleville QLD 13 K13 15 D14
Charleyong NSW 30 D5
Charleys Creek VIC 39 J9
Charlotte Pass NSW 30 H1 43 D14
Charlton VIC 41 K9
Charlwood QLD 5 J13
Charmhaven NSW 20 B2
Charnwood ACT 32 B2
Charra SA 64 C2 68 K7
Charters Towers QLD 8 B4 11 J13
Chasm Island NT 87 F12
Chatsbury NSW 22 K6 30 B5
Chatswood NSW 19 D5 21 C8
Chatswood West NSW 19 D5
Chatsworth NSW 25 D13
Chatsworth VIC 38 F7
Cheadanup Nature Res WA 75 F11
Cheepie QLD 15 E11
Chelmer QLD 3 F3
Chelsea VIC 35 H5 37 F8
Cheltenham NSW 19 C3 21 D8
Cheltenham SA 59 E2
Cheltenham VIC 35 G4 37 E8
Cherbourg QLD 7 D11
Chermside QLD 3 C4 4 E7
Chermside West QLD 3 C3
Cherry Gardens SA 60 H3 61 C7
Cherry Tree Hill NSW 25 D8
Cherry Tree Pool WA 73 A11
Cherrybrook NSW 19 C3 20 D7
Cherrypool VIC 38 C5
Cherryville SA 60 F4
Cheshunt VIC 42 E7
Chester Hill NSW 21 D9
Chesterton Range Nat Park QLD 6 D2
Chetwynd VIC 38 D3
Cheviot VIC 42 G4
Cheviot Island QLD 9 E10
Chewton VIC 39 C12
Cheyne Bay WA 75 J8
Cheyne Beach WA 74 J7
Cheynes Bridge VIC 43 K8 45 B9 46 D3
Chichester NSW 23 C10
Chiddarcooping Nature Res WA 74 A7 77 J8
Chidlow WA 72 E3
Chifley ACT 32 F3
Chifley NSW 21 B9
Chifley WA 77 J12 83 F2
Childers QLD 7 B11
Childers VIC 44 E6 46 F1
Childowlah NSW 30 C2
Chillagoe QLD 11 D11
Chillagoe-Mungana Caves Nat Park QLD 11 D11
Chilli Beach QLD 16 E4
Chillingham NSW 25 A13
Chillingollah VIC 28 H5 41 E8
Chiltern VIC 29 K12 43 B8
Chiltern-Mt Pilot Nat Park VIC 29 K12 43 B8
Chinaman Creek SA 62 G1 65 E9
Chinaman Flat VIC 28 K3 40 H3
Chinaman Island VIC 37 H10
Chinamans Wells SA 63 D10
Chinbi QLD 13 B10
Chinchilla QLD 7 E8
Chinderah NSW 25 A14
Chinkapook VIC 28 H5 40 E7
Chinocup Nature Res WA 74 F7
Chipping Norton NSW 21 D9
Chisholm ACT 32 J4
Chittaway Point NSW 20 B3
Chorregon QLD 13 D9
Chowerup WA 73 C13
Chowilla Reg Res SA 28 E1 62 A4 65 G13
Christies Beach SA 60 J1 61 C5
Christmas Creek QLD 5 E14
Christmas Hills TAS 54 C2
Christmas Hills VIC 37 B10
Christmas Island TAS 54 A6
Chudleigh TAS 54 G7
Chum Creek VIC 37 B11
Church Point NSW 19 A7 20 B6
Churchill VIC 45 E8 46 G2
Churchill Island VIC 37 K10
Churchill Nat Park VIC 37 E9 44 C3
Chute VIC 39 D9
City Beach WA 71 F2
Clackline WA 72 D2 74 C4 76 K5
Clairview QLD 9 F9
Clandulla NSW 22 E6
Clapham SA 59 J4
Clare QLD 8 B5
Clare SA 62 F4 65 G10
Claremont TAS 50 B5 53 F10
Claremont WA 71 G2
Claremont Isles Nat Park QLD 16 G4
Clarence Gardens SA 59 H3
Clarence Point TAS 56 C2
Clarence Town NSW 23 D11
Clarendon NSW 20 G7
Clarendon SA 60 J2 61 C6 62 F7 65 J10
Clarendon TAS 55 G10 56 K6
Clarendon VIC 39 F11
Clareville NSW 20 B6
Clarina QLD 10 E6
Clarke Island TAS 55 B13
Clarkefield VIC 39 E13 42 H1
Clarkes Hill Nature Res NSW 30 F1 43 A13
Claude Road TAS 54 F7
Claverton QLD 15 F13
Clayfield QLD 3 D4
Claymore WA 73 G11
Clayton SA 63 E8 65 K10
Clayton VIC 35 F5 37 E8
Clear Island Waters QLD 5 B13
Clear Lake VIC 38 C4
Clear Mountain QLD 3 A1
Clear Ridge NSW 29 E13
Clearview SA 59 E4
Cleland Con Park SA 59 H6 60 G3 61 A7
Clematis VIC 37 E11
Clements Gap Con Park SA 62 G3 65 F9
Clermont QLD 8 G6
Cleve SA 62 K4 64 G7
Cleveland QLD 5 C8
Cleveland TAS 53 A11 55 H11
Clifton NSW 21 C12
Clifton QLD 7 H10
Clifton Beach QLD 11 D13
Clifton Beach TAS 51 E8 53 G11
Clifton Creek VIC 43 K11 45 B13 46 D6
Clifton Gardens NSW 19 E6
Clifton Springs VIC 36 G4 39 G13
Clinton SA 62 G5 65 H9
Clinton Centre SA 62 G5 65 H9
Cloncurry QLD 10 K5 12 A5
Clonmel Island VIC 45 H9 46 H3
Clontarf NSW 19 E6 21 B8
Clouds Creek NSW 25 F11
Clovelly NSW 21 B9
Clovelly Park SA 59 J3
Cloverdale WA 71 G6
Cluan TAS 55 G9 56 J3
Club Terrace VIC 47 C10
Clunes NSW 25 B14
Clunes VIC 39 D10
Clybucca NSW 25 J12
Clyde VIC 37 G10 44 D3
Clyde River Nat Park NSW 30 E5
Clydebank VIC 45 D11 46 E4
Coal Creek VIC 37 K14
Coalcliff NSW 21 C12
Coaldale NSW 25 D12
Coalseam Con Park WA 76 F4
Coalstoun Lakes QLD 7 C11
Cobains VIC 45 D11 46 E4
Cobaki NSW 5 A14
Cobar NSW 27 H10
Cobargo NSW 30 G5
Cobark NSW 23 B10
Cobaw VIC 39 D13 42 G1
Cobbadah NSW 24 F7
Cobba-da-mana QLD 7 J9 25 A8
Cobbannah VIC 43 J10 45 A11 46 C4
Cobbity NSW 21 F11
Cobbora NSW 22 C5
Cobby Cobby Island QLD 5 B10
Cobden VIC 39 H8
Cobdogla SA 62 B5 65 H12
Cobera SA 62 B6 65 J12
Coboco NSW 22 B3
Cobourg Peninsula NT 86 B5
Cobram VIC 29 K10 42 A4
Cobrico VIC 39 H8
Cobungra VIC 43 G10 46 A5
Coburg VIC 35 C3 36 C7 39 F14 42 K2 44 B1
Cocamba VIC 40 E7
Cocata Con Park SA 64 F5
Cocata Con Res SA 64 F5
Cochranes Creek VIC 39 B9
Cockaleechie SA 64 G6
Cockatoo VIC 37 E11 42 K4 44 C4
Cockatoo WA 80 E5
Cockatoo Island WA 80 E5
Cockatoo Tank WA 75 B9 77 K9
Cockatoo Valley SA 60 C5
Cockburn SA 26 K1 28 A1 65 D14
Cockermouth Island QLD 9 C9
Cockle Creek TAS 53 K9

96 Cocklebiddy Motel – Deeford

Cocklebiddy Motel WA 83 G4
Coconut Grove NT 84 B2
Cocoparra Nat Park NSW 29 F11
Cocoparra Nature Res NSW 29 E11
Codrington VIC 38 H5
Coen QLD 16 H3
Coffin Bay SA 64 H5
Coffin Bay Nat Park SA 64 H5
Coffs Harbour NSW 25 G13
Coghills Creek VIC 39 D10
Cohuna VIC 28 K7 41 H11
Coila Creek NSW 30 F5
Cokum VIC 41 G9
Colac VIC 39 H10
Colbinabbin VIC 39 A13 42 D1
Coldstream VIC 37 C10 42 K3 44 B3
Coleambally NSW 29 G10
Colebee NSW 21 F8
Colebrook TAS 53 E10
Coledale NSW 21 C13 23 J8
Coleraine VIC 38 E4
Coles Bay TAS 53 C14 55 K14
Coleyville QLD 5 J11
Colignan VIC 28 G4 40 B5
Colinroobie NSW 29 F12
Colinton NSW 30 F3
Collarenebri NSW 24 D2
Collaroy NSW 19 C7 20 B7
Collector NSW 30 C4
Collerina NSW 27 D12
Colley SA 64 E4
Collie NSW 22 A2
Collie WA 73 E9 74 F3
Collie Cardiff WA 73 E10
Collier Bay WA 80 E6
Collier Range Nat Park WA 78 H6 82 K5
Collingullie NSW 29 H12
Collingwood VIC 35 D4 37 D8
Collins WA 73 F14
Collins Cap TAS 50 C3 53 F10
Collins Island QLD 9 F10
Collinsvale TAS 50 C4 53 F10
Collinsville QLD 8 C6
Colly Blue NSW 22 A7 24 K5
Colo NSW 20 G5
Colo Heights NSW 20 H5 23 F8
Colo Vale NSW 22 K7
Colton QLD 7 B12
Colton SA 64 F4
Columboola QLD 7 E8
Colyton NSW 21 F8
Comara NSW 25 H11
Comaum SA 38 D1 63 A12
Combaning NSW 22 J1 29 F14
Combara NSW 24 J1
Combienbar VIC 47 C11
Combo Waterhole Con Park QLD 12 B7
Combogolong NSW 24 G1
Comboyne NSW 23 A12
Come-By-Chance NSW 24 G1
Comerong Island Nature Res NSW 30 C7
Comet QLD 8 H7
Comet Vale WA 77 G11
Comleroy Road NSW 20 H6
Commodore Heights NSW 20 B5
Como NSW 19 J3 21 C10
Como WA 71 H4
Conara TAS 53 A11 55 H11
Conargo NSW 29 H9 41 F14
Concord NSW 19 E4 21 C8
Concordia SA 60 B4
Condah VIC 38 G4
Condamine QLD 6 E7
Condell Park NSW 21 D9
Conder ACT 32 K4
Condingup WA 75 G14 83 J2
Condobolin NSW 29 C13
Condong NSW 25 A14
Condowie SA 62 F4 65 G9
Congelin WA 72 C7
Congo NSW 30 F6
Congupna VIC 42 C3
Conimbla NSW 22 G3
Conimbla Nat Park NSW 22 H3
Coningham TAS 50 G5
Coniston NSW 21 C14
Conjola NSW 30 D6
Conjola Nat Park NSW 30 D7
Conmurra SA 63 C12
Connells Lagoon Con Res NT 89 F12
Connells Point NSW 19 H4
Connemurra NSW 22 A6 24 K5
Connewarre VIC 36 H3
Connewirrecoo VIC 38 D3
Conoble NSW 29 C8
Conondale QLD 4 H1 7 E12
Conondale Nat Park QLD 4 J1 7 E12
Contine WA 72 B7
Conway Beach QLD 9 C8
Conway Nat Park QLD 9 C8
Coober Pedy SA 66 G4
Coobowie SA 62 H7 65 J8
Coochiemudlo Island QLD 5 C9
Coochin Creek QLD 4 E3
Coodanup WA 72 G6
Cooee TAS 54 D5
Coogee NSW 19 G6 21 B9
Coojar VIC 38 D4
Cook ACT 32 D3
Cook SA 68 H3
Cookamidgera NSW 22 F2
Cookardinia NSW 29 J13
Cooke Plains SA 63 D8 65 K11
Cookernup WA 73 G8
Cooks Gap NSW 22 C6
Cooktown QLD 11 A12 16 K7
Coolabah NSW 27 G12
Coolabunia QLD 7 E11
Coolac NSW 29 G14 30 C1
Cooladdi QLD 15 E12
Coolah NSW 22 B6
Coolah Tops Nat Park NSW 22 B7
Coolamon NSW 29 G13
Coolana QLD 5 J8
Coolangatta QLD 5 A14 7 H13 25 A14
Coolaroo VIC 35 A2 36 B7
Coolatai NSW 24 D7
Coolbaggie Nature Res NSW 22 B4
Coolbinia WA 71 E4
Coolgardie WA 75 A12 77 J10
Coolimba WA 76 G3
Coolmunda Dam QLD 7 J9 25 A8
Coolongolook NSW 23 C12
Cooltong SA 28 F1 62 B5 65 G13
Cooltong Con Park SA 62 B5 65 H13
Coolum Beach QLD 7 E13
Coolumbooka Nature Res NSW 30 J3 47 A12
Coolup WA 72 G7 74 E3
Cooma NSW 30 G3
Cooma VIC 41 K14 42 C2
Coomallo Nature Res WA 76 H4
Coomandook SA 63 D8 65 K11
Coomba NSW 23 C12
Coombabah QLD 5 B12
Coombah NSW 28 C2
Coomera QLD 5 C11 7 H13
Coomera Island QLD 5 B11
Coominya QLD 4 K7 7 G12
Coonabarabran NSW 24 J3
Coonalpyn SA 63 C9
Coonamble NSW 24 H1
Coonana WA 77 J13 83 F2
Coonawarra SA 38 D1 63 B12
Coondle WA 72 D1
Coongie Lake SA 14 F3 67 D13
Coongoola QLD 15 G13
Coonooer Bridge VIC 39 A9 41 K9
Cooperabung Creek Nature Res NSW 25 K12
Coopernook NSW 23 B13
Coopers Creek VIC 45 C8 46 E2
Coopers Plains QLD 3 G4
Cooplacurripa NSW 23 A11
Coopracambra Nat Park VIC 30 K3 47 B12
Coorabakh Nat Park NSW 23 B12
Coorabie SA 68 K5
Cooran QLD 7 D12
Cooranbong NSW 20 C1 23 F10
Cooranga North QLD 7 E10
Cooranup WA 73 C13
Cooriemungle VIC 39 J8
Coornartha Nature Res NSW 30 G3
Coorong Nat Park SA 63 D9
Coorow WA 76 G5
Cooroy QLD 7 E12
Coorparoo QLD 3 F4
Cootamundra NSW 22 K2 29 G14 30 B1
Coothalla QLD 15 E13
Cooyal NSW 22 D6
Cooyar QLD 7 F11
Copacabana NSW 20 B4
Cope Cope VIC 41 K8
Copeton Dam NSW 25 E8
Copeville SA 62 C6 65 J12
Copley SA 65 A10 67 K10
Copmanhurst NSW 25 E12
Coppabella QLD 8 E7
Copperfield QLD 8 G6
Copperfield Mining Centre WA 77 F10
Copperhannia Nature Res NSW 22 H4
Copping TAS 51 B12 53 F12
Cora Lynn VIC 37 G12 44 D4
Corack VIC 41 J8
Corack East VIC 41 J8
Corackerup Nature Res WA 74 H7
Coragulac VIC 39 H9
Coraki NSW 7 K13 25 C13
Coral Bay WA 78 G1
Coral Coast QLD 7 A12 9 K13
Coral Sea QLD 11 A14
Coramba NSW 25 G12
Cordalba QLD 7 B11
Cordering WA 73 C10
Coree NSW 29 J9
Coreen NSW 29 J11
Corella Creek NT 89 E11
Corfield QLD 13 C9
Coridhap VIC 39 F10
Corinda QLD 3 G3
Corindi Beach NSW 25 F13
Corinella VIC 37 K11 44 F3
Corinna TAS 54 G2
Corio VIC 36 F3
Cornella VIC 39 A13 42 E1
Corner Inlet VIC 44 H7
Cornucopia VIC 37 F12
Cornwall TAS 55 G13
Cornwallis NSW 20 G7
Corny Point SA 62 J7 64 J7
Corobimilla NSW 29 G11
Coromandel East SA 59 K5
Coromandel Valley SA 59 K4 60 H3 61 B6
Coromby VIC 38 A6
Coronation Beach WA 76 F3
Coronation Islands WA 80 C7
Coronet Bay VIC 37 K11
Corop VIC 41 K13 42 D1
Cororooke VIC 39 H9
Corowa NSW 29 K11 42 A7
Corridgery NSW 22 F1 29 D14
Corrigin WA 74 D6
Corrimal NSW 21 C14 23 J8 30 B7
Corroboree Park Inn NT 85 D3 86 D4
Corroboree Rock Con Res NT 91 F9
Corrowong NSW 30 J2
Corryong VIC 29 K14 43 C12
Cosgrove VIC 42 C4
Cosmo Newberry WA 77 E12 83 C2
Cossack WA 78 E4 82 C2
Costerfield VIC 39 B13 42 F1
Cottage Point NSW 20 C6
Cottan-Bimbang Nat Park NSW 23 A12 25 K10
Cottesloe WA 71 G1
Cottles Bridge VIC 37 B9
Couchy Creek Nature Res NSW 25 A13
Cougal NSW 25 A13
Coulomb Point Nature Res WA 79 A8 80 G3
Coulson QLD 5 H12
Coulston Park QLD 9 E8
Coulta SA 64 H5
Councillor Island TAS 54 B7
Countegany NSW 30 G4
Courabyra Nature Res NSW 29 J14
Couta Rocks TAS 54 E1
Coutts Crossing NSW 25 E12
Cowabbie West NSW 29 F12
Cowan NSW 20 D6
Cowan Cowan QLD 4 B5
Cowangie VIC 28 H2 40 E2 65 K14
Cowaramup WA 73 J12 74 G2
Coward Springs SA 66 H7
Cowell SA 62 J4 64 G7
Cowes VIC 37 K9 44 F3
Cowley QLD 11 E13
Cowper NSW 25 E13
Cowra NSW 22 H3
Cowwarr VIC 45 D9 46 E3
Cox Peninsula NT 85 C1 86 D3
Cox Scrub Con Park SA 61 F7
Crab Island QLD 16 C1
Crabtree TAS 50 E2 53 G9
Crace ACT 32 B5
Cracow QLD 7 B8
Cradle Mountain - Lake St Clair Nat Park TAS 52 A5 54 H5
Cradle Valley TAS 54 G5
Cradoc TAS 50 H2 53 H9
Cradock SA 65 C10
Crafers SA 59 J6 60 G3 61 B7
Crafers West SA 59 J6
Craiggiemore WA 77 F12 83 D2
Craigie NSW 30 J3 47 A11
Craigie VIC 39 C10
Craigie WA 71 B2
Craigieburn VIC 36 B7 39 E14 42 J2 44 A1
Craiglie QLD 11 C12
Cramenton VIC 28 G4 40 D6
Cramps TAS 53 A9 55 H9
Cramsie QLD 8 H1 13 E10
Cranbourne VIC 35 K7 37 G9 44 D3
Cranbrook TAS 53 B13 55 J13
Cranbrook WA 74 H6
Cranebrook NSW 21 G8
Craneford SA 60 C7
Craven NSW 23 C11
Cravensville VIC 43 C11
Crawley WA 71 G3
Crayfish Creek TAS 54 C4
Creek Junction VIC 42 E5
Creek View VIC 39 A13 42 D1
Cremorne NSW 19 E6 21 B8
Cremorne TAS 51 E8 53 G11
Crescent Head NSW 25 J12
Cressy TAS 55 G9 56 K5
Cressy VIC 39 G10
Crestmead QLD 3 K5 5 E10
Crestwood NSW 32 F7
Creswick VIC 39 D11
Crib Point VIC 37 J9
Croajingolong Nat Park VIC 47 D12
Crocodile Hole WA 79 A14 81 F13
Croftby QLD 5 J14
Croker Island NT 86 B6
Cromer Con Park SA 60 E6
Cronulla NSW 19 K5 21 B10
Crooble NSW 24 C6
Crooked River VIC 43 H9 46 B4
Crookwell NSW 22 K5 30 B4
Croppa Creek NSW 24 C6
Cross SA 60 F2
Crossdale QLD 4 J5
Crossman WA 72 D7
Crow Mountain NSW 24 G7
Crowdy Bay Nat Park NSW 23 B13
Crowes VIC 39 K9
Crowlands VIC 39 C8
Crows Nest NSW 19 E5
Crows Nest QLD 7 F11
Crows Nest Nat Park QLD 7 F11
Croxton East VIC 38 F5
Croydon QLD 10 F7
Croydon SA 59 F3 60 F2
Croydon VIC 37 C10 42 K3 44 B3
Crusoe Island QLD 5 B10
Crymelon VIC 40 J5
Cryon NSW 24 F2
Crystal Brook SA 62 G3 65 F9
CSA Mine NSW 27 H10
Cuballing WA 72 A7 74 E5
Cubbaroo NSW 24 F3
Cuckoo TAS 55 E11
Cudal NSW 22 F3
Cudgee VIC 38 H7
Cudgegong NSW 22 E6
Cudgen NSW 25 A14
Cudgen Nature Res NSW 25 A14
Cudgera Creek NSW 25 A14
Cudgewa VIC 29 K14 43 B12
Cudgewa North VIC 43 B12
Cudlee Creek SA 60 F5
Cudlee Creek Con Park SA 60 F5
Cudmore Nat Park QLD 8 G4 13 D13
Cue WA 76 D7
Culbin WA 73 C9
Culburra NSW 30 C7
Culburra SA 63 C9
Culcairn NSW 29 J12
Culgoa VIC 28 J5 41 G8
Culgoa Floodplain Nat Park QLD 6 K1 27 B12
Culgoa Nat Park NSW 6 K1 27 C12
Culgoora NSW 24 F4
Culham WA 72 D1
Cullacabardee WA 71 C4
Cullen NT 85 G4 86 F5
Cullen Bullen NSW 22 F6
Cullendulla NSW 30 E6
Cullendulla Creek Nature Res NSW 30 E5
Cullerin NSW 30 C4
Cullulleraine VIC 28 F2 40 B3 65 H14
Cumborah NSW 27 D14
Cummins SA 64 H5
Cumnock NSW 22 E3
Cundare VIC 39 G10
Cundeelee WA 77 J13 83 F2
Cunderdin WA 72 A2 74 C5 76 K6
Cundinup WA 73 G12
Cungena SA 64 D4
Cunliffe SA 62 H5 65 G9
Cunnamulla QLD 15 H13
Cunnawarra Nat Park NSW 25 H10
Cunningham SA 62 H5 65 H9
Cunningham Islands NT 87 C12
Cunninyeuk NSW 28 H7 41 E10
Cuprona TAS 54 D6
Curacoa Island QLD 11 G14
Curban NSW 22 A3 24 K2
Curdie Vale VIC 38 J7
Curdimurka SA 67 H8
Curl Curl NSW 19 D7 20 B7
Curlew Island QLD 9 E9
Curlewis NSW 24 J6
Curlewis VIC 36 G4
Curlwaa NSW 28 F3 40 A4
Currabubula NSW 24 J6
Curramulka SA 62 H6 65 J8
Currarong NSW 30 D7
Currawang NSW 30 C4
Currawarna NSW 29 H12
Currawinya Nat Park QLD 15 J10 26 B7
Currency Creek SA 63 F8 65 K10
Currie TAS 54 B6
Curries VIC 38 H3
Currimundi QLD 4 D2
Currumbin QLD 5 A14
Currumbin Valley QLD 5 B14
Currumbin Waters QLD 5 B14
Curtin ACT 32 F3
Curtin WA 75 A13 77 J11 83 F1
Curtin Airport WA 80 G6
Curtin Springs NT 90 J5
Curtis Island QLD 9 H11
Curtis Island Nat Park QLD 9 H11
Curyo VIC 28 K5 40 H7
Cuttabri NSW 24 G3
Cuumbean Nature Res NSW 30 D4
Cygnet TAS 50 H3 53 H9
Cygnet River SA 63 H8 65 K8
Cynthia QLD 7 B9

D

D'Aguilar QLD 4 G3
D'Aguilar Nat Park QLD 4 G6 7 F12
D'Entrecasteaux Nat Park WA 73 G14 74 J3
Daandine QLD 7 F9
Dadswells Bridge VIC 38 B6
Daguragu NT 88 D3
Dahlen VIC 38 A5
Daintree QLD 11 C12
Daintree Nat Park QLD 11 C12
Daisy Dell TAS 54 G6
Daisy Hill QLD 3 J7 5 D9
Daisy Hill State Forest QLD 3 J7
Dajarra QLD 12 C3
Dakabin QLD 4 F5
Dalbeg QLD 8 B5
Dalby QLD 7 F9
Dale Bridge WA 72 C4
Dale Con Park WA 72 E4 74 D4
Dales Creek VIC 36 A2
Dalgety NSW 30 H2
Dalkeith WA 71 H2
Dallarnil QLD 7 B11
Dalma QLD 9 H10
Dalmeny NSW 30 G5
Dalmore VIC 37 G11
Dalmorton NSW 25 F11
Dalrymple Nat Park QLD 8 B4 11 J13
Dalton NSW 22 K4 30 C3
Dalwallinu WA 76 H5
Daly River NT 85 G1 86 F3
Daly Waters NT 86 K7 88 B7
Dalyston VIC 44 G4
Dampier WA 78 E4 82 C1
Dananbilla Nature Res NSW 22 J3 30 A2
Dandaloo NSW 22 C1 27 K13 29 A13
Dandaragan WA 74 A2 76 J4
Dandenong VIC 35 G7 37 E9 44 C2
Dandenong North VIC 35 G7
Dandenong Ranges Nat Park VIC 37 D10 42 K3 44 C3
Dandenong South VIC 35 H7
Dandongadale VIC 43 E8
Dangarfield NSW 23 C9
Dangarsleigh NSW 25 H9
Dangelong Nature Res NSW 30 G4
Danggali Con Park SA 28 D1 62 A3 65 F13
Dangin WA 72 A4 74 D5 76 K6
Danyo VIC 28 H2 40 F2
Dapper Nature Res NSW 22 C5
Dapto NSW 23 K8 30 B7
Daradgee QLD 11 E13
Darawank Nature Res NSW 23 C12
Darbalara NSW 29 H14 30 C1
Darbys Falls NSW 22 H4
Darch Island NT 86 B6
Dardadine WA 73 C9
Dardanup WA 73 G10 74 F3
Dareton NSW 28 F3 40 A4
Dargo VIC 43 H10 46 C4
Dark Corner NSW 22 F6
Darkan WA 73 C9 74 F4
Darke Peak SA 64 F6
Darkes Forest NSW 21 D12
Darkwood NSW 25 G12
Darley VIC 36 B3
Darling Harbour NSW 18 C1
Darling Point NSW 19 F6
Darlinghurst NSW 18 D3 19 F6
Darlington QLD 5 E14
Darlington SA 59 K3
Darlington TAS 53 E13
Darlington VIC 39 G8
Darlington Point NSW 29 G10
Darlu Darlu WA 79 A14 81 G14
Darnick NSW 28 C6
Darnum VIC 44 E6
Daroobalgie NSW 22 F2 29 D14
Darr QLD 8 G1 13 E10
Darra QLD 3 G2
Darradup WA 73 H13
Darraweit Guim VIC 39 D14 42 H1
Darriman VIC 45 F10 46 G3
Dartmoor VIC 38 G3 63 A14
Dartmouth QLD 8 H2 13 E11
Dartmouth VIC 43 D11
Darwin NT 85 C1 86 D3
Darwin CBD NT 84
Dattening WA 72 C6
Davenport Range Nat Park NT 89 J10 91 A10
Daveyston SA 60 A5
Davidson NSW 19 C5 20 C7
Davies Creek Nat Park QLD 11 D12
Davies Plain VIC 43 E13
Davis Creek NSW 23 C9
Davistown NSW 20 B4
Davyhurst WA 77 H10
Daw Island WA 83 J3
Dawes Point NSW 18 A2
Dawesley SA 60 H6
Dawesville WA 72 G6
Dawson SA 62 E2 65 E10
Dawsons Hill NSW 23 C9
Dayboro QLD 4 G5 7 F12
Daydream Island QLD 9 B8
Daylesford VIC 39 D11
Daymar QLD 6 J5 24 B3
Daysdale NSW 29 J11
Daytrap VIC 28 H5 40 E7
Daytrap Corner VIC 28 H5 40 F7
De La Poer Range Nature Res WA 77 D12 83 C2
De Salis NSW 32 G7
De Witt Island TAS 52 K7
Dead Horse Gap NSW 30 H1 43 D13
Deagon QLD 3 A5
Deakin ACT 31 D1 32 F4
Deakin WA 68 H1 83 F7
Dean VIC 39 E11
Dean Park NSW 21 F8
Deanmill WA 73 F13 74 H3
Deans Marsh VIC 39 H11
Deception Bay QLD 4 E5 7 F13
Deddington TAS 55 G11
Dederang VIC 43 D9
Dee Why NSW 19 C7 20 B7
Deeford QLD 9 J10

Deep Creek Con Park – Exmouth 97

Deep Creek Con Park SA 61 K2 63 G8 65 K9
Deep Lead VIC 38 C7
Deepwater NSW 25 D10
Deepwater Nat Park QLD 9 J12
Deer Park VIC 36 C6 39 F13 42 K1
Deer Vale NSW 25 G11
Deeragun QLD 8 A4 11 H14
Deeral QLD 11 D13
Delamere SA 61 J2 63 G8 65 K9
Delaneys Creek QLD 4 G4
Delatite VIC 42 G6 46 A1
Delegate NSW 30 J3 47 A10
Delegate River VIC 30 J2 47 A10
Delfin Island SA 59 E1
Dellicknora VIC 47 A10
Dellyanine WA 73 B10
Deloraine TAS 55 F8 56 H1
Delungra NSW 24 E7
Demon Nature Res NSW 25 C11
Denham WA 76 B1 78 K1
Denham Group Nat Park QLD 16 C3
Denham Island QLD 10 D3
Denham Sound WA 76 B1
Denial Bay SA 64 C2 68 K7
Denicull Creek VIC 38 D7
Deniliquin NSW 29 J9 41 G14
Denman NSW 23 D8
Denman SA 68 H2
Denmark WA 74 K5
Dennes Point TAS 50 G6 53 G10
Dennington VIC 38 H6
Deptford VIC 43 J11 45 A13 46 C6
Depuch Island WA 78 E4 82 C3
Derby TAS 55 E12
Derby VIC 39 A11
Derby WA 79 A10 80 G5
Dereel VIC 39 F10
Dergholm VIC 38 D2 63 A13
Dergholm State Park VIC 38 D2 63 A12
Dering VIC 40 F5
Deringulla NSW 22 A5 24 K4
Dernancourt SA 59 E6
Deroora QLD 8 H2 13 F11
Derrinallum VIC 39 G8
Derriwong NSW 29 C13
Derwent Bridge TAS 52 C6 54 K6
Desault Bay WA 79 C8 80 K2
Desdemona WA 77 F11 83 E1
Desert Camp Con Res SA 63 B10
Detpa VIC 40 J4
Deua Nat Park NSW 30 F5
Devenish VIC 42 C5
Devils Marbles Con Res NT 89 J9 91 A9
Devoit TAS 55 E9 56 E3
Devon VIC 45 G9 46 H2
Devon Meadows VIC 37 G10
Devoncourt QLD 12 B4
Devonian Reef Con Park WA 79 B11 81 H8
Devonport TAS 54 E7
Dewars Pool WA 72 E1
Dhalinybuy NT 87 D12
Dharawal Nature Res NSW 21 D12
Dharawal State Con Area NSW 21 D12
Dharug Nat Park NSW 20 E4 23 G9
Diamantina Nat Park QLD 12 F6
Diamond Creek VIC 35 A6 37 B9 39 E14 42 J2 44 B2
Dianella WA 71 D4
Diapur VIC 40 K3
Dickson ACT 32 C5
Dicky Beach QLD 4 D2
Didleum Plains TAS 55 F11
Digby VIC 38 F3
Digby Island QLD 9 D9
Diggers Rest VIC 36 B5 39 E13 42 J1
Dillalah Ridge QLD 15 E13
Dillcar QLD 13 D9
Dillon Bay WA 75 J9
Dilpurra NSW 28 H6 41 E10
Dilston TAS 55 F9 56 F4
Dimboola VIC 38 A5 40 K5
Dimbulah QLD 11 D12
Dingee VIC 41 K12
Dingley Village VIC 35 G5 37 E8
Dingo QLD 9 H8
Dingup WA 73 E13
Dingwall VIC 28 K6 41 H10
Dinmore QLD 5 G9
Dinner Plain VIC 43 F10 46 A5
Dinninup WA 73 D11 74 G4
Dinoga NSW 24 F7
Dinyarrak VIC 40 K2
Dipperu Nat Park QLD 8 E7
Direk SA 59 A4 60 D2
Dirk Hartog Island WA 76 B1 78 K1
Dirnaseer NSW 22 K1 29 G14
Dirranbandi QLD 6 J4 24 A1
Disaster Bay NSW 30 K5 47 B14
Discovery Bay VIC 38 H2
Discovery Bay Coastal Park VIC 38 H2 63 A14
Diwarra NSW 28 B4
Dixie VIC 39 H8
Dixons Creek VIC 37 B11 42 J3 44 A3
Djugerari WA 79 C11 81 K8
Djukbinj Nat Park NT 85 C3 86 D4
Dobbyn QLD 10 J4
Docker VIC 42 D7
Docker River (Kaltukatjara) NT 79 J14 83 A7
Doctors Flat VIC 43 H12 46 B6
Dodges Ferry TAS 51 C9 53 F11
Dodnun WA 79 A12 81 E10
Dolphin Island WA 78 D4 82 C2
Dolphin Island Nature Res WA 78 D3 82 B1
Don TAS 54 E7
Don Valley VIC 37 C12
Donald VIC 41 K8
Donalds Well SA 68 A5 90 K6
Doncaster VIC 35 C6 37 C9
Dongara WA 76 G3
Donnelly River WA 73 F13
Donnybrook QLD 4 E4
Donnybrook VIC 36 A7
Donnybrook WA 73 G10 74 G3
Doo Town TAS 51 F13
Dooboobetic VIC 41 K8
Doodenanning WA 72 B3
Doodlakine WA 74 C6 76 K7
Dooen VIC 38 A5
Dookie VIC 42 C4
Doolandella QLD 3 J3
Doomadgee QLD 10 F2
Doomben QLD 3 D5 4 E7
Doon Doon Roadhouse WA 79 A14 81 E13
Doonside NSW 21 E8
Dooragan Nat Park NSW 23 B13
Dooralong NSW 20 C2
Doreen NSW 24 F4
Doreen VIC 37 B9 39 E14 42 J2 44 A2
Dorodong VIC 38 D2
Dorre Island WA 76 A1 78 J1
Dorrigo NSW 25 G12
Dorrigo Nat Park NSW 25 G12
Dorset Vale SA 60 J3 61 C7
Double Bridges (site) VIC 43 J12 45 A14 46 C7
Double Sandy Point Coastal Res TAS 55 D10 56 A7
Doubtful Islands Bay WA 75 H9
Doughboy NSW 30 D4
Douglas VIC 38 C4
Douglas Apsley Nat Park TAS 53 A13 55 H13
Douglas Park NSW 21 E12
Douglas River TAS 53 A14 55 H14
Dover TAS 53 J9
Dover Heights NSW 19 F7 21 B8
Doveton VIC 35 G7
Dowerin WA 74 B5 76 J6
Downer ACT 32 C5
Downfall Nature Res NSW 29 J14
Downside NSW 29 H13
Doyalson NSW 20 B1 23 F10
Dragon Rocks Nature Res WA 75 E8
Dragon Tree Soak Nature Res WA 79 D9
Drake NSW 25 C11
Dreeite VIC 39 H9
Drewvale QLD 3 J4
Driffield VIC 44 E7 46 F1
Drik Drik VIC 38 G3
Drillham QLD 6 E7
Dripstone NSW 22 D4
Dromana VIC 36 J7 39 H14 44 E1
Dromedary TAS 50 A4 53 F10
Dronfield QLD 12 B4
Drouin VIC 37 G14 44 D5
Drouin South VIC 37 G14 44 D5
Drouin West VIC 37 F14
Drovers Cave Nat Park WA 76 H3
Drumborg VIC 38 G3
Drummond QLD 8 H5
Drummoyne NSW 19 E5 21 C8
Drung Drung VIC 38 B6
Dry Creek SA 59 D4
Dry Creek VIC 42 F5
Dryander Nat Park QLD 8 B7
Drysdale VIC 36 G4 39 G13
Drysdale Island NT 87 B11
Drysdale River Nat Park WA 81 C11
Duaringa QLD 9 H9
Dubbo NSW 22 C3
Dubelling WA 72 A4
Dublin SA 62 F5 65 H9
Duchess QLD 12 B4
Duck Island VIC 36 H5
Duddo VIC 28 H2 40 E2
Dudinin WA 74 E6
Dudley VIC 44 G4
Dudley Con Park SA 63 G9
Dudley Park SA 59 E4
Duff Creek SA 66 F6
Duffholme VIC 38 B4
Duffy ACT 32 F2
Duffys Forest NSW 19 B5 20 C6
Duke Islands QLD 9 E10
Duke of Orleans Bay WA 83 J2
Dulacca QLD 6 E7
Dularcha Nat Park QLD 4 F2
Dulbolla QLD 5 F14
Dulbydilla QLD 6 D2
Dulcie Ranges Nat Park NT 91 D11
Dululu QLD 9 H10
Dulwich SA 59 G5
Dumaresq NSW 25 G9
Dumbalk VIC 44 G6 46 H1
Dumbalk North VIC 44 G7 46 G1
Dumberning WA 73 B8
Dumbleyung WA 74 F6
Dumbleyung Lake Nature Res WA 74 F6
Dumosa VIC 28 K5 41 H8
Dunalley TAS 51 D12 53 F12
Duncraig WA 71 C2
Dundas NSW 21 D8
Dundas QLD 4 J6
Dundas TAS 52 A4 54 H4
Dundas Nature Res WA 75 D14 83 H1
Dundas Valley NSW 19 D3
Dundee NSW 25 E10
Dundee Beach NT 86 D3
Dundonnell VIC 39 F8
Dundurrabin NSW 25 G11
Dunedoo NSW 22 B5
Dunggir Nat Park NSW 25 H12
Dungog NSW 23 D11
Dungowan NSW 25 J8
Dunk Island QLD 11 F13
Dunkeld NSW 22 F5
Dunkeld QLD 6 E3
Dunkeld VIC 38 E6
Dunlop ACT 32 B2
Dunluce QLD 13 A10
Dunmarra NT 88 C7
Dunmore NSW 22 D2 29 B14
Dunn Rock Nature Res WA 75 F9
Dunnstown VIC 39 E11
Dunolly VIC 39 B10
Dunoon NSW 25 B13
Dunorlan TAS 54 F7
Dunrobbin Bridge TAS 53 E8
Dunrobin VIC 38 E3
Dunsborough WA 73 J11 74 G1
Dunwich QLD 5 B8 7 G13
Durack QLD 3 H3
Dural NSW 19 B3 20 D7
Duramana NSW 22 F5
Duranillin WA 73 C10 74 G4
Durdidwarrah VIC 36 D1 39 F11
Durham QLD 11 F9
Durham Lead VIC 39 F10
Durham Ox VIC 28 K7 41 J10
Duri NSW 24 J7
Durong South QLD 7 D9
Durras NSW 30 E6
Durundur QLD 4 G3
Dutton SA 62 E5 65 H11
Dutton Park QLD 3 F4
Duval Nature Res NSW 25 G9
Duverney VIC 39 G9
Dwarda WA 72 C7 74 E4
Dwellingup WA 72 F7 74 E3
Dwyers NSW 27 F11
Dykehead QLD 7 C9
Dynnyrne TAS 49 D1
Dysart QLD 8 F7
Dysart TAS 53 E10

E

Eagle Bay WA 73 K10 74 G1
Eagle Bore SA 68 A5 90 K5
Eagle Farm QLD 3 D5
Eagle Heights QLD 5 D12
Eagle on the Hill SA 59 H6
Eagle Point VIC 43 K11 45 C13 46 E6
Eagle Vale NSW 21 E11
Eagleby QLD 5 D10
Eaglehawk VIC 39 A12
Eaglehawk Neck TAS 51 F13 53 G13
Eaglevale VIC 43 H9 46 B4
Earlston VIC 42 D4
Earlwood NSW 21 C9
East Brisbane QLD 3 E4
East Fremantle WA 71 H2
East Gosford NSW 20 B4
East Guyong NSW 22 F5
East Haydon QLD 10 F6
East Hills NSW 19 H2 21 D10
East Islands QLD 16 C3
East Kangaroo Island TAS 55 C8
East Killara NSW 19 D5
East Kurrajong NSW 20 G6
East Lynne NSW 30 E6
East Melbourne VIC 34 C4
East Palmerston QLD 11 E13
East Perth WA 70 B4 71 F4
East Point NT 84 C1
East Ryde NSW 19 E4
East Sassafras TAS 55 E8
East Strait Island QLD 16 B2
East Vernon Island NT 85 B2 86 C4
East Victoria Park WA 71 G5
East Yuna Nature Res WA 76 E4
Eastbrook WA 73 F14
Easter Group WA 76 F2
Eastern Creek NSW 21 E8
Eastern Group WA 83 J3
Eastern View VIC 39 J11
Eastwood NSW 19 D3 21 D8
Eastwood SA 58 D3
Eaton WA 73 G9
Eatons Hill QLD 3 B2
Eba Island SA 64 E3
Ebenezer NSW 20 F6
Ebor NSW 25 G11
Eccleston NSW 23 C10
Echo Hill SA 66 B1 68 B6
Echuca VIC 29 K8 41 J13 42 B1
Echunga SA 60 J4 62 E7 65 J10
Ecklin South VIC 39 H8
Eddington QLD 10 K7 12 A6
Eddington VIC 39 B10
Eden NSW 30 J5 47 A14
Eden Hill WA 71 E5
Eden Hills SA 59 K4 60 H2 61 B6
Eden Island QLD 5 B10
Eden Valley SA 60 C7 62 E6 65 H11
Edenhope VIC 38 C2 63 A12
Edensor Park NSW 21 E9
Edgecliff NSW 21 B8
Edgeroi NSW 24 F5
Edgewater WA 71 A2
Edi VIC 42 E7
Ediacara Con Res SA 65 A9 67 K9
Edillilie SA 64 H5
Edith NSW 22 H6
Edith Creek TAS 54 D2
Edithburgh SA 62 H7 65 J8
Edithvale VIC 35 H5 37 F8 39 G14 44 D2
Edjudina Mine WA 77 G12 83 E2
Edmondson Park NSW 21 E10
Edmonton QLD 11 D13
Edmund Kennedy Nat Park QLD 11 F13
Edrom NSW 30 K5 47 A14
Edungalba QLD 9 H9
Edward Island NT 87 G11
Edwards Creek SA 66 F6
Edwardstown SA 59 J3
Egan Peaks Nature Res NSW 30 J4 47 A13
Egg Island TAS 50 G2
Egg Lagoon TAS 54 A6
Eidsvold QLD 7 B9
Eight Mile WA 79 B11 81 J9
Eight Mile Plains QLD 3 H5 5 E9
Eildon VIC 42 G5
Eimeo QLD 9 D8
Einasleigh QLD 11 G10
El Alamein SA 62 H1 65 D8
El Arish QLD 11 E13
Elaine VIC 39 F11
Elalie QLD 9 E9
Elands NSW 23 B12
Elanora Heights NSW 19 B7 20 B7
Elbow Hill SA 62 K4 64 G7
Elcho Island NT 87 C11
Elcombe NSW 24 E6
Elderslie TAS 53 E9
Eldon TAS 53 E11
Eldorado VIC 42 C7
Electrona TAS 50 G5 53 G10
Elgin WA 73 H10
Elgin Vale QLD 7 D11
Elimbah QLD 4 F4
Elizabeth SA 59 A5 60 D3 62 F6 65 J10
Elizabeth East SA 59 A6
Elizabeth Grove SA 59 A6
Elizabeth Island VIC 37 K10
Elizabeth Town TAS 55 F8
Ella Bay Nat Park QLD 11 E13
Ellam VIC 40 J5
Ellenborough NSW 23 A12 25 K11
Ellenbrook WA 71 B6
Ellendale TAS 53 E8
Ellerslie NSW 28 E3
Ellerslie VIC 38 G7
Ellerslie Nature Res NSW 29 H14
Ellerston NSW 23 B10
Ellery Creek Nature Park NT 90 F7
Elliminyt VIC 39 H10
Ellinbank VIC 37 H14 44 E6
Elliot Price Con Park SA 67 F8
Elliott NT 89 D8
Elliott QLD 7 A12 9 K13
Elliott TAS 54 D5
Elliott Heads QLD 7 A12 9 K13
Elliston SA 64 F4
Elmhurst VIC 39 C9
Elmore VIC 39 A13 41 K13 42 D1
Elong Elong NSW 22 C4
Elphin TAS 56 G5
Elphinstone QLD 8 D7
Elphinstone VIC 39 C12
Elsey Nat Park NT 86 H7
Elsmore NSW 25 E8
Eltham NSW 25 B14
Eltham VIC 35 B6 37 C9 39 F14 42 J2 44 B2
Elura Mine NSW 27 G10
Elwood VIC 35 E3
Emerald QLD 8 H7
Emerald VIC 37 E11 42 K3 44 C3
Emerald Beach NSW 25 G13
Emerald Hill NSW 24 H5
Emerald Springs NT 85 G4 86 F5
Emily and Jessie Gaps Nature Park NT 91 F8
Emita TAS 55 B8
Emmaville NSW 25 D9
Emmdale NSW 26 J7
Emmet QLD 8 K1 13 G11
Empire Bay NSW 20 B5
Empire Vale NSW 25 C14
Emu VIC 39 B9
Emu Bay SA 63 H8 65 K8
Emu Downs SA 62 E4 65 G10
Emu Flat VIC 39 C13 42 G1
Emu Junction SA 68 E5
Emu Park QLD 9 G11
Emu Plains NSW 21 G8
Emuford QLD 11 E12
Endeavour River Nat Park QLD 11 A12 16 K7
Enderby Island WA 78 E3 82 C1
Endyalgout Island NT 85 A6 86 C6
Eneabba WA 76 G4
Enfield NSW 19 F4 21 C9
Enfield SA 59 E4 60 F2
Enfield VIC 39 F10
Enfield State Park VIC 39 F10
Engadine NSW 19 K2 21 C10
Engawala NT 91 D9
Englefield VIC 38 D4
English Town TAS 55 G11
Enmore NSW 21 C9 25 H9
Enngonia NSW 27 C10
Enoggera QLD 3 D3
Ensay VIC 43 H12 46 B7
Ensay North VIC 43 H12 46 B7
Ensay South VIC 43 H12 46 B6
Eppalock VIC 39 B12
Epping NSW 19 D3 21 D8
Epping VIC 35 A4 37 B8 39 E14 42 J2 44 A2
Epping Forest TAS 53 A11 55 H10
Epping Forest Nat Park QLD 8 F4 13 C14
Epsom QLD 9 D8
Epsom VIC 39 A12
Ercildoun VIC 39 D10
Eribung NSW 22 D1 29 B14
Eric Bonython Con Park SA 61 K3
Erica VIC 44 C7 46 E1
Erigolia NSW 29 E11
Erikin WA 74 C6 76 K7
Erina NSW 20 B4
Erindale SA 59 G6
Erldunda NT 90 H7
Ermington NSW 19 E3 21 D8
Ernabella (Pukatja) SA 68 A5
Ernest QLD 5 B12
Ernest Henry Mine QLD 10 K5
Eromanga QLD 15 E8
Erriba TAS 54 F6
Erringibba Nat Park QLD 6 F7
Errinundra VIC 47 B10
Errinundra Nat Park VIC 30 K2 47 B10
Errolls WA 77 D8
Erskine Island QLD 9 H12
Erskine Park NSW 21 F9
Erskineville NSW 21 B9
Esk QLD 4 K6 7 F11
Eskdale VIC 43 D10
Esmond VIC 29 K11 42 B6
Esperance WA 75 G13 83 J1
Esperance Bay WA 75 G13 83 J1
Essendon VIC 35 C2 36 C7
Estcourt VIC 37 E12
Eton QLD 9 D8
Ettalong Beach NSW 20 B5
Ettrick NSW 7 J12 25 B12
Etty Bay QLD 11 E13
Euabalong NSW 29 C11
Euabalong West NSW 29 C11
Eubenangee Swamp Nat Park QLD 11 E13
Euchareena NSW 22 E4
Eucla WA 68 K1 83 G7
Eucla Nat Park WA 68 K1 83 G7
Eucumbene Cove NSW 30 G2
Eudlo QLD 4 F1
Eudlo Creek Nat Park QLD 4 F1
Eudunda SA 62 E5 65 H11
Eugenana TAS 54 E7
Eugowra NSW 22 F3
Eulo QLD 15 H11
Eumundi QLD 7 E13
Eumungerie NSW 22 B3
Eungai NSW 25 H12
Eungella QLD 8 D7
Eungella Nat Park QLD 8 C7
Eurack VIC 39 G10
Eurambeen VIC 39 D9
Euramo QLD 11 F13
Eurelia SA 62 F1 65 D10
Eurilla Con Park SA 60 G3 61 A7
Eurimbula Nat Park QLD 9 J12
Euroa VIC 42 E4
Eurobin VIC 43 E9
Eurobodalla NSW 30 G5
Eurobodalla Nat Park NSW 30 F6
Eurong QLD 7 B13
Eurongilly NSW 29 G14
Euston NSW 28 G4 40 C7
Evandale TAS 55 G10 56 J6
Evans Crown Nature Res NSW 22 G6
Evans Head NSW 7 K13 25 C14
Evans Island SA 64 D2
Evansford VIC 39 D10
Evanston SA 60 C4
Evanston WA 77 G9
Evatt ACT 32 B3
Everard Junction WA 79 J11 83 A4
Everett Island NT 87 C12
Eversley VIC 39 D8
Everton VIC 42 C7
Everton Hills QLD 3 C2
Everton Park QLD 3 C3 4 E7
Ewaninga Rock Carvings Con Res NT 91 F8
Ewens Ponds SA 38 G1
Exeter NSW 22 K7 30 B6
Exeter TAS 55 E9 56 E3
Exford VIC 36 C4
Exmouth WA 78 F1

98 Exmouth Gulf – Goomadeer

Exmouth Gulf WA 78 F2
Expedition Nat Park QLD 6 B5 9 K8
Exton TAS 55 G8 56 H1
Eyre Island SA 64 D2
Eyre Peninsula SA 62 K3 64 E5

F

Fadden ACT 32 H4
Failford NSW 23 C12
Fair Cape QLD 16 E3
Fairbank VIC 37 K14
Fairfax Islands QLD 9 J13
Fairfield NSW 19 F1 21 D9
Fairfield West NSW 19 F1
Fairhaven VIC 36 K1 37 J10 39 J11 47 C13
Fairholme NSW 29 D13
Fairley VIC 41 G10
Fairneyview QLD 5 H8
Fairview Con Park SA 63 B11
Fairview Park SA 59 C7
Fairy Hill NSW 25 B13
Fairy Meadow NSW 21 C14
Fairyland Mine WA 77 E10
Falcon WA 72 H6 74 E2
Falls Creek NSW 30 C7
Falls Creek Alpine Village VIC 43 F10
Falmouth TAS 55 G14
False Cape Bossut WA 79 B8 80 J2
Family Islands Nat Park QLD 11 F13
Fannie Bay NT 84 D1
Fantome Island QLD 11 G14
Faraday VIC 39 C12
Farina SA 67 J10
Farleigh QLD 9 D8
Farnham NSW 22 E4
Farrar WA 73 B12
Farrell Flat SA 62 E4 65 G10
Farrer ACT 32 G4
Fassifern QLD 5 J12
Faulconbridge NSW 21 H8
Faulkland NSW 23 C11
Faure Island WA 76 B2 78 K2
Fawcett VIC 42 G4
Fawkner VIC 35 B3
Federal NSW 25 B14
Feilton TAS 50 B1
Felixstow SA 59 F5
Feluga QLD 11 E13
Fentonbury TAS 53 E8
Fentons Creek VIC 39 A9
Ferguson SA 64 A4 66 K4
Ferguson VIC 39 J9
Fern Tree TAS 50 D5 53 G10
Fernances NSW 20 F3
Fernbank VIC 43 K10 45 C12 46 E5
Fernbrook WA 73 F9
Ferndale NSW 29 J12
Ferndale VIC 37 J14
Ferndale WA 71 H5
Ferndene TAS 54 E6
Fernihurst VIC 41 J10
Fernlees QLD 8 H7
Fernshaw VIC 37 B12
Ferntree Gully VIC 37 D10
Fernvale QLD 5 H8
Ferny Glen QLD 5 D13
Ferny Grove QLD 3 C1 4 F7
Ferny Hills QLD 3 C2
Ferries McDonald Con Park SA 62 E7 65 K11
Ferryden Park SA 59 E3
Fiddletown NSW 20 D6
Field Island NT 85 B5 86 C6
Fiery Flat VIC 41 K10
Fifes Knob Nature Res NSW 25 J11
Fifield NSW 29 B13
Fig Tree NSW 21 D14
Fig Tree Pocket QLD 3 F2
Finch Hatton QLD 8 C7
Findon SA 59 F2 60 F1
Fine Flower NSW 25 D12
Fingal NSW 5 A14 25 A14
Fingal TAS 55 G13
Finger Post NSW 22 D4
Finke (Apatula) NT 91 J9
Finke Bay NT 85 B4 86 C5
Finke Gorge Nat Park NT 90 G7
Finley NSW 29 J10
Finniss SA 63 E8 65 K10
Finniss Con Park SA 61 F7
Finucane Is Nat Park QLD 10 E4
Fish Creek VIC 44 H6
Fish Point VIC 41 F10
Fish River Res NT 85 J2 86 G3
Fisher ACT 32 G3
Fisher SA 68 H4
Fisherman Islands QLD 3 C7 4 D7
Fishermens Bend VIC 35 D2
Fiskville VIC 36 B2
Fitzgerald TAS 53 F8
Fitzgerald WA 75 G9
Fitzgerald River Nat Park WA 75 H9
Fitzgibbon QLD 3 B4
Fitzroy SA 58 A2 59 F4
Fitzroy VIC 34 A4 35 D3
Fitzroy Crossing WA 79 B11 81 J8
Fitzroy Falls NSW 22 K7 30 B6
Fitzroy Island QLD 11 D13
Fitzroy Island Nat Park QLD 11 D13
Five Day Creek NSW 25 H11
Five Ways NSW 27 J12 29 A12
Fiveways VIC 37 G10
Flaggy Rock QLD 9 E9
Flagstaff Hill SA 59 K4 60 H2 61 B6
Flat Rocks WA 73 A12
Flat Witch Island TAS 52 K7
Flaxley SA 60 J5
Flaxton QLD 4 F1
Fleurieu Peninsula SA 61 J3 63 F8
Flinders QLD 5 H11
Flinders VIC 37 K8 39 J14 44 F2
Flinders Bay WA 73 J14 74 J2
Flinders Chase Nat Park SA 63 K9
Flinders Group Nat Park QLD 16 H5
Flinders Island QLD 16 H5
Flinders Island SA 64 G3
Flinders Island TAS 55 B9
Flinders Park SA 59 F3
Flinders Ranges Nat Park SA 65 B10
Flintstone TAS 53 B9 55 J9
Flora River Nature Park NT 85 J4 86 H5
Floreat WA 71 F2
Florey ACT 32 B3
Florida NSW 27 H11
Florida WA 72 H6
Florieton SA 62 D4 65 G11
Flowerdale TAS 54 D5
Flowerdale VIC 42 H3
Flowerpot TAS 50 J5 53 H10
Flowery Gully TAS 55 E9 56 E2
Fluorspar QLD 11 D11
Flynn ACT 32 B3
Fog Bay NT 86 D2
Foleyvale QLD 9 H9
Footscray VIC 35 D2 36 C6
Forbes NSW 22 F2 29 D14
Forcett TAS 51 B10 53 F11
Forde ACT 32 A5
Fords Bridge NSW 27 D9
Forest TAS 54 C3
Forest Den Nat Park QLD 8 E2 13 C12
Forest Glen NSW 20 E6
Forest Lake QLD 3 J2 5 F9
Forest Range SA 60 G4
Forest Reefs NSW 22 G4
Forestdale QLD 3 K3 5 E9
Forester TAS 55 D12
Foresters Beach NSW 20 B4
Forestier Peninsula TAS 51 D13 53 G13
Forestville NSW 19 D6 20 C7
Forge Creek VIC 43 K11 45 C13 46 E6
Forrest ACT 31 D2 32 E5
Forrest VIC 39 J10
Forrest WA 83 F6
Forrest Beach QLD 11 G14
Forrest Lakes WA 68 F1 83 E7
Forrestfield WA 71 G7
Forreston SA 60 E5
Forsayth QLD 11 G9
Forster NSW 23 C12
Forsyth Island QLD 10 D3
Forsyth Island TAS 55 A14
Forsyth Islands QLD 10 D3
Fort Glanville Con Park SA 60 F1
Fort Lytton Nat Park QLD 3 D6 4 D7
Fortescue River Roadhouse WA 78 E3 82 D1
Forth TAS 54 E7
Fortis Creek Nat Park NSW 25 D12
Fortitude Valley QLD 2 A3 3 E4
Forty Mile Scrub Nat Park QLD 11 F11
Foster VIC 44 G7 46 H1
Fosterton NSW 23 D11
Fosterville VIC 39 A12
Four Mile Creek TAS 55 G14
Fowlers Bay SA 68 K6
Fowlers Bay Con Res SA 68 K6
Fowlers Gap NSW 26 G2
Foxdale QLD 8 C7
Foxhow VIC 39 G9
Framlingham VIC 38 H7
Frampton NSW 22 K1 29 G14
Frances SA 38 B1 63 A11
Francois Peron Nat Park WA 76 B2 78 K1
Frank Hann Nat Park WA 75 E10
Frankford TAS 55 F8 56 F2
Frankland WA 73 B14 74 H5
Franklin ACT 32 B5
Franklin TAS 50 G1 53 H9
Franklin - Gordon Wild Rivers Nat Park TAS 52 D5 54 K5
Franklin Harbor Con Park SA 62 J4 64 G7
Franklin Island SA 64 D2
Franklin Vale QLD 5 K10
Franklinford VIC 39 D11
Frankston VIC 35 K5 37 G8 39 G14 44 D2
Frankton SA 62 E5 65 H11
Fraser ACT 32 A3
Fraser Island QLD 7 B13 9 K14
Freeling SA 62 E5 65 H10
Freemans Reach NSW 20 F6
Freemans Waterhole NSW 23 E10
Freemantle Nature Res NSW 22 F5
Freeth Junction SA 66 B6 91 K11
Fregon (Kaltjiti) SA 68 B5
Fremantle WA 71 J1 72 G4 74 D2 76 K4
French Island VIC 37 J10 44 E3
French Island Nat Park VIC 37 J10 44 E3
French Park NSW 29 H12
Frenchmans VIC 39 C8
Frenchs Forest NSW 19 C6 20 B7
Freshwater Creek VIC 36 H2 39 H12
Freshwater Nat Park QLD 4 F5
Frewhurst QLD 11 F11
Freycinet Nat Park TAS 53 C14 55 K14
Freycinet Peninsula TAS 53 C14
Friday Island QLD 16 B1
Frogmore NSW 22 J4 30 A3
Fulham SA 59 G2 60 F1
Fulham Gardens SA 59 F2
Fulham Island TAS 51 D11
Fulham Vale QLD 4 K4
Fullarton SA 59 H5 60 G2 61 A6
Fullerton NSW 22 J5 30 A4
Fumina VIC 42 K6 44 C6 46 E1
Furner SA 63 C13
Furracabad NSW 25 E9
Fyans Creek VIC 38 C6
Fyansford VIC 36 G2
Fyshwick ACT 32 F6

G

Gabba Island QLD 16 A2
Gabo Island VIC 47 C14
Gads Sugarloaf Nature Res NSW 25 H11
Gaffneys Creek VIC 42 H6 46 C1
Gagebrook TAS 50 A5 53 F10
Gagudju Cooinda Lodge NT 85 D6 86 D6
Gailes QLD 3 J1 5 F9
Gairdner WA 75 H8
Galah VIC 28 H4 40 E5
Galaquil VIC 40 J6
Galaquil East VIC 40 J6
Gale ACT 32 H7
Galeru Gorge WA 79 C12 81 J9
Galga SA 62 C6 65 J12
Galiwinku NT 87 C11
Galong NSW 22 K3 30 B2
Galore NSW 29 H12
Galston NSW 19 A3 20 D7
Gama VIC 40 G6
Gan Gan NT 87 E11
Ganay Nature Res NSW 25 G12
Ganmain NSW 29 G12
Gannawarra VIC 28 J7 41 G11
Gapsted VIC 43 D8
Gapuwiyak NT 87 D11
Garah NSW 6 K6 24 C4
Garden Island SA 59 C2 60 E2
Garden Island TAS 50 K3
Garden Island WA 72 G4 74 D2
Garden Island Creek TAS 50 K3 53 H10
Gardens Of Stone Nat Park NSW 22 F7
Gardners Bay TAS 50 J3 53 H10
Garema NSW 22 G1 29 D14
Garfield VIC 37 F13 44 D4
Garfield North VIC 37 F12
Gargett QLD 9 D8
Garie NSW 21 C11 23 J9
Garig Gunak Barlu Nat Park NT 85 A4 86 B5
Garigal Nat Park NSW 19 C5 23 H9
Garland NSW 22 G4
Garnpung Lake NSW 28 D5
Garra NSW 22 F3
Garran ACT 32 F4
Garrawilla NSW 24 J4
Garrthalala NT 87 D12
Garvoc VIC 38 H7
Gary Junction WA 79 F11
Gascoyne Junction WA 76 A3 78 J2
Gatton QLD 7 G11
Gatum VIC 38 D4
Gaven QLD 5 C12
Gawler SA 60 B4 62 E6 65 H10
Gawler TAS 54 E6
Gawler Ranges Con Res SA 64 D4
Gawler Ranges Nat Park SA 64 D5
Gayndah QLD 7 C10
Gaythorne QLD 3 D3
Gazette VIC 38 G5
Gecko Mine NT 89 G8
Geebung QLD 3 C4
Geehi NSW 30 G1 43 C13
Geelong VIC 36 G3 39 G12
Geera QLD 8 H3 13 F12
Geeralying WA 73 B8
Geeveston TAS 50 J1 53 H9
Geikie Gorge Nat Park WA 79 B12 81 H9
Gelantipy VIC 43 G13 47 A8
Gellibrand VIC 39 J10
Gembrook VIC 37 E12 44 C4
Gemoka QLD 11 K9 13 A8
Genoa VIC 47 C13
Geoffrey Bay WA 79 C8 80 K2
Geographe Bay WA 73 J10 74 G2
George Fisher Mine QLD 10 K3 12 A3
George Town TAS 55 D9 56 C2
Georges Creek Nature Res NSW 25 H10
Georges Hall NSW 21 D9
Georges Junction NSW 25 H10
Georges Plains NSW 22 G5
Georges River Nat Park NSW 19 H2
Georgetown QLD 11 F9
Georgetown SA 62 F3 65 F10
Georgica NSW 25 B13
Gepps Cross SA 59 D4 60 F2
Geraldton WA 76 F3
Gerang Gerung VIC 40 K4
Geranium SA 63 C8 65 K12
Gerard SA 62 B5 65 H13
German Creek Mine QLD 8 G7
Gerogery NSW 29 K12 43 A9
Gerringhap VIC 36 F2
Gerringong NSW 23 K8 30 C7
Gerroa NSW 30 C7
Getullai Island QLD 16 A2
Geurie NSW 22 D4
Gherang VIC 36 J1
Ghin-Doo-Ee Nat Park NSW 23 C11
Gibinbell QLD 7 J8 24 B7
Gibraltar Nature Res NSW 25 C9
Gibraltar Range Nat Park NSW 25 E11
Gibson Desert Nature Res WA 79 J11 83 A4
Gibson Island QLD 3 D6
Gidgegannup WA 72 E2
Gidginbung NSW 29 F13
Giffard VIC 45 F10 46 G4
Gilbert River QLD 11 F8
Gilberton SA 58 A3
Gilderoy VIC 37 D13
Gilead NSW 21 E11
Giles Meteorological Station WA 79 J13 83 A7
Gilgai NSW 25 E8
Gilgandra NSW 22 A3
Gilgooma NSW 24 H2
Gilgunnia NSW 27 K10 29 B10
Gilles Plains SA 59 E5 60 F3
Gilliat QLD 10 K6 12 A6
Gillingall VIC 43 H13 47 B8
Gilmore ACT 32 H5
Gilston QLD 5 C13
Gin Gin NSW 22 B2 27 J14
Gin Gin QLD 7 A11 9 K12
Gina SA 66 J4
Gindalbie WA 77 H11 83 F1
Gindie QLD 8 H7
Gingilup Swamps Nature Res WA 73 H14 74 H2
Gingin WA 72 G1 74 B3 76 K4
Gippsland Lakes Coastal Park VIC 45 D12 46 F6
Gipsy Point VIC 47 C13
Giralang ACT 32 B4
Girgarre VIC 41 K14 42 C2
Girilambone NSW 27 G12
Girral NSW 29 E12
Girralang Nature Res NSW 22 F5
Girraween NSW 21 E8
Girraween Nat Park QLD 7 K11 25 B10
Girrawheen WA 71 C3
Girringun Nat Park QLD 11 F13
Giru QLD 8 A5
Girvan NSW 23 D11
Gisborne VIC 39 E13
Gladesville NSW 19 E4
Gladfield VIC 41 J11
Gladstone NSW 25 J12
Gladstone QLD 9 H11
Gladstone SA 62 F3 65 F10
Gladstone TAS 55 D13
Gladysdale VIC 37 D12 42 K4 44 B4
Glamis NSW 23 A11
Glamorgan Vale QLD 5 J8
Glance Creek TAS 54 D5
Glandore SA 59 H3
Glass House Mountains QLD 4 F3
Glass House Mountains Nat Park QLD 4 F3 7 F12
Glastonbury QLD 7 D12
Glaziers Bay TAS 50 H2 53 H9
Glebe NSW 19 F5 21 C8
Glebe TAS 49 B2
Glen Alice NSW 22 E7
Glen Alvie VIC 37 K12 44 F4
Glen Davis NSW 22 F7
Glen Eagle WA 72 E5
Glen Elgin NSW 25 E10
Glen Forbes VIC 37 K12
Glen Gallic NSW 23 D8
Glen Helen Resort NT 90 F6
Glen Huon TAS 50 F1 53 G9
Glen Innes NSW 25 E9
Glen Morrison NSW 25 J9
Glen Osmond SA 59 H5 60 G3 61 A7
Glen Patrick VIC 39 C9
Glen Roy Con Park SA 38 D1 63 B12
Glen Valley VIC 43 F11
Glen Waverley VIC 35 E6 37 D9
Glenaire VIC 39 K9
Glenaladale VIC 43 K10 45 B11 46 D5
Glenalbyn VIC 39 A10
Glenalta SA 59 J5
Glenariff NSW 27 G12
Glenaroua VIC 39 C14 42 G2
Glenbrae VIC 39 D9
Glenbrook NSW 21 H9 23 H8
Glenburn VIC 42 H3
Glenburnie SA 38 F1 63 B14
Glencairn VIC 42 J7 45 A8 46 C2
Glencoe NSW 25 F9
Glencoe SA 63 B13
Glencoe West SA 63 B13
Glendambo SA 64 A5
Glenden QLD 8 D7
Glendevie TAS 50 K1 53 H9
Glendon Brook NSW 23 D10
Gleneagle QLD 5 F12
Glenelg SA 59 J2 60 G1 61 A5 62 F7 65 J10
Glenelg North SA 59 H2
Glenfern QLD 4 J3
Glenfern TAS 50 B1 53 F9
Glenfield NSW 21 E10
Glenfyne VIC 39 H8
Glengarrie NSW 5 B14
Glengarry NSW 27 D14
Glengarry TAS 55 F9 56 F2
Glengarry VIC 45 D8 46 F2
Glengower VIC 39 D10
Glengowrie SA 59 J2
Glenhaven NSW 20 E7
Glenhope VIC 39 C13 42 G1
Glenisla VIC 38 D5
Glenlee VIC 40 K4
Glenlofty VIC 39 C8
Glenlusk TAS 50 B4 53 F10
Glenlyon VIC 39 D12
Glenmaggie VIC 43 K8 45 C9 46 E3
Glenmore NSW 21 G11
Glenmore VIC 36 C2
Glenmore Park NSW 21 G9
Glenmorgan QLD 6 F6
Glennie Group VIC 44 K7 46 K1
Glenora TAS 53 E9
Glenoran WA 73 F13
Glenorchy TAS 50 C5 53 F10
Glenorchy VIC 38 B7
Glenore QLD 10 E6
Glenore TAS 55 G9 56 J3
Glenore Grove QLD 5 K8
Glenorie NSW 19 A2 20 E6
Glenormiston North VIC 39 G8
Glenormiston South VIC 39 H8
Glenreagh NSW 25 F12
Glenrowan VIC 42 D6
Glenroy SA 38 D1
Glenside SA 59 G5
Glenstuart QLD 8 J2 13 G12
Glenthompson VIC 38 E6
Glentulloch WA 73 E12
Glenunga SA 59 H5
Glenusk QLD 8 J3 13 G12
Glenwarrin NSW 23 A12
Glenwood NSW 21 E8
Glenwood QLD 7 C12
Glossodia NSW 20 G6
Glossop SA 62 B5 65 H13
Gloucester NSW 23 C11
Gloucester Island QLD 8 B7
Gloucester Island Nat Park QLD 8 B7
Gloucester Nat Park WA 73 F14 74 J3
Gnangara WA 71 B4
Gnarpurt VIC 39 G9
Gnarwarree VIC 36 G1
Gnotuk VIC 39 H8
Gnowangerup WA 74 G6
Goangra NSW 24 F1
Goat Island SA 64 D2 68 K7
Gobarralong NSW 30 C1
Gobur VIC 42 F4
Gochin Jiny Jirra NT 87 C9
Gocup NSW 29 H14 30 D1
Godfreys Creek NSW 22 J3 30 A2
Godwin Beach QLD 4 E4
Gogango QLD 9 H9
Gogeldrie NSW 29 G11
Gol Gol NSW 28 F3 40 A5
Golconda TAS 55 E10 56 D7
Gold Coast QLD 5 A12 7 H14
Golden Bay WA 72 G5
Golden Beach QLD 4 E2
Golden Beach VIC 45 E12 46 F5
Golden Grove SA 59 C7 60 E3
Golden Ridge WA 75 A13 77 J11 83 F1
Golden Valley TAS 55 G8 56 K1
Goldfields Woodlands Con Park WA 75 A11 77 J10
Goldfields Woodlands Nat Park WA 75 A10 77 J10
Goldsborough VIC 39 B10
Goldsmith TAS 53 B10 55 J10
Goldsmith Island QLD 9 C8
Goldsworthy WA 78 D6 82 B6
Gollan NSW 22 C4
Golspie NSW 22 J5 30 A4
Gomersal SA 60 B5
Goneaway Nat Park QLD 13 F8
Gongolgon NSW 27 E12
Goobang Nat Park NSW 22 E3
Good Hope NSW 30 C2
Goodedulla Nat Park QLD 9 G9
Goodger QLD 7 E10
Goodlands Nature Res WA 76 G6
Goodna QLD 3 J1 5 F9
Goodnight NSW 41 D9
Goodnight Scrub Nat Park QLD 7 B11
Goodooga NSW 6 K2 27 B13
Goods Island QLD 16 B1
Goodwood QLD 7 B12
Goodwood SA 59 H4
Goohi NSW 24 J5
Goold Island QLD 11 F13
Goold Island Nat Park QLD 11 F13
Goolgowi NSW 29 E10
Goolma NSW 22 C5
Goolmangar NSW 25 B13
Gooloogong NSW 22 G3
Goolwa SA 63 F8 65 K10
Goomadeer NT 87 C8

Goomalibee – Homebush Bay 99

Goomalibee VIC 42 D5
Goomalling WA 74 B4 76 J6
Goombi QLD 7 E8
Goombungee QLD 7 F10
Goomeri QLD 7 D11
Goon Nure VIC 45 C12 46 E5
Goonawarra Nature Res NSW 29 E8
Goondah NSW 22 K3 30 B2
Goondiwindi QLD 7 8J 24 A6
Goonengerry Nat Park NSW 25 B14
Goongarrie WA 77 H10
Goongarrie Nat Park WA 77 G11 83 E1
Goongee VIC 40 E2
Goongerah VIC 30 K2 47 B10
Goonook Nature Res NSW 23 B12
Goonumbla NSW 22 E2 29 C14
Goonyella Mine QLD 8 E6
Goorabin NSW 29 J11
Gooram VIC 42 F4
Goorambat VIC 42 C5
Goorawin NSW 29 E10
Goornong VIC 39 A12
Gooroc VIC 39 A8 41 K8
Goorooyarroo Nature Res NSW 30 D4
Goose Island TAS 55 C8
Gooseberry Hill Nat Park WA 72 F3
Goovigen QLD 9 J10
Goowarra QLD 9 H8
Gorae VIC 38 H3
Gorae West VIC 38 H3
Goranba QLD 7 F8
Gordon ACT 32 K4
Gordon NSW 19 D5 20 C7
Gordon TAS 50 K4 53 H10
Gordon VIC 36 A1 39 E11
Gordon Park QLD 3 D4
Gordon Ruins SA 65 D9
Gordonvale QLD 11 D13
Gormandale VIC 45 E9 46 F3
Gormanston TAS 52 B4 54 J4
Gorokan NSW 20 B2
Goroke VIC 38 B3
Goschen VIC 28 J6 41 F9
Gosford NSW 20 B4 23 G9
Goshen TAS 55 E13
Gosnells WA 71 K6
Gosse Bore SA 66 A1 68 A6 90 K7
Gostwyck NSW 25 H9
Goughs Bay VIC 42 G6
Goulburn NSW 22 K6 30 C5
Goulburn Islands NT 86 B7
Goulburn River Nat Park NSW 22 C7
Goulburn Weir VIC 39 A14 42 E2
Goulds Country TAS 55 E13
Gourock Nat Park NSW 30 F4
Gove Peninsula NT 87 D13
Gowanford VIC 41 F8
Gowar East VIC 39 A9
Gowrie ACT 32 H4
Gowrie Park TAS 54 F6
Goyura VIC 40 H6
Grabben Gullen NSW 22 K5 30 B4
Gracefield WA 73 A13
Gracemere QLD 9 H10
Gracetown WA 73 K12 74 H1
Graceville QLD 3 F3
Gradgery NSW 27 G14
Gradule QLD 6 J5 24 A3
Grafton NSW 25 E12
Graham NSW 22 J4 30 A3
Grahamstown NSW 29 H14 30 D1
Grahamvale VIC 42 C3
Graman NSW 24 D7
Grampians Nat Park VIC 38 C6
Grandchester QLD 5 K10
Grange QLD 3 D3
Grange SA 59 F2 60 F1
Granite Flat VIC 43 D10
Granite Island SA 61 J6
Granite Island VIC 44 H7 46 J2
Granite Point Con Area TAS 55 D11 56 A7
Granite Tor Con Area TAS 52 A5 54 H5
Granny Smith Mine WA 77 F12 83 D1
Grant (site) VIC 43 H9 46 B4
Grant Island NT 86 B7
Granton TAS 50 A4 53 F10
Granton VIC 37 A13
Grantville VIC 37 K11 44 F4
Granville NSW 19 E2 21 D8
Granville Harbour TAS 52 A2 54 H2
Granya VIC 43 B10
Grass Flat VIC 38 A4
Grass Hut NSW 27 D10
Grass Patch WA 75 F13 83 J1
Grass Valley WA 72 C2 74 C4 76 K6
Grassdale VIC 38 F4
Grassmere VIC 38 H6
Grasstree QLD 9 D8
Grassy TAS 54 C6
Grassy Head NSW 25 H12
Grattai NSW 22 D5
Gravelly Beach TAS 55 E9 56 E4
Gravesend NSW 24 E6
Grawin NSW 27 D14
Gray TAS 55 G14
Grays Point NSW 19 K3
Graytown VIC 39 B14 42 E2
Great Australian Bight Marine Park SA 68 K4 83 G7
Great Barrier Reef QLD 9 C11 11 C13 16 F5
Great Basalt Wall Nat Park QLD 8 B2 11 J12
Great Dog Island TAS 55 C9
Great Keppel Island QLD 9 G11
Great Lake TAS 53 A8 55 H8
Great Palm Island QLD 11 G14
Great Sandy Island Nature Res WA 78 E3
Great Sandy Nat Park QLD 7 D13
Great Victoria Desert Nature Res WA 68 F1 83 E6
Great Western VIC 38 C7
Great Western Tiers Con Park TAS 53 B10 55 J10 56 K1
Greater Bendigo Nat Park VIC 39 A12
Gredgwin VIC 41 H10
Green Cape NSW 30 K5 47 B14
Green Fields SA 59 C4
Green Head WA 76 H3
Green Island QLD 4 C7 11 D13
Green Island TAS 50 J5
Green Island Nat Park QLD 11 D13
Green Lake VIC 38 B5
Green Pigeon NSW 25 B13
Green Point NSW 20 B4
Green Valley NSW 21 E9
Greenacre NSW 19 G3 21 C9
Greenacres SA 59 E5
Greenbank QLD 5 F10
Greenbushes WA 73 F12 74 G3
Greendale NSW 21 G10
Greendale VIC 36 A2 39 E12
Greenethorpe NSW 22 H3
Greengrove NSW 20 D4
Greenhill QLD 9 E9
Greenhill SA 59 G6 60 K4
Greenhill Island NT 85 A5 86 B5
Greenhills WA 72 B3 74 C5 76 K6
Greenmount QLD 7 G10
Greenmount VIC 45 G9 46 H3
Greenmount Nat Park WA 72 F3
Greenock SA 60 A6 62 E5 65 H10
Greenough WA 76 F3
Greenpatch SA 64 H5
Greens Beach TAS 55 D8 56 C1
Greens Creek VIC 39 C8
Greensborough VIC 35 B5 37 C8
Greenslopes QLD 3 F4
Greenvale NSW 29 H11
Greenvale QLD 11 G12
Greenvale VIC 35 A2 36 B6
Greenwald VIC 38 G3
Greenway ACT 32 J3
Greenways SA 62 D6 63 C12 65 J11
Greenwell Point NSW 30 C7
Greenwich NSW 21 C8
Greenwich Park NSW 22 K6 30 B5
Greenwith SA 59 B7
Greenwood WA 71 C2
Gregors Creek QLD 4 K3
Gregory WA 76 E2
Gregory Downs QLD 10 G3
Gregory Mine QLD 8 G7
Gregory Nat Park NT 86 K3 88 B3
Greigs Flat NSW 30 J5 47 A14
Grenfell NSW 22 H2 29 E14
Grenville VIC 39 F10
Gresford NSW 23 D10
Greta VIC 42 D6
Greta West VIC 42 D6
Gretna TAS 53 E9
Grevillia NSW 25 A12
Grey Peaks Nat Park QLD 11 D13
Greystanes NSW 19 E1 21 E8
Griffin QLD 4 E6
Griffith ACT 32 F5
Griffith NSW 29 F11
Griffiths Island VIC 38 H6
Griffiths Nature Res WA 75 F12
Grimwade WA 73 F11 74 G3
Gringegalgona VIC 38 E4
Grogan NSW 22 J1 29 F14
Grong Grong NSW 29 G12
Gronos Point NSW 20 F6
Groote Eylandt NT 87 F12
Groper Creek QLD 8 A6
Grose Island NT 86 D3
Grose Vale NSW 20 H7
Grose Wold NSW 20 G7
Grove TAS 50 E3 53 G10
Grove Hill NT 85 F3 86 F4
Grovedale VIC 36 H2
Grovely QLD 3 C2
Gruyere VIC 37 C11
Guanaba QLD 5 C12
Gubbata NSW 29 D11
Gubbata Nature Res NSW 29 D12
Guilderton WA 72 H1 74 B2 76 K4
Guildford NSW 19 F2 21 D9
Guildford TAS 54 F5
Guildford VIC 39 C11
Guildford WA 71 E6
Gulaga Nat Park NSW 30 G5
Gular NSW 24 K1
Gulargambone NSW 24 K1
Gulera QLD 7 F9
Gulf of Carpentaria 10 B3 87 E14
Gulf St Vincent SA 59 G1 60 H1 61 B3 62 G6 65 J9
Gulgong NSW 22 C5
Gulguer Nature Res NSW 21 G10 23 H8
Gull Creek NSW 24 F7
Gulnare SA 62 F3 65 F10
Guluguba QLD 6 D7
Guluwuru Island NT 87 B12
Gum Creek NSW 26 G9
Gum Flat VIC 36 J1
Gum Lagoon Con Park SA 63 C10
Gum Lake NSW 28 B5
Gumble NSW 22 E3
Gumdale QLD 3 F6
Gumeracha SA 60 E5 62 E6 65 J10
Gumlu QLD 8 B6
Gunalda QLD 7 D12
Gunbalanya (Oenpelli) NT 85 C7 86 D7
Gunbar NSW 29 E9
Gunbower VIC 29 K8 41 H12
Gunbower Island VIC 41 H12
Gundabooka Nat Park NSW 27 F10
Gundagai NSW 29 H14 30 D1
Gundaroo NSW 30 C3
Gunderman NSW 20 E5
Gundowring VIC 43 D9
Gundy NSW 23 B9
Gunebang NSW 29 C12
Gungahlin ACT 32 A5
Gungal NSW 23 C8
Gunnary NSW 22 J4 30 A2
Gunnedah NSW 24 J6
Gunner VIC 28 H3 40 E4
Gunnewin QLD 6 C4
Gunning NSW 30 C3
Gunning Grach NSW 30 H3
Gunningbland NSW 22 F1 29 C14
Gunns Plains TAS 54 E6
Gunpowder QLD 10 J3
Gununa QLD 10 D3
Gunyarra QLD 8 C7
Gurley NSW 24 E5
Gurrai SA 28 H1 62 B7 65 J13
Gurrbalgun WA 79 A9 80 F4
Gurrumuru NT 87 D12
Gurulmundi QLD 6 D7
Gutha WA 76 F4
Guthalungra QLD 8 B6
Guthega NSW 30 G1 43 C14
Guy Fawkes River Nat Park NSW 25 F11
Guy Fawkes River Nature Res NSW 25 G11
Guyra NSW 25 F9
Guys Forest VIC 43 B11
Gwabegar NSW 24 G3
Gwambygine WA 72 C3
Gwandalan NSW 20 A1
Gwandalan TAS 51 F10 53 G12
Gwenneth Lakes WA 79 E11
Gwindinup WA 73 G10
Gymbowen VIC 38 B3
Gymea NSW 21 C10
Gympie QLD 7 D12
Gypsum VIC 28 H4 40 F6

H

H1 Yandicoogina Mine WA 78 G6 82 F5
Hackett ACT 32 C5
Hackham SA 60 K1 61 D5
Hackney SA 58 B3 59 F5
Haddon VIC 39 E10
Haddon Corner QLD SA 12 K6 14 C4 67 A14
Haden QLD 7 F11
Hadleigh NSW 24 D6
Hadspen TAS 55 F9 56 H4
Hagley TAS 55 F9 56 H3
Hahndorf SA 60 H5 62 E7 65 J10
Haig WA 83 F4
Haigslea QLD 5 J9
Haines Junction VIC 39 J10
Halbury SA 62 F5 65 G10
Hale Con Park SA 60 C5
Halekulani NSW 20 A2
Halfway Creek NSW 25 F13
Halidon SA 62 C7 65 J12
Halifax QLD 11 G14
Halifax Bay QLD 11 G14
Halifax Bay Wetlands Nat Park QLD 11 G14
Halinor Lake SA 68 F3
Hall ACT 32 A3
Hall NSW 19 G2 30 D3
Hallett SA 62 E3 65 F10
Hallett Cove SA 60 J1 61 C5
Hallett Cove Con Park SA 60 H1 61 C5
Hallidays Point NSW 23 C12
Hallora VIC 37 H14
Halls Creek WA 79 B13 81 J12
Halls Gap VIC 38 C6
Hallston VIC 44 F6
Halton NSW 23 C10
Hambidge Con Park SA 64 F6
Hamel WA 72 F7
Hamelin Bay WA 73 K13 74 H1
Hamelin Pool Marine Nature Res WA 76 B2 78 K2
Hamersley WA 71 D3 72 C2
Hamilton QLD 3 D4
Hamilton SA 62 E5 65 H10
Hamilton TAS 53 E9
Hamilton VIC 38 F5
Hamilton Downs Youth Camp NT 90 F7
Hamilton Hill WA 71 K2
Hamilton Island QLD 9 C8
Hamley Bridge SA 62 F5 65 H10
Hammond SA 62 F1 65 D9
Hammond Island QLD 16 B2
Hampshire TAS 54 E5
Hampton NSW 22 G6
Hampton QLD 7 G11
Hanging Rock NSW 23 A9 25 K8
Hann River Roadhouse QLD 11 A10 16 K5
Hann Tableland Nat Park QLD 11 D12
Hannahs Bridge NSW 22 B6
Hannan NSW 29 D11
Hannaville QLD 9 D8
Hansborough SA 62 E5 65 H10
Hanson SA 62 E4 65 G10
Hansonville VIC 42 D6
Hanwood NSW 29 F11
Happy Valley QLD 7 B13
Happy Valley SA 60 J2 61 C6
Happy Valley VIC 28 G4 40 C7 43 D8 43 H9 46 B4
Harcourt VIC 39 C11
Harden NSW 22 K3 30 B1
Hardwicke Bay SA 62 H6 65 J8
Harefield NSW 29 H13
Harford TAS 55 E8
Hargraves NSW 22 E5
Harlin QLD 7 F11
Harman ACT 32 F6
Harrietville VIC 43 F9
Harrington NSW 23 B13
Harris Nature Res WA 75 E8
Harrismith WA 74 E6
Harrison ACT 32 B5
Harrisville QLD 5 H11
Harrogate SA 60 G7 62 E7 65 J10
Harrow VIC 38 D3
Hart SA 62 F4 65 G10
Hartley NSW 22 G7
Hartley SA 60 K7
Harts Range NT 91 E10
Hartz Mountains Nat Park TAS 53 H8
Harvey WA 73 G8 74 F3
Harwood NSW 25 D13
Haslam SA 64 D3
Hassell Nat Park WA 74 J7
Hastings TAS 53 J9
Hastings VIC 37 J9 39 H14 44 E2
Hastings Point NSW 25 A14
Hat Head Nat Park NSW 25 J12
Hatfield NSW 28 E6
Hatherleigh SA 63 C13
Hattah VIC 28 G4 40 D5
Hattah-Kulkyne Nat Park VIC 28 G4 40 C5
Hatton Vale QLD 5 K9
Havanna Island QLD 11 G14
Havelock VIC 39 C10
Haven VIC 38 B5
Hawker ACT 32 C2
Hawker SA 65 C10
Hawkesbury Island QLD 16 B2
Hawkesdale VIC 38 G6
Hawkesdale West VIC 38 G5
Hawknest Island NT 87 F12
Hawks Nest NSW 23 E11
Hawley Beach TAS 55 E8
Hawthorn VIC 35 D4
Hawthorndene SA 59 K5
Hawthorne QLD 3 E4
Hay NSW 29 F8 41 B13
Hay Point QLD 9 D8
Haydens Bog VIC 47 A10
Hayes TAS 50 A2 53 F9
Hayes Creek NT 85 F3 86 F4
Hayman Island QLD 9 B8
Haysdale VIC 28 G5 41 D8
Hazelbrook NSW 21 J9
Hazeldean QLD 4 J4
Hazelmere WA 71 E7
Hazelwood VIC 44 E7 46 F1
Hazelwood Island QLD 9 B8
Hazelwood Park SA 59 G5
Healesville VIC 37 B11 42 J4 44 B4
Hearson WA 78 E4 82 C1
Heartlea WA 73 D13
Heath Hill VIC 37 H13
Heathcote NSW 19 K2 21 C11 23 J9
Heathcote VIC 39 B13 42 F1
Heathcote Nat Park NSW 19 K2 21 D11 23 J8
Heathcote-Graytown Nat Park VIC 39 B13 42 E1
Heathfield SA 59 K7 60 H4 61 B7
Heathlands QLD 16 D2
Heathmere VIC 38 H4
Heathwood QLD 3 J3
Hebden NSW 23 D9
Hebel QLD 6 K3 27 B14
Hectorville SA 59 F6
Heggaton Con Res SA 62 K3 64 F7
Heidelberg VIC 35 C4 37 C8
Heirisson Island WA 70 D4
Heka TAS 54 E6
Helensburgh NSW 21 C12 23 J9
Helensvale QLD 5 C12
Helenvale QLD 11 B12 16 K7
Helidon QLD 7 G11
Hell Hole Gorge Nat Park QLD 13 J10 15 B10
Hells Gate Roadhouse QLD 10 E2
Hellyer TAS 54 C4
Hellyer Gorge State Res TAS 54 E4
Hemmant QLD 3 E6
Henbury Meteorite Con Res NT 90 G7
Hendon QLD 7 H11
Henley Beach SA 59 F2 60 F1 61 A5
Henley Brook WA 71 B6
Henrietta TAS 54 E5
Henry Freycinet Harbour WA 76 C2
Hensley Park VIC 38 E5
Henty NSW 29 J12
Henty VIC 38 F3
Hepburn Springs VIC 39 D11
Herbert Wash WA 77 B14 79 K10 83 A3
Herberton QLD 11 E12
Heritage Park QLD 3 K5
Hermannsburg NT 90 F6
Hermidale NSW 27 H12
Hernani NSW 25 G11
Herne Hill WA 71 C7
Heron Island QLD 9 H12
Herons Creek NSW 23 A13
Herrick TAS 55 D12
Hervey Bay QLD 7 A12 7 B13
Hesso SA 65 D8
Hester WA 73 E12
Hewetsons Mill NSW 25 A11
Hewitt NSW 21 F9
Hexham VIC 38 G7
Hexham Island QLD 9 E10
Hexham Swamp Nature Res NSW 23 E10
Heybridge TAS 54 D6
Heyfield VIC 45 C9 46 E3
Heywood VIC 38 H4
Heywood Islands WA 80 C7
Hicks Island QLD 16 D3
Hidden Island WA 80 E5
Hidden Vale QLD 5 K10
Hidden Valley QLD 11 G13
Higgins ACT 32 C2
Higginsville WA 75 C13 77 K11 83 G1
Higginsville Mine WA 75 C13 77 K11 83 G1
High Island QLD 11 D13
High Peak Island QLD 9 E10
High Range NSW 22 J7 30 B6
High Wycombe WA 71 F7
Highbury SA 59 E6 60 F3
Highbury WA 73 A8 74 F5
Highclere TAS 54 E5
Highcroft TAS 51 H11 53 H12
Higher McDonald NSW 20 F3
Highgate WA 71 F4
Highlands VIC 42 G3
Highton VIC 36 G2
Hilgay VIC 38 E3
Hill End NSW 22 E5
Hill End VIC 44 D6 46 E1
Hillarys WA 71 B1
Hillbank SA 59 B6
Hillcrest QLD 3 K4
Hillcrest SA 59 E5
Hillgrove NSW 25 H10
Hillier SA 60 C3
Hillman WA 73 C9
Hillside VIC 43 K11 45 C12 46 D5
Hillston NSW 29 D10
Hilltop NSW 21 G14
Hilltown SA 62 F4 65 G10
Hillview QLD 5 E14
Hillwood TAS 55 E9 56 E4
Hilton WA 71 J2
Hilton Mine QLD 10 K3 12 A3
Hinchinbrook Island QLD 11 F13
Hinchinbrook Island Nat Park QLD 11 F13
Hincks Con Park SA 64 G6
Hincks Con Res SA 64 G5
Hindmarsh SA 59 F3 60 F2
Hindmarsh Island SA 63 E8 65 K10
Hindmarsh Valley SA 61 H6
Hinnomunjie VIC 43 F11 46 A6
Hivesville QLD 7 D10
Hiway Inn NT 86 K7 88 B7
HMAS Cerberus VIC 37 J9
Hobart TAS 49 C2 50 C5 53 F10
Hobart CBD TAS 49
Hobbys Yards NSW 22 G5
Hocking WA 71 A3
Hoddles Creek VIC 37 D12
Hodgson QLD 6 E4
Hoffman WA 73 F8
Hogarth Range Nature Res NSW 25 C12
Holbrook NSW 29 J13
Holden Hill SA 59 E6
Holder ACT 32 F3
Holey Plains State Park VIC 45 E10 46 F3
Holgate NSW 20 B4
Holland Landing VIC 45 D12 46 E5
Holland Park QLD 3 F4
Hollow Tree TAS 53 E9
Holmwood NSW 22 H4
Holsworthy NSW 19 H1 21 D10
Holt ACT 32 C2
Holt Rock WA 75 E9
Holts Flat NSW 30 H3
Holwell TAS 55 E8 56 E2
Home Hill QLD 8 A5
Home Rule NSW 22 D6
Homebush NSW 21 D9
Homebush QLD 9 D8
Homebush Bay NSW 19 E3 21 D8

100 Homecroft - Ki Ki

Homecroft VIC 40 J6
Homerton VIC 38 G4
Homestead QLD 8 B3 11 K13
Homevale Nat Park QLD 8 D7
Homewood VIC 42 G3
Honeymoon Beach WA 81 A10
Hook Island QLD 9 B8
Hookina SA 65 C9
Hope Campbell Lake WA 77 F13 83 E2
Hope Vale QLD 11 A12 16 K7
Hope Valley SA 59 D6 60 E3
Hopefield NSW 29 K11 42 A7
Hopetoun VIC 28 J4 40 G6
Hopetoun WA 75 G10
Hopetoun West VIC 40 G5
Hopevale VIC 28 K4 40 H5
Hoppers Crossing VIC 36 D5
Horfield VIC 41 H11
Horn Island QLD 16 B2
Hornsby NSW 19 B3 20 D7 23 H9
Hornsby Heights NSW 19 B4
Horrocks WA 76 E3
Horsham VIC 38 B5
Horsley Park NSW 21 E9
Horsnell Gully Con Park SA 59 G7 60 G3 61 A7
Hortons Creek Nature Res NSW 25 F12
Hoskinstown NSW 30 E4
Hoskyn Islands QLD 9 H13
Hotham Heights Alpine Village VIC 43 F10
Hotspur VIC 38 G3
Hotspur Island QLD 9 D10
Houtman Abrolhos WA 76 F2
Howard QLD 7 B12
Howard Island NT 87 C10
Howard Springs NT 85 C2 86 D4
Howden TAS 50 F5 53 G10
Howes Valley NSW 23 E8
Howick Group Nat Park QLD 16 H6
Howick Island QLD 16 H6
Howlong NSW 29 K12 43 A8
Howqua VIC 42 G6 46 B1
Howqua Hills VIC 42 G7 46 A1
Howth TAS 54 D6
Hoxton Park NSW 21 E9
Hoyleton SA 62 F4 65 G10
Hugh River NT 91 G8
Hughenden QLD 8 C1 11 K10 13 A10
Hughes ACT 32 F4
Hughes SA 68 H2 83 F7
Hull Heads QLD 11 F13
Humbug Point Con Area TAS 55 E14
Hume ACT 32 H5
Hume Weir NSW 29 K12 43 B9
Humevale VIC 37 A9 39 E14 42 H3 44 A2
Humpty Doo NT 85 C2 86 D4
Humula NSW 29 J14
Hungerford QLD 15 K10 26 B7
Hunter VIC 41 K12
Hunter Island TAS 54 A1
Hunters Hill NSW 19 E5 21 C8
Huntingdale WA 71 K6
Huntly VIC 39 A12
Huonville TAS 50 F2 53 G9
Hurstbridge VIC 35 A6 37 B9 39 E14 42 J3 44 A2
Hurstville NSW 19 H4 21 C9
Huskisson NSW 30 D7
Hyden WA 75 D8
Hyland Bay NT 86 F2
Hynam SA 38 C1 63 B12

I

Iandra NSW 22 H3 30 A1
Ida Bay TAS 53 J9
Idalia Nat Park QLD 8 K2 13 H11 15 A11
Ifould Lake SA 68 H5
Iga Warta SA 65 A11 67 K11
Iguana Creek VIC 43 K10 45 B12 46 D5
Ikuntji (Haasts Bluff) NT 90 E5
Ilbilbie QLD 9 E8
Ilbunga SA 91 K10
Ile du Golfe TAS 52 K7
Ilford NSW 22 E6
Ilfracombe QLD 8 H1 13 F11
Ilfraville TAS 55 E9 56 D2
Ilkurlka WA 83 D6
Illabarook VIC 39 F10
Illabo NSW 29 G14
Illalong Creek NSW 22 K3 30 C2
Illamurta Con Res NT 90 G6
Illawong WA 76 G3
Illili NT 90 E5
Illilliwa NSW 29 F9 41 B14
Illowa VIC 38 H6
Illpurta NT 90 G6
Iltur SA 68 C3
Iluka NSW 25 D13
Ilykuwaratja SA 66 A1 68 A6 90 K7
Imanpa NT 90 H6
Imbil QLD 7 E12
Imintji WA 79 A11 81 G8
Immarna SA 68 H5
Impadna NT 91 H8
Inala QLD 3 H2 5 F9
Inarki SA 68 A2 90 K2
Indented Head VIC 36 G5 39 G13
Indooroopilly QLD 3 F3
Indulkana (Iwantja) SA 66 C1 68 B7
Indwarra Nature Res NSW 25 F8
Ingalba Nature Res NSW 29 F13
Ingebyra NSW 30 H2 43 E14
Ingham QLD 11 G13
Ingle Farm SA 59 D5 60 E3
Ingleburn NSW 21 E10
Inglegar NSW 27 H14
Ingleside NSW 19 B6 20 B6
Inglewood QLD 7 J9 25 A8
Inglewood SA 60 E4
Inglewood VIC 39 A10
Inglewood WA 71 E4
Inglis Island NT 87 C12
Ingliston VIC 36 B2
Ininti NT 79 G14 90 E1
Injarrtnama NT 90 F7
Injinoo QLD 16 B2
Injune QLD 6 C4
Inkerman QLD 8 A6
Inkerman SA 62 G5 65 H9
Inman Valley SA 61 H5 63 F8 65 K10
Innaloo WA 71 E2
Innamincka SA 14 G3 67 E14
Innamincka Reg Res SA 14 F3 67 D13
Inner Sister Island TAS 55 A8
Innes Nat Park SA 62 J7 64 K7
Innisfail QLD 11 E13
Innisplain QLD 5 F14
Innot Hot Springs QLD 11 E12
Interlaken TAS 53 C10 55 K10
Inveralochy NSW 30 C4
Inverell NSW 25 E8
Invergordon VIC 42 B4
Inverleigh VIC 36 G1 39 G11
Inverloch VIC 44 G5
Investigator Group Con Park SA 64 G3
Investigator Strait SA 63 J8
Iona VIC 37 G13 44 D5
Ipolera NT 90 F6
Ipswich QLD 5 G9 7 G12
Irishtown TAS 54 C3
Irishtown WA 72 D1
Irkini NT 68 A1 79 K14 83 B7 90 K2
Iron Baron SA 62 J2 65 E8
Iron Knob SA 62 J1 65 E8
Iron Range QLD 16 F3
Iron Range Nat Park QLD 16 E4
Ironbank SA 59 K6 60 H3 61 B7
Ironbark Nature Res NSW 24 G7
Ironmungy Nature Res NSW 30 H2
Ironwood Bore SA 68 B5
Irrapatana SA 66 G7
Irrewarra VIC 39 H10
Irrewillipe VIC 39 H9
Irrilirre NT 91 D10
Irrmarne NT 91 C12
Irrunytju (Wingellina) WA 68 A1 90 K1
Irvinebank QLD 11 E12
Irymple VIC 28 F3 40 A5
Isaacs ACT 32 G4
Isabella NSW 22 H5
Isabella Plains ACT 32 J4
Isis TAS 53 A10 55 H10
Isis Junction QLD 7 B12
Isisford QLD 8 J1 13 G11
Isla Gorge Nat Park QLD 6 B7
Island Bend NSW 30 G2 43 C14
Island Lagoon SA 64 B7
Isle of the Dead TAS 51 H13
Isle Woodah NT 87 E12
Israelite Bay WA 83 J3
Ivanhoe NSW 28 C7
Iveragh QLD 9 J11

J

Jaaningga Nature Res NSW 25 H12
Jabiru NT 85 D7 86 D6
Jabuk SA 63 C8 65 K12
Jack River VIC 45 G8 46 H2
Jackadgery NSW 25 E11
Jackeys Marsh TAS 55 G8 56 K1
Jackie Junction WA 79 K12 83 A5
Jackson QLD 6 E6
Jacobs Well QLD 5 B11
Jacobs Well WA 72 A4
Jalbarragup WA 73 H12
Jallukar VIC 38 D7
Jallumba VIC 38 C4
Jam Jerrup VIC 37 J11
Jamberoo NSW 23 K8 30 B7
Jambin QLD 9 J10
Jamboree Heights QLD 3 G2
Jamestown SA 62 F3 65 F10
Jamieson VIC 42 H6 46 B1
Jamieson (Mantamaru) WA 79 K13 83 A6
Jamisontown NSW 21 G8
Jan Juc VIC 36 J2 39 H12
Jancourt VIC 39 H8
Jancourt East VIC 39 H8
Jandabup WA 71 A4
Jandakot WA 71 K4 72 G4
Jandowae QLD 7 E9
Jannali NSW 19 J3
Japoonvale QLD 11 E13
Jaraga QLD 8 B6
Jardee WA 73 E14
Jardine River Nat Park QLD 16 C2
Jardine Valley QLD 8 C1 13 A10
Jarklin VIC 41 K11
Jarlmadangah WA 79 B10 80 H6
Jarra Jarra NT 88 J7 90 A7
Jarrahdale WA 72 F5 74 D3
Jarrahwood WA 73 G11 74 G3
Jasper Hill/Dominion WA 77 F11
Jasper Nature Res NSW 23 A12 25 K11
Jaspers Brush NSW 30 C7
Jeetho VIC 37 J13
Jeffcott North VIC 41 K8
Jennacubbine WA 72 C1
Jennapullin WA 72 C1
Jenolan Caves NSW 22 H6
Jeogla NSW 25 H10
Jeparit VIC 40 J4
Jerangle NSW 30 F4
Jerdacuttup Lakes Nature Res WA 75 G10
Jericho QLD 8 H4 13 F13
Jericho TAS 53 D10
Jericho VIC 42 J6 44 A7 46 C1
Jerilderie NSW 29 H10
Jerrabomberra NSW 32 G7
Jerralong Nature Res NSW 30 D5
Jerramungup WA 75 G8
Jerrawa NSW 30 C3
Jerrawangala Nat Park NSW 30 C6
Jerrys Plains NSW 23 D9
Jerseyville NSW 25 J12
Jervis Bay NSW 30 D7
Jervis Bay Nat Park NSW 30 C7
Jervois SA 62 D7 65 K11
Jetsonville TAS 55 D11
Jigalong WA 78 G7
Jil Jil VIC 28 K5 41 H8
Jilbadji Nature Res WA 75 C9 77 K9
Jilkminggan NT 86 H7
Jilliby NSW 20 C2
Ji-Marda NT 87 C9
Jimaringle NSW 28 H7 41 F11
Jimbalakudunj WA 79 B11 80 H7
Jimblebar Mine WA 78 G7 82 H7
Jimboomba QLD 5 E11 7 H13
Jimbour QLD 7 F9
Jimenbuen NSW 30 J2
Jimna QLD 4 K1 7 E12
Jincumbilly NSW 30 H3
Jindabyne NSW 30 H2
Jindalee QLD 3 G2 5 F8
Jindera NSW 29 K12 43 A9
Jindivick VIC 37 F14 44 D5
Jindivick North VIC 37 F14
Jindivick West VIC 37 F14
Jindong WA 73 J11
Jingalup WA 73 B12
Jingellic NSW 29 K14 43 A12
Jingellic Nature Res NSW 29 K14 43 A12
Jingera NSW 30 F4
Jingili NT 84 B3
Jinglemoney NSW 30 E4
Jip Jip Con Park SA 63 C10
Jitarning WA 74 E6
Joadja NSW 22 K7 30 B6
Joadja Nature Res NSW 22 J7 30 B6
Joanna SA 38 C1 63 B12
Joel VIC 39 C8
Johanna VIC 39 K9
John Forrest Nat Park WA 72 F3 74 C3 76 K5
Johnburgh SA 62 E1 65 D10
Johns River NSW 23 B13
Jolimont WA 71 F3
Jondaryan QLD 7 F10
Joondalup WA 71 A2
Joondanna WA 71 E3
Josbury WA 73 C8
Joseph Banks (Round Hill Head) Con Park QLD 9 J12
Joseph Bonaparte Gulf WA NT 81 B13 86 G1
Josephville QLD 5 F13
Joycedale QLD 8 H4 13 F13
Joyces Creek VIC 39 C11
Judbury TAS 50 E1 53 G9
Jueburra QLD 12 B4
Jugiong NSW 30 C1
Julatten QLD 11 C12
Julia SA 62 E5 65 G10
Julia Creek QLD 10 K7 12 A7
Julimar Con Park WA 72 E1
Jumbunna VIC 37 K13 44 F5
Junction Bay NT 87 C8
Jundah QLD 13 H9 15 A8
Junee NSW 29 G13
Junee Nat Park QLD 9 G8
Junee Reefs NSW 22 K1 29 G13
Jung VIC 38 A6
Junjuwa WA 79 B11 81 H9
Junortoun VIC 39 B12
Junuy Juluum Nat Park NSW 25 G11
Jurema QLD 8 G6
Jurien Bay WA 76 H3
Juugawaarri Nature Res NSW 25 H12

K

Kaarimba VIC 42 B3
Kaban QLD 11 E12
Kabelbara QLD 8 G6
Kabra QLD 9 H10
Kadina SA 62 H4 65 G8
Kadjina WA 79 C11 80 K7
Kadnook VIC 38 C3
Kadungle NSW 22 D1 29 B13
Kagara QLD 5 F11
Kaimkillenbun QLD 7 F10
Kainton SA 62 G5 65 G9
Kainton Corner SA 62 G5 65 G9
Kairi QLD 11 D12
Kaiserstuhl Con Park SA 60 B7
Kajabbi QLD 10 J4
Kajuligah Nature Res NSW 29 B8
Kakadu Nat Park NT 85 C6 86 D6
Kalamunda WA 72 F3 74 C3 76 K5
Kalamunda Nat Park WA 72 F3 74 C3 76 K5
Kalang NSW 25 G12
Kalangadoo SA 38 E1 63 B13
Kalannie WA 76 H6
Kalarka QLD 9 F9
Kalaru NSW 30 J5
Kalbar QLD 5 J12 7 H12
Kalbarri WA 76 D2
Kalbarri Nat Park WA 76 D2
Kaleen ACT 32 C4
Kaleentha NSW 28 B5
Kalgoorlie WA 75 A12 77 J11 83 F1
Kalimna West VIC 43 K12 45 C14 46 E7
Kalka SA 68 A1 79 K14 83 B7 90 K1
Kalkallo VIC 36 A7 39 E14 42 J2 44 A1
Kalkaringi NT 88 D3
Kalkee VIC 38 A5
Kallangur QLD 4 E6
Kallaroo WA 71 B1
Kallista VIC 37 D10
Kalorama VIC 37 D10
Kalpi SA 68 C5
Kalpowar QLD 7 A10 9 K11
Kaltukatjara (Docker River) NT 90 H1
Kalumburu WA 81 B10
Kalyan SA 62 C7 65 J12
Kamarah NSW 29 F12
Kamarooka VIC 39 A12 41 K12
Kambah ACT 32 G3
Kambalda WA 75 B13 77 J11 83 G1
Kambalda Nature Res WA 75 A12 77 J11 83 F1
Kambalda West WA 75 B13 77 J11 83 G1
Kamber NSW 22 A3 24 K2
Kamona TAS 55 E12
Kampurarr Pirti WA 79 K13 83 B6
Kanagulk VIC 38 C4
Kanangra-Boyd Nat Park NSW 22 H6 30 A5
Kandanga QLD 7 D12
Kandat Djaru WA 79 C14 81 K13
Kandiwal WA 81 C9
Kandos NSW 22 E6
Kangarilla SA 60 K3 61 D7 62 F7 65 J10
Kangaroo Creek Res SA 60 F4
Kangaroo Flat SA 60 B3
Kangaroo Flat VIC 39 B11
Kangaroo Ground VIC 35 B7 37 B9
Kangaroo Island QLD 5 B10
Kangaroo Island SA 63 J9
Kangaroo Island TAS 54 B1
Kangaroo Point QLD 2 C4
Kangaroo Valley NSW 22 K7 30 C7
Kangarooby NSW 22 G3
Kangawall VIC 38 B3
Kangy Angy NSW 20 C3
Kaniva VIC 40 K2 63 A10
Kanmantoo SA 60 H7
Kanowna WA 77 H11 83 F1
Kanpa WA 79 K11 83 B4
Kanpi SA 68 A2 90 K3
Kanumbra VIC 42 F4
Kanunnah Bridge TAS 54 D2
Kanwal NSW 20 B2
Kanya VIC 39 B8
Kanyaka Ruins SA 65 C9
Kaoota TAS 50 F4 53 G10
Kapinnie SA 64 G5
Kapunda SA 62 E5 65 H10
Karabar NSW 32 G7
Karabeal VIC 38 E5
Karadoc VIC 28 F4 40 B5
Karana Downs QLD 5 G8
Karanja TAS 53 E9
Karara QLD 7 H10 25 A9
Karatta SA 63 J9
Karawatha QLD 3 J5
Karawinna VIC 28 F3 40 B3
Kardella VIC 37 K14
Kardella South VIC 37 K14
Kardinya WA 71 J3
Kareela NSW 19 J3 21 C10
Kariah VIC 39 H8
Karijini Nat Park WA 78 G5 82 F4
Kariong NSW 20 C4
Karkoo SA 64 G5
Karlgarin WA 75 D8
Karonie WA 75 A14 77 J12 83 F2
Karonie Mine WA 75 A14 77 J12 83 F2
Karook VIC 39 A14 42 D2
Karoola TAS 55 E10 56 E5
Karoon QLD 8 C2 13 A11
Karoonda SA 62 C7 65 J12
Karping WA 72 B6
Karragarra Island QLD 5 B9
Karrakatta WA 71 G2
Karramomus North VIC 42 D4
Karratha WA 78 E4 82 C2
Karratha Roadhouse WA 78 E4 82 C1
Karridale WA 73 J13 74 H2
Karrinyup WA 71 D2
Karrku WA 79 J13
Karroun Hill Nature Res WA 76 G7
Kars Springs NSW 23 B8
Karte SA 28 H1 62 B7 65 J13
Karte Con Park SA 28 H1 62 B7 65 K13
Karuah NSW 23 D11
Karuah Nature Res NSW 23 D11
Karukaki NT 79 J14 90 H2
Karumba QLD 10 E5
Karween VIC 28 F2 40 B2
Katamatite VIC 29 K10 42 B4
Katandra VIC 42 B4
Katanning WA 74 G5
Katherine NT 85 J5 86 G6
Katoomba NSW 21 K9 22 G7
Katrine WA 72 D2
Kattyoong VIC 28 H3 40 E4
Katunga VIC 29 K10 42 A4
Katyil VIC 40 K5
Kau Rock Nature Res WA 75 F14 83 J1
Kawana Waters QLD 4 D1
Kawarren VIC 39 J10
Kayena TAS 55 E9 56 D3
Kedron QLD 3 C4 4 E7
Keep River Nat Park NT 81 E14 86 J1 88 A1
Keera NSW 24 F7
Keilor VIC 35 B1 36 C6 39 F13 42 J1 44 B1
Keilor North VIC 35 B1
Keith SA 63 B10
Kellalac VIC 40 K6
Kellatier TAS 54 D4
Kellerberrin WA 74 C6 76 K7
Kellevie TAS 51 B12 53 F12
Kellidie Bay Con Park SA 64 H5
Kelly Hill Caves Con Park SA 63 J9
Kellys Creek NSW 22 H3
Kellyville NSW 19 B1 20 E7
Kelmscott WA 72 F4 74 D3
Kelso TAS 55 D8 56 C2
Kelvin NSW 24 H6
Kelvin Grove QLD 2 A2 3 E3
Kembla Heights NSW 21 D14
Kemps Creek NSW 21 F9
Kempsey NSW 25 J12
Kempton TAS 53 E10
Kendall NSW 23 B13
Kendenup WA 74 J6
Kenebri NSW 24 H3
Kenilworth QLD 7 E12
Kenley VIC 41 D9
Kenmare VIC 28 K4 40 H5
Kenmore QLD 3 F2 5 F8
Kenmore Hills QLD 3 F2
Kennedy QLD 11 F13
Kennedy Range Nat Park WA 78 H2
Kennedys Creek VIC 39 J9
Kenneth Stirling Con Park SA 60 G4
Kennett River VIC 39 K10
Kenny ACT 32 B5
Kennys Creek NSW 22 J4 30 B3
Kensington NSW 21 B9
Kensington SA 59 G5 60 G3 61 A7
Kensington VIC 35 D3
Kensington WA 71 G4
Kensington Gardens SA 59 G6
Kent Town SA 58 C3
Kentbruck VIC 38 H3
Kenthurst NSW 19 B2
Kentlyn Ruse NSW 21 E11
Kenton Valley SA 60 F5
Kentucky NSW 25 H9
Kentville QLD 5 K8
Kenwick WA 71 J6
Keperra QLD 3 D2 4 F7
Keppel Bay Islands Nat Park QLD 9 G11
Keppel Sands QLD 9 H10
Keppoch SA 63 B11
Kerang VIC 28 J7 41 G10
Kerang East VIC 41 H11
Kerang South VIC 41 H11
Kerein Hills NSW 29 B12
Kergunyah VIC 43 C9
Kernot VIC 37 K12 44 F4
Kerrabee NSW 22 D7
Kerrisdale VIC 42 G3
Kerriwah NSW 27 K13 29 B13
Kerrs Creek NSW 22 E4
Kerry QLD 5 E13
Kersbrook SA 60 E5 62 E6 65 J10
Keswick SA 58 D1
Kettering TAS 50 H5 53 H10
Kevin SA 64 C1 68 K6
Kevington VIC 42 H6 46 B1
Kew NSW 23 B13
Kew VIC 35 D4
Kewdale WA 71 G6
Kewell VIC 38 A6
Keyneton SA 62 E6 65 H11
Keysborough VIC 35 H6 37 F9
Keysbrook WA 72 F5
Khancoban NSW 29 K14 30 G1 43 C13
Khappinghat Nature Res NSW 23 C13
Khatambuhl Nature Res NSW 23 B11
Kholo QLD 5 H8
Ki Ki SA 63 D8 65 K11

Kia Ora – Lamplough 101

Kia Ora VIC 38 E7
Kiacatoo NSW 29 C12
Kiah NSW 30 K5 47 B14
Kialla NSW 22 K5 30 B4
Kialla VIC 42 D3
Kiama NSW 23 K8 30 C7
Kiamal VIC 28 H4 40 D5
Kiandra NSW 30 F2 43 A14
Kianga NSW 30 G5
Kianga QLD 9 K9
Kiata VIC 40 K4
Kidman Park SA 59 F2
Kidston QLD 11 G10
Kielpa SA 64 F6
Kiewa VIC 43 C9
Kikoira NSW 29 D12
Kilburn SA 59 E4 60 F2
Kilcoy QLD 4 J3 7 F12
Kilcunda VIC 44 G4
Kilcunda Road VIC 37 K13
Kilkenny SA 59 F3
Kilkivan QLD 7 D11
Killabakh NSW 23 B12
Killabakh Nature Res NSW 23 B12
Killara NSW 19 D5 20 C7
Killara VIC 37 C11
Killarney QLD 7 J11 25 A11
Killarney VIC 38 H6
Killarney Heights NSW 19 D6 20 C7
Killarney Nature Res NSW 23 C11
Killarney Vale NSW 20 B3
Killcare NSW 20 B5 23 G10
Killi Killi WA 79 D14
Killiecrankie TAS 55 A8
Kilmany VIC 45 D10 46 F3
Kilmore VIC 39 D14 42 G2
Kimba SA 62 K2 64 E6
Kimberley TAS 54 F7
Kimbriki NSW 23 B12
Kimburra QLD 8 C3 11 K12
Kin Kin QLD 7 D12
Kinalung NSW 26 K3 28 A3
Kinchega Nat Park NSW 26 K3 28 B3
Kinchela Creek NSW 25 J12
Kincumber NSW 20 B4
Kindee NSW 23 A12 25 K11
Kindred TAS 54 E7
King Ash Bay NT 87 K12 89 A12
King George Island TAS 51 E12
King Island QLD 16 H5
King Island TAS 54 B6
King Leopold Ranges Con Park WA 79 A11 81 G9
King Sound WA 79 A10 80 F5
King Valley VIC 42 E7
Kingaroy QLD 7 E10
Kingfisher Bay QLD 7 B13
Kingfisher Island WA 80 E6
Kinglake VIC 37 A10 42 J3 44 A3
Kinglake Central VIC 37 A10 42 H3 44 A3
Kinglake East VIC 37 A10
Kinglake Nat Park VIC 37 A10 39 D14 42 H3 44 A3
Kinglake West VIC 42 H3
Kingoonya SA 64 A5 66 K5
Kingower VIC 39 A10
Kings Cross NSW 18 C3 21 B8
Kings Langley NSW 19 C1
Kings Plains Nat Park NSW 25 E9
Kings Point NSW 30 E6
Kingsborough QLD 11 D12
Kingsbury VIC 35 B4 37 C8
Kingscliff NSW 7 J14 25 A14
Kingscote SA 63 H8 65 K8
Kingsdale NSW 22 K6 30 B4
Kingsford NSW 19 G6 21 B9
Kingsholme QLD 5 C11
Kingsley WA 71 B2
Kingston ACT 31 D4 32 E5
Kingston QLD 3 K5 5 E9
Kingston TAS 50 E6 53 G10
Kingston VIC 39 D11
Kingston OM SA 62 B5 65 H12
Kingston SE SA 63 D11
Kingstown NSW 25 G8
Kingsvale NSW 22 J2 30 B1
Kingswood NSW 21 G8
Kingswood SA 59 H4
Kinimakatka VIC 40 K3
Kinlyside ACT 32 A3
Kinnabulla VIC 40 H7
Kinrara Nat Park QLD 11 F12
Kioloa NSW 30 E6
Kirkstall VIC 38 H6
Kirramingly Nature Res NSW 24 E5
Kirrawee NSW 19 J3
Kirup WA 73 F11 74 G3
Kitchener WA 77 J14 83 F3
Kithbrook VIC 42 E5
Kiwirrkurra WA 79 G13
Klemzig SA 59 E5
Knight Island QLD 9 D9
Knorrit Flat NSW 23 B11
Knowsley VIC 39 B13
Knoxfield VIC 37 D9
Kobyboyn VIC 42 F3
Koetong VIC 29 K13 43 B11
Kogan QLD 7 F8
Kogarah NSW 19 H4
Koimbo VIC 28 H5 40 D7
Kojonup WA 73 A11 74 G5
Kokotungo QLD 9 J9
Koloona NSW 24 E7
Koloro VIC 38 G7
Komungla NSW 30 C4
Kondalilla Nat Park QLD 4 G1
Kondinin WA 74 D7
Kongal SA 63 B10
Kongorong SA 63 B14
Kongwak VIC 44 G5
Konongwootong VIC 38 E4
Konupa QLD 8 K1 13 H10 15 A10
Kookaburra NSW 25 J11
Kookynie WA 77 G11 83 E1
Koolamarra QLD 10 J4
Koolan WA 80 E6
Koolan Island WA 80 E6
Koolewong NSW 20 C4
Koolgera Con Res SA 64 D4
Kooloonong VIC 28 G5 41 D8
Kooltandra QLD 9 G9
Koolunga SA 62 F3 65 F9
Koolyanobbing WA 75 A9 77 J9
Koombooloomba QLD 11 E12
Koonda VIC 28 H2 40 E3 42 D5
Koondoola WA 71 C4
Koondrook VIC 28 J7 41 G11
Koongawa SA 64 F6
Koonibba SA 64 C2 68 K7
Koonibba Community SA 64 C2 68 K7
Koonoomoo VIC 42 A4
Koonunga SA 62 E5 65 H10
Koonwarra VIC 44 G6
Koonya TAS 51 G12 53 G12
Kooraban Nat Park NSW 30 G5
Koorabye WA 80 J7
Kooragang Nature Res NSW 23 E11
Kooralbyn QLD 5 G13
Koorarawalyee WA 75 B10 77 J9
Koorawatha NSW 22 H3
Koorawatha Nature Res NSW 22 H3 30 A2
Koorboora QLD 11 E11
Koorda WA 74 A5 76 J6
Koorebang Nature Res NSW 23 A12 25 K11
Kooreh VIC 39 A9
Kooringal QLD 4 B7
Koorkab VIC 28 G5 41 D8
Koorlong VIC 28 F3 40 A5
Kooroocheang VIC 39 D11
Koorrabye WA 79 C11
Kootingal NSW 25 J8
Koo-wee-rup VIC 37 H11 44 E4
Koo-wee-rup North VIC 37 G11
Kooyoora State Park VIC 39 A10
Kopi SA 64 F5
Koppio SA 64 H6
Korbel WA 74 C7 76 K7
Koreelah Nat Park NSW 25 A11
Koriella VIC 42 G4
Korobeit VIC 36 A3
Koroit VIC 38 H6
Korong Vale VIC 41 K10
Koroop VIC 41 G11
Korora NSW 25 G13
Korrak Korrak VIC 41 G10
Korumburra VIC 37 K13 44 F5
Korumburra South VIC 37 K14
Korunye SA 60 A1
Kosciuszko Nat Park NSW 30 G1 43 C14
Kotta VIC 41 J12
Kotupna VIC 41 J14 42 B2
Koukandowie Nature Res NSW 25 F12
Koumala QLD 9 E8
Koumala South QLD 9 E8
Kowanyama QLD 10 A7 16 K1
Kowguran QLD 6 D7
Kowtah WA 77 F11 83 D1
Kowulka SA 64 C1 68 K6
Koyuga VIC 41 J13 42 B1
Krambach NSW 23 C12
Kroombit Tops Nat Park QLD 9 J11
Krowera VIC 37 K12 44 F4
Kudardup WA 73 J13 74 H1
Kudla SA 60 C3
Kukerin WA 74 F7
Kulail NT 79 J14 90 H1
Kulde SA 62 D7 65 K11
Kulger Rail Head NT 90 J7
Kulgera NT 66 A1 68 A6 90 J7
Kulgera Rail Head NT 66 A2 68 A7
Kulikup WA 73 C11
Kulin WA 74 E7
Kulingalimpa NT 88 F4
Kulitjara SA 68 C5
Kulja WA 76 H6
Kulkami SA 62 B7 65 K12
Kulkyne VIC 28 G4 40 C6
Kulliparu Con Park SA 64 E4
Kulliparu Con Res SA 64 F4
Kulnine VIC 28 F2 40 A3
Kulnine East VIC 28 F2 40 A3
Kulnura NSW 20 D2 23 F9
Kulpara SA 62 G5 65 G9
Kulpi QLD 7 F10
Kulpitarra NT 90 F5
Kultanaby SA 64 A5
Kulwin VIC 28 H4 40 E6
Kulyalling WA 72 B5
Kumarina Roadhouse WA 78 H6 82 K6
Kumarl WA 75 E12 83 H1
Kumbarilla QLD 7 F9
Kumbatine Nat Park NSW 25 J11
Kumbia QLD 7 E10
Kunamata SA 68 B2
Kunapula NT 79 J14 83 A7 90 H1
Kunat VIC 41 G9
Kunatjara SA 68 B1 79 K14 83 B7 90 K1
Kunawarara QLD 9 G10
Kunawarritji WA 79 F11
Kunayangku NT 89 H8
Kundabung NSW 25 K12
Kundana WA 77 H11
Kundip Nature Res WA 75 G10
Kundora QLD 12 B4
Kungala NSW 25 F12
Kunghur NSW 7 J13 25 B13
Kunlara SA 62 C6 65 J12
Kunmunya Mission WA 80 D7
Kununurra WA 81 D14
Kunytjanu SA 68 B1 83 B7
Kupungarri WA 79 A12 81 F9
Kuraby QLD 3 J5 5 E9
Kuranda QLD 11 D12
Kurbayia QLD 12 B4
Kuri Bay WA 80 D7
Kuridala QLD 12 B5
Ku-ring-gai Chase Nat Park NSW 19 A6 20 C6 23 G9
Kurkatingara NT 79 J14 83 A7
Kurkutjara NT 68 A1 90 K1
Kurmond NSW 20 G6
Kurnbrunin VIC 28 K3 40 H4
Kurnell NSW 19 J6 21 B10
Kurnwill VIC 28 G2 40 B2
Kurraca VIC 39 A10
Kurraca West VIC 39 A9
Kurrajong NSW 20 H7 23 G8
Kurrajong WA 77 F10
Kurrajong Heights NSW 20 H6
Kurralta Park SA 59 H3
Kurrawang WA 75 A12 77 J11 83 F1
Kurri Kurri NSW 23 E10
Kurrimine QLD 11 E13
Kurrimine Beach Nat Park QLD 11 E13
Kuruala WA 83 C6
Kurumbul QLD 7 J8 24 B7
Kurwongbah QLD 4 G6
Kutjurntari WA 79 J14 83 A7
Kutkabubba WA 77 B9 78 K7
Kuttabul QLD 9 D8
Kwiambal Nat Park NSW 7 K9 25 C8
Kwinana WA 72 G5 74 D2
Ky Valley VIC 41 K14 42 C2
Kyabram VIC 41 K14 42 C2
Kyalite NSW 28 H6 41 D9
Kyancutta SA 64 E5
Kybeyan NSW 30 G4
Kybeyan Nature Res NSW 30 G4
Kybunga SA 62 F4 65 G10
Kybybolite SA 38 B1 63 A11
Kydra NSW 30 H4
Kyeamba NSW 29 J13
Kyeema Con Park SA 61 E7
Kylie WA 73 B10
Kyndalyn VIC 40 C7
Kyneton VIC 39 D12
Kynuna QLD 12 B7
Kyogle NSW 7 J13 25 B13
Kywong NSW 29 H12

L

La Perouse NSW 19 H6 21 B9
Laanecoorie VIC 39 B11
Laang VIC 38 H7
Labertouche VIC 37 F13 44 D5
Labrador QLD 5 B12
Lacepede Islands WA 79 A8 80 F3
Lachlan TAS 50 C2 53 F9
Lachlan Island TAS 53 E13
Lackrana TAS 55 B9
Lacmalac NSW 30 D1
Lacrosse Island WA 81 C13
La-Djardarr Bay WA 79 A9 80 F5
Lady Annie Mine QLD 10 J3
Lady Barron TAS 55 C9
Lady Bay SA 61 H3
Lady Elliot Island QLD 9 J13
Lady Jane – Orabanda Mine WA 77 H10
Lady Julia Percy Island VIC 38 J5
Lady Musgrave Island QLD 9 J13
Ladys Pass VIC 39 B13 42 E1
Laen VIC 40 K7
Laggan NSW 22 J5 30 B4
Lagoon Island QLD 5 C10
Lagrange Bay WA 79 C8 80 J2
Laguna Quays QLD 9 C8
Lah VIC 40 J6
Lah-Arum VIC 38 C6
Laheys Creek NSW 22 C5
Laidley QLD 5 K9 7 G11
Lajamanu NT 88 E3
Lake Ace Nature Res WA 75 E9
Lake Acraman SA 64 C5
Lake Aerodrome WA 79 H8
Lake Albacutya VIC 28 K3 40 G4
Lake Albacutya Park VIC 28 J3 40 G4
Lake Albert SA 63 E8
Lake Alexandrina SA 63 E8 65 K10
Lake Altibouka NSW 26 D4
Lake Amadeus NT 90 H3
Lake Anec WA 79 H13
Lake Annean WA 76 C7 78 K5
Lake Anthony SA 66 J1 68 G7
Lake Argyle WA 79 A14 81 E14
Lake Argyle Village WA 81 E14
Lake Auld WA 79 F10
Lake Austin WA 76 D7
Lake Awoonga QLD 9 J11
Lake Ballard WA 77 G10
Lake Barlee WA 77 F9
Lake Bathurst NSW 30 C4
Lake Bedford WA 77 B13 79 K9
Lake Bennett NT 90 E4
Lake Betty WA 79 D12
Lake Biddy WA 75 E8
Lake Bindegolly Nat Park QLD 15 H10
Lake Blair WA 79 J11
Lake Blanche SA 67 G12
Lake Blanche WA 79 F9
Lake Boga VIC 28 J6
Lake Bolac VIC 38 F7
Lake Boonderoo WA 77 J14 83 G3
Lake Breaden WA 79 K11 83 A4
Lake Bremner WA 77 A13 79 J9 83 A2
Lake Brewster NSW 29 D11
Lake Bring SA 66 J1 68 G6
Lake Brown WA 74 A7 76 J7
Lake Buchanan QLD 8 E3 13 B13
Lake Buchanan WA 77 A13 79 J9 83 A2
Lake Buck NT 88 G3
Lake Buloke VIC 40 K7 41 K8
Lake Burnside WA 79 J9
Lake Burragorang NSW 21 H11 22 H7
Lake Cadibarrawirracanna SA 66 G5
Lake Callabonna SA 67 H13
Lake Campion Nature Res WA 74 A7 77 J8
Lake Carey WA 77 F12 83 D1
Lake Cargelligo NSW 29 D11
Lake Carnegie WA 77 B12 79 K9 83 B2
Lake Cathie NSW 23 A13 25 K12
Lake Cawndilla NSW 28 B3
Lake Charm VIC 28 J6 41 G10
Lake Christopher WA 79 J13
Lake Clifton WA 72 G7
Lake Cootabarlow SA 67 J13
Lake Corangamite VIC 39 H9
Lake Cowal NSW 29 D13
Lake Cowan WA 75 C13 77 K12
Lake Dalrymple QLD 8 C5 13 A14
Lake Dartmouth VIC 43 D11
Lake Deborah East WA 75 A9 77 H9
Lake Deborah West WA 75 A8 77 H8
Lake Dennis WA 79 E14
Lake Dey Dey SA 68 F4
Lake Disappointment WA 79 G9
Lake Dora WA 79 F9
Lake Dundas WA 83 H1
Lake Eildon VIC 42 G5
Lake Eildon Nat Park VIC 42 G5
Lake Etamunbanie SA 14 D2 67 B12
Lake Eucumbene NSW 30 G2
Lake Everade SA 64 B4
Lake Eyre Nat Park SA 67 F8
Lake Eyre North SA 67 F8
Lake Eyre South SA 67 G8
Lake Farnham WA 79 J13
Lake Frome SA 65 A12
Lake Frome Con Park SA 63 C13
Lake Frome Reg Res SA 65 A12 67 K12
Lake Gairdner SA 64 C6
Lake Gairdner Nat Park SA 64 B6
Lake Galilee QLD 8 F3 13 D13
Lake George NSW 30 D4
Lake George WA 79 F10
Lake Gillen WA 79 K10 83 B3
Lake Gilles SA 62 J1
Lake Gilles Con Park SA 62 K2 64 E7
Lake Gilmore WA 75 E12 83 H1
Lake Gleeson QLD 8 A5
Lake Goldsmith VIC 39 E9
Lake Gordon TAS 52 F6
Lake Goyder SA 14 F3 67 C13
Lake Grace WA 74 F7
Lake Gregory SA 67 G11
Lake Gregory WA 79 D13
Lake Griselda SA 67 C8
Lake Gruszka WA 79 J11 83 A4
Lake Hancock WA 79 J11
Lake Hanson SA 64 A6
Lake Harris SA 64 A5
Lake Harry SA 67 H10
Lake Hart SA 64 B6
Lake Hazlett WA 79 F14
Lake Hindmarsh VIC 40 J4
Lake Hoar WA 79 J10
Lake Hope WA 75 D10
Lake Hopkins WA 79 H14 90 G1
Lake Howitt SA 67 D10
Lake Hume NSW VIC 29 K13 43 B9
Lake Hurlstone Nature Res WA 75 E9
Lake Innes Nature Res NSW 23 A13 25 K12
Lake Jindabyne NSW 30 G2
Lake Johnston WA 75 D11
Lake Jones WA 79 J10
Lake Julius QLD 10 J4
Lake Keene WA 77 A13 79 J9 83 A3
Lake Keepit NSW 24 H6
Lake King WA 75 F9
Lake King Nature Res WA 75 F9
Lake King William TAS 52 C7 54 K7
Lake Koodnanie SA 67 D11
Lake Labyrinth SA 64 A4 66 K4
Lake Lanagan WA 79 D12
Lake Leagur NSW 28 D5
Lake Leake TAS 53 B12 55 J12
Lake Lefroy WA 75 B13
Lake Lockhart WA 75 F8
Lake Logue Nature Res WA 76 G4
Lake Macdonald WA 79 H14
Lake MacFarlane SA 64 C7
Lake Mackay WA 79 F14 90 D1
Lake MacLeod WA 78 H1
Lake Macquarie NSW 23 F10
Lake Magenta WA 75 F8
Lake Magenta Nature Res WA 75 G8
Lake Maraboon QLD 8 H6
Lake Marmal VIC 41 J9
Lake Marmion WA 77 G11 83 E1
Lake Mason WA 77 D9
Lake Maurice SA 68 F4
Lake McLernon WA 79 D12
Lake Meering VIC 28 K6 41 H10
Lake Menindee NSW 28 B3
Lake Meramangye SA 68 E5
Lake Milkengay NSW 28 D3
Lake Mindona NSW 28 D3
Lake Minigwal WA 83 E2
Lake Mipia QLD 12 H4 14 A1
Lake Miranda WA 77 D10
Lake Mokoan VIC 42 D6
Lake Moondarra QLD 10 K4
Lake Moore WA 76 G6
Lake Muck NSW 26 E1
Lake Muir WA 73 C14 74 J4
Lake Muir Nature Res WA 73 C14 74 J4
Lake Mulwala NSW 29 K11 42 A6
Lake Mundi VIC 38 E2
Lake Mungo NSW 28 E5
Lake Munmorah NSW 20 A1
Lake Murphy Con Park QLD 6 B6
Lake Nabberu WA 78 J7
Lake Neale NT 90 G2
Lake Newell WA 79 J12
Lake Newland Con Park SA 64 F4
Lake Noondie WA 77 E8
Lake Owen WA 77 H10
Lake Pedder TAS 52 G6
Lake Philipi QLD 12 G3
Lake Phillipson SA 66 H3
Lake Pure QLD 14 E4
Lake Raeside WA 77 G11
Lake Rason WA 77 F14 83 D3
Lake Rebecca WA 77 H12 83 E1
Lake Roe WA 75 A14 77 H12 83 F2
Lake Rowan VIC 42 C5
Lake Seabrook WA 75 A9 77 J9
Lake Shaster Nature Res WA 75 G11
Lake Sorell TAS 53 B10 55 J10
Lake St Clair TAS 52 B6 54 J6
Lake Starvation SA 26 F1 67 K14
Lake Sunshine WA 78 H7
Lake Surprise NT 88 H5
Lake Tallacootra SA 68 J5
Lake Tandou NSW 28 B3
Lake Tay WA 75 E11
Lake Teague WA 77 B10 78 K7
Lake Tobin WA 79 F11
Lake Torrens SA 65 A9 67 K9
Lake Torrens Nat Park SA 65 A9 67 K9
Lake Tourquinie QLD 12 G2
Lake Tyers VIC 43 K13 46 E7
Lake Tyers State Park VIC 43 K12 46 D7
Lake Tyrrell VIC 28 J5 40 F7
Lake Ulenia NSW 26 E3
Lake Uloowaranie SA 14 D1 67 B12
Lake Urana NSW 29 H11
Lake Urana Nature Res NSW 29 H11
Lake Varley Nature Res WA 75 E9
Lake Victoria NSW 28 E2
Lake View SA 62 G4 65 F9
Lake Waukarlycarly WA 79 E8
Lake Way WA 77 C10 78 K7
Lake Wells WA 77 C13 83 B2
Lake White WA 79 E14
Lake Wilderness WA 78 H7
Lake Wills WA 79 E14
Lake Windabout SA 65 B8
Lake Winifred WA 79 G9
Lake Wivenhoe QLD 4 J6 7 F12
Lake Woods NT 88 D7
Lake Wyangala NSW 22 H4
Lake Wyangan NSW 29 F11
Lake Yamma Yamma QLD 12 K7 14 D5
Lake Yindarlgooda WA 83 F1
Lake Younghusband SA 64 A6 66 K6
Lakefield Nat Park QLD 11 A10 16 J5
Lakeland QLD 11 B11
Lakeland Nature Res WA 75 F8
Lakemba NSW 21 C9
Lakes Entrance VIC 43 K12 45 C14 46 E7
Lakeside VIC 37 E11
Lal Lal VIC 39 E11
Lalbert VIC 28 J6 41 G9
Lalbert Road VIC 41 G9
Lalla TAS 55 E10 56 E5
Lalor Park NSW 21 E8
Lamb Island QLD 5 B9
Lameroo SA 63 B8 65 K13
Lamington Nat Park QLD 5 D14 7 J13 25 A13
Lamplough VIC 39 C9

102 Lana – Margate

Lana QLD 13 C9
Lancaster VIC 41 K14 42 C2
Lancefield VIC 39 D13 42 G1
Lancelin WA 74 A2 76 J4
Lancevale QLD 8 H3 13 F13
Landed at Last Mine WA 77 F12 83 D1
Landsborough QLD 4 F2 7 E12
Landsborough VIC 39 C8
Landsdale WA 71 B4
Landsdowne NSW 23 B12
Lane Cove NSW 19 E5 21 C8
Lane Cove Nat Park NSW 19 D4
Lane Poole Con Park WA 72 F7 73 E8 74 E3
Lane Poole Con Res WA 73 E8 74 F4
Lang Lang VIC 37 H12 44 E4
Langford WA 71 J5
Langhorne Creek SA 63 E8 65 K10
Langi-Ghiran State Park VIC 39 D8
Langkoop VIC 38 C2 63 A12
Langlo Crossing QLD 13 K12 15 D13
Langtree NSW 29 E10
Langtree Nature Res NSW 29 D10
Langwarrin VIC 37 G9
Lankeys Creek NSW 29 K14 43 A11
Lannercost QLD 11 G13
Lansdowne NSW 19 F2
Lansvale NSW 21 D9
Lapaku WA 79 J13 83 A6
Lapoinya TAS 54 D4
Lappa QLD 11 E11
Lapstone NSW 21 G9
Lara VIC 36 F3 39 G12
Lara Lake VIC 39 G12
Laramba NT 90 D6
Laravale QLD 5 F13
Lardner VIC 37 H14
Largs Bay SA 59 D1 60 E1
Lark Quarry Env Park QLD 13 E8
Larpent VIC 39 H9
Larrakeyah NT 84 E1
Larras Lee NSW 22 E4
Larrimah NT 86 J7 88 A7
Lascelles VIC 28 J4 40 G6
Laterite Con Park WA 81 C9
Latham ACT 32 B2
Latham WA 76 G5
Lathami Con Park SA 63 J8 65 K8
Latrobe TAS 54 E7
Lauderdale TAS 51 D8 53 G11
Launceston TAS 55 F10 56 G5
Launching Place VIC 37 C12 42 K4 44 B4
Laura QLD 11 B11 16 K5
Laura SA 62 F2 65 F9
Laura Bay SA 64 D2 68 K7
Laurieton NSW 23 B13
Lauriston VIC 39 D12
Lavers Hill VIC 39 K9
Laverton VIC 36 D6 39 F13 42 K1
Laverton WA 77 F12 83 D1
Lavington NSW 29 K12 43 B9
Lavinia Nature Res TAS 54 A6
Lawler VIC 40 K7
Lawlers WA 77 E10
Lawlers Mine WA 77 E10
Lawley River Nat Park WA 81 B9
Lawloit VIC 40 K3
Lawnton QLD 4 F6
Lawrence NSW 25 E13
Lawrenny TAS 53 E8
Lawson ACT 32 C4
Lawson NSW 21 J9 22 G7
Lawson Island NT 86 A6
Leadville NSW 22 B5
Leaghur VIC 28 K6 41 H10
Leaghur State Park VIC 28 K7 41 H10
Learmonth VIC 39 D10
Learmonth WA 78 F1
Lebrina TAS 55 E10 56 D6
Ledge Point WA 74 B2 76 J4
Lednapper Crossing NSW 27 D11
Lednapper Nature Res NSW 27 C11
Leedawooloo WA 79 B13 81 J12
Leeka TAS 55 B8
Leeman WA 76 H3
Leeming WA 71 J4
Leeor VIC 40 K2
Leeton NSW 29 G11
Leeuwin-Naturaliste Nat Park WA 73 K13 74 G1
Lefroy TAS 55 D9 56 C4
Legana TAS 55 F9 56 F4
Legendre Island WA 78 D4 82 B2
Legerwood TAS 55 E12
Legume NSW 25 A11
Legunia TAS 55 E12
Leicester Island QLD 9 F10
Leichhardt NSW 19 F5 21 C9
Leigh Creek SA 65 A10 67 K10
Leigh Creek Coalfield SA 67 K10
Leighton SA 62 E4 65 G10
Leinster WA 77 E10
Leinster Mine WA 77 D10
Leitchville VIC 28 K7 41 H12
Leith TAS 54 E7
Leitpar VIC 28 H4 40 E6
Lemana TAS 55 G8
Lemon Tree Passage NSW 23 E11
Lemont TAS 53 D11 55 K11
Leneva VIC 29 K12 43 C9
Lennox Head NSW 7 K14 25 C14
Lenswood SA 60 F5
Leonards Hill VIC 39 D11
Leonay NSW 21 G9
Leongatha VIC 37 K14 44 F6
Leongatha South VIC 44 G5
Leonora WA 77 F11 83 D1
Leopold VIC 36 G4 39 H12
Leppington NSW 21 E10
Leprena TAS 53 K9
Lerderderg State Park VIC 36 A3 39 E12
Leslie Manor VIC 39 G9
Leslie Vale TAS 50 E5 53 G10
Lesmurdie Nat Park WA 71 G7 72 F3
Lesueur Con Park SA 63 G9
Lesueur Nat Park WA 76 H3
Letchworth NSW 32 G7
Lethbridge VIC 36 E1 39 G11
Leumeah NSW 21 E11
Leura NSW 21 K9 22 G7
Leven Beach Con Park SA 62 J7 65 J8
Levendale TAS 53 E11
Lewana WA 73 F12
Lewisham TAS 51 C9 53 F11
Lewiston SA 60 B2
Lexia WA 71 B5
Lexton VIC 39 D9
Leyburn QLD 7 H10
Liamana NSW 22 B5
Liawenee TAS 53 A8 55 H8
Licola VIC 43 J8 45 A9 46 C2
Lidcombe NSW 19 F3 21 D9
Liddell NSW 23 D9
Liena TAS 54 G6
Lietinna TAS 55 E11
Liffey TAS 55 G9 56 K2
Light Pass SA 60 A7
Lightning Ridge NSW 27 C14
Liguanea Island SA 64 J5
Lija NT 89 D10
Likkaparta NT 89 G9
Lileah TAS 54 D3
Lilli Pilli NSW 21 C10
Lillimur VIC 40 K2
Lillimur South VIC 38 A2 40 K2
Lilydale TAS 55 E10 56 E6
Lilydale VIC 37 C10 42 K3 44 B3
Lilyvale NSW 21 C12
Lima VIC 42 E5
Lima South VIC 42 E5
Limbri NSW 25 J8
Lime Bay Nature Res TAS 51 E11 53 G12
Lime Lake WA 73 A10
Limeburners Creek Nature Res NSW 23 A14 25 K12
Limekilns NSW 22 F6
Limerick NSW 22 J5 30 A4
Limestone VIC 42 G4
Limevale QLD 7 J9 25 B8
Limmen Nat Park (Proposed) 87 J10 89 A10
Limpinwood Nature Res NSW 25 A13
Lincoln Con Res SA 64 J5
Lincoln Gap SA 62 H1 65 E8
Lincoln Nat Park SA 64 J6
Lind Nat Park VIC 47 C10
Linda TAS 52 B4 54 J4
Lindeman Island QLD 9 C8
Lindeman Islands Nat Park QLD 9 C8
Linden NSW 21 J8
Lindenow VIC 43 K10 45 C12 46 D5
Lindfield NSW 19 D5 20 C7
Lindisfarne TAS 50 C6 53 F10
Lindsay Island VIC 40 A2
Linga VIC 28 H3 40 E3
Lingnoonganee Island QLD 10 C4
Linke Lakes WA 77 B13 79 K9 83 A2
Linne Islands QLD 9 C8
Linton VIC 39 F9
Linton Nature Res NSW 24 G7
Linville QLD 7 E11
Lipson SA 64 H6
Liptrap VIC 44 H5
Lisarow NSW 20 B4
Lisle TAS 55 E10 56 E7
Lismore NSW 7 K13 25 C13
Lismore VIC 39 G9
Liston NSW 25 B10
Litchfield VIC 40 K7
Litchfield Nat Park NT 85 E1 86 E3
Lithgow NSW 22 G7
Littabella Nat Park QLD 9 K12
Little Adolphus Island QLD 16 B2
Little Billabong NSW 29 J13
Little Desert Nat Park VIC 38 A3 63 A11
Little Dip Con Park SA 63 D12
Little Dog Island TAS 55 C9
Little Forest NSW 22 F5
Little Green Island TAS 55 C9
Little Llangothlin Nature Res NSW 25 F9
Little Mulgrave QLD 11 D13
Little Plain NSW 24 E7
Little River VIC 36 E4 39 G12
Little Snake Island VIC 45 H8 46 H2
Little Swanport TAS 53 D12
Littlehampton SA 60 H5
Littlemore QLD 9 K11
Liverpool NSW 19 G1 21 D9 23 H8
Liveseys WA 72 A2
Livingstone Nat Park NSW 29 H13
Lizard Island Nat Park QLD 16 J7
Llandaff TAS 53 B14 55 J13
Llandilo NSW 21 G8
Llangothlin NSW 25 F9
Lloyd Bay QLD 16 F4
Loamside QLD 5 H10
Lobethal SA 60 F5 62 E7 65 J10
Loch VIC 37 J13 44 F5
Loch Sport VIC 45 D13 46 E6
Lochaber SA 63 B11
Lochern Nat Park QLD 13 F9
Lochiel NSW 30 J5 47 A13
Lochiel SA 62 G4 65 G9
Lochinvar NSW 23 D10
Lochnagar QLD 8 H3 13 F12
Lock SA 64 F5
Lockhart NSW 29 H12
Lockhart River QLD 16 F4
Lockington VIC 41 K12
Lockleys SA 59 G2 60 G1 61 A5
Lockridge WA 71 D6
Lockrose QLD 5 K8
Locksley VIC 42 E3
Lockwood VIC 39 B11
Lockwood South VIC 39 B11
Loddon QLD 15 E12
Loddon Vale VIC 28 K7 41 H11
Loftus NSW 19 K3 21 C10
Logan QLD 7 G13
Logan VIC 39 A9
Logan Central QLD 3 J5
Logan Village QLD 5 E11
Loganholme QLD 3 K7 5 D10
Loganlea QLD 3 K6 5 D10
Lombadina WA 79 A9 80 E4
Londonderry NSW 20 G7
Long Beach NSW 30 E6
Long Flat NSW 23 A12 25 K11
Long Gully VIC 37 B11
Long Island QLD 4 E3 5 B10 9 C8 9 F9
Long Island TAS 55 A13
Long Island WA 78 F2
Long Plains SA 62 F5 65 H9
Long Plains VIC 40 F7
Long Pocket QLD 3 F3
Longerenong VIC 38 B6
Longford TAS 55 G10 56 J5
Longford VIC 45 E11 46 F4
Longlea VIC 39 B12
Longley TAS 50 E4 53 G10
Longreach QLD 8 H1 13 E10
Longwarry VIC 37 G13 44 D5
Longwarry North VIC 37 F13
Longwood SA 59 K7 60 H3 61 B7
Longwood VIC 42 E3
Lonnavale TAS 53 G9
Lonsdale SA 60 J1 61 C5
Looma WA 79 B10 80 H6
Loomberah NSW 25 J8
Loongana TAS 54 F6
Loongana WA 83 F5
Loorana TAS 54 B6
Lorinna TAS 54 G6
Lorne NSW 23 B13
Lorne SA 62 G5 65 H9
Lorne VIC 39 J11
Lorquon VIC 40 J4
Lostock NSW 23 C10
Lota QLD 3 E7
Lottah TAS 55 E13
Loughnan Nature Res NSW 29 D10
Louisville TAS 53 E12
Louth NSW 27 F9
Louth Bay SA 64 H6
Louth Island SA 64 H6
Loveday SA 62 B5 65 H13
Lovett Bay NSW 19 A7
Low Head TAS 55 D9 56 B2
Low Hill SA 64 D7
Lowan Con Park SA 62 D6 65 J11
Lowana TAS 52 C3 54 K3
Lowden WA 73 F10 74 G3
Lowdina TAS 53 E11
Lower Barrington TAS 54 E7
Lower Beechmont QLD 5 D13
Lower Bendoc VIC 47 A11
Lower Beulah TAS 54 F7
Lower Bucca NSW 25 F13
Lower Creek NSW 25 H11
Lower Cresswell QLD 4 K4
Lower Frankland WA 73 B14
Lower Gellibrand VIC 39 K9
Lower Glenelg Nat Park VIC 38 G3 63 A14
Lower Hawkesbury NSW 20 E5
Lower Hermitage SA 60 E4
Lower Heytesbury VIC 39 J8
Lower Light SA 60 B1 62 F6 65 H9
Lower Longley TAS 50 E3
Lower Mangrove NSW 20 D4
Lower Marshes TAS 53 D10
Lower Molonglo Nature Res ACT 32 D2
Lower Mookerawa NSW 22 E4
Lower Mount Hicks TAS 54 D5
Lower Mount Walker QLD 5 J10
Lower Norton VIC 38 B5
Lower Portland NSW 20 F5
Lower Turners Marsh TAS 55 E10 56 D5
Lower Wilmot TAS 54 E6
Lowesdale NSW 29 J11 42 A7
Lowlands NSW 20 G7 29 C9
Lowmead QLD 9 K12
Lowood QLD 5 J8 7 G12
Loxton SA 62 B6 65 H13
Loxton North SA 28 G1 62 B6 65 H13
Loy Yang VIC 45 E8 46 F2
Loyetea TAS 54 E5
Lubeck VIC 38 B6
Lucas Heights NSW 19 J2 21 D10
Lucaston TAS 50 E2 53 G9
Lucinda QLD 11 G14
Lucindale SA 63 B12
Lucknow NSW 22 F4
Lucknow VIC 43 K11 45 C13 46 D6
Lucky Bay SA 62 J4 64 G7
Lucky Flat NSW 24 G4
Lucyvale VIC 43 C11
Luddenham NSW 21 G10
Ludlow WA 73 H11 74 G2
Ludmilla NT 84 C2
Lue NSW 22 D6
Lugarno NSW 21 C10
Luina TAS 54 F3
Lul-Tju NT 88 E3
Lulworth TAS 55 D9 56 B4
Lumeah WA 73 A12
Lumuku WA 79 A14 81 G13
Lunawanna TAS 53 J10
Lune River TAS 53 J9
Lupton Con Park WA 72 C5 74 D4
Lurg VIC 42 D6
Lurnea NSW 21 E10
Luscombe QLD 5 D11
Lutwyche QLD 3 D4
Lymington TAS 50 J2 53 H9
Lymwood TAS 54 C6
Lynchford TAS 52 C4 54 K4
Lyndbrook QLD 11 E11
Lyndhurst NSW 22 G4
Lyndhurst SA 67 J10
Lyndhurst VIC 35 H7 37 F9 44 D2
Lyndoch SA 60 B5 62 E6 65 H10
Lyneham ACT 32 C5
Lyons ACT 32 F3
Lyons SA 64 A3 66 K3 68 H7
Lyons VIC 38 G3
Lyonville VIC 39 D12
Lyrup SA 28 F1 62 B5 65 H13
Lysterfield Lake Park VIC 37 E10 42 K3
Lytton QLD 3 D6 4 D7

M

Maaroom QLD 7 C13
Maatsuyker Group TAS 52 K7
Maatsuyker Island TAS 52 K7
Mabuiag Island QLD 16 A2
Mac Clark (Acacia Peuce) Con Res NT 91 H10
Macalister QLD 7 F9
Macarthur ACT 32 H5
Macarthur VIC 38 G5
Macclesfield SA 60 K5 62 E7 65 J10
Macclesfield VIC 37 D11
Macedon VIC 39 D13
Macgregor ACT 32 B2
MacGregor QLD 3 G5 5 E9
Mackay QLD 9 D8
MacKenzie QLD 3 G6
Macksville NSW 25 H12
Maclean NSW 25 D13
Macleay Island QLD 5 B9
Macleod VIC 35 B5 37 C8
Macorna VIC 28 K7 41 H11
Macquarie ACT 32 C3
Macquarie Fields NSW 21 E10
Macquarie Marshes Nature Res NSW 27 F13
Macquarie Pass Nat Park NSW 23 K8 30 B7
Macquarie Plains TAS 53 F9
Macrossan QLD 8 B4 11 J14
Macumba Oil Well SA 66 B7
Maddarr WA 79 A9 80 F5
Maddington WA 71 J7
Madora WA 72 G5
Madura WA 83 G5
Mafeking VIC 38 D6
Maffra NSW 30 H3
Maffra VIC 45 C10 46 E4
Maggea SA 62 C6 65 H12
Magill SA 59 F6 60 F3
Magnetic Island QLD 11 G14
Magnetic Island Nat Park QLD 11 G14
Magra TAS 50 A2 53 F9
Magrath Flat SA 63 D9
Maharatta NSW 30 J3 47 A12
Maianbar NSW 21 B10
Maida Vale WA 71 F7
Mailers Flat VIC 38 H6
Maimuru NSW 22 J2 30 A1
Main Beach QLD 5 B12
Main Creek NSW 23 C11
Main Range Nat Park QLD 5 K13 7 H11 25 A11
Maindample VIC 42 F5
Mainoru Store NT 87 F8
Mairjimmy NSW 29 J10
Maitland NSW 23 E10
Maitland SA 62 H5 65 H8
Major Plains VIC 42 C5
Majorca VIC 39 C10
Majors Creek NSW 30 E5
Majura ACT 32 C6
Makiri SA 68 C4
Makowata QLD 9 K12
Makurapiti SA 68 B1 83 B7
Malabar NSW 19 H6
Malaburra WA 79 A9 80 F5
Malaga WA 71 D5
Malanda QLD 11 E13
Malangan WA 79 B14 81 G14
Malbina TAS 50 B3 53 F10
Malbon QLD 12 B5
Malbooma SA 64 A3 66 K3
Malcolm WA 77 F11 83 D1
Maldon NSW 21 F12
Maldon VIC 39 C11
Malebelling WA 72 B3
Malebo NSW 29 H13
Maleny QLD 4 G1 7 E12
Malinong SA 63 D8 65 K11
Mallacoota VIC 47 C13
Mallala SA 62 F5 65 H10
Mallanganee NSW 25 C12
Mallanganee Nat Park NSW 7 K12 25 C12
Mallee Cliffs Nat Park NSW 28 F4 40 A6
Mallison Island NT 87 C12
Malmsbury VIC 39 C12
Malua Bay NSW 30 F6
Malvern SA 59 H4
Malvernton QLD 8 J2 13 G12
Mamboo QLD 8 H5 13 F14
Mambray Creek SA 62 G2 65 E9
Mammoth Mines QLD 10 J3
Manangatang VIC 28 H5 40 E7
Mandagery NSW 22 F3
Mandalong NSW 20 C1
Mandalup WA 73 E12
Mandorah NT 85 C1 86 D3
Mandurah WA 72 G6 74 E2
Mandurama NSW 22 G4
Mangalo SA 62 K3 64 F7
Mangalore QLD 15 E13
Mangalore TAS 53 E10
Mangalore VIC 39 B14 42 F3
Mangana TAS 55 G12
Mangkili Claypan Nature Res WA 77 A14 79 J10 83 A3
Mangoplah NSW 29 H13
Mangrove Creek NSW 20 D4
Mangrove Mountain NSW 20 D3 23 F9
Manguri SA 66 G3
Manildra NSW 22 F3
Manilla NSW 24 H7
Maninga Marley WA 77 E9
Maningrida NT 87 C9
Manjimup WA 73 E13 74 H3
Manly NSW 19 D7 20 B7 23 H9
Manly QLD 3 D7 5 D8
Manly Vale NSW 19 D6 20 B7
Manly West QLD 3 E7
Manmoyi NT 87 D8
Mann River Nature Res NSW 25 E10
Mannahill SA 62 C1 65 D12
Mannanarie SA 62 F2 65 E10
Mannerim VIC 36 H4
Mannering Park NSW 20 B1
Manning WA 71 H4
Manns Beach VIC 45 G9 46 H3
Mannum SA 62 D7 65 J11
Mannus NSW 29 J14 43 A12
Manobalai Nature Res NSW 23 C8
Manoora SA 62 E4 65 G10
Manor VIC 36 E4 39 F13
Manorina VIC 47 D10
Manowar Island QLD 10 C3
Mansfield QLD 3 G5
Mansfield VIC 42 F6 46 A1
Manton Dam Park NT 85 D2 86 E4
Mantung SA 62 C6 65 H12
Manuka ACT 32 F5
Manumbar QLD 7 D11
Many Peaks QLD 9 K11
Manyallaluk (Eva Valley) NT 85 H7 86 G6
Manyirkanga SA 68 A4 90 K4
Manypeaks WA 74 J7
Manyung QLD 7 D11
Mapleton QLD 7 E12
Mapoon QLD 16 D1
Mapurru NT 87 C10
Maralinga SA 68 G4
Marama SA 62 C7 65 K12
Marananga SA 60 A6
Maranboy NT 85 J7 86 G6
Marandoo Mine WA 78 G5 82 F4
Marangaroo WA 71 C3
Marathon QLD 13 A9
Marathon South QLD 13 A9
Maraylya NSW 20 F6
Marayong NSW 21 E8
Marble Bar WA 78 E6 82 D6
Marble Hill SA 60 F4
Marble Island QLD 9 E10
Marburg QLD 5 J9 7 G12
Marchagee WA 76 H5
Marchinbar Island NT 87 B12
Marcus Hill VIC 36 H4 39 H12
Mardan VIC 44 F6 46 G1
Mardella WA 72 F5
Mareeba QLD 11 D12
Marengo VIC 39 K10
Maret Islands WA 81 B8
Margaret River WA 73 K12 74 H1
Margate QLD 4 E6

Margate - Mornington 103

Margate TAS 50 F5 53 G10
Margooya VIC 28 G5 40 D7
Maria Island NT 87 H11
Maria Island TAS 53 F13
Maria Island Nat Park TAS 53 E13
Maria Nat Park NSW 25 J12
Mariala Nat Park QLD 13 K12 15 C11
Marian QLD 9 D8
Marimo QLD 10 K5 12 A5
Marino SA 59 K2 60 H1 61 B5
Marino Con Park SA 60 H1 61 B5
Marion SA 59 J3 60 H2 61 B6
Marion Bay SA 62 J7 64 K7
Mark Oliphant Con Park SA 60 H3 61 B7
Markwood VIC 42 D7
Marla SA 66 D2 68 C7
Marlborough QLD 9 G9
Marlee NSW 23 B12
Marleston SA 59 G3
Marley Pool WA 72 C3
Marlinja NT 88 D7
Marlo VIC 43 K14 47 D9
Marma VIC 38 B6
Marmion WA 71 C1
Marmion Marine Park WA 76 K4
Marmor QLD 9 H10
Marnoo VIC 38 A7
Marnoo East VIC 39 A8
Marong VIC 39 B11
Maroochydore QLD 4 D1 7 E13
Maroon QLD 5 H14
Maroona VIC 38 E7
Maroota NSW 20 E5
Maroota South NSW 20 E6
Maroubra NSW 19 G6 21 B9
Marp VIC 38 F2
Marraba QLD 12 A4
Marrabel SA 62 E5 65 G10
Marradong WA 72 D7 74 E4
Marramarra Nat Park NSW 20 D5 23 G9
Marrar NSW 29 G13
Marrawah TAS 54 C1
Marraweeny VIC 42 E4
Marree SA 67 H9
Marrickville NSW 21 C9
Marryat SA 66 B2 68 B7 90 K7
Marsden NSW 22 G1 29 E13
Marsden QLD 3 K5 5 E10
Marsden Park NSW 20 F7
Marsfield NSW 19 D4 21 C8
Marshall VIC 36 H3
Marshdale NSW 23 D11
Martin Washpool Con Park SA 63 D10
Martindale NSW 23 D8
Marton QLD 11 A2
Marulan NSW 22 K6 30 C5
Marunbabidi WA 81 D10
Marvel Loch WA 75 B9 77 K9
Mary Kathleen QLD 10 K4 12 A4
Mary River Con Park NT 85 C4
Mary River Con Res NT 86 D5
Mary River Nat Park NT 85 D4 86 D5
Mary River Roadhouse NT 85 F5 86 F5
Mary Seymour Con Park SA 63 B12
Maryborough QLD 7 C12
Maryborough VIC 39 C10
Maryfarms QLD 11 C12
Maryknoll VIC 37 F12
Maryland Nat Park NSW 25 A10
Marysville VIC 37 A13 42 H5 44 A5
Maryvale NSW 22 D4
Mascot NSW 19 G5 21 B9
Maslin Beach SA 61 E5 62 F7 65 K9
Massey VIC 40 J7
Masthead Island QLD 9 H12
Matakana NSW 29 C10
Mataranka NT 85 K7 86 H7
Mataranka Homestead NT 86 H7
Matcham NSW 20 B4
Matheson NSW 25 E9
Mathiesons VIC 39 A14 42 D2
Mathinna TAS 55 F12
Mathoura NSW 29 K8 41 H13 42 A1
Matlock VIC 42 J6 44 A7 46 C1
Matong NSW 29 G12
Matraville NSW 19 H6 21 B9
Maude NSW 28 F7 41 B12
Maude VIC 36 E1 39 G11
Maudsland QLD 5 C12
Mawbanna TAS 54 D3
Mawson ACT 32 G4
Mawson WA 72 A3
Mawson Lakes SA 59 C4
Maxwelton QLD 11 K8 13 A8
Maya WA 76 G5
Mayanup WA 73 D12 74 G4
Mayberry TAS 54 G7
Maybole NSW 25 F9
Maydena TAS 53 F8
Mayfield Bay Con Area TAS 53 C13 55 K13
Maylands WA 71 F5
Maynard Bore SA 68 C5
Mayrung NSW 29 J9
Maytown QLD 11 B10
Mazeppa Nat Park QLD 8 F5
McAlinden WA 73 E10
McCluer Island NT 86 A7
McCoys Bridge VIC 41 J14 42 B2
McCrae VIC 36 J7
McCullys Gap NSW 23 C9
McDowall QLD 3 C3
McGraths Hill NSW 20 F7
McKellar ACT 32 B3
McKenzie Creek VIC 38 B5
McKillops Bridge VIC 43 G14 47 A9
McKinlay QLD 12 B6
McKinnon VIC 35 F4
McLaren Creek NT 89 J9
McLaren Flat SA 60 K2 61 D6
McLaren Vale SA 60 K2 61 E5 62 F7 65 K10
McIntyre VIC 39 A10
McMahons Creek VIC 37 C14 42 J5 44 B5
McMahons Reef NSW 22 K3 30 B2
McMasters Beach NSW 20 B4
McMillans VIC 41 H11
McPhail NSW 22 D2
Mead VIC 41 H11
Meadow Flat NSW 22 G6
Meadows SA 60 K4 62 F7 65 K10
Meandarra QLD 6 F7
Meander TAS 55 G8
Mears WA 72 A5
Meatian VIC 41 G9
Mebbin Nat Park NSW 7 J13 25 A13
Meckering WA 72 B2 74 C5 76 K6
Medina WA 72 G4
Medindie SA 58 A3
Medlow Bath NSW 21 K9
Meeandah QLD 3 D5
Meekatharra WA 76 C7 78 K5
Meelup WA 73 K10
Meenaar WA 72 C2
Meeniyan VIC 44 G6
Meerlieu VIC 45 D12 46 E5
Megan NSW 25 G12
Mekaree QLD 8 K2 13 G11
Melba ACT 32 B3
Melba Gully State Park VIC 39 K9
Melbourne VIC 35 D3 36 C7 39 F14 42 K2 44 B1
Melbourne CBD VIC 34
Meldale QLD 4 E4
Mella TAS 54 C2
Melros WA 72 H6
Melrose NSW 29 B12
Melrose SA 62 F2 65 E9
Melrose TAS 54 E7
Melrose Park SA 59 J4
Melton SA 62 G5 65 G9
Melton VIC 36 B4 39 E13
Melton Mowbray TAS 53 D10
Melton South VIC 36 C4
Melville WA 71 J2
Melville Forest VIC 38 E4
Melville Island NT 85 A1 86 B3
Melville Range Nature Res NSW 24 J6
Melwood VIC 43 K11 45 B12 46 D5
Memana TAS 55 B9
Memerambi QLD 7 D10
Mena Park VIC 39 E9
Menai NSW 19 J2 21 D10
Menangle NSW 21 E12
Menangle Park NSW 21 E11
Mendooran NSW 22 B4
Mengha TAS 54 C3
Menindee NSW 26 K4 28 B4
Meningie SA 63 D9 65 K11
Mentone VIC 35 G5 37 E8 39 G14 44 C2
Menzies WA 77 G10
Menzies Creek VIC 37 E11
Mepunga East VIC 38 J7
Mepunga West VIC 38 J7
Merah North NSW 24 F4
Merbein VIC 28 F3 40 A4
Merbein South VIC 28 F3 40 A4
Merbein West VIC 40 A4
Mercunda SA 62 C6 65 J12
Merebene NSW 24 H3
Meredith VIC 36 D1 39 F11
Meribah SA 28 G1 40 C1 62 A6 65 J13
Merimbula NSW 30 J5
Merinda QLD 8 B7
Meringandan QLD 7 G11
Meringur VIC 28 F2 40 B2 65 H14
Meringur North VIC 28 F2 40 B2
Merino VIC 38 F3
Mermaid Beach QLD 5 B13
Mernda VIC 37 B8 39 E14 42 J2 44 A2
Mernot Nature Res NSW 23 A10
Meroo Nat Park NSW 30 E6
Merredin WA 74 B7 76 K7
Merriang VIC 43 D8
Merriangaah Nature Res NSW 30 H3
Merricks VIC 37 J8 39 H14 44 F2
Merricks Beach VIC 37 K8
Merricks North VIC 37 J8
Merrigum VIC 41 K14 42 C2
Merrijig VIC 42 G6 46 A1
Merrimac QLD 5 B13
Merrinee VIC 28 F3 40 B4
Merrinee North VIC 28 F3 40 B4
Merriton SA 62 G3 65 F9
Merriwa NSW 22 C7
Merriwagga NSW 29 E10
Merrygoen NSW 22 B5
Merrylands NSW 19 E2 21 D8
Merryvale QLD 5 J11
Merrywinebone NSW 24 E2
Merseylea TAS 54 F7
Merton NSW 29 K11 42 A6
Merton VIC 42 F4
Messent Con Park SA 63 D9
Messines QLD 25 B10
Metcalfe VIC 39 C12
Methul NSW 29 G13
Metricup WA 73 J11
Metung VIC 43 K12 45 C14 46 E7
Meunna TAS 54 D4
Mia Mia VIC 39 C13
Miallo QLD 11 C12
Miami QLD 5 B13
Miandetta NSW 27 H12
Miara QLD 7 A11 9 K12
Michaelmas and Upolu Cays Nat Park QLD 11 C13
Michelago NSW 30 E3
Mickleham VIC 36 A7
Middingbank NSW 30 G2
Middle Beach SA 62 F6 65 H9
Middle Brother Nat Park NSW 23 B13
Middle Camp NSW 20 A1
Middle Dural NSW 19 A2
Middle Island QLD 9 E10
Middle Island WA 83 J2
Middle Lagoon WA 79 A9 80 F4
Middle Park QLD 5 F9
Middle Point NT 85 C3 86 D4
Middle Swan WA 71 D7
Middlecamp Hills Con Park SA 62 K4 64 F7
Middlemount QLD 8 G7
Middleton QLD 12 D6
Middleton SA 61 H7 63 F8 65 K10
Middleton TAS 50 K5 53 H10
Midge Point QLD 9 C8
Midkin Nature Res NSW 24 D5
Midland WA 71 D7 72 F3 74 C3 76 K5
Midway Point TAS 51 B8 53 F11
Miena TAS 53 B8 55 J8
Miepoll VIC 42 D4
Miga Lake VIC 38 C3
Mike O/P Mine WA 79 F8
Mil Lel SA 38 F1 63 B14
Mila NSW 30 J3 47 A11
Milabena TAS 54 D4
Milang SA 63 E8 65 K10
Milawa VIC 42 D7
Milbrulong NSW 29 H12
Milchomi NSW 24 G2
Mildura VIC 28 F3 40 A5
Mile End SA 58 C1 59 G3
Miles QLD 6 E7
Milford QLD 5 H13
Milguy NSW 24 D6
Milikapiti NT 86 B3
Miling WA 76 H5
Milingimbi NT 87 C10
Mill Park VIC 35 A4
Millaa Millaa QLD 11 E13
Millaroo QLD 8 B5
Millbank NSW 25 H11
Millchester QLD 8 B4 11 J14
Miller NSW 21 E10
Millers Point NSW 18 A1
Millfield NSW 23 E9
Millgrove VIC 37 C12 42 K4 44 B4
Millicent SA 63 C13
Millie NSW 24 E4
Millmerran QLD 7 H9
Millner NT 84 B2
Milloo VIC 41 K12
Millstream Chichester Nat Park WA 78 E4 82 D2
Millstream Falls Nat Park QLD 11 E12
Millswood SA 59 H4
Millthorpe NSW 22 G4
Milltown VIC 38 G4
Millwood NSW 29 H13
Milparinka NSW 26 D2
Milperra NSW 19 G2 21 D9
Milton NSW 30 D6
Milton QLD 5 F8
Milvale NSW 22 J2 29 F14
Milyakburra NT 87 F12
Milyu Nature Res WA 70 D1
Mimili (Everard Park) SA 68 C6
Mimosa Rocks Nat Park NSW 30 H5
Mincha VIC 41 H11
Mindarie SA 62 C6 65 J12
Minden QLD 5 J8
Miners Rest VIC 39 E10
Minerva QLD 8 J6
Minerva Hills Nat Park QLD 8 J6
Mingary SA 65 D13
Mingay VIC 39 F9
Mingela QLD 8 B4 11 J14
Mingenew WA 76 G4
Mingoola QLD 25 C9
Minhamite VIC 38 G6
Minilya Roadhouse WA 78 H1
Minimay VIC 38 B2
Mininera VIC 39 E8
Miniyeri NT 87 H8
Minjah VIC 38 G6
Minjary Nat Park NSW 29 H14 30 D1
Minjilang NT 86 B6
Minlaton SA 62 H6 65 J8
Minnamurra NSW 23 K8
Minnie Water NSW 25 E13
Minnipa SA 64 E4
Minore NSW 22 C3
Mintabie SA 66 D1 68 C6
Mintaro SA 62 F4 65 G10
Minto NSW 21 E10
Minyip VIC 38 A6 40 K6
Miralie VIC 28 H5 41 E9
Miram VIC 40 K2
Miram South VIC 38 A3 40 K3
Miranda NSW 19 J4 21 C10
Mirani QLD 9 D8
Mirannie NSW 23 D10
Mirboo VIC 44 F7 46 G1
Mirboo North VIC 44 F7 46 G1
Miriam Vale QLD 9 J12
Mirikata SA 66 H5
Mirima (Hidden Valley) Nat Park WA 81 D14
Mirimbah VIC 42 G7 46 A2
Mirirrinyunga (Duck Ponds) NT 88 F4
Miriwinni QLD 11 E13
Mirrabooka QLD 15 F13
Mirrabooka WA 71 D4
Mirranatwa VIC 38 D6
Mirrindi NT 88 F4
Mirrnatja NT 87 D10
Mirrool NSW 29 F12
Missabotti NSW 25 H12
Mission Beach QLD 11 E13
Missouri Mine WA 77 H10
Mistake Creek NT 79 A14 81 G14 88 C1
Mitakooki QLD 12 A4
Mitcham SA 59 J4 60 G2 61 A6
Mitcham VIC 35 D7
Mitchell ACT 32 C5
Mitchell QLD 6 D3
Mitchell - Alice Rivers Nat Park QLD 10 A7 16 K2
Mitchell River Nat Park VIC 43 J10 45 A12 46 C5
Mitchell River Nat Park WA 81 C9
Mitchells (site) VIC 42 H7 46 B1
Mitchellville SA 62 J3 65 F8
Mitchelton QLD 3 D2
Mitiamo VIC 41 J12
Mitre VIC 38 B4
Mitta Mitta VIC 43 D10
Mittagong NSW 22 K7 30 B6
Mittyack VIC 28 H4 40 E6
Moa Island QLD 16 A2
Moama NSW 29 K8 41 J13 42 B1
Moana SA 60 K1 61 D5
Moana Sands Con Park SA 60 K1 61 D5
Mobrup WA 73 B13
Mockinya VIC 38 C5
Modbury SA 59 D6 60 E3
Modbury Heights SA 59 C6
Modbury North SA 59 D6
Modella VIC 37 G13 44 E5
Modewarre VIC 36 H1
Moe VIC 44 D7 46 F1
Moganemby VIC 42 D4
Moggill QLD 3 H1 5 F9
Mogo NSW 30 F6
Mogriguy NSW 22 C3
Mogumber WA 74 A3 76 J5
Moil NT 84 B3
Moina TAS 54 F6
Mokepilly VIC 38 C7
Mokola Con Park SA 62 E3 65 F10
Mole Creek TAS 54 G7
Mole Creek Karst Nat Park TAS 54 G7
Mole River NSW 7 K10 25 C9
Molesworth TAS 50 B3 53 F10
Molesworth VIC 42 G4
Moliagul VIC 39 B10
Molka VIC 42 E3
Molle Islands Nat Park QLD 9 B8
Mollerin Nature Res WA 76 H6
Mollymook NSW 30 D6
Molong NSW 22 F4
Moltema TAS 55 F8
Molyullah VIC 42 D6
Mona Vale NSW 19 B7 20 B6 23 G9
Mona Vale TAS 53 B11 55 J11
Monadnocks Con Res WA 72 E5 74 D3
Monak NSW 28 F4 40 A5
Monarto Con Park SA 60 K7
Monash ACT 32 H4
Monash SA 62 B5 65 H13
Monbulk VIC 37 D11 42 K3 44 C3
Moncrieff ACT 32 A4
Mondrain Island WA 75 H14
Monduran Dam QLD 7 A11 9 K12
Monea VIC 42 E3
Monegeetta VIC 39 D13 42 H1
Monga NSW 30 E5
Monga Nat Park NSW 30 E5
Mongarlowe NSW 30 E5
Mongers Lakes WA 76 G6
Monkerai Nature Res NSW 23 C11
Monkey Mia WA 76 B2 78 K1
Monkeycot Nature Res NSW 23 B10
Monogorilby QLD 7 D9
Monomeith VIC 37 H11
Monsildale QLD 4 K1
Montacute SA 59 F7 60 F4
Montacute Con Park SA 60 F4
Montagu TAS 54 C2
Montagu Bay TAS 49 B4
Montagu Island TAS 54 C2
Montague WA 77 D9
Montague Island NSW 30 G6
Montague Island Nature Res NSW 30 G6
Montana TAS 55 G8
Monteagle NSW 22 J2 30 A1
Montebello Islands WA 78 D3
Montebello Islands Con Park WA 78 D3
Montefiores NSW 22 D4
Monterey NSW 19 H5 21 B9
Montesquieu Islands WA 81 A9
Montgomery Islands WA 80 D6
Monto QLD 7 A9 9 K11
Montumana TAS 54 D4
Montville QLD 4 F1 7 E12
Mooball NSW 7 J14 25 A14
Mooball Nat Park NSW 7 J13 25 A14
Moockra SA 62 F1 65 D10
Moodiarrup WA 73 C10
Moodlu QLD 4 F4
Moogara TAS 53 F9
Moogerah QLD 5 J13
Moogerah Peaks Nat Park QLD 5 J13
Moojeeba QLD 16 H4
Moolap VIC 36 G3
Mooloolaba QLD 4 D1 7 E13
Mooloolah QLD 4 F2
Mooloolah River Nat Park QLD 4 E1
Moolort VIC 39 C11
Moolpa NSW 28 H6 41 D10
Moomba SA 14 H2 67 E13
Moombooldool NSW 29 F12
Moombra QLD 4 K6
Moona Plains NSW 25 J10
Moonambel VIC 39 C9
Moonan Flat NSW 23 B9
Moonaran NSW 24 H7
Moonbah NSW 30 H2 43 D14
Moonbi NSW 25 J8
Moonda Lake QLD 12 K5 14 C3 67 A13
Moondarra VIC 44 D7 46 E1
Moondarra State Park VIC 44 D7 46 E1
Moondyne Nature Res WA 72 F2 74 B3 76 K5
Moonee Beach NSW 25 G13
Mooney Mooney NSW 20 C5
Moonford QLD 7 A9 9 K11
Moongardie WA 79 C12 81 K10
Moongobulla QLD 11 G14
Moonie QLD 7 G8
Moonlight Flat SA 64 E4
Moonta SA 62 H5 65 G8
Moonta Bay SA 62 H4 65 G8
Moonyoonooka WA 76 F3
Moora WA 74 A3 76 J5
Moorabbin VIC 35 F5 37 E8 39 G14 42 K2 44 C2
Moorabool VIC 36 F2
Mooralla VIC 38 D5
Moore QLD 7 F11
Moore Creek NSW 24 J7
Moore Park QLD 7 A12 9 K13
Moore River Nat Park WA 74 B2 76 J4
Moorebank NSW 19 G1 21 D9
Mooree VIC 38 D3
Mooreville TAS 54 D5
Moorilim VIC 42 D3
Moorina TAS 55 E12
Moorine Rock WA 75 B8 77 J8
Moorland NSW 23 B13
Moorlands SA 63 D8 65 K11
Moorleah TAS 54 D4
Moormbool VIC 39 B14 42 E2
Moorooduc VIC 37 H8
Moorook SA 62 B5 65 H12
Moorooka QLD 3 G4
Mooroongga Island NT 87 C10
Mooroopna VIC 42 C3
Moorrinya Nat Park QLD 8 D2 13 B11
Moorumbine WA 72 A6
Moorundie Wildlife Park SA 65 H11
Mopoke Hut VIC 28 G3
Moppin NSW 24 C5
Morago NSW 29 H8 41 F13
Moranbah QLD 8 E6
Morangarell NSW 22 J1 29 F14
Morans Crossing NSW 30 H4
Morawa WA 76 G5
Morayfield QLD 4 F5
Morchard SA 62 F1 65 E10
Mordalup WA 73 C14
Mordialloc VIC 35 H5 37 F8 39 G14 44 D2
Morea (Carpolac) VIC 38 B2
Moree NSW 24 D5
Morella QLD 13 E10
Moresby QLD 11 E13
Moreton Bay QLD 3 A6 4 C6 7 F13
Moreton Island QLD 4 B5 7 F13
Moreton Island Nat Park QLD 4 B5 7 F13
Moreton Telegraph Station QLD 16 E2
Morgan SA 62 D5 65 G11
Morgan Con Park SA 62 C5 65 G11
Morgan Island NT 87 E11
Moriac VIC 36 H1 39 H11
Morialpa SA 65 D12
Morialta Con Park SA 59 F7 60 F3 65 J10
Moriarty TAS 54 E7
Morisset NSW 20 B1 23 F10
Morisset Park NSW 20 B1
Morkalla VIC 28 F2 40 B2
Morley WA 71 D5
Morna Point NSW 23 E11
Morningside QLD 3 E5
Mornington VIC 36 H7 39 H14 44 E2

104 Mornington Island – Netherby

Mornington Island QLD 10 C3
Mornington Peninsula VIC 37 J8 39 H14 44 E2
Mornington Peninsula Nat Park VIC 36 K7 39 H13 44 F1
Morongla Creek NSW 22 H3
Mororo Creek Nature Res NSW 25 D13
Morphett Vale SA 60 J1 61 C5 62 F7 65 J10
Morphettville SA 59 J3
Morratta Con Park SA 62 F7
Morri Morri VIC 38 B7
Morrisons VIC 36 C1 39 F11
Morrisons Lake Nature Res NSW 28 C7
Morse Island NT 85 A5 86 B6
Mortchup VIC 39 E9
Mortdale NSW 21 C9
Mortlake VIC 38 G7
Morton Nat Park NSW 30 C6
Morton Plains VIC 28 K5 40 J7
Morundah NSW 29 G11
Moruya NSW 30 F5
Moruya Heads NSW 30 F6
Morven NSW 29 J13
Morven QLD 6 D2
Morwell VIC 45 E8 46 F2
Morwell Nat Park VIC 45 F8 46 G2
Moselle QLD 11 K9 13 A9
Mosman NSW 19 E6 21 B8
Mosman Park WA 71 H1
Moss Vale NSW 22 K7 30 B6
Mossgiel NSW 29 D8
Mossiface VIC 43 K12 45 B14 46 D6
Mossman QLD 11 C12
Mossy Point NSW 30 F6
Moulamein NSW 28 H7 41 E11
Moule SA 64 C2 68 K7
Mount Aberdeen Nat Park QLD 8 B6
Mount Adolphus Island QLD 16 B2
Mount Alford QLD 5 J13
Mount Annan NSW 21 E11
Mount Arapiles - Tooan State Park VIC 38 B4
Mount Archer Nat Park QLD 9 H10
Mount Augustus (Burringurrah) Nat Park WA 78 H4 82 J2
Mount Barker SA 60 H5 62 E7 65 J10
Mount Barker WA 74 J6
Mount Barker Junction SA 60 H5
Mount Barkly NT 90 B6
Mount Barney Nat Park QLD 7 J12 25 A12
Mount Bauple Nat Park QLD 7 C12
Mount Baw Baw Alpine Village VIC 42 K6 44 B7 46 D1
Mount Beauty VIC 43 E9
Mount Benson SA 63 D12
Mount Beppo QLD 4 K5
Mount Boothby Con Park SA 63 D9
Mount Brown Con Park SA 62 G1 65 D9
Mount Bryan SA 62 E3 65 F10
Mount Buangor State Park VIC 39 D8
Mount Buffalo Chalet VIC 43 E8
Mount Buffalo Nat Park VIC 43 E8
Mount Buller Alpine Village VIC 42 G7 46 A2
Mount Burnett VIC 37 E11
Mount Burr SA 63 B13
Mount Bute VIC 39 F9
Mount Camel VIC 39 B13 42 E1
Mount Carbine QLD 11 C12
Mount Catt NT 87 F9
Mount Chapple Island TAS 55 C8
Mount Christie Corner SA 66 J2 68 H7
Mount Christie Siding SA 66 K1 68 H7
Mount Claremont WA 71 F2
Mount Clifford Nature Res NSW 30 G3
Mount Clunie Nat Park NSW 7 J12 25 A11
Mount Colah NSW 19 B4 20 C7
Mount Colosseum Nat Park QLD 9 J12
Mount Compass SA 61 F6 63 F8 65 K10
Mount Cook Nat Park QLD 11 A12 16 K6
Mount Coolon QLD 8 D5
Mount Coot-tha QLD 3 E2 5 F8
Mount Cotton QLD 5 D9
Mount Cottrell VIC 36 C5 39 F13
Mount Crosby QLD 5 G8
Mount Cuthbert Mine QLD 10 J4
Mount Damper SA 64 E4
Mount Dandenong VIC 37 D10
Mount Dangar QLD 8 B7
Mount David NSW 22 H5
Mount Direction TAS 55 E9 56 E4
Mount Dowling Nature Res NSW 30 F3
Mount Druit NSW 21 F8
Mount Drummond SA 64 H5
Mount Duneed VIC 36 H3 39 H12
Mount Dutton SA 66 E5
Mount Ebenezer NT 90 H6
Mount Eccles VIC 44 F6
Mount Eccles Nat Park VIC 38 G4
Mount Eckersley VIC 38 G4
Mount Egerton VIC 36 B1 39 E11
Mount Eliza VIC 37 G8 39 H14 44 E2
Mount Emu VIC 39 E9
Mount Ernest Island QLD 16 A2
Mount Etna Caves Nat Park QLD 9 G10
Mount Field Nat Park TAS 53 E8
Mount Fitton SA 67 J11
Mount Frankland Nat Park WA 74 J5
Mount Gambier SA 38 F1 63 B14
Mount Garnet QLD 11 E12
Mount George NSW 23 B12
Mount Gipps NSW 26 J2 28 A2
Mount Glorious QLD 4 G6
Mount Granya State Park VIC 29 K13 43 B10
Mount Gravatt QLD 3 G5 5 E8
Mount Grenfell Historic Site NSW 27 H9
Mount Gunson Mine SA 65 B8
Mount Hawthorn WA 71 E3
Mount Helen VIC 39 E10
Mount Hill SA 64 G6
Mount Hope NSW 29 C10
Mount Hope SA 64 G5
Mount Hope Res VIC 41 H11
Mount Hunter NSW 21 F11
Mount Hyland Nature Res NSW 25 F11
Mount Hypipamee Nat Park QLD 11 E12
Mount Ida WA 77 F10
Mount Imlay Nat Park NSW 30 K4 47 A13
Mount Irvine NSW 20 K6
Mount Isa QLD 10 K3 12 A3
Mount Jerusalem Nat Park NSW 7 J13 25 B14
Mount Kaputar Nat Park NSW 24 F6
Mount Keith Mine WA 77 C10
Mount Kelly Mine QLD 10 J3
Mount Kokeby WA 72 B4
Mount Kororoit VIC 36 B5
Mount Kuring-gai NSW 19 A5 20 D6
Mount Larcom QLD 9 H11
Mount Lawley WA 71 F4
Mount Lawson State Park VIC 29 K13 43 B11
Mount Leura Con Park QLD 8 H6
Mount Leyson Mine QLD 8 B4 11 J14
Mount Liebig NT 90 E4
Mount Lion NSW 25 A13
Mount Lloyd TAS 50 C1 53 F9
Mount Lonarch VIC 39 D9
Mount Macedon VIC 39 D13
Mount Mackenzie Nature Res NSW 25 C10
Mount Magnet WA 76 E7
Mount Magnificent Con Park SA 61 F7
Mount Manning Nature Res WA 77 G9
Mount Margaret WA 77 F12 83 D1
Mount Martha VIC 36 H7 39 H14 44 E1
Mount Mary SA 62 D5 65 G11
Mount Mee QLD 4 G4
Mount Mercer VIC 39 F10
Mount Molloy QLD 11 C12
Mount Morgan QLD 9 H10
Mount Morgans WA 77 F12 83 D1
Mount Moriac VIC 36 H1
Mount Mort QLD 5 K11
Mount Napier State Park VIC 38 G5
Mount Nathan QLD 5 C12
Mount Nebo QLD 4 G7
Mount Neville Nature Res NSW 25 D12
Mount Nothofagus Nat Park NSW 25 A12
Mount O'Connell Nat Park QLD 9 G9
Mount Olive NSW 23 D9
Mount Ommaney QLD 3 G2
Mount Ossa QLD 9 D8
Mount Ossa Nat Park QLD 9 D8
Mount Oxide Mine QLD 10 H3
Mount Perry QLD 7 B10
Mount Pikapene Nat Park NSW 7 K12 25 C12
Mount Pleasant QLD 4 G5
Mount Pleasant SA 60 E7 62 E6 65 J10
Mount Pleasant WA 71 H3
Mount Pritchard NSW 19 G1 21 E9
Mount Remarkable Nat Park SA 62 G2 65 E9
Mount Rescue Con Park SA 63 B9
Mount Richmond Nat Park VIC 38 H3
Mount Royal Nat Park NSW 23 C9
Mount Russell NSW 24 E7
Mount Samaria State Park VIC 42 F6
Mount Samson QLD 4 G6
Mount Scott Con Park SA 63 C11
Mount Seaview NSW 23 A11 25 K10
Mount Seaview Nature Res NSW 23 A12
Mount Selwyn NSW 30 F1 43 A14
Mount Seymour TAS 53 D11
Mount Shaugh Con Park SA 28 K1 40 H1 63 A9
Mount Stirling Alpine Resort VIC 42 G7 46 A2
Mount Surprise QLD 11 F11
Mount Tamborine QLD 5 D12
Mount Tarampa QLD 5 K8
Mount Taylor VIC 43 K11 45 B13 46 D6
Mount Torrens SA 60 F6 62 E7 65 J10
Mount Vernon NSW 21 F9
Mount Victoria NSW 22 G7
Mount Walker QLD 5 J11
Mount Wallace VIC 36 C2 39 F12
Mount Walsh Nat Park QLD 7 C11
Mount Warning Nat Park NSW 7 J13 25 A13
Mount Waverley VIC 35 E6
Mount Webb Nat Park QLD 11 A12 16 J6
Mount Wedge SA 64 F5
Mount White NSW 20 D4
Mount William Nat Park TAS 55 D14
Mount Wilson NSW 20 K7 22 G7
Mount Worth State Park VIC 44 E6
Mount Yarrowyck Nature Res NSW 25 G8
Mountain Creek NSW 29 J13 43 A10
Mountain Creek QLD 4 E1
Mountain River TAS 50 E3 53 G10
Mountain View VIC 37 H14
Moura QLD 9 K9
Mourilyan QLD 11 E13
Mourilyan Harbour QLD 11 E13
Moutajup VIC 38 E5
Mowanjum WA 79 A10 80 G6
Mowbray TAS 56 G5
Mowbray Park NSW 21 G12
Mowen WA 73 J12
Moyarra VIC 37 K13
Moyhu VIC 42 D7
Moyston VIC 38 D7
Muchea WA 72 F2 74 C3 76 K5
Muckadilla QLD 6 E4
Muckatah VIC 29 K10 42 A4
Mud Island QLD 4 C7
Mud Island VIC 36 H6
Mudamuckla SA 64 D3
Mudgee NSW 22 D5
Mudgeeraba QLD 5 C13 7 H13
Mudgegonga VIC 43 D8
Mudjarn Nature Res NSW 30 D1
Mudludja WA 79 B12 81 H9
Muiron Islands WA 78 F2
Mukinbudin WA 74 A7 76 J7
Mulan WA 79 D13
Mulanggari ACT 32 B5
Mulbring NSW 23 E10
Mulcra VIC 28 H2 40 E2
Mulga Bore SA 68 B5
Mulgildie QLD 7 A9 9 K11
Mulgoa NSW 21 G9
Mulgowrie NSW 22 J4 30 A3
Mulgrave NSW 20 F7
Mulgrave VIC 37 E9
Mullaley NSW 24 J5
Mullaloo WA 71 A1 72 G2 74 C2 76 K4
Mullalyup WA 73 F11
Mullaway NSW 25 F13
Mullengandra Village NSW 29 K13 43 A10
Mullengudgery NSW 27 J13
Mullewa WA 76 F4
Mulline WA 77 G10
Mullion Creek NSW 22 F4
Mullumbimby NSW 7 J13 25 B14
Mulpata SA 62 B7 65 K12
Mulurulu Lake NSW 28 C6
Mulwala NSW 29 K11 42 A6
Mulyandry NSW 22 G2 29 D14
Mulyati NT 79 J14 83 A7
Mumballup WA 73 F10 74 G3
Mumbannar VIC 38 G2
Mumberkine WA 72 D1
Mumbil NSW 22 D4
Mumbleberry Lake QLD 12 G2
Mummel Gulf Nat Park NSW 23 A11 25 K9
Mummulgum NSW 7 K12 25 C12
Mumu QLD 13 A10
Mundaring WA 72 F3 74 C3 76 K5
Mundaring Weir WA 72 E3
Mundarlo NSW 29 H14
Munderoo NSW 29 K14 43 A12
Mundijong WA 72 F5 74 D3
Mundiwindi WA 78 H7 82 H7
Mundoona VIC 42 B3
Mundoonen Nature Res NSW 30 C3
Mundoora SA 62 G3 65 F9
Mundowey NSW 24 H7
Mundrabilla WA 83 F6
Mundrabilla Motel WA 83 G6
Mundubbera QLD 7 B9
Mundulla SA 40 K1 63 B10
Mungalawurru NT 89 G8
Mungallala QLD 6 D3
Mungana QLD 11 D11
Mungar QLD 7 C12
Mungaroona Range Nature Res WA 78 F5 82 E4
Mungerannie Roadhouse SA 67 E10
Mungeriba NSW 22 C2 29 A14
Mungeribar NSW 27 K14
Munghorn Gap Nature Res NSW 22 D6
Mungindi NSW 6 K5 24 C3
Mungkan Kandju Nat Park QLD 16 G3
Munglinup WA 75 G11
Mungo Brush NSW 23 D12
Mungo Nat Park NSW 28 E5
Mungunburra QLD 8 B3 11 K13
Mungungo QLD 7 A9 9 K11
Munjina (Auski) Roadhouse WA 78 F5 82 F5
Munmorah State Con Area NSW 20 A1 23 F10
Munno Para SA 60 C3
Munro VIC 43 K9 45 C11 46 E4
Muntadgin WA 74 C7 77 K8
Muntz Nature Res WA 75 G14 83 J2
Munyaroo Con Park SA 62 J3 65 F8
Muogamarra Nature Res NSW 20 D6 23 G9
Muradup WA 73 B12
Muralug QLD 16 B2
Murarrie QLD 3 E6
Murbko SA 62 D5 65 H11
Murcheboluc VIC 36 G1
Murchison VIC 42 D3
Murchison East VIC 42 D3
Murchison Roadhouse WA 76 C4
Murdinga SA 64 G5
Murdoch WA 71 J3
Murdunna TAS 51 E13 53 G12
Muresk WA 72 C2
Murga NSW 22 F3
Murgenella NT 85 A7 86 B6
Murgon QLD 7 D11
Murninnie SA 62 H3 65 F8
Muronbung NSW 22 C4
Murphys Creek QLD 7 G11
Murra Warra VIC 40 K5
Murrabit VIC 28 J7 41 G11
Murradoc VIC 36 G5
Murramarang Nat Park NSW 30 E6
Murrami NSW 29 F11
Murrawal NSW 22 A5 24 K4
Murray Bridge SA 62 D7 65 J11
Murray River Nat Park SA 28 F1 62 B6 65 H13
Murray – Sunset Nat Park VIC 28 G2 40 D3 62 A6 65 J14
Murray Town SA 62 G2 65 E9
Murray-Kulkyne Park VIC 28 G4 40 C6
Murrayville VIC 28 J2 40 F2 63 A8 65 K14
Murrigal QLD 11 F13
Murrin Bridge NSW 29 C11
Murrindal VIC 43 H13 47 B8
Murrindindi VIC 42 H4
Murringo NSW 22 J3 30 A2
Murroon VIC 39 J10
Murrumbateman NSW 30 C3
Murrumburrah NSW 22 K2 30 B1
Murrungowar VIC 47 C10
Murrurundi NSW 23 B8
Murtoa VIC 38 A6
Murun Murula NT 89 F14
Murweh QLD 15 E13
Murwillumbah NSW 7 J13 25 A14
Musselboro TAS 55 F11
Musselroe Bay Con Res TAS 55 C13
Muswellbrook NSW 23 C9
Mutarnee QLD 11 G13
Mutawintji Nat Park NSW 26 H4
Mutawintji Nature Res NSW 26 G4
Mutchilba QLD 11 D12
Mutdapilly QLD 5 H10
Muttaburra QLD 8 F1 13 D11
Muttama NSW 29 G14 30 C1
Mutton Bird Island TAS 52 J5
Myall VIC 41 G11
Myall Lakes Nat Park NSW 23 D12
Myalla TAS 54 D4
Myalla Nature Res NSW 30 H3
Myalup WA 73 G8 74 F2
Myamyn VIC 38 G4
Mylestom NSW 25 G12
Mylor SA 60 H4 62 F7 65 J10
Myola VIC 39 A13 42 D1
Mypolonga SA 62 D7 65 J11
Myponga SA 61 G5 63 F8 65 K10
Myponga Beach SA 61 F4 63 F8 65 K9
Myponga Con Park SA 61 G4
Myrla SA 62 B6 65 H12
Myrniong VIC 36 B3 39 E12
Myrrhee VIC 42 E6
Myrtle Bank SA 59 H5
Myrtle Bank TAS 55 E10 56 E7
Myrtle Scrub NSW 23 A11 25 K10
Myrtleford VIC 43 D8
Myrtletown QLD 3 C6
Myrtleville NSW 22 K6 30 B5
Mysia VIC 41 J10
Mystery Bay NSW 30 G5
Mystic Park VIC 41 G10
Myubee QLD 12 B4

N

N'dhala Gorge Nature Park NT 91 F9
Nabageena TAS 54 D3
Nabarlek NT 86 D7
Nabawa WA 76 F3
Nabiac NSW 23 C12
Nabowla TAS 55 E11 56 D7
Nackara SA 62 D2 65 E11
Nadgee Nature Res NSW 30 K5 47 C14
Nadgigomar Nature Res NSW 30 D5
Nagambie VIC 39 B14 42 E2
Nagoorin QLD 9 J11
Nailsworth SA 59 E4
Nairana Nat Park QLD 8 E5 13 B14
Nairne SA 60 H6 62 E7 65 J10
Nakara NT 84 A3
Nala TAS 53 D11
Nalangil VIC 39 H9
Nalinga VIC 42 C4
Nalya WA 72 A5
Namadgi Nat Park ACT 30 E3 32 K1
Nambour QLD 7 E13
Nambrok VIC 45 D10 46 E3
Nambucca Heads NSW 25 H12
Nambung Nat Park WA 74 A1 76 H4
Namming Nature Res WA 74 A2 76 J4
Nana Glen NSW 25 F12
Nanango QLD 7 E11
Nanarup WA 74 K7
Nandaly VIC 28 H4 40 F7
Nanga WA 72 F7
Nangalala NT 87 D10
Nangana VIC 37 D11
Nangar Nat Park NSW 22 F3
Nangiloc VIC 28 G4 40 B5
Nangkita SA 61 F7
Nangus NSW 29 H14
Nangwarry SA 38 E1 63 B13
Nannine WA 76 C7
Nannup WA 73 G12 74 H3
Nantawarra SA 62 G4 65 G9
Nanutarra Roadhouse WA 78 F3
Napier Broome Bay WA 81 A10
Napperby SA 62 G2 65 F9
Napranum QLD 16 E1
Nar Nar Goon VIC 37 F12 44 D4
Nar Nar Goon North VIC 37 F12
Naracoopa TAS 54 B7
Naracoorte SA 38 C1 63 B12
Naracoorte Caves Nat Park SA 38 C1 63 B12
Naradhan NSW 29 D11
Narangba QLD 4 F5
Narara NSW 20 C4
Narawntapu Nat Park TAS 55 D8 56 C1
Narbethong VIC 37 A12 42 J4 44 A4
Nardoo QLD 15 G13
Nareen VIC 38 D3
Narellan NSW 21 F11
Narellan Vale NSW 21 F11
Narembeen WA 74 C7 76 K7
Naretha WA 83 F3
Nariel Creek VIC 43 C12
Naringal VIC 38 H7
Narioka VIC 41 J14 42 B2
Narooma NSW 30 G5
Narrabarba NSW 30 K5 47 B13
Narrabeen NSW 19 C7 20 B7
Narrabri NSW 24 G5
Narrabri West NSW 24 G5
Narrabundah ACT 32 F5
Narraburra NSW 22 J1 29 F14
Narran Lake NSW 27 D13
Narran Lake Nature Res NSW 27 D13
Narrandera NSW 29 G11
Narraport VIC 28 K5 41 H8
Narrawa NSW 22 J4 30 B3
Narrawallee NSW 30 D6
Narraweena NSW 19 C7 20 B7
Narrawong VIC 38 H4
Narre Warren VIC 37 F10
Narre Warren East VIC 37 E10
Narre Warren North VIC 37 E10
Narrewillock VIC 41 J9
Narridy SA 62 F3 65 F9
Narrien Range Nat Park QLD 8 G5 13 D14
Narrikup WA 74 J6
Narrogin WA 72 A7 74 E5
Narromine NSW 22 C2
Narrung SA 63 E8 65 K11
Narrung VIC 28 G5 41 C8
Narrungar SA 64 B7
Nashdale NSW 22 F4
Nathalia VIC 29 K9 41 J14 42 B3
Nathan QLD 3 G4
Natimuk VIC 38 B4
National Park TAS 53 F8
Natone TAS 54 E5
Nattai NSW 21 H12 22 H7 30 A6
Nattai Nat Park NSW 21 H13 22 J7 30 A6
Nattai State Con Area NSW 21 H12
Natte Yallock VIC 39 B9
Natural Bridge QLD 5 C14
Naturi SA 62 D7 65 K11
Natya VIC 28 H5 41 D8
Nauiyu NT 85 G1 86 F3
Navarre VIC 39 B8
Nayook VIC 37 E14 42 K5 44 C6
Nea NSW 24 J6
Neale Junction WA 83 D4
Neale Junction Nature Res WA 83 D4
Nearie Lake Nature Res NSW 28 D3
Nebo QLD 8 E7
Nectar Brook SA 62 G1 65 E9
Nedlands WA 71 G2
Neds Corner VIC 28 F2 40 A2
Needles TAS 55 G8
Neerabup Nat Park WA 72 G2 74 C2 76 K4
Neeralin Pool WA 73 A8
Neerim VIC 44 C6
Neerim South VIC 44 D6
Neeworra NSW 24 C3
Neilrex NSW 22 A5
Nelia QLD 11 K8 12 A7
Nelligen NSW 30 E5
Nelshaby SA 62 G2 65 E9
Nelson NSW 20 E7
Nelson VIC 38 G2 63 A14
Nelson Bay NSW 23 E11
Nemingha NSW 24 J7
Nene Valley Con Park SA 63 B14
Nepabunna SA 65 A11 67 K11
Nepean Nickel Mine WA 75 B12 77 J10
Neptune Islands SA 64 K6
Nerang QLD 5 C12 7 H13
Neranwood QLD 5 C14
Nerriga NSW 30 D5
Nerrigundah NSW 30 G5
Nerrin Nerrin VIC 39 F8
Nest Hill Nature Res NSW 29 J13
Netherby VIC 40 J3

Nethercote – Pawleena 105

Nethercote NSW 30 J5 47 A14
Netherdale QLD 8 D7
Netherton SA 63 C8 65 K12
Netley SA 59 G3
Neuarpur VIC 38 B2
Neunman NT 90 F2
Neurea NSW 22 D4
Neurum QLD 4 H3
Neutral Bay NSW 19 E6
Nevertire NSW 20 D2 22 B1 27 J14
Neville NSW 22 G5
New Angledool NSW 6 K3 27 B14
New Beith QLD 5 F10
New England Nat Park NSW 25 G11
New Farm QLD 3 E4 5 E8
New Italy NSW 25 D13
New Looma WA 79 B10 80 H6
New Mollyann NSW 22 A5 24 K3
New Norcia WA 74 A3 76 J5
New Norfolk TAS 50 B2 53 F9
New Residence SA 62 B5 65 H12
New Town TAS 49 A1
New Year Island TAS 54 A6
Newbridge NSW 22 G5
Newbridge VIC 39 B11
Newburn WA 71 G6
Newbury VIC 39 D12
Newcastle NSW 23 E11
Newcastle Waters NT 88 D7
Newdegate WA 75 F8
Newell QLD 11 C12
Newfield VIC 39 J8
Newham VIC 39 D13
Newhaven VIC 44 F3
Newland Head Con Park SA 61 K5 63 F8 65 K10
Newlands WA 73 G11
Newlands Mine QLD 8 D6
Newlyn VIC 39 D11
Newman WA 78 G6 82 H6
Newmarket QLD 3 D3
Newmerella VIC 43 K14 47 D9
Newnes NSW 22 F7
Newport NSW 19 A7 20 B6
Newport VIC 35 E2 36 D6
Newry VIC 43 K8 45 C10 46 E3
Newry Islands Nat Park QLD 9 C8
Newrybar NSW 25 B14
Newstead QLD 3 E4
Newstead VIC 39 C11
Newton SA 59 F6
Newton Boyd NSW 25 E11
Newtown NSW 19 F5
Newtown VIC 36 G3
Ngadang Nature Res NSW 30 H2
Ngalingkadji WA 79 C11 81 J9
Ngallo VIC 40 F1
Ngambaa Nature Res NSW 25 H12
Nganggganawili WA 77 C10 78 K7
Ngarkat Con Park SA 28 K1 40 H1 63 B9 65 K13
Ngarngurr NT 90 J2
Ngarutjara SA 68 A4 90 K5
Nguiu NT 85 A1 86 C3
Ngukurr NT 87 H9
Ngulin Nature Res NSW 23 A10 25 K9
Ngumpan WA 79 C12 81 K9
Ngunjiwirri WA 79 C13 81 K11
Ngunnawal ACT 32 A4
Ngurtuwarta WA 79 B11 81 J8
Nhill VIC 40 K3
Nhulunbuy NT 87 C13
Niagara WA 77 G11 83 E1
Niagara Park NSW 20 C3
Niangala NSW 25 K8
Nicholls ACT 32 A4
Nicholls Rivulet TAS 50 J3 53 H10
Nicholson VIC 43 K11 45 C13 46 D6
Nicholson Camp WA 79 B13 81 J12
Nicol Island NT 87 E12
Nicoll Scrub Nat Park QLD 5 B14
Niemur NSW 28 H7 41 E11
Nierinna TAS 50 F4 53 G10
Nietta TAS 54 F6
Night Island QLD 16 F4
Nightcap Nat Park NSW 7 J13 25 B13
Nightcliff NT 84 B2
Nildottie SA 62 D6 65 J11
Nile TAS 55 G10 56 K7
Nilgen Nature Res WA 74 A2 76 J4
Nillahcootie VIC 42 F6
Nimaru QLD 15 D13
Nimbin NSW 7 J13 25 B13
Nimmitabel NSW 30 H3
Nimmo Nature Res NSW 30 G2
Ninda VIC 40 F7
Nindigully QLD 6 H5 24 A2
Ninety Mile Tank WA 75 E11
Ningaloo Marine Park WA 78 F1
Ningi QLD 4 E4
Ninnes SA 62 G4 65 G9
Ninth Island TAS 55 C10
Nirranda VIC 38 J7
Nirranda East VIC 38 J7
Nirranda South VIC 38 J7
Nirrippi NT 90 D3
Nitmiluk Nat Park NT 85 H6 86 G6
Nixon Skinner Con Park SA 61 G4
Noah Beach QLD 11 B12
Noarlunga Centre SA 60 J1 61 D5
Nobby QLD 7 H10
Noble Park VIC 35 G6 37 E9
Noccundra QLD 14 G7
Nocoleche Nature Res NSW 26 D7
Noggerup WA 73 E10 74 G3
Nollamara WA 71 D3
Nombinnie Nature Res NSW 29 C10
Nome QLD 8 A5 11 H14
Nonda QLD 11 K8 13 A8
Nongra Lake NT 88 E2
Noogoora QLD 5 H8
Noojee VIC 42 K5 44 C6
Nook TAS 54 F7
Noonamah NT 85 D2 86 D4
Noondoo QLD 6 J4 24 B1
Noonkanbah WA 79 B11 80 J7
Noorat VIC 39 H8
Noorinbee VIC 47 C11
Noorinbee North VIC 47 C11
Noosa Heads QLD 7 D13
Noosa Nat Park QLD 7 D13
Nora Creina SA 63 D12
Noradjuha VIC 38 B4
Norah Head NSW 20 A2 23 F10
Noranda WA 71 D5
Noraville NSW 20 A2
Nords Wharf NSW 20 A1
Norlane VIC 36 F3
Normanhurst NSW 20 D7
Normanton QLD 10 E6
Normanville SA 61 G3 63 G8 65 K9
Nornalup WA 74 K4
Norseman WA 75 D13 83 H1
North Adelaide SA 58 A2 59 F4
North Bannister WA 72 D6
North Beach WA 71 D1
North Bondi NSW 21 B8
North Bourke NSW 27 E10
North Bruny Island TAS 50 H6 53 H10
North Dandalup WA 72 F6
North East Island QLD 9 E10
North East Isles NT 87 F13
North Fremantle WA 71 H1
North Goonyella QLD 8 E7
North Goonyella Mine QLD 8 E6
North Haven NSW 23 B13
North Haven SA 59 C2 60 E1
North Hobart TAS 49 B1
North Ipswich QLD 5 H9
North Isis QLD 7 B11
North Island NT 87 J13 89 A13
North Island WA 76 E2
North Karlgarin Nature Res WA 74 D7
North Keppel Island QLD 9 G11
North Lilydale TAS 56 D6
North Maclean QLD 5 E10
North Molle Island QLD 9 B8
North Motton TAS 54 E6
North Parkes Mine NSW 22 E2 29 C14
North Perth WA 71 F4
North Pinjarra WA 72 F6
North Point Island NT 87 F12
North Richmond NSW 20 G7
North Riverside TAS 55 F9 56 G4
North Ryde NSW 19 D4 21 C8
North Scottsdale TAS 55 D11
North Shields SA 64 H6
North Shore VIC 36 F3
North Solitary Island NSW 25 F13
North St Ives NSW 20 C7
North Star NSW 7 K8 24 C6
North Stradbroke Island QLD 5 B9 7 G13
North Sydney NSW 19 E6 21 B8
North Tamborine QLD 5 D12
North Turramurra NSW 19 B5
North West Cape WA 78 F1
North West Crocodile Island NT 87 B10
North West Island QLD 9 H12
North Willoughby NSW 19 D6
North Wollongong NSW 21 C14
Northam WA 72 D2 74 C4 76 K6
Northampton WA 76 E3
Northbridge NSW 19 E6
Northbridge WA 70 A2 71 F4
Northcliffe WA 74 J3
Northcote VIC 35 C4 37 C8
Northdown TAS 54 E7
Northfield SA 59 E5 60 F3
Northumberland Islands QLD 9 D9
Northumberland Islands Nat Park QLD 9 D9
Norton Summit SA 59 G7 60 G4 61 A7
Norval Park QLD 9 K12
Norwood SA 59 G5 60 G3 61 A6
Norwood TAS 56 G5
Notley Hills TAS 55 F9 56 F3
Notts Well SA 62 C6 65 H12
Novar Gardens SA 59 I12
Nowa Nowa VIC 43 K13 46 D7
Nowendoc NSW 23 A11 25 K9
Nowendoc Nat Park NSW 23 A10 25 K9
Nowingi VIC 28 G3 40 C5
Nowley NSW 24 F3
Nowra NSW 30 C7
Nubeena TAS 51 H11 53 H12
Nudgee QLD 3 C5 4 E7
Nudgee Beach QLD 3 B5 4 E7
Nuga Nuga Nat Park QLD 6 A5 8 K7
Nugent TAS 51 A11 53 F12
Nullagine WA 78 F7 82 E7
Nullamanna NSW 25 E8
Nullarbor Motel SA 68 J4
Nullarbor Nat Park SA 68 J2 83 G7
Nullarbor Reg Res SA 68 J3 83 G7
Nullavale VIC 39 C13 42 G1
Nullawarre VIC 38 J7
Nullawil VIC 28 K5 41 H8
Number One NSW 23 B11
Numbla Vale NSW 30 H2
Numbugga NSW 30 H4
Numbulwar NT 87 G11
Numeralla NSW 30 G4
Numeralla Nature Res NSW 30 G4
Numinbah Nature Res QLD 25 A13
Numinbah Valley QLD 5 C14
Numurkah VIC 29 K9 42 B3
Nunamara TAS 55 F10 56 G7
Nundah QLD 3 C4
Nundle NSW 23 A9 25 K8
Nunga VIC 28 H4 40 E6
Nungarin WA 74 B6 76 J7
Nungatta NSW 30 K4 47 B12
Nungatta South VIC 47 B12
Nunjikompita SA 64 D3
Nunniong Plains VIC 43 G12 46 A7
Nunnyah Con Res SA 64 C3
Nurina WA 83 F5
Nuriootpa SA 60 A6 62 E6 65 H10
Nurrabiel VIC 38 B5
Nurrai Lakes SA 68 F2
Nutfield VIC 37 B9
Nuyts Archipelago Con Park SA 64 D2
Nuyts Reef Con Park SA 68 K5
Nuytsland Nature Res WA 83 H3
NW Vernon Island NT 85 B2 86 C4
Nyabing WA 74 G7
Nyah VIC 28 H6 41 E9
Nyah West VIC 28 H6 41 E9
Nyamup WA 73 E14
Nyapari SA 68 A2 90 K3
Nyarrin VIC 40 F7
Nyerimilang State Park VIC 45 C14 46 E7
Nyikukura SA 68 A1 79 K14 83 B7 90 K1
Nyintjilan WA 83 B6
Nymagee NSW 27 J11 29 A11
Nymboi-Binderay Nat Park NSW 25 F12
Nymboida NSW 25 F12
Nymboida Nat Park NSW 25 E11
Nyngan NSW 27 H13
Nyora NSW 29 J10
Nyora VIC 37 J12 44 E4
Nypo VIC 28 J3 40 G5

O

O'Connell NSW 22 G6
O'Connor ACT 32 D5
O'Connor WA 71 J2
O'Malley ACT 32 F4
O'Malley SA 68 H4
O'Reillys QLD 7 H13 25 A13
O'Sullivan Beach SA 60 J1 61 C5
Oak Beach QLD 11 C12
Oak Creek Nature Res NSW 30 C2
Oak Valley SA 68 F3
Oakbank SA 60 G5
Oakey QLD 7 G10
Oakey Creek NSW 22 A6 24 K4
Oakhurst NSW 21 F8
Oaklands NSW 29 J11
Oaklands Park SA 59 J3
Oakleigh VIC 35 F5 37 E8 39 F14 42 K2 44 C2
Oaks TAS 55 G9 56 J4
Oaks Estate ACT 32 F7
Oakvale VIC 41 H9
Oakville NSW 20 F7
Oakwood NSW 25 E8
Oakwood TAS 51 H12 53 H12
Oaky Creek Mine QLD 8 G7
Oasis Roadhouse QLD 11 G11
Oatlands NSW 21 D8
Oatlands TAS 53 D10 55 K10
Oatley NSW 21 C10
OB Flat SA 38 G1 63 B14
Oban NSW 25 F10
Oberne NSW 29 J14
Oberon NSW 22 G6
Obley NSW 22 D3
Ocean Grove VIC 36 H4 39 H12
Ocean Reef WA 71 A1
Ocean Shores NSW 25 B14
Ocean View QLD 4 G5
Offham QLD 15 G13
Officer VIC 37 F11
Officer Ck SA 68 B5
Ogmore QLD 9 F9
Olary SA 62 B1 65 D13
Old Adaminaby NSW 30 F2
Old Aparawilinitja SA 68 C5
Old Bar NSW 23 C13
Old Beach TAS 50 A5 53 F10
Old Bonalbo NSW 25 B12
Old Grevillia NSW 25 A12
Old Halls Creek WA 79 B13 81 J12
Old Junee NSW 29 G13
Old Noarlunga SA 60 K1 61 D5 62 F7 65 J10
Old Onslow Historic Ruin WA 78 F2
Old Tyabb VIC 37 H9
Old Warburton VIC 37 C13
Old Warrah NSW 23 A8
Oldina TAS 54 D4
Olinda NSW 22 E7
Olinda VIC 37 D10 42 K3 44 C3
Olio QLD 13 C9
Olive Island Con Park SA 64 E3
Olympic Dam SA 66 K7
Ombersley VIC 39 H10
Omeo VIC 43 G11 46 A6
Ondit VIC 39 H10
One Arm Point WA 80 E5
One Mile Rocks Nature Res WA 75 F10
One Tree NSW 29 F8 41 A13
One Tree Hill SA 60 D4
One Tree Island QLD 9 H12
Ongerup WA 74 H7
Onkaparinga River Nat Park SA 60 K2 61 D6 62 F7 65 J10
Onslow WA 78 F2
Oodla Wirra SA 62 E2 65 E11
Oodnadatta SA 66 D5
Oolambeyan Nat Park NSW 29 G9
Oolarinna Oil Well SA 66 A7
Ooldea SA 68 H5
Oolloo Crossing NT 85 H2 86 F4
Ooma North NSW 22 G2 29 D14
Oombulgurri WA 81 C12
Oonah TAS 54 E4
Oondooroo QLD 13 C9
Oorindi QLD 10 K6 12 A6
Ootann QLD 11 E11
Ootha NSW 29 C13
Opalton QLD 13 E8
Ophir NSW 22 E5
Opossum Bay TAS 50 E7 53 G11
Ora Banda WA 77 H10
Oran Park NSW 21 F10
Orange NSW 22 F4
Orange Grove WA 71 H7
Orangeville NSW 21 G11
Oranmeir NSW 30 E4
Orbost VIC 43 K14 47 D9
Orchard Hills NSW 21 F8
Orchid Beach QLD 7 A13 9 K14
Orchid Valley WA 73 B12
Ord River Nature Res WA 81 C14
Orford TAS 53 E12
Orford VIC 38 H5
Organ Pipes Nat Park VIC 36 B6 39 E13 42 J1
Orielton TAS 51 A8 53 F11
Orkabie QLD 9 E9
Ormeau QLD 5 C11
Ormiston QLD 5 C8
Orpheus Island Nat Park QLD 11 G14
Orroroo SA 62 F1 65 E10
Orrvale VIC 42 C3
Osborne NSW 29 H12
Osborne SA 59 C1
Osborne Mine QLD 12 C5
Osborne Park WA 71 E2
Osborne Well NSW 29 J10
Osmington WA 73 J12
Osterley TAS 53 D8
Otago TAS 50 B5 53 F10
Otford NSW 21 C12
Ottoway SA 59 D2
Otway Nat Park VIC 39 K10
Ourimbah NSW 20 B3 23 F10
Ournie NSW 29 K14 43 A12
Ouse TAS 53 D8
Outer Harbor SA 59 B2 60 E1 62 F6 65 J10
Outer Sister Island TAS 55 A9
Ouyen VIC 28 H4 40 E5
Ovens VIC 43 D8
Overland Corner SA 62 B5 65 H12
Overland Telegraph Station Reserve NT 89 G9
Overlander Roadhouse WA 76 C3 78 K2
Owen SA 62 F5 65 H10
Owens Gap NSW 23 B8
Owingup Nature Res WA 74 K4
Oxenford QLD 5 C11
Oxford Falls NSW 19 C6 20 B7
Oxley ACT 32 H3
Oxley NSW 28 F7 41 A11
Oxley QLD 3 G2 5 F9
Oxley VIC 42 D7
Oxley Island NT 86 A6
Oxley Wild Rivers Nat Park NSW 25 J10
Oyster Bay NSW 21 C10
Oyster Cove TAS 50 G4 53 H10
Ozenkadnook VIC 38 B3

P

Pacific Palms NSW 23 D12
Packsaddle NSW 26 F3
Padbury WA 71 B2
Paddington NSW 18 D3 21 B8
Paddington QLD 3 E3
Paddington Siding WA 77 H11 83 F1
Paddys Ranges State Park VIC 39 C10
Paddys River NSW 22 K7 30 B6
Padstow NSW 19 H3 21 D9
Padstow Heights NSW 19 H3
Padthaway SA 63 B11
Padthaway Con Park SA 63 B11
Page ACT 32 C3
Pagewood NSW 21 B9
Pago Mission WA 81 A11
Paignie VIC 28 H3 40 E5
Pains Island QLD 10 D3
Pakenham VIC 37 F11 44 D4
Pakenham South VIC 37 G11
Pakenham Upper VIC 37 F11
Palana TAS 55 A8
Palarang NSW 30 J3
Palgarup WA 73 E13
Pallamallawa NSW 24 D6
Pallamana SA 62 E7 65 J11
Pallara QLD 3 J3
Pallarang VIC 28 H2 40 E2
Pallarenda QLD 8 A5 11 H14
Pallarup Nature Res WA 75 F9
Palm Beach NSW 20 B5 23 G9
Palm Beach QLD 5 A13
Palm Cove QLD 11 D13
Palm Grove NSW 20 C3
Palmdale NSW 20 C3
Palmer SA 62 E7 65 J11
Palmer River Roadhouse QLD 11 C11
Palmers Oakey NSW 22 F6
Palmerston ACT 32 B5
Palmerston NT 85 C2 86 D3
Palmgrove Nat Park QLD 6 A6 9 K8
Palmview QLD 4 E1
Palmwoods QLD 4 F1
Palmyra WA 71 J2
Paloona TAS 54 E7
Paluma QLD 11 G13
Paluma Range Nat Park QLD 11 G13
Palumpa NT 86 G2
Pambula NSW 30 J5 47 A14
Pambula Beach NSW 30 J5 47 A14
Pandanus Park WA 79 B10 80 H6
Pandappa Con Park SA 62 E3 65 F11
Panitya VIC 28 H1 40 F1
Panmure VIC 38 H7
Pannawonica WA 78 F3 82 E1
Pannikin Island QLD 5 C9
Panorama SA 59 J4
Pantijan WA 81 E8
Panton Hill VIC 37 B9 42 J3 44 A3
Paper Beach TAS 55 E9 56 E4
Pappinbarra NSW 23 A12 25 K11
Papunya NT 90 E5
Para Hills SA 59 C5 60 E3
Para Vista SA 59 D6
Para Wirra Rec Park SA 62 E6 65 J10
Paraburdoo WA 78 G4 82 G3
Parachilna SA 65 B10
Paracombe SA 60 F4
Paradise SA 59 E6
Paradise TAS 54 F7
Paradise Beach VIC 45 E12 46 F5
Paradise Point QLD 5 B11
Parafield SA 59 C5 60 E2
Parafield Gardens SA 59 C4
Paralowie SA 59 B4
Parap NT 84 D2
Paraparap VIC 36 H2
Paratoo SA 62 D1 65 E11
Parattah TAS 53 D11
Parawa SA 61 J4
Pardoo Roadhouse WA 78 D6 82 B6
Parenna TAS 54 B6
Parham SA 62 G5 65 H9
Parilla SA 63 B8 65 K13
Paringa SA 28 F1 62 A5 65 H13
Paris Creek SA 60 K4
Park Holme SA 59 J3 60 G2 61 A5
Park Orchards VIC 35 C7
Park Ridge QLD 5 E10
Parkes ACT 31 C3 32 E5
Parkes NSW 22 F2 29 C14
Parkham TAS 55 F8
Parkhurst QLD 9 H10
Parkinson QLD 3 J4
Parkside SA 58 D3 59 G4 60 G2 61 A6
Parkville NSW 23 B9
Parkwood QLD 5 B12
Parkwood WA 71 J5
Parma NSW 30 C6
Parnabal QLD 9 H8
Parndana SA 63 J9
Parnngurr (Cotton Creek) WA 79 G9
Paroo Siding WA 77 C9 78 K6
Paroo-Darling Nat Park NSW 26 G6
Parrakie SA 63 C8 65 K12
Parramatta NSW 19 E2 21 D8 23 H9
Parrawe TAS 54 E4
Parry Lagoons Nature Res WA 81 D13
Parsons Beach SA 62 H6 65 J8
Partridge Island TAS 53 J10
Paru NT 85 A1 86 C3
Paruna SA 28 G1 62 B6 65 J13
Parwan VIC 36 C3 39 F12
Pascoe Vale VIC 36 C7
Paskeville SA 62 G4 65 G9
Pasminco Century Mine QLD 10 G2
Passage Island TAS 55 A14
Pastoria VIC 39 D13
Pata SA 62 B6 65 H13
Patchewollock VIC 28 J4 40 F5
Pateena TAS 55 G10 56 J5
Paterson NSW 23 D10
Patersonia TAS 55 F10 56 F6
Patho VIC 29 K8 41 H12
Patonga NSW 20 C5
Patterson Lakes VIC 37 F9
Paupong NSW 30 H2
Paupong Nature Res NSW 30 H2
Paw Paw SA 68 C5
Pawleena TAS 51 A9 53 F11

106 Pawtella - Reid

Pawtella TAS 53 C11 55 K11
Paxton NSW 23 E9
Payne QLD 8 G1 13 E10
Payneham SA 59 F5 60 F3
Paynes Crossing NSW 23 E9
Paynes Find WA 76 G7
Paynesville VIC 45 C13 46 E6
Peachester QLD 4 F2
Peachna Con Res SA 64 G5
Peak Charles Nat Park WA 75 E12
Peak Creek Siding SA 66 E5
Peak Crossing QLD 5 H11
Peak Downs Mine QLD 8 F7
Peak Hill NSW 22 D2
Peak Hill WA 77 A8 78 J5
Peak Range Nat Park QLD 8 F6
Peak View NSW 30 F4
Peake SA 63 C8 65 K12
Peakhurst NSW 19 H3
Pearce ACT 32 G3
Pearcedale VIC 37 G9 44 E2
Pearl Beach NSW 20 B5
Pearsall WA 71 B3
Pearshape TAS 54 C6
Pearson Isles SA 64 G3
Peats Ridge NSW 20 D3 23 F9
Pebbly Beach NSW 30 E6
Pedirka SA 66 B5
Pee Dee Nature Res NSW 25 H11
Peebinga SA 28 H1 40 D1 62 A7 65 J13
Peebinga Con Park SA 28 H1 40 E1 62 A7 65 J13
Peechelba VIC 42 B6
Peel NSW 22 F5
Peel Island QLD 5 B8
Peelwood NSW 22 J5 30 A4
Peerabeelup WA 73 G14
Peery Lake NSW 26 F6
Pegarah TAS 54 B6
Pekina SA 62 F2 65 E10
Peko Mine NT 89 H9
Pelham TAS 53 E9
Pelican Lagoon Con Park SA 63 H9
Pelican Waters QLD 4 E2
Pella VIC 28 K3 40 H4
Pelorus Island QLD 11 G14
Pelsaert Group WA 76 F2
Pelverata TAS 50 G3 53 G10
Pemberton WA 73 F14 74 J3
Pembroke NSW 23 A13 25 K12
Penarie NSW 28 F6 41 B9
Pencil Pine TAS 54 G5
Pender Bay WA 79 A9 80 F4
Penfield SA 60 C2
Penguin TAS 54 D6
Penguin Island WA 72 G5
Penna TAS 51 B8 53 F11
Pennant Hills NSW 19 C3 20 D7
Penneshaw SA 63 G8 65 K9
Penola SA 38 E1 63 B13
Penong SA 64 C1 68 K6
Penrice SA 60 A7
Penrith NSW 21 G8 23 H8
Penshurst VIC 38 F6
Pental Island VIC 41 F10
Pentland QLD 8 C3 11 K12 13 A12
Penwortham SA 62 F4 65 G10
Penzance TAS 51 F13
Peppermint Grove WA 71 G2
Peppers Plains VIC 40 J5
Peppimenarti NT 86 G2
Peranga QLD 7 F10
Percival Lakes WA 79 E10
Percy Isles QLD 9 E10
Percy Isles Nat Park QLD 9 E10
Perekerten NSW 28 H7 41 D10
Perenjori WA 76 G5
Perenna VIC 40 J4
Perforated Island SA 64 H4
Pericoe NSW 30 K4 47 A13
Perisher NSW 30 G1 43 D14
Perkins Island TAS 54 C2
Pernatty Lagoon SA 65 B8
Peron Island North NT 86 E2
Peron Island South NT 86 E2
Perponda SA 62 C7 65 J12
Perth TAS 55 G10 56 J5
Perth WA 71 F4 72 G3 74 C3 76 K4
Perth CBD WA 70
Perthville NSW 22 G5
Petcheys Bay TAS 50 J2 53 H9
Peterborough SA 62 E2 65 E10
Peterborough VIC 38 J7
Peterhead SA 59 D2
Peters Island QLD 8 A6
Petersville SA 62 G5 65 H9
Petford QLD 11 E12
Petina SA 64 D3
Petrie QLD 4 F6 7 F13
Petrie Terrace QLD 2 B1
Pettavel VIC 36 H2
Pheasant Creek VIC 42 H3
Pheasants Nest NSW 23 J8 30 A7
Phegans Bay NSW 20 C5
Phillip ACT 32 F4
Phillip Bay NSW 21 B9
Phillip Island VIC 37 K9 39 J14 44 F2
Phillott QLD 15 H13
Phils Creek NSW 22 J4 30 A3
Phosphate Hill Mine QLD 12 C4
Piallamore NSW 25 J8
Piallaway NSW 24 J6
Pialligo ACT 32 E6
Piambie VIC 28 G5 41 D8
Piangil VIC 28 H5 41 E9
Piangil West VIC 41 E8
Piccadilly SA 59 J7 60 G4
Piccaninnie Ponds Con Park SA 38 G1 63 B14
Pickanjinnie QLD 6 E5
Pickering Brook WA 72 F4
Pickertaramoor NT 85 A2 86 C3
Picnic Point NSW 29 K9 41 H14 42 A2
Picola VIC 41 H14 42 A2
Picton NSW 21 F12 23 J8 30 A7
Picton WA 73 G9 74 F3
Piedmont VIC 37 E14
Piednippie SA 64 E3
Pielegia NT 88 F3
Pieman River State Res TAS 54 G3
Pier Millan VIC 28 H4 40 E7
Piesseville WA 73 A9 74 F5
Pigeon Hole NT 88 C4
Pigeon Ponds VIC 38 D4
Piggabeen NSW 5 B14
Pikedale QLD 7 J10 25 B9
Pilakatal NT 90 J2
Pilgna SA 68 C3
Pilkinga SA 68 C4
Pillar Valley NSW 25 E13
Pilliga NSW 24 G2
Pilliga Nature Res NSW 24 H4
Pimba SA 64 B7
Pimpama QLD 5 C11
Pimpinio VIC 38 A5
Pinchgut Junction VIC 36 K1
Pindar WA 76 E4
Pine Clump NSW 24 K1 27 H14
Pine Corner SA 62 K4 64 F6
Pine Creek NT 85 G4 86 F5
Pine Gap NT 91 F8
Pine Hill QLD 8 H5 13 F14
Pine Lodge VIC 42 C4
Pine Peak Island QLD 9 E10
Pine Point SA 62 G6 65 H9
Pine Ridge NSW 23 A8 24 K6
Pinery SA 62 F5 65 H10
Piney Range NSW 22 H2 29 E14
Pingaring WA 74 E7
Pingelly WA 72 B6 74 E5
Pingrup WA 74 G7
Pinjarra WA 72 G6 74 E3
Pinjarra Hills QLD 3 G1
Pinjarrega Nature Res WA 76 H4
Pink Lakes State Park VIC 65 J14
Pinkawillinie Con Park SA 64 E5
Pinkawillinie Con Res SA 64 E5
Pinkenba QLD 3 D6
Pinnacle QLD 8 D7
Pinnaroo SA 28 H1 40 F1 63 A8 65 K13
Pioneer TAS 55 D13
Pioneer WA 75 C13 77 K11 83 G1
Pioneer Bay VIC 37 J11
Pipalyatjara SA 68 A1 79 K14 83 B7 90 K1
Pipeclay Nat Park QLD 7 D13
Pipers Brook TAS 55 D10 56 C6
Pipers River TAS 55 D9 56 C4
Pipon Island QLD 16 H5
Piries VIC 42 G6 46 A1
Pirlangimpi NT 86 B3
Pirlta VIC 28 F3 40 B4
Pirrinuan QLD 7 F9
Pirron Yallock VIC 39 H9
Pirrulpakalarintja NT 90 J3
Pitalu NT 79 J14 90 J2
Pitarpunga Lake NSW 28 F6 41 B9
Pitfield VIC 39 F9
Pithara WA 76 H5
Pitt Town NSW 20 F6
Pitt Water TAS 51 B8
Pittong VIC 39 E9
Pittsworth QLD 7 G10
Plainland QLD 5 K9
Planchonella Nature Res NSW 24 C7
Platts NSW 30 J3 47 A12
Pleasant Hills NSW 29 J12
Plenty TAS 50 A1 53 F9
Plenty VIC 35 A5 37 B8 39 E14 42 J2 44 B2
Plumpton NSW 21 F8
Plumridge Lakes WA 83 E4
Plumridge Lakes Nature Res WA 83 E4
Plympton SA 59 H3 60 G1 61 A5
Plympton Park SA 59 H3
Pmara Jutunta NT 90 C7
Poatina TAS 53 A9 55 H9
Poeppel Corner NT QLD SA 12 K2 67 A9 91 K14
Point Bell Con Res SA 64 D1 68 K6
Point Clare NSW 20 C4
Point Cook VIC 36 E6 39 F13 42 K1
Point Davenport Con Park SA 62 H7 65 J8
Point Denison WA 76 G3
Point Leo VIC 37 K8 39 H14 44 F2
Point Lonsdale VIC 36 H5 39 H13
Point Lookout QLD 4 A7 7 G14
Point Pass SA 62 E5 65 G10
Point Samson WA 78 E4 82 C2
Point Souttar SA 62 J6 65 J8
Point Stuart Coastal Res NT 85 B4 86 C5
Point Turton SA 62 H7 65 J8
Pokataroo NSW 24 D2
Pokolbin NSW 23 E9
Police Point TAS 50 K2 53 H9
Policemans Point SA 63 D9
Poltalloch SA 63 E8 65 K11
Pomborneit VIC 39 H9
Pomborneit North VIC 39 H9
Pomona QLD 7 D12
Pomonal VIC 38 D7
Pompapiel VIC 41 K11
Pontville TAS 53 E10
Poochera SA 64 E4
Pooginagoric SA 38 A1 40 K1
Pooginook Con Park SA 62 C5 65 G12
Poolaijelo VIC 38 D2
Poolawanna No. 1 Oil Well SA 67 B9
Poole TAS 55 C14
Poona QLD 7 C13
Poona Nat Park QLD 7 C12
Pooncarie NSW 28 D4
Poonindie SA 64 H6
Pooraka SA 59 D5 60 E3
Pootilla VIC 39 E11
Pootnoura SA 66 F3
Poowong VIC 37 J13 44 E5
Poowong East VIC 37 J14 44 E5
Poowong North VIC 37 J13
Popanyinning WA 72 B6 74 E5
Popilta Lake NSW 28 C3
Popran Nat Park NSW 20 D4 23 F9
Porcupine Gorge Nat Park QLD 8 C1 11 K11
Porepunkah VIC 43 E9
Pormpuraaw QLD 10 A6 16 J1
Porongurup WA 74 J6
Porongurup Nat Park WA 74 J6
Porphyry Mine WA 77 G12 83 E1
Port Adelaide SA 59 E2 60 E1 62 F6 65 J10
Port Albert VIC 45 G9 46 H3
Port Alma QLD 9 H11
Port Arthur TAS 51 H12 53 H12
Port Augusta SA 62 H1 65 D9
Port Botany NSW 19 H6
Port Broughton SA 62 G3 65 F9
Port Campbell VIC 39 J8
Port Campbell Nat Park VIC 39 J8
Port Clinton Con Park SA 62 G5 65 G9
Port Davis SA 62 G3 65 F9
Port Douglas QLD 11 C12
Port Elliot SA 61 J7 63 F8 65 K10
Port Fairy VIC 38 H5
Port Fairy – Warrnambool Coastal Park VIC 38 H6
Port Franklin VIC 44 H7 46 H1
Port Gawler SA 60 C1 62 F6 65 J9
Port Gawler Con Park SA 60 C1 62 F6 65 H9
Port Germein SA 62 G2 65 E9
Port Gibbon SA 62 K4 64 G7
Port Hacking NSW 19 K4
Port Hedland WA 78 D5 82 B4
Port Hughes SA 62 H6 65 G8
Port Huon TAS 50 H1 53 H9
Port Jackson NSW 19 E7
Port Julia SA 62 G6 65 H9
Port Kembla NSW 21 C14 23 K8 30 B7
Port Kenny SA 64 E4
Port Latta TAS 54 C3
Port Lincoln SA 64 J6
Port MacDonnell SA 38 G1 63 B14
Port Macquarie NSW 23 A13 25 K12
Port Melbourne VIC 35 D3
Port Minlacowie SA 62 H6 65 J8
Port Moorowie SA 62 H7 65 J8
Port Neill SA 64 G6
Port Noarlunga SA 60 K1 61 D5 62 F7 65 J10
Port Phillip Bay VIC 36 F6 39 G13 44 D1
Port Pirie SA 62 G2 65 F9
Port Rickaby SA 62 H6 65 H8
Port Roper NT 87 H10
Port Sorell TAS 55 E8
Port Stewart QLD 16 H4
Port Victoria SA 62 H6 65 H8
Port Vincent SA 62 G6 65 J9
Port Wakefield SA 62 G5 65 H9
Port Welshpool VIC 45 H8 46 H2
Port Willunga SA 61 E5
Portarlington VIC 36 G5 39 G13
Porters Retreat NSW 22 H6
Portland NSW 22 F6
Portland VIC 38 H4
Portland Bay VIC 38 H4
Portland Roads QLD 16 E4
Portsea VIC 36 J5 39 H13
Possession Island Nat Park QLD 16 B2
Potato Point NSW 30 G5
Potts Point NSW 18 B4
Pottsville NSW 7 J14 25 A14
Pound Creek VIC 44 G5
Powelltown VIC 37 D13 42 K5 44 C5
Powers Creek VIC 38 D2
Powlathanga QLD 8 B4 11 J13
Powlett Plains VIC 41 K10
Poynter Island QLD 9 E9
Prahran VIC 35 E4 37 D8
Prairie QLD 8 C1 11 K11 13 A11
Prairie VIC 41 K12
Precipice Nat Park QLD 6 B7
Premaydena TAS 51 G11 53 G12
Premer NSW 22 A6 24 K5
Preolenna TAS 54 D4
Prescott Lakes WA 79 E11
Preservation Island TAS 55 A13
Preston TAS 54 E6
Preston VIC 35 B4 36 C7
Preston Beach WA 72 H7 74 E2
Pretty Beach NSW 20 B5
Pretty Gully NSW 25 B11
Pretty Pine NSW 29 J8 41 F13
Prevelly WA 73 K12 74 H1
Price SA 62 G5 65 H9
Price Island SA 64 H5
Priestdale QLD 3 H6
Prime Seal Island TAS 55 B8
Primrose Sands TAS 51 D10 53 G12
Prince of Wales Island QLD 16 B1
Prince Regent Nature Res WA 81 D8
Princess Charlotte Bay QLD 16 H4
Princetown VIC 39 K8
Princhester QLD 9 G9
Priors Pocket QLD 3 H1
Priory TAS 55 E14
Probable Island NT 87 C11
Propodollah VIC 40 K3
Proserpine QLD 8 C7
Prospect NSW 19 E1 21 E8
Prospect SA 59 F4 60 F2
Prospect TAS 56 H5
Proston QLD 7 D10
Prubi QLD 13 C9
Prudhoe Island QLD 9 D9
Pucawan NSW 29 F13
Pucawan Nature Res NSW 29 F13
Puckapunyal VIC 39 C14 42 F2
Pudman Creek NSW 22 K4 30 B3
Pukatja (Ernabella) SA 90 K6
Pullabooka NSW 22 G1 29 E14
Pullen Island SA 61 J7
Pullen Island Con Park SA 61 J7
Pullenvale QLD 5 F8
Pulletop NSW 29 J13
Pulletop Nature Res NSW 29 E10
Pullut VIC 40 J5
Pumphreys Bridge WA 72 C6
Punchbowl NSW 19 G3 21 C9
Punmu WA 79 F9
Punthari SA 62 D6 65 J11
Pura Pura VIC 39 F8
Pureba Con Park SA 64 C3
Pureba Con Res SA 64 C3 68 K7
Purfleet NSW 23 B12
Purga QLD 5 H10
Purlewaugh NSW 24 K4
Purnim VIC 38 H7
Purnong SA 62 D6 65 J11
Purnululu Con Res WA 79 B14 81 H13
Purnululu Nat Park WA 79 B14 81 G13
Purrumbete South VIC 39 H8
Puta Puta NT 90 H2
Putaputa SA 68 A1 90 K2
Putty NSW 20 J1 23 E8
Pyalong VIC 39 C13 42 G1
Pyap SA 62 B6 65 H13
Pyengana TAS 55 E13
Pygery SA 64 E5
Pymble NSW 19 C5 20 C7
Pymurra QLD 10 K5 12 A5
Pyramid Hill VIC 28 K7 41 J11
Pyramul NSW 22 E5

Q

Quaama NSW 30 H5
Quail Island NT 86 D3
Quail Island QLD 9 F9
Quail Island VIC 37 H10 44 E3
Quairading WA 72 A3 74 C5 76 K6
Quakers Hill NSW 21 E8
Qualco SA 62 C5 65 G12
Qualeup WA 73 C11
Quambatook VIC 28 K6 41 H9
Quambone NSW 27 G14
Quamby QLD 10 K5
Quamby Brook TAS 55 G8 56 J1
Quanda Nature Res NSW 27 J12
Quandialla NSW 22 H1 29 E14
Quangallin WA 73 A9
Quantong VIC 38 B5
Quarram Nature Res WA 74 K4
Queanbeyan NSW 30 D3 32 G7
Queen Victoria Spring Nature Res WA 77 H13 83 F2
Queens Lake Nature Res NSW 23 A13
Queenscliff NSW 20 B7
Queenscliff VIC 36 H5 39 H13
Queensferry VIC 37 K11
Queenstown TAS 52 B4 54 J4
Quellington WA 72 C2
Quidong Nature Res NSW 30 J3
Quilberry QLD 15 F13
Quilpie QLD 15 E10
Quinalow QLD 7 F10
Quindalup WA 73 J11
Quindanning WA 73 D8 74 F4
Quindinup Nature Res WA 73 C14 74 H5
Quinninup WA 73 E14
Quinns Rocks WA 72 G2 74 C2 76 K4
Quipolly NSW 23 A8 24 K7
Quirindi NSW 23 A8 24 K7
Quobba WA 78 H1
Quoin Island NT 86 H1
Quondong NSW 26 K3 28 A3
Quorn SA 62 G1 65 D9

R

Rabbit Flat Roadhouse NT 88 H2
Rabbit Island QLD 9 C8
Rabuma Island NT 87 C10
Raby NSW 21 E10
Raglan QLD 9 H11
Raglan VIC 39 D9
Ragul Waajaarr Nature Res NSW 25 G11
Railton TAS 54 F7
Rainbow VIC 28 K3 40 H4
Rainbow Beach QLD 7 C13
Rainbow Valley Con Res NT 91 G8
Raine Island QLD 16 D5
Raleigh NSW 25 G12
Raluana VIC 38 A7
Ramco SA 62 C5 65 H12
Raminea TAS 53 J9
Ramingining NT 87 D10
Ramornie Nat Park NSW 25 E12
Ramsgate NSW 21 B9
Ranceby VIC 37 J14 44 F5
Rand NSW 29 J12
Randalls Mine WA 75 A13 77 J12 83 F1
Randell WA 75 A14 77 J12 83 F1
Randwick NSW 19 G6 21 B9
Ranelagh TAS 50 F2 53 G9
Ranga TAS 55 C9
Rangal QLD 9 H8
Rangelands QLD 13 C9
Rankins Springs NSW 29 E11
Rannes QLD 9 J9
Rannock NSW 29 G13
Ransome QLD 3 E7
Rapanyup South VIC 38 B7
Rapid Bay SA 61 J2 63 G8 65 K9
Rapid Creek NT 84 B2
Rappville NSW 25 C12
Raragala Island NT 87 B12
Ratcatchers Lake NSW 28 A5
Rathdowney QLD 5 G14 7 H12 25 A12
Rathscar VIC 39 C9
Ravensdale NSW 20 D2
Ravenshoe QLD 11 E12
Ravensthorpe WA 75 G10
Ravenswood QLD 8 B5 11 J14
Ravenswood VIC 39 B11
Ravenswood WA 72 G6
Ravensworth NSW 23 D9
Ravine NSW 43 A14
Rawbelle QLD 7 A9 9 K10
Rawdon Creek Nature Res NSW 23 A13 25 K12
Rawdon Vale NSW 23 C10
Rawlinna WA 83 F4
Rawson VIC 45 C8 46 E2
Raymond Island VIC 45 C13 46 E6
Raymond Terrace NSW 23 E10
Raywood VIC 39 A11
Razorback Nature Res NSW 22 H5 30 A4
Recherche Archipelago Nature Res WA 75 H14 83 J1
Red Banks SA 60 A2
Red Banks Con Park SA 62 E4 65 G11
Red Bluff Nature Res VIC 28 K2 40 H1 63 A9
Red Cap Creek VIC 38 E2
Red Cliffs VIC 28 F3 40 B5
Red Hill ACT 32 F5
Red Hill QLD 2 A1 3 E3 5 E8
Red Hill VIC 37 J8
Red Hill South VIC 37 J8
Red Hills TAS 55 G8
Red Range NSW 25 E10
Red Rock NSW 25 F13
Redbank VIC 39 B9 43 E9
Redbank Plains QLD 5 G9
Redbanks SA 62 E4 65 G11
Redcliffe QLD 4 D6 7 F13
Redcliffe WA 71 F5
Redesdale VIC 39 C12
Redfern NSW 19 F6 21 B9
Redhill SA 62 G3 65 F9
Redland Bay QLD 5 C9 7 G13
Redlynch QLD 11 D13
Redmond WA 74 K6
Redpa TAS 54 C1
Redwood Park SA 59 C7
Reedy Creek QLD 5 B13
Reedy Creek SA 63 C12
Reedy Creek VIC 39 D14 42 G2
Reedy Dam VIC 28 K4 40 H7
Reedy Flat VIC 43 H12 46 B7
Reedy Marsh TAS 55 F8 56 G1
Reef Hills Regional Park VIC 42 D5
Reefton NSW 29 F13
Reefton VIC 37 B14 42 J5 44 B5
Reekara TAS 54 B6
Reeves Plains SA 60 A2
Reevesby Island SA 64 H6
Regatta Point TAS 52 C3 54 K3
Regency Park SA 59 E3
Regents Park NSW 19 F2 21 D9
Regents Park QLD 3 K4
Regentville NSW 21 G9
Reid ACT 31 A4 32 D5

Reid – Smithfield 107

Reid **WA** 83 F6
Reid River **QLD** 8 A5 11 J14
Reids Creek **VIC** 43 C8
Reids Flat **NSW** 22 J4 30 A3
Relbia **TAS** 55 F10 56 H6
Rendlesham **SA** 63 C13
Renison Bell **TAS** 52 A4 54 H4
Renmark **SA** 28 F1 62 A5 65 H13
Renner Springs **NT** 89 E8
Rennie **NSW** 29 K11 42 A6
Research **VIC** 35 B6
Reservoir **VIC** 35 B4 36 C7
Retreat **TAS** 55 E10 56 D5
Retro **QLD** 8 G6
Revesby **NSW** 19 H3 21 D9
Reynella **SA** 60 J2 61 C5 62 F7 65 J10
Reynolds Island **TAS** 53 A8 55 H8
Reynolds Neck **TAS** 53 A8 55 H8
Rheban **TAS** 53 E13
Rheola **VIC** 39 A10
Rhodes **NSW** 21 D8
Rhyll **VIC** 37 K10 44 F3
Rhyndaston **TAS** 53 D11
Rhynie **SA** 62 F5 65 G10
Riana **TAS** 54 E6
Rich Avon **VIC** 38 A7 40 K7
Richardson **ACT** 32 J4
Richlands **NSW** 22 J6 30 A5
Richlands **QLD** 3 H2
Richmond **NSW** 20 G7 23 G8
Richmond **QLD** 11 K9 13 A9
Richmond **SA** 59 G3 60 G2 61 A6
Richmond **TAS** 50 A7 53 F11
Richmond **VIC** 35 D4 37 D8
Richmond Range Nat Park **NSW** 7 J12 25 B12
Rickeys **WA** 72 B3
Riddells Creek **VIC** 39 E13 42 H1
Ridgehaven **SA** 59 D7
Ridgelands **QLD** 9 G10
Ridgeway **TAS** 50 D5
Ridgley **TAS** 54 E5
Rifle Creek **QLD** 12 A3
Rimbanda **QLD** 13 D10
Rimbija Island **NT** 87 A13
Ringa **WA** 72 D2
Ringarooma **TAS** 55 E12
Ringarooma Coastal Res **TAS** 55 C13
Ringwood **VIC** 35 D7 37 D9 42 K3 44 B2
Ripley **QLD** 5 G10
Ripplebrook **VIC** 37 H13 44 E5
Risdon Vale **TAS** 50 B6 53 F10
Rita Island **QLD** 8 A6
River Heads **QLD** 7 B13
Riverhills **QLD** 3 G1
Riverside **TAS** 56 G5
Riverside Mine **QLD** 8 E6
Riverstone **NSW** 20 F7
Riverton **SA** 62 E5 65 H10
Riverton **WA** 71 H5
Rivervale **WA** 71 G5
Riverview **QLD** 5 G9
Riverwood **NSW** 19 H3 21 C9
Rivett **ACT** 32 F2
Roadvale **QLD** 5 H12
Rob Roy Nature Res **ACT** 32 K4
Robbins Island **TAS** 54 B2
Robe **SA** 63 D12
Roberts Point **TAS** 50 H5
Robertson **NSW** 23 K8 30 B7
Robertson **QLD** 3 G4
Robertstown **SA** 62 E4 65 G11
Robigana **TAS** 55 E9 56 E3
Robin Hood **VIC** 37 F14
Robina **QLD** 5 B13
Robinson River **NT** 89 C13
Robinvale **VIC** 28 G5 40 C7
Rochedale **QLD** 3 G6 5 D9
Rochedale South **QLD** 3 H6
Rocherlea **TAS** 55 F10 56 F5
Rochester **VIC** 41 K13 42 C1
Rochford **VIC** 39 D13 42 H1
Rock Flat **NSW** 30 G3
Rockbank **VIC** 36 C5 39 F13 42 K1
Rockdale **NSW** 19 H4 21 C9
Rockhampton **QLD** 9 H10
Rockingham **WA** 72 G5 74 D2
Rocklands Reservoir **VIC** 38 D5
Rocklea **QLD** 3 G3 5 E8
Rockleigh **SA** 60 G7 62 E7 65 J10
Rockley **NSW** 22 G5
Rocklyn **VIC** 39 D11
Rocksberg **QLD** 4 G4
Rockton **NSW** 30 K3 47 A12
Rockvale **NSW** 25 G10
Rocky Cape **TAS** 54 C4
Rocky Cape Nat Park **TAS** 54 C4
Rocky Creek **NSW** 24 F6
Rocky Glen **NSW** 24 J4
Rocky Gully **WA** 73 B14 74 J5
Rocky Hall **NSW** 30 J4
Rocky Island **QLD** 10 C3
Rocky River **NSW** 25 H9
Rocky River **SA** 63 K9
Rodds Bay **QLD** 9 J11
Rodinga **NT** 91 G8
Roebourne **WA** 78 E4 82 C2
Roebuck Bay **WA** 79 B8 80 H3
Roebuck Plains Roadhouse **WA** 79 B9 80 H4
Roelands **WA** 73 G9
Roger Corner **SA** 62 H7 65 J8
Roger River **TAS** 54 D2
Roger River West **TAS** 54 D2
Rokeby **TAS** 50 D7 53 G11
Rokeby **VIC** 37 F14 44 D6
Rokewood **VIC** 39 F10
Rokewood Junction **VIC** 39 F10
Roland **TAS** 54 F7
Rollands Plains **NSW** 23 A13 25 K12
Rolleston **QLD** 8 J7
Rollingstone **QLD** 11 G14
Roma **QLD** 6 E5
Romsey **VIC** 39 D13 42 H1
Rookhurst **NSW** 23 B11
Rooty Hill **NSW** 21 F8
Roper Bar **NT** 87 H9
Rorruwuy **NT** 87 C12
Rosa Glen **WA** 73 J12
Rosanna **VIC** 37 C8
Rose Bay **NSW** 21 B8
Rose Bay **TAS** 49 A4
Rosebank **NSW** 25 B14
Roseberry **VIC** 28 K4 40 H6
Roseberry East **VIC** 40 H6
Rosebery **TAS** 52 A4 54 H4
Rosebrook **VIC** 38 H5
Rosebud **VIC** 36 J7 39 H13 44 F1
Rosedale **QLD** 9 K12
Rosedale **SA** 60 B5
Rosedale **VIC** 45 E9 46 F3
Rosegarland **TAS** 53 E9
Rosehill **NSW** 19 E3
Rosemary Island **WA** 78 D3 82 C1
Rosemeadow **NSW** 21 E11
Roses Gap **VIC** 38 C6
Roses Tier **TAS** 55 F12
Rosevale **QLD** 5 K11
Rosevale **TAS** 55 F9 56 G3
Rosevears **TAS** 55 E9 56 F4
Roseville **NSW** 19 D5 21 C8
Rosewater **SA** 59 E2
Rosewhite **VIC** 43 D9
Rosewood **NSW** 29 J14
Rosewood **QLD** 5 J9 7 G12
Rosewood Island **QLD** 9 F9
Roseworthy **SA** 60 A4 62 F6 65 H10
Roseworthy College **SA** 60 A3
Roslyn **NSW** 22 K5 30 B4
Roslyn Bay **QLD** 9 G11
Roslynmead **VIC** 41 J12
Rosny **TAS** 49 B4
Rosny Park **TAS** 49 B4
Ross **TAS** 53 B11 55 J11
Ross River **NT** 91 F9
Rossarden **TAS** 55 G12
Rossbridge **VIC** 38 E7
Rossi **NSW** 30 E4
Rossiter Bay **WA** 75 G14 83 J1
Rossmore **NSW** 21 F10
Rossmore **WA** 72 C1
Rossmoyne **WA** 71 H4
Rossville **QLD** 11 B12
Rostrevor **SA** 59 F6 60 F3
Rostron **VIC** 39 B8
Rothwell **QLD** 4 E5
Rothwell **VIC** 36 E3
Roto **NSW** 29 C9
Rottnest Island **WA** 72 H3 74 C2 76 K4
Rouchel Brook **NSW** 23 C9
Round Corner **NSW** 19 B2 20 E7
Round Hill Island **NT** 87 E12
Round Hill Nature Res **NSW** 29 C11
Round Island **WA** 83 J3
Rouse Hill **NSW** 20 E7
Rowella **TAS** 55 E9 56 D3
Rowena **NSW** 24 E3
Rowland Flat **SA** 60 B6
Rowles Lagoon Nature Res **WA** 77 H10
Rowsley **VIC** 36 C3 39 F12
Rowville **VIC** 37 E9
Roxby Downs **SA** 64 A7 66 K7
Roxby Island **SA** 64 H6
Royal George **TAS** 53 A12 55 H12
Royal Nat Park **NSW** 19 K3 21 C11 23 J9
Royal Park **SA** 59 E2
Royalla **NSW** 30 E3
Roydon Island **TAS** 55 B8
Roysalt Siding **WA** 75 B12 77 J11 83 G1
Royston Park **SA** 59 F5
Rozelle **NSW** 21 C8
Rubunja **NT** 90 E7
Ruby **VIC** 37 K14
Ruby Gap Nature Park **NT** 91 F10
Rubyvale **QLD** 8 H6
Rudall **SA** 64 G6
Rudall River Nat Park **WA** 79 F9
Ruffy **VIC** 42 F4
Rufus River **NSW** 28 F2 40 A2 65 G14
Rugby **NSW** 22 J4 30 B3
Rules Beach **QLD** 9 K12
Rules Point **NSW** 30 E2
Rum Island **TAS** 55 A13
Rum Jungle **NT** 85 E2 86 E4
Rumbalara **NT** 91 J9
Rumula **QLD** 11 C12
Runaway Bay **QLD** 5 B12
Runcorn **QLD** 3 H5
Rundle Range Nat Park **QLD** 9 H11
Rungoo **QLD** 11 F13
Running Creek Nature Res **NSW** 23 C11
Running Stream **NSW** 22 E6
Runnymede **TAS** 53 E11
Runnymede **VIC** 39 A13 42 D1
Rupanyup **VIC** 38 A7
Rupanyup North **VIC** 38 A7
Rushworth **VIC** 39 A14 42 D2
Rushy Lagoon **TAS** 55 C13
Russell **ACT** 31 C4 32 E5
Russell Island **QLD** 5 B10
Russell River Nat Park **QLD** 11 D13
Russell Vale **NSW** 21 D13
Rutherglen **VIC** 29 K11 42 B7
Ryan **NSW** 29 J12
Ryans Creek **VIC** 42 E6
Rydalmere **NSW** 19 E3 21 D8
Ryde **NSW** 19 E4 21 C8
Rye **VIC** 36 J6 39 H13 44 F1
Rye Park **NSW** 22 K4 30 B3
Rylstone **NSW** 22 E6
Ryton **VIC** 44 G7 46 H1

S

Sackville **NSW** 20 F6
Sackville North **NSW** 20 F5
Saddleworth **SA** 62 F5 65 G10
Safety Bay **WA** 72 G5 74 D2
Safety Beach **VIC** 36 H7
St Agnes **SA** 59 D7
St Albans **NSW** 20 F3 23 F9
St Albans **VIC** 35 C1 36 C6
St Andrews **VIC** 37 B10
St Arnaud **VIC** 39 A9
St Arnaud Range Nat Park **VIC** 39 B9
St Bees Island **QLD** 9 D9
St Clair **NSW** 21 F9 23 D9
St Clair Island **QLD** 5 C9
St Fillans **VIC** 37 A12 42 J4 44 A4
St Francis Island **SA** 64 D2
St George **QLD** 6 H5
St Germains **VIC** 41 J14 42 C3
St Helena Island **QLD** 4 C7
St Helena Island Nat Park **QLD** 4 C7
St Helens **TAS** 55 F14
St Helens **VIC** 38 H5
St Helens Island **TAS** 55 F14
St Helens Point Con Area **TAS** 55 E14
St Helier **VIC** 37 J12
St Ives **NSW** 19 C5 20 C7
St Ives Chase **NSW** 20 C7
St Ives Mine **WA** 75 B13 77 K11 83 G1
St James **VIC** 42 C5
St Kilda **SA** 59 A3 60 D1 62 F6 65 J10
St Kilda **VIC** 35 E3 36 D7 39 F14 42 K2 44 C1
St Kitts **SA** 62 E5 65 H11
St Lawrence **QLD** 9 F9
St Leonards **NSW** 21 C8
St Leonards **TAS** 55 F10 56 G6
St Leonards **VIC** 36 G5 39 G13
St Lucia **QLD** 3 F3 5 E8
St Margaret Island **VIC** 45 G9 46 H3
St Marys **NSW** 21 F8
St Marys **SA** 59 J4
St Marys **TAS** 55 G13
St Patricks River **TAS** 55 F11 56 F7
St Peter Island **SA** 64 D2 68 K7
St Peters **NSW** 21 B9
St Peters **SA** 59 F5 60 F3
Sale **VIC** 45 D10 46 F4
Salisbury **NSW** 23 C10
Salisbury **QLD** 3 G4
Salisbury **SA** 59 B5 60 D3 62 F6 65 J10
Salisbury **VIC** 40 K4
Salisbury Downs **SA** 59 B4
Salisbury East **SA** 59 C6
Salisbury Heights **SA** 59 B6
Salisbury Island **WA** 83 K2
Salisbury North **SA** 59 A5
Salisbury South **SA** 59 C5
Salisbury West **VIC** 39 A11
Sallys Flat **NSW** 22 E5
Salmon Gums **WA** 75 E13 83 H1
Salt Creek **SA** 63 D10
Salt Lake **NSW** 26 E3
Salter Point **WA** 71 H4
Saltern **QLD** 8 H2 13 F12
Saltwater Nat Park **NSW** 23 C13
Saltwater River **TAS** 51 F11 53 G12
Samford **QLD** 7 G12
Samford State Forest **QLD** 3 C1
Samford Valley **QLD** 4 G7
Samford Village **QLD** 3 B1
Samson **WA** 71 J2
Samsonvale **QLD** 4 G6
San Remo **VIC** 44 G3
Sanctuary Cove **QLD** 5 B11
Sand Hill **WA** 78 G6 82 F6
Sandalwood **SA** 62 C7 65 J12
Sanderston **SA** 62 E6 65 J11
Sandfire Roadhouse **WA** 78 D7
Sandfly **TAS** 50 E4 53 G10
Sandford **TAS** 51 E8 53 G11
Sandford **VIC** 38 E3
Sandgate **QLD** 3 A4 4 E6
Sandigo **NSW** 29 G12
Sandilands **SA** 62 H6 65 H8
Sandon **NSW** 25 E13
Sandringham **NSW** 19 J4
Sandringham **VIC** 35 G4 36 E7
Sandsmere **VIC** 40 K2
Sandstone **WA** 77 E8
Sandstone Point **QLD** 4 D4
Sandy Bay **TAS** 49 D2
Sandy Beach **NSW** 25 F13
Sandy Blight Junction **NT** 90 E2
Sandy Cape **TAS** 54 F1
Sandy Creek **SA** 60 B5
Sandy Creek **VIC** 43 C9
Sandy Creek Con Park **SA** 60 B5
Sandy Hill **NSW** 25 C11
Sandy Hollow **NSW** 23 C8
Sandy Island **NT** 87 G11
Sandy Point **NSW** 19 H2
Sandy Point **VIC** 44 H6 46 J1
Sandys Bore **SA** 68 C5
Sangar **NSW** 29 J11
Sans Souci **NSW** 21 C10
Santa Teresa **NT** 91 G9
Sapphire **NSW** 25 E8
Sapphire **QLD** 8 H6
Sarah Island **TAS** 52 D3
Saraji Mine **QLD** 8 F7
Saratoga **NSW** 20 B4
Sarina **QLD** 9 D8
Sarsfield **VIC** 43 K11 45 B13 46 D6
Sassafras **NSW** 30 D6
Sassafras **TAS** 54 E7
Sassafras **VIC** 37 D10
Sassie Island **QLD** 16 A3
Saunders Beach **QLD** 11 H14
Savage River **TAS** 54 F3
Savage River Nat Park **TAS** 54 E4
Savernake **NSW** 29 J11
Sawtell **NSW** 25 G13
Sayers Lake **NSW** 28 B5
Scabby Range Nature Res **NSW** 30 F2
Scaddan **WA** 75 F13 83 J1
Scamander **TAS** 55 F14
Scarborough **NSW** 21 C12 23 J9
Scarborough **QLD** 4 D5
Scarborough **WA** 71 E2 72 G3 74 C2 76 K4
Scarsdale **VIC** 39 E10
Scawfell Island **QLD** 9 C9
Sceale Bay **SA** 64 E3
Scheyville **NSW** 20 F7
Scheyville Nat Park **NSW** 20 F6 23 G8
Schofields **NSW** 20 E7
School Hill **VIC** 36 K7
Schouten Island **TAS** 53 D14
Scone **NSW** 23 C8
Scoresby **VIC** 35 E7 37 D9
Scorpion Springs Con Park **SA** 28 J1 40 G1 63 A8 65 K13
Scotia **WA** 77 H11
Scotia Mine **WA** 77 H11 83 F1
Scotland Island **NSW** 19 A7
Scotsburn **VIC** 39 E11
Scott Con Park **SA** 61 G7
Scott Creek **SA** 60 H3 61 B7
Scott Creek Con Park **SA** 60 J3 61 C7
Scott Nat Park **WA** 73 J13 74 H2
Scott Nature Res **NSW** 30 D4
Scotts Creek **VIC** 39 J8
Scotts Head **NSW** 25 H12
Scottsdale **TAS** 55 E11
Scottville **QLD** 8 C6
Scullin **ACT** 32 C2
Sea Bird **WA** 74 B2 76 J4
Sea Elephant **TAS** 54 B7
Sea Lake **VIC** 28 J5 40 F7
Sea View **VIC** 37 H14
Seabrook **TAS** 54 D5
Seacliff **SA** 59 K2 60 H1 61 B5
Seacliff Park **SA** 59 K2
Seacombe **VIC** 45 D12 46 F5
Seacombe Gardens **SA** 59 K3
Seaford **SA** 60 K1 61 D5
Seaford **VIC** 35 K6 37 G8
Seaforth **NSW** 21 B8
Seaforth **QLD** 9 C8
Seaham **NSW** 23 D10
Seal Bay Con Park **SA** 63 J9
Seal Island **SA** 61 J6 63 J8 64 K7
Seal Rocks **NSW** 23 D12
Seal Rocks State Res **TAS** 54 C6
Searcy Bay **SA** 64 E3
Seaspray **VIC** 45 F11 46 G4
Seaton **SA** 59 F2 60 F1
Seaton **VIC** 45 C9 46 E2
Seaview **VIC** 44 E6
Seaview Downs **SA** 59 K2
Sebastopol **NSW** 22 K1 29 G13
Sebastopol **VIC** 39 E10
Second Valley **SA** 61 H2 63 G8 65 K9
Sedan **SA** 62 D6 65 H11
Sedan Dip **QLD** 10 J6
Sedgwick **VIC** 39 B12
Sefton **NSW** 21 D9
Seisia **QLD** 16 B2
Selbourne **TAS** 55 F9 56 G3
Sellheim **QLD** 8 B4 11 J14
Sellicks Beach **SA** 61 F4 63 F8 65 K9
Sellicks Hill **SA** 61 F5
Selwyn **QLD** 12 B5
Selwyn Mine **QLD** 12 C5
Semaphore **SA** 59 D1 60 F1
Semaphore Park **SA** 59 E1
Seppeltsfield **SA** 60 A6
Serpentine **VIC** 41 K11
Serpentine **WA** 72 F5
Serpentine Lakes **SA** 83 D7
Serpentine Nat Park **WA** 72 F5 74 D3
Serpentine Nature Res **NSW** 25 G10
Serviceton **VIC** 40 K1 63 A10
Seven Hills **NSW** 19 D1 21 E8
Seven Mile Beach **TAS** 51 C8 53 F11
Seven Mile Beach Nat Park **NSW** 30 C7
Sevenhill **SA** 62 F4 65 G10
Seventeen Seventy **QLD** 9 J12
Severn River Nature Res **NSW** 25 D9
Seville **VIC** 37 C11 42 K4 44 B3
Seymour **TAS** 53 A14 55 H14
Seymour **VIC** 39 C14 42 F2
Shackleton **WA** 74 C6 76 K7
Shadforth **NSW** 22 F4
Shailer Park **QLD** 3 J7 5 D9
Shallow Crossing **NSW** 30 E6
Shanes Park **NSW** 21 F8
Shannon **TAS** 53 B8 55 J8
Shannon Con Res **SA** 64 G5
Shannon Nat Park **WA** 73 D14 74 J4
Shannon Vale **NSW** 25 E10
Shannons Flat **NSW** 30 F3
Shark Bay **WA** 76 A1
Shark Bay Marine Park **WA** 76 A1 78 J1
Shaw Island **QLD** 9 C8
Shay Gap **WA** 78 D7 82 B7
Shay Gap Mining Settlement **WA** 78 D7 82 C7
Sheans Creek **VIC** 42 E4
Shearwater **TAS** 54 E7
Sheep Hills **VIC** 40 K6
Sheffield **TAS** 54 F7
Shelbourne **VIC** 39 B11
Shelburne Bay **QLD** 16 D3
Sheldon **QLD** 3 H7
Shelford **VIC** 39 G11
Shell Harbour **NSW** 30 B7
Shelley **VIC** 29 K13 43 B11
Shelley **WA** 71 H4
Shelley Beach **NSW** 20 A3
Shellharbour **NSW** 23 K8
Shelly Beach **QLD** 4 D2
Shenton Park **WA** 71 F2
Sheoak Hill Con Park **SA** 62 K3 64 F7
Sheoak Hill Con Res **SA** 62 J3
Sheoak Log **SA** 60 A5
Sheoaks **VIC** 36 D1
Shepparton **VIC** 42 C3
Sheringa **SA** 64 G5
Sherlock **SA** 63 D8 65 K11
Sherwood **NSW** 25 J12
Sherwood **QLD** 3 F3
Sherwood Nature Res **NSW** 25 F13
Shinfield **QLD** 9 D8
Shoal Cape **WA** 75 G12
Shoalhaven Heads **NSW** 30 C7
Shoalwater Bay **QLD** 9 F10
Shoalwater Bay Con Park **QLD** 9 F10
Shooters Hill **NSW** 22 H6
Shoreham **VIC** 37 K8
Shorncliffe **QLD** 3 B5 4 E6
Short Island **QLD** 5 B10
Shotts **WA** 73 E10
Shute Harbour **QLD** 9 B8
Sidmouth **TAS** 55 E9 56 D3
Silkwood **QLD** 11 E13
Silky Oak **QLD** 11 F13
Silvan **VIC** 37 D11
Silver Sands **SA** 61 F4
Silver Spur **QLD** 7 K9 25 B8
Silver Swan **WA** 77 H11 83 F1
Silverdale **NSW** 21 G10
Silverdale **QLD** 5 J11
Silverton **NSW** 26 J1 28 A1 65 C14
Silverwater **NSW** 19 E3
Simmie **VIC** 41 K13 42 C1
Simpson **VIC** 39 J8
Simpson Con Res **SA** 63 G9
Simpson Desert Con Park **SA** 12 K1 67 B9 91 K13
Simpson Desert Nat Park **QLD** 12 J2 67 A10 91 J14
Simpson Desert Reg Res **SA** 67 C8 91 K12
Simpsons Bay **TAS** 53 J10
Single Nat Park **NSW** 25 F9
Singleton **NSW** 23 D9
Singleton **WA** 72 G5
Sinnamon Park **QLD** 3 G2
Sir Edward Pellew Group **NT** 87 J13 89 A12
Sir George Hope Islands **NT** 86 B5
Sir Graham Moore Islands **WA** 81 A10
Sir Joseph Banks Group Con Park **SA** 64 H6
Sisters Beach **TAS** 54 C4
Sisters Creek **TAS** 54 D4
Skenes Creek **VIC** 39 K10
Skillion Nature Res **NSW** 25 J12
Skipton **VIC** 39 F9
Skye **SA** 59 G6
Skye **VIC** 35 K7 37 G9
Slacks Creek **QLD** 3 J6
Slade Point **QLD** 9 D8
Slaty Creek **VIC** 39 A9
Sliding Rock Mine **SA** 65 A10 67 K10
Sloping Island **TAS** 51 E10 53 G11
Smeaton **VIC** 39 D11
Smeaton Grange **NSW** 21 F11
Smiggin Holes **NSW** 30 G2 43 D14
Smith Islands Nat Park **QLD** 9 C8
Smithfield **NSW** 19 E1 21 E9

108 Smithfield – The Channon

Smithfield SA 60 C3 62 F6 65 J10
Smithton TAS 54 C3
Smithtown NSW 25 J12
Smokers Bank TAS 54 C3
Smoky Bay SA 64 D3
Smooth Island TAS 51 E11 53 G12
Smythesdale VIC 39 E10
Snake Island VIC 45 H8 46 J2
Snake Range Nat Park QLD 8 J6
Snake Valley VIC 39 E10
Snobs Creek VIC 42 G5
Snowtown SA 62 F4 65 G9
Snowy River Nat Park VIC 30 K1 43 G14 47 B9
Snug TAS 50 G5 53 G10
Snuggery SA 63 B13
Sofala NSW 22 F6
Somers VIC 37 J9 39 H14 44 F2
Somersby NSW 20 C3
Somerset TAS 54 D5
Somerset Dam QLD 4 J5 7 F12
Somerton NSW 24 H7
Somerton VIC 35 A3 36 B7
Somerton Park SA 59 J2 60 H1 61 B5
Somerville VIC 37 H9 39 H14 44 E2
Sommariva QLD 6 D1 13 K14 15 D14
Sorell TAS 51 B9 53 F11
Sorrento VIC 36 J6 39 H13
Sorrento WA 71 C1 72 G3
South Arm TAS 50 F7 53 G11
South Bank QLD 2 C2
South Blackwater Mine QLD 9 J8
South Brisbane QLD 2 D1 3 E4
South Bruny Island TAS 53 J10
South Bruny Nat Park TAS 53 J10
South Bukalong NSW 30 J3
South Cape TAS 53 K8
South Coogee NSW 19 G7
South Cumberland Island Nat Park QLD 9 C9
South East Cape TAS 53 K8
South East Forests Nat Park NSW 30 J4 47 A12
South East Isles WA 83 K2
South Eneabba Nature Res WA 76 H4
South Forest TAS 54 C3
South Franklin TAS 50 H1 53 H9
South Fremantle WA 71 J1
South Glen QLD 7 F8
South Grafton NSW 25 E12
South Guildford WA 71 E6
South Hedland WA 78 D5 82 B4
South Hobart TAS 49 D1
South Island QLD 9 E10
South Johnstone QLD 11 E13
South Kilkerran SA 62 H5 65 H8
South Kolan QLD 7 A11 9 K12
South Kumminin WA 74 D7
South Lake WA 71 K3
South Maclean QLD 5 E11
South Melbourne VIC 34 D2 35 D3
South Molle Island QLD 9 B8
South Morang VIC 37 B8 39 E14 42 J2 44 A2
South Mount Cameron TAS 55 D13
South Nietta TAS 54 F6
South Perth WA 70 D2 71 G4
South Preston TAS 54 E6
South Riana TAS 54 E6
South Springfield TAS 55 E11
South Stradbroke Island QLD 5 B11 7 H14
South Wellesley Islands QLD 10 D3
South West Cape TAS 52 K6
South West Island NT 87 J12 89 A12
South West Rocks NSW 25 J12
Southbank VIC 34 D1
Southend QLD 9 H11
Southend SA 63 C13
Southern Beekeepers Nature Res WA 76 H3
Southern Brook WA 72 C1
Southern Cross QLD 8 B4 11 J13
Southern Cross WA 75 B9 77 J9
Southern Moreton Bay Islands Nat Park QLD 5 B11
Southern River WA 71 K6
Southport QLD 5 B12 7 H13
Southport TAS 53 J9
Southwest Con Area TAS 52 E3
Southwest Nat Park TAS 52 H6
Southwood QLD 6 G7
Southwood Nat Park QLD 6 G7
Sovereign Island QLD 5 B11
Spalding SA 62 F3 65 F10
Spalford TAS 54 E6
Spargo Creek VIC 39 E11
Spearwood WA 71 K2
Speed VIC 28 J4 40 F6
Speewa VIC 28 H6 41 E9
Spence ACT 32 B3
Spencer NSW 20 D5
Spencer Gulf SA 62 J5 64 G7
Spencers Brook WA 72 C2
Spicers Creek NSW 22 C4
Spilsby Island SA 64 H6
Spinnaker Island ACT 31 B1
Sprent TAS 54 E6
Spreyton TAS 54 E7
Spring Beach TAS 53 E12
Spring Creek QLD 11 H12
Spring Farm NSW 21 F11
Spring Hill NSW 22 F4
Spring Hill QLD 2 A2 3 E4
Spring Mount Con Park SA 61 G5
Spring Ridge NSW 22 A7 22 C5 24 K6
Springbank Island ACT 31 B1
Springbrook QLD 5 C14 7 H13 25 A13
Springbrook Nat Park QLD 5 C14 25 A14
Springcreek QLD 8 A3
Springdale NSW 22 K1 29 F14
Springfield QLD 3 K1 5 F9
Springfield SA 59 H5
Springfield TAS 55 E11
Springfield Lakes QLD K1
Springhurst VIC 42 B7
Springsure QLD 8 J7
Springton SA 60 D7 62 E6 65 J11
Springvale VIC 35 G6 37 E8
Springwood NSW 21 H8 23 G8
Springwood QLD 3 J6 5 D9
Staaten River Nat Park QLD 11 C8
Stack Island TAS 54 B1
Stafford QLD 3 C3 4 E7
Staffordshire Reef VIC 39 F10
Stalker VIC 39 K9
Stamford QLD 13 B10
Stanage QLD 9 F9
Stanborough NSW 25 F8
Stanhope VIC 41 K14 42 D2
Stanley TAS 54 C3
Stanley VIC 43 C8
Stanley Island QLD 16 H5
Stanmore QLD 4 G3
Stannifer NSW 25 E8
Stannum NSW 25 D10
Stansbury SA 62 H7 65 J9
Stanthorpe QLD 7 J10 25 B10
Stanwell QLD 9 H10
Stanwell Park NSW 21 C12 23 J9
Stapylton QLD 5 C10
Starcke Nat Park QLD 11 A12 16 J6
Starling Gap VIC 42 K5 44 B5
Staughton Vale VIC 30 F12 36 D2
Stavely VIC 38 E7
Staverton TAS 54 F6
Stawell VIC 38 C7
Steels Creek VIC 37 A10
Steep Island TAS 54 B1
Steiglitz QLD 5 C10
Steiglitz VIC 36 D1 39 F11
Steiglitz Historic Park VIC 36 D1
Stenhouse Bay SA 62 J7 64 K7
Stephens QLD 5 B13
Stephens Creek NSW 26 J2
Steppes TAS 53 B9 55 J9
Stevens Island NT 87 B12
Stieglitz TAS 55 F14
Stirling ACT 32 F3
Stirling SA 59 J7 60 H4 61 B7 62 F7 65 J10
Stirling VIC 43 H11 46 C6
Stirling WA 71 D3
Stirling North SA 62 G1 65 D9
Stirling Range Nat Park WA 74 H6
Stockdale VIC 43 K10 45 B11 46 D4
Stockinbingal NSW 22 K1 29 F14
Stockleigh QLD 5 E10
Stockmans Reward VIC 42 J5 44 A6
Stockport SA 62 F5 65 H10
Stockton NSW 23 E11
Stockyard Gully Nat Park WA 76 H3
Stockyard Hill VIC 39 E9
Stockyard Point QLD 9 G11
Stokes Bay SA 63 J8 65 K8
Stokes Nat Park WA 75 G11
Stone Hut SA 62 F2 65 E9
Stonefield SA 62 D5 65 H11
Stonehaven VIC 36 G2
Stonehenge NSW 25 E9
Stonehenge QLD 13 G9
Stonehenge TAS 53 D11
Stoney Point NSW 29 F11
Stoneyford VIC 39 H9
Stonor TAS 53 D11
Stony Batter Creek Nature Res NSW 25 G8
Stony Creek VIC 44 G6
Stony Creek Nature Res ACT 32 E1
Stony Crossing NSW 28 H6 41 E9
Stony Point VIC 37 J9 44 F2
Stonyfell SA 59 G6 60 G3 61 A7
Stoodley TAS 54 F7
Store Creek NSW 22 E4
Storm Bay TAS 51 H9 53 H11
Stormlea TAS 51 J11 53 H12
Storys Creek TAS 55 G12
Stowport TAS 54 D5
Strachan WA 73 D14
Stradbroke VIC 45 E10 46 G4
Stradbroke West VIC 45 E10 46 F3
Strahan TAS 52 C3 54 K3
Strangways Springs SA 66 G7
Stratford NSW 23 C11
Stratford VIC 45 C11 46 E4
Strath Creek VIC 42 G3
Strathalbyn SA 62 E7 65 K10
Stratham WA 73 H10 74 G2
Strathblane TAS 53 J9
Strathbogie NSW 25 D9
Strathbogie VIC 42 E4
Strathdownie VIC 38 F2
Stratherne WA 72 A6
Strathewen VIC 37 A10
Strathfield NSW 19 F3 21 C9
Strathfieldsaye VIC 39 B12
Strathgordon TAS 52 F6
Strathkellar VIC 38 F5
Strathmerton VIC 29 K10 42 A4
Strathpine QLD 3 A3 4 F6 7 F13
Straun SA 38 C1
Streaky Bay SA 64 E3
Streatham VIC 39 E8
Stretton QLD 3 J5
Strickland TAS 53 D8
Strickland Bay WA 80 E5
Strike-a-Light Nature Res NSW 30 F3
Stroud NSW 23 D11
Stroud Road NSW 23 D11
Struan SA 63 B12
Strzelecki VIC 37 J14 44 E5
Strzelecki Nat Park TAS 55 C9
Strzelecki Reg Res SA 14 K2 67 G12
Stuart QLD 8 A5 11 H14
Stuart Creek Opal Deposit SA 67 J8
Stuart Mill VIC 39 B9
Stuart Park NT 84 D2
Stuart Town NSW 22 E4
Stuarts Point NSW 25 H12
Stuarts Well NT 90 G7
Sturt Nat Park NSW 14 K5 26 C1 67 G14
Suarji Island QLD 16 A2
Subiaco WA 71 F3
Suggan Buggan VIC 43 F14
Sulphur Creek TAS 54 D6
Summerfield VIC 39 A12
Summerholm QLD 5 K9
Summerland VIC 37 K9 39 J14 44 F2
Summerland Point NSW 20 A1
Summertown SA 59 H7 60 G4 61 A7
Sumner QLD 3 G2
Sunbury VIC 36 A5 39 E13 42 J1
Sunday Creek VIC 39 D14 42 G2
Sunday Island VIC 45 H8 46 H2
Sunday Island WA 80 E5
Sundown Nat Park QLD 7 K10 25 B9
Sunny Cliffs VIC 40 A5
Sunny Corner NSW 22 F6
Sunnybank QLD 3 H5
Sunnybank Hills QLD 3 H4
Sunnyside NSW 25 C10
Sunnyside TAS 54 F7
Sunrise Mine WA 77 F12 83 D2
Sunshine NSW 20 B1
Sunshine VIC 35 D1 36 C6
Sunshine Coast QLD 4 D1 7 E13
Surat QLD 6 F5
Surfers Paradise QLD 5 B12 7 H13
Surges Bay TAS 50 K1 53 H9
Surrey Downs SA 59 C7
Surveyor Generals Corner NT SA WA 68 A1 79 K14 83 B7 90 K1
Surveyors Bay TAS 53 H9
Sussex Inlet NSW 30 D7
Sussex Mill WA 73 G12
Sutherland NSW 19 J3 21 C10 23 H9
Sutherland Creek VIC 36 F2
Sutherlands SA 62 D5 65 H11
Sutton NSW 30 D3
Sutton VIC 41 G8
Sutton Forest NSW 22 K7 30 B6
Sutton Grange VIC 39 C12
SW Vernon Island NT 85 B2 86 C4
Swain Reefs Nat Park QLD 9 E13
Swan Hill VIC 28 J6 41 F9
Swan Island TAS 55 C13
Swan Island VIC 36 H5 39 H13
Swan Marsh VIC 39 H9
Swan Reach SA 62 D6 65 H11
Swan Reach VIC 43 K12 45 C14 46 D7
Swan Reach Con Park SA 62 D6 65 H11
Swan Regional Park WA 71 D7
Swanbourne WA 71 G1
Swanpool VIC 42 E5
Swansea NSW 23 F10
Swansea TAS 53 C13 55 K13
Sweers Island QLD 10 D3
Swifts Creek VIC 43 H11 46 B6
Swim Creek Con Res NT 85 C4 86 D5
Sydenham NSW 19 G5 21 C9
Sydenham VIC 36 C6 39 F13 42 J1
Sydney NSW 19 F6 21 B8 23 H9
Sydney CBD NSW 18
Sydney Harbour Nat Park NSW 19 E7 21 B8 23 H9
Sydney Island QLD 10 D3
Sylvania NSW 19 J4 21 C10
Symonston ACT 32 F6

T

Tabbara VIC 43 K14 47 D9
Tabberabbera VIC 43 J10 45 A12 46 C5
Tabbimoble Swamp Nature Res NSW 25 D13
Tabbita NSW 29 E10
Tabby Tabby Island QLD 5 B10
Table Top NSW 29 K12 43 A9
Tabor VIC 38 F5
Tabourie Lake NSW 30 E6
Tabulam NSW 25 C12
Tacoma NSW 20 B2
Taggerty VIC 42 H4
Tahara VIC 38 F4
Tahara Bridge VIC 38 F4
Tahmoor NSW 21 F13 23 J8 30 A7
Taigum QLD 3 B4
Tailem Bend SA 62 D7 65 K11
Takone TAS 54 E4
Takone West TAS 54 E4
Talapa Con Park SA 63 B11
Talarm NSW 25 H12
Talawa TAS 55 E12
Talawahl Nature Res NSW 23 C12
Talbingo NSW 30 E1
Talbot VIC 39 C10
Talbot Brook WA 72 C3
Talbotville (site) VIC 43 H9 46 B4
Taldra SA 28 F1 40 B1 62 A5 65 H13
Talgarno VIC 43 B10
Talia SA 64 F4
Talislier Con Park SA 61 K1
Tallaganda Nat Park NSW 30 F4
Tallageira VIC 38 B2
Tallai QLD 5 C13
Tallanalla WA 73 F8
Tallandoon VIC 43 C10
Tallangatta VIC 29 K13 43 C10
Tallangatta Valley VIC 43 C10
Tallaringa Con Park SA 66 F2 68 E7
Tallarook VIC 39 C14 42 F2
Tallawudjah Nature Res NSW 25 F12
Tallebudgera QLD 5 B14
Tallebudgera Valley QLD 5 C14
Tallebung NSW 29 B11
Tallegalla QLD 5 J9
Tallimba NSW 29 E12
Tallong NSW 22 K6 30 C5
Tallygaroopna VIC 42 C3
Talmalmo NSW 29 K13 43 A11
Talmo NSW 30 C2
Talwood QLD 6 J6 24 A4
Tamarang NSW 22 A7 24 K5
Tambar Springs NSW 24 K5
Tambelin SA 60 C3
Tambellup WA 74 H6
Tambo QLD 8 K4 13 H13 15 A14
Tambo Crossing VIC 43 J12 45 A14 46 C7
Tambo Upper VIC 43 K12 45 B14 46 D7
Tamboon VIC 47 D11
Tamborine QLD 5 D11 7 H13
Tamborine Nat Park QLD 5 D11
Tamboy NSW 23 D12
Tamleugh VIC 42 D4
Tammin WA 74 C5 76 K6
Tampa WA 77 F11 83 E1
Tamrookum QLD 5 F14
Tamworth NSW 24 J7
Tanami Mine NT 88 H2
Tanara West VIC 38 F4
Tanawha QLD 4 E1
Tandarra VIC 41 K12
Tangalooma QLD 4 B5 7 F13
Tangambalanga VIC 43 C9
Tangmangaroo NSW 22 K3 30 B2
Tangorin QLD 8 E1 13 C10
Tanja NSW 30 H5
Tanjil Bren VIC 42 K6 44 B7 46 D1
Tankaanu SA 68 B2 90 K3
Tankerton VIC 37 J10 44 F3
Tannum Sands QLD 9 J11
Tansey QLD 7 D11
Tantanoola SA 63 B13
Tanunda SA 60 A6 62 E6 65 H10
Tanwood VIC 39 C9
Tanybryn VIC 39 J10
Taparoo VIC 40 B1
Taperoo SA 59 C2
Tapin Tops Nat Park NSW 23 B12
Taplan SA 28 G1 40 C1 62 A6 65 H13
Tara NT 91 B9
Tara QLD 7 F8
Taradale VIC 39 C12
Tarago NSW 30 D4
Tarago VIC 37 F14
Taragoola QLD 9 J11
Taralga NSW 22 J6 30 B5
Tarana NSW 22 G6
Taranna TAS 51 G13 53 G12
Tarawi Nature Res NSW 28 D1 62 A3
Tarcoola SA 64 A4 66 K4
Tarcoon NSW 27 E12
Tarcowie SA 62 F2 65 E10
Tarcutta NSW 29 H14
Tardun WA 76 F4
Taree NSW 23 B12
Tareleton TAS 54 E7
Taren Point NSW 19 J4 21 B10
Targa TAS 55 E11 56 F7
Tarin Rock Nature Res WA 74 F7
Taringa QLD 3 F3
Tarlee SA 62 E5 65 H10
Tarlo NSW 22 K6 30 B5
Tarlo River Nat Park NSW 22 K6 30 B5
Tarnagulla VIC 39 B10
Tarneit VIC 36 D5
Tarnma SA 62 E5 65 H10
Tarnook VIC 42 D5
Taroborah QLD 8 H6
Tarome QLD 5 K12
Taroom QLD 6 C7
Taroon VIC 38 H7
Taroona TAS 50 E6 53 G10
Tarpeena SA 38 F1 63 B13
Tarra-Bulga Nat Park VIC 45 F8 46 G2
Tarragal VIC 38 H3
Tarragindi QLD 3 F4
Tarraleah TAS 52 D7 54 K7
Tarrango VIC 28 G3 40 B3
Tarranyurk VIC 40 J5
Tarraville VIC 45 G9 46 H3
Tarrawarra VIC 37 B11
Tarrawingee VIC 42 C7
Tarrayoukyan VIC 38 D3
Tarrington VIC 38 F5
Tarvano QLD 13 B9
Tarwin VIC 44 G6
Tarwin Lower VIC 44 H5
Tarwin Meadows VIC 44 H5
Tarwin Middle VIC 44 G5
Tarzali QLD 11 E12
Tasman Island TAS 51 K14 53 H13
Tasman Nat Park TAS 51 J13 53 H12
Tasman Peninsula TAS 51 H12 53 H12
Tate River Tin Mine QLD 11 E11
Tatham NSW 25 C13
Tathra NSW 30 H5
Tathra Nat Park WA 76 G4
Tatong VIC 42 E6
Tatura VIC 42 C3
Tatyoon VIC 39 E8
Tatyoon North VIC 39 E8
Taunton Nat Park QLD 9 H8
Tawonga VIC 43 E10
Tawonga South VIC 43 E10
Tayene TAS 55 F11
Tayetea Bridge TAS 54 D3
Taylor ACT 32 A4
Taylor Island SA 64 J6
Taylors Arm NSW 25 H12
Taylors Flat NSW 22 J4 30 A3
Tchanning QLD 6 E6
Tea Gardens NSW 23 D11
Tea Tree TAS 53 F10
Tea Tree Gully SA 59 D7 60 E4
Teddywaddy VIC 41 J9
Teddywaddy West VIC 41 J8
Teds Beach TAS 52 F6
Teesdale VIC 39 G11
Teeta Bore SA 68 C5
Telangatuk VIC 38 C5
Telegraph Point NSW 23 A13 25 K12
Telfer Mine WA 79 F8
Telford SA 67 K10
Telford VIC 42 B5
Telita TAS 55 E12
Telopea Downs VIC 40 J2 63 A10
Telowie Gorge Con Park SA 62 G2 65 E9
Temma TAS 54 E1
Temora NSW 22 J1 29 F13
Tempe NSW 19 G5
Temple Bay QLD 16 E3
Temple Island QLD 9 E9
Templer Island NT 86 B6
Templers SA 60 A4
Templestowe VIC 35 C6 37 C9
Templin QLD 5 H12
Tempy VIC 40 F6
Ten Mile Lake WA 78 J7
Tenby Pt VIC 37 K11
Tenindewa WA 76 F4
Tennant Creek NT 89 G9
Tennyson NSW 19 E4 20 G6
Tennyson SA 59 F1 60 F1
Tennyson VIC 41 K12
Tent Hill NSW 25 D9
Tent Hill SA 62 H1 65 D8
Tent Island Nature Res WA 78 F2
Tenterfield NSW 7 K11 25 C10
Teodter O/P Mine WA 77 C8
Tepko SA 62 E7 65 J11
Terang VIC 39 H8
Teridgerie NSW 24 H2
Teringie SA 59 G7
Terip Terip VIC 42 F4
Termeil NSW 30 E6
Terminal Lake WA 78 H7
Terowie NSW 22 D1 27 K14 29 B14
Terowie SA 62 E2 65 F10
Terranora NSW 25 A14
Terrey Hills NSW 19 B6 20 C7
Terrick Terrick Nat Park VIC 41 J11
Terrigal NSW 20 B4 23 G10
Terry Hie Hie NSW 24 E6
Teryaweynya Lake NSW 26 K5 28 A5
Tetoora Road VIC 37 H14
Teutonic Bore WA 77 E10
Tevan NSW 7 K13 25 C14
Teviotville QLD 5 H12
Tewantin QLD 7 D13
Tewkesbury TAS 54 E5
Texas QLD 7 K9 25 B8
Thalaba NSW 22 J5 30 A4
Thalanga QLD 8 B3 11 K13
Thalia VIC 41 J8
Thallon QLD 6 J5 24 B2
Thangool QLD 9 K10
Tharbogang NSW 29 F10
Thargomindah QLD 15 H9
Tharwa NSW 30 E3
The Banca TAS 55 D12
The Basin VIC 37 D10
The Basin Nature Res NSW 25 F8
The Bump VIC 37 D13
The Casties Nature Res NSW 25 J11
The Caves QLD 9 G10
The Channon NSW 25 B13

The Charcoal Tank – Wagerup 109

The Charcoal Tank Nature Res NSW 29 E13
The Cove VIC 38 J7
The Dutchmans Stern Con Park SA 65 D9
The English Company's Islands NT 87 C12
The Entrance NSW 20 A3 23 F10
The Gap QLD 3 D2 4 F7
The Gap SA 62 H5 65 H8
The Gap VIC 36 A5
The Gardens NT 84 D1
The Gardens TAS 55 E14
The Glen TAS 55 E9 56 D4
The Glen Nature Res NSW 23 C11
The Granites Mine NT 88 J3 90 A3
The Gums QLD 6 F7
The Gurdies VIC 37 J12
The Heart VIC 45 D11 46 F4
The Knoll Con Park SA 60 H3 61 B7
The Lakes WA 72 E3 74 C4 76 K5
The Lakes Nat Park VIC 45 C14 46 E6
The Lynd Junction QLD 11 G11
The Monument QLD 12 C4
The Narrows NT 84 C2
The Oaks NSW 21 G12 23 J8 30 A7
The Peak Goldmine NSW 27 H10
The Plug Range Con Res SA 62 K3 64 F7
The Risk NSW 25 A13
The Rock NSW 29 H13
The Rock Nature Res NSW 29 H12
The Rocks NSW 18 A2
The Sisters VIC 38 H7
The Triangle VIC 42 J6 44 B6 46 C1
The Vines WA 71 A7
Thebarton SA 59 G3 60 F2 61 A6
Theebine QLD 7 C12
Theodore ACT 32 K4
Theodore QLD 6 A7 9 K9
Theresa Park NSW 21 G11
Thevenard SA 64 D2 68 K7
Thirlmere NSW 21 G13 23 J8 30 A7
Thirlmere Lakes Nat Park NSW 21 G13 22 J7 30 A6
Thirlstane TAS 55 E8
Thirroul NSW 21 C13 23 J8
Thistle Island SA 64 J6
Thologolong VIC 43 A10
Thomas Bay WA 80 E4
Thomastown VIC 35 A4
Thomson Bay WA 72 H3
Thooloora Island QLD 4 E3
Thoona VIC 42 C6
Thora NSW 25 G12
Thornbury VIC 35 C4
Thorneside QLD 3 E7
Thorngate SA 58 A2
Thornlands QLD 5 C9
Thornleigh NSW 19 C3 20 D7
Thornlie WA 71 J6
Thornton VIC 42 G5
Thornton Beach QLD 11 C12
Thorpdale VIC 44 E7 46 F1
Thowgla VIC 43 C12
Thowgla Upper VIC 43 C12
Thredbo NSW 30 H1 43 D14
Three Bridges VIC 37 D13
Three Hummock Island TAS 54 A2
Three Moon QLD 7 A9 9 K11
Three Springs WA 76 G4
Three Ways NT 89 G9
Throsby ACT 32 B6
Thrushton Nat Park QLD 6 G3
Thuddungra NSW 22 J2 29 F14 30 A1
Thulloo NSW 29 D12
Thurgoona NSW 29 K12 43 B9
Thuringowa QLD 8 A5 11 H14
Thurla VIC 28 F3 40 B5
Thursday Island QLD 16 B2
Tia NSW 25 J9
Tiaro QLD 7 C12
Tibarri QLD 10 K6 12 A6
Tibbuc NSW 23 B11
Tibooburra NSW 26 C3
Tichborne NSW 22 F2 29 C14
Tickera SA 62 H4 65 G8
Tidal River VIC 44 K7 46 K1
Tieri QLD 8 G7
Tilba Tilba NSW 30 G5
Tilbuster NSW 25 G9
Tilley Swamp Con Park SA 63 C10
Tilligerry Nature Res NSW 23 E11
Tilmouth Roadhouse NT 90 D6
Tilpa NSW 26 G7
Timbarra VIC 43 H12 46 B7
Timbarra Nat Park NSW 25 C11
Timber Creek NT 86 J3 88 B3
Timberoo VIC 28 H4 40 E5
Timberoo South VIC 28 H3 40 E5
Timbillica NSW 30 K4 47 C13
Timboon VIC 39 J8
Timor NSW 23 B9
Timor VIC 39 C10
Timor West VIC 39 C10
Tin Can Bay QLD 7 C13
Tin Kettle Island TAS 55 C9
Tinamba VIC 45 C10 46 E3
Tinaroo Falls QLD 11 D12
Tindal NT 85 J5 86 G6
Tinderbox TAS 53 G10
Tinderry Nature Res NSW 30 E3
Tindo QLD 8 C1 13 A11
Tingalpa QLD 3 E6 5 D8
Tingaringi NSW 30 J2
Tingha NSW 25 F8
Tingoora QLD 7 D10
Tinonee NSW 23 B12
Tintaldra VIC 29 K14 43 B12
Tintinara SA 63 C9
Tirranaville NSW 30 C4
Titjikala NT 91 H8
Ti-Tree NT 90 C7
Tittybong VIC 41 G9
Tiwi NT 84 A3
Tjintalka SA 68 A2 79 K14 90 K2
Tjinturritjan WA 83 B6
Tjirrkarli WA 79 K11 83 A4
Tjukayirla Roadhouse WA 77 C14 83 C3
Tjukurla WA 79 H14 90 G1
Tjuninanta NT 79 J14 90 H1
Tjunti NT 79 J14 90 H2
Tjuntjuntjarra WA 83 E5
Tjuwaliyn (Douglas Hot Springs Nature Park) NT 85 G3 86 F4
Tnorala Con Res NT 90 F6
Tocal QLD 13 F9
Tocumwal NSW 29 K10 42 A4
Tods TAS 53 B9 55 J8
Togari TAS 54 C2
Togganoggera NSW 30 E4
Toilberry TAS 55 G9 56 J4
Tolga QLD 11 D12
Tollingo Nature Res NSW 29 B12
Tolmie VIC 42 F6
Tolmies QLD 8 H7
Tom Groggin NSW 30 H1 43 D13
Tom Price WA 78 G5 82 F3
Tomahawk TAS 55 C12
Tomakin NSW 30 F6
Tomalla NSW 23 B10
Tomalla Nature Res NSW 23 A10 25 K8
Tomaree Nat Park NSW 23 E11
Tombong NSW 30 J3
Tomboy NSW 30 D5
Tomerong NSW 30 D7
Tomingley NSW 22 D2
Tonebridge WA 73 C13
Tongala VIC 41 J14 42 C2
Tonganah TAS 55 E11
Tonghi Creek VIC 47 C11
Tongio VIC 43 G11 46 A6
Tongio West VIC 43 G11 46 B6
Tonimbuk VIC 37 F13
Tooan VIC 38 B4
Tooan East VIC 38 B4
Toobanna QLD 11 G13
Toobeah QLD 6 J7 24 A5
Tooborac VIC 39 C13 42 F1
Toodyay WA 72 D1 74 B4 76 K5
Toogong NSW 22 F3
Toogoolawah QLD 7 F11
Toolakea QLD 11 H14
Toolamba VIC 42 D3
Toolangi VIC 37 A11 42 J4 44 A3
Toolern Vale VIC 36 B4 39 E13
Tooleybuc NSW 28 H6 41 E9
Tooligie SA 64 G5
Tooligie Hill SA 64 G5
Toolleen VIC 39 B13 42 E1
Toolondo VIC 38 C4
Toolong VIC 38 H5
Toolonga Nature Res WA 76 C3
Tooloom NSW 25 B11
Tooloom Nat Park NSW 7 J11 25 A11
Tooloombah QLD 9 G9
Tooloon NSW 24 J1
Tooma NSW 29 K14 30 F1 43 A13
Toombul QLD 3 C5
Toompine QLD 15 F10
Toomula QLD 11 G14
Toongabbie NSW 19 D1 21 E8
Toongabbie VIC 45 D8 46 E2
Toongi NSW 22 D3
Toonpan QLD 8 A5 11 H14
Toonumbar NSW 25 B12
Toonumbar Nat Park NSW 7 J12 25 B12
Tooperang SA 61 G7
Toora VIC 44 G7 46 H1
Tooradin VIC 37 H10 44 E3
Toorak VIC 35 E4
Toorak Gardens SA 59 G5
Toorale East NSW 27 F9
Tooraweenah NSW 22 A4 24 K2
Toorbul QLD 4 E4
Toorloo Arm VIC 43 K12 46 D7
Toorongo VIC 42 K6 44 B6 46 D1
Tootgarook VIC 36 J6
Tootool NSW 29 H12
Toowong QLD 3 E3
Toowoomba QLD 7 G11
Toowoon Bay NSW 20 A3
Top Springs NT 88 B5
Topgallant Island SA 64 G4
Torbanlea QLD 7 B12
Torbay Bay WA 74 K6
Torndirrup Nat Park WA 74 K7
Toronto NSW 23 E10
Torquay VIC 36 J2 39 H12
Torrens ACT 32 G4
Torrens Creek QLD 8 C2 11 K12 13 A11
Torrens Island SA 59 C2 60 E1
Torrens Island Con Park SA 59 B2 60 D1
Torrens Park SA 59 H4
Torrens Vale SA 61 H4
Torrensville SA 59 G3
Torres Strait QLD 16 A2
Torrington NSW 25 D9
Torrita VIC 28 H3 40 E4
Torrumbarry VIC 29 K8 41 J12
Tostaree VIC 43 K13 47 D8
Tottenham NSW 27 K13 29 A13
Tottington VIC 39 B8
Toukley NSW 20 A2
Towallum NSW 25 F12
Towamba NSW 30 J4 47 A13
Towaninny VIC 41 H9
Towarri Nat Park NSW 23 B8
Tower Hill TAS 55 G12
Townshend Island QLD 9 F10
Townsville QLD 8 A5 11 H14
Towong VIC 29 K14 43 B12
Towra Point Nature Res NSW 19 J5
Towradgi NSW 21 C14
Towrang NSW 22 K6 30 B5
Trafalgar VIC 44 E7 46 F1
Tragowel VIC 41 H11
Trangie NSW 22 B2 27 J14 29 A14
Tranmere SA 59 F6
Traralgon VIC 45 E8 46 F2
Traralgon South VIC 45 E8 46 F2
Travellers Lake NSW 28 D3
Trawalla VIC 39 D9
Trawool VIC 39 C14 42 G3
Trayning WA 74 A6 76 J7
Trebonne QLD 11 G13
Treesville WA 73 E9
Treeton WA 73 J12
Trefoil Island TAS 54 B1
Tregole Nat Park QLD 6 D2
Trenah TAS 55 E12
Trentham VIC 39 D12
Trentham East VIC 39 D12
Trephina Gorge Nature Park NT 91 F9
Tresco VIC 41 F10
Trevallyn NSW 23 D10
Trevallyn State Rec Area TAS 56 G5
Trewalla VIC 38 H3
Trewilga NSW 22 E2
Triabunna TAS 53 E12
Trial Harbour TAS 52 B3 54 H3
Trida NSW 29 C9
Trigg WA 71 D1
Trigg Island WA 71 D1
Trinita VIC 40 D5
Trinital VIC 28 H4
Trinity Beach QLD 11 D13
Trinity Gardens SA 59 F5
Troubridge Island Con Park SA 62 G7 65 J9
Troughton Island WA 81 A10
Trowutta TAS 54 D2
Truant Island NT 87 B13
Truganina VIC 36 D5
Trundle NSW 22 E1 29 C14
Trunkey Creek NSW 22 H5
Truro SA 62 E5 65 H11
Truslove Townsite Nature Res WA 75 F13 83 J1
Tryon Island QLD 9 G12
Tryphinia QLD 9 H9
Tuan QLD 7 C13
Tuart Forest Nat Park WA 73 H10 74 G2
Tuart Hill WA 71 E3
Tubbul NSW 22 J2 29 F14
Tubbut VIC 43 G14 47 A9
Tucabia NSW 25 E13
Tuckanarra WA 76 C7
Tuckean Nature Res NSW 25 C13
Tucklan NSW 22 C5
Tudor VIC 28 H5 41 E8
Tuena NSW 22 H5
Tugan QLD 5 A14
Tuggalong NSW 22 J7 30 B6
Tuggerah NSW 20 B3
Tuggerah Lake NSW 20 B2
Tuggeranong ACT 32 J4
Tuggeranong NSW 30 E3
Tuggerawong NSW 20 B2
Tuggolo Creek Nature Res NSW 23 A10 25 K9
Tulburrerr Island QLD 10 D3
Tulendeena TAS 55 E12
Tulka SA 64 J5
Tullagri QLD 7 F8
Tullah TAS 52 A4 54 G4
Tullamarine VIC 35 B2 36 B6
Tullamore NSW 22 D1 29 B13
Tullibigeal NSW 29 D12
Tullich VIC 38 E2
Tully QLD 11 F13
Tully Gorge Nat Park QLD 11 E13
Tully Heads QLD 11 F13
Tumbarumba NSW 29 J14 30 F1 43 A13
Tumbi Umbi NSW 20 B3
Tumblong NSW 29 H14
Tumbulgum NSW 25 A14
Tumby Bay SA 64 H6
Tumorrama NSW 30 D2
Tumoulin QLD 11 E12
Tumut NSW 29 H14 30 D1
Tunart VIC 28 G2 40 B2
Tunbridge TAS 53 C11 55 K11
Tuncurry NSW 23 C12
Tungamah VIC 42 B5
Tungkillo SA 60 E7 62 E6 65 J10
Tunnack TAS 53 D11
Tunnel TAS 56 D6
Tunnel Creek Nat Park WA 79 B11 81 G8
Tunney WA 73 A13
Tuppal NSW 29 J9
Tupul SA 68 A4 90 K4
Tura Beach NSW 30 J5
Turill NSW 22 C6
Turkey Beach QLD 9 J12
Turkey Creek WA 81 G13
Turlinjah NSW 30 F5
Turner ACT 32 D5
Turners Beach TAS 54 E7
Turners Marsh TAS 55 E10 56 E5
Turon Nat Park NSW 22 F6
Turondale NSW 22 F5
Tuross Head NSW 30 F6
Tuross Lake NSW 30 G6
Turramurra NSW 19 C4 20 D7
Turrawan NSW 24 G5
Turriff VIC 40 F6
Turtle Group Nat Park QLD 16 J6
Turtle Head Island QLD 16 B3
Tusmore SA 59 G5
Tutanning Nature Res WA 72 A6 74 D5
Tutunup WA 73 H11
Tutye VIC 28 H2 40 E3
Tweed Heads NSW 5 A14 7 H14 25 A14
Twelve Mile NSW 22 D5
Two Mile Flat NSW 22 D5
Two Peoples Bay WA 74 K7
Two Peoples Bay Nature Res WA 74 K7
Two Rocks WA 72 H1 74 B2 76 K4
Two Wells SA 60 B1 62 F6 65 H10
Twofold Bay NSW 30 K5 47 A14
Twyford QLD 11 C12
Tyaak VIC 39 D14 42 G2
Tyabb VIC 37 H9 39 H14 44 E2
Tyagarah Nature Res NSW 25 B14
Tyagong NSW 22 H2 30 A1
Tyalgum NSW 7 J13 25 A13
Tyalla VIC 28 H2 40 E3
Tycannah NSW 24 E5
Tyenna TAS 53 F8
Tyers VIC 45 D8 46 F2
Tylden VIC 39 D12
Tyndale NSW 25 E13
Tynong VIC 37 F12 44 D4
Tynong North VIC 37 F12
Tyntynder Central VIC 28 H6 41 E9
Tyntynder South VIC 28 H6 41 F9
Tyrendarra VIC 38 H4
Tyrendarra East VIC 38 H4
Tyringham NSW 25 G11
Tyrrell Downs VIC 28 J5 40 F7

U

Uarbry NSW 22 B6
Ubobo QLD 9 J11
Ukatjupa NT 79 K14 90 K1
Uki NSW 7 J13 25 A13
Ulamambri NSW 24 J4
Ulan NSW 22 C6
Ulandra Nature Res NSW 22 K2 29 G14
Ulaypai SA 68 A4 90 K5
Uleybury SA 60 C4
Ulidarra Nat Park NSW 25 G13
Ulidia NSW 25 B12
Ulinda NSW 22 A5 24 K4
Ulkiya SA 68 B3 90 K4
Ulladulla NSW 30 E6
Ullina VIC 39 D10
Ullswater VIC 38 C3
Ulmarra NSW 25 E13
Ulong NSW 25 G12
Ultima VIC 28 J6 41 F8
Ultimo NSW 18 D1
Uluṟu - Kata Tjuṯa Nat Park NT 90 J4
Ulverstone TAS 54 E6
Umagico QLD 16 B2
Umbakumba NT 87 F13
Umerina SA 66 C1 68 B6
Umina NSW 20 B5
Umpukula SA 68 A3
Umpukulunga SA 90 K3
Umuwa SA 68 B5
Unanderra NSW 21 D14
Undara Volcanic Nat Park QLD 11 F11
Undera VIC 42 C3
Underbool VIC 28 H3 40 E4
Underwood QLD 3 H5
Underwood TAS 55 E10 56 E6
Undina QLD 10 K6 12 A5
Ungarie NSW 29 D12
Ungarra SA 64 G6
Ungo QLD 8 K1 13 H10
Unicup Nature Res WA 73 C14 74 H4
Unley SA 58 D2 59 G4 60 G2 61 A6
Unnamed Con Park SA 68 E2 83 E7
Upper Bingara NSW 24 F7
Upper Blessington TAS 55 F11
Upper Bowman NSW 23 B11
Upper Caboolture QLD 4 F5
Upper Castra TAS 54 F6
Upper Colo NSW 20 G5
Upper Coomera QLD 5 C11
Upper Esk TAS 55 F12
Upper Ferntree Gully VIC 37 E10 42 K3 44 C3
Upper Hermitage SA 60 E4
Upper Horton NSW 24 F6
Upper Kedron QLD 3 D1
Upper Manilla NSW 24 H7
Upper McDonald NSW 20 F3
Upper Mount Gravatt QLD 3 G5
Upper Mount Hicks TAS 54 D5
Upper Myall NSW 23 C12
Upper Nariel VIC 43 D12
Upper Natone TAS 54 E5
Upper Orara NSW 25 G12
Upper Plenty VIC 39 D14 42 H2
Upper Rollands Plains NSW 25 K11
Upper Scamander TAS 55 F14
Upper Stone QLD 11 G13
Upper Stowport TAS 54 E5
Upper Sturt SA 59 K6
Upper Swan WA 72 F2 74 C3 76 K5
Upper Tallebudgera QLD 5 C14
Upper Yarra Dam VIC 37 B14 42 J5 44 B5
Uraidla SA 59 H7 60 G4 62 F7 65 J10
Uralla NSW 25 H9
Urana NSW 29 H11
Urandangi QLD 12 C2
Urangeline NSW 29 J12
Urangeline East NSW 29 J12
Urania SA 62 H6 65 H8
Uranquinty NSW 29 H13
Urapunga NT 87 G9
Urapuntja (Utopia) NT 91 C9
Urawa Nature Res WA 76 E4
Urbenville NSW 7 J12 25 A12
Urilpila NT 90 J3
Urlampe NT 12 D1 91 D14
Urrbrae SA 59 H5
Urunga NSW 25 G12
Useless Loop WA 76 B1 78 K1
Utah Lake NSW 27 E8
Uxbridge TAS 53 F9

V

Vacy NSW 23 D10
Valencia Island NT 86 B6
Valley Heights NSW 21 H8
Valley View SA 59 D5
Van Diemen Gulf NT 85 A4 86 C5
Vanderlin Island NT 87 J13 89 A13
Vandyke Creek Con Park QLD 8 J6
Vansittart Bay WA 81 A10
Vansittart Island TAS 55 C10
Varley WA 75 E9
Vasey VIC 38 D4
Vasse WA 73 J11
Vaucluse NSW 19 F7 21 B8
Vectus VIC 38 B5
Veitch SA 62 B6 65 J13
Venman Bushland Nat Park QLD 3 J7 5 D9
Ventnor VIC 37 K9 39 J14 44 F2
Venus Bay SA 64 F4
Venus Bay VIC 44 G5
Venus Bay Con Park SA 64 F3
Venus Bay Con Res SA 64 E3
Verdun SA 60 H4
Veresdale QLD 5 F12
Vermont VIC 37 D9
Verona NSW 30 H5
Verona Sands TAS 53 H10
Verran SA 64 G6
Vervale VIC 37 G12
Victor Harbor SA 61 J6 63 F8 65 K10
Victoria Park WA 71 G4
Victoria Point QLD 5 C9
Victoria River NT 86 J4 88 A4
Victoria Rock Nature Res WA 75 B11 77 J10
Victoria Valley TAS 53 D8 55 K8
Victoria Valley VIC 38 E6
Victory Well SA 68 C5
Villawood NSW 19 F2
Villeneuve QLD 4 H3
Vincentia NSW 30 D7
Vineyard NSW 20 F7
Vinifera VIC 28 H6 41 E9
Violet Town VIC 42 D4
Virginia QLD 3 C5
Virginia SA 60 C2 62 F6 65 H10
Vista SA 59 D7
Vite Vite VIC 39 F8
Vite Vite North VIC 39 F9
Vivonne SA 63 J9
Vivonne Bay Con Park SA 63 J9
Vokes Hill Corner SA 68 E3
Vulkathuna-Gammon Ranges Nat Park SA 65 A11 67 K11

W

Waaia VIC 42 B3
Waarre VIC 39 J8
Wabba Wilderness Park VIC 43 C11
Wabma Kadarbu Mound Springs Con Park SA 66 H7
Wacol QLD 3 H1 5 F9
Wadbilliga NSW 30 G4
Waddamana TAS 53 C8 55 K8
Waddi NSW 29 G10
Waddikee SA 64 F6
Wadeye NT 86 G1
Waeel WA 72 B2
Wagaman NT 84 B3
Wagant VIC 28 H4 40 E6
Wagerup WA 72 F7

110 Wagga Wagga – Wilmington

Wagga Wagga NSW 29 H13
Waggabundi QLD 10 H3
Waggarandall VIC 42 C5
Wagin WA 73 A9 74 F5
Wagonga NSW 30 G5
Wahgunyah VIC 42 B7
Wahgunyah Con Res SA 68 K5
Wahroonga NSW 19 C4 20 C7
Waikerie SA 62 C5 65 H12
Wail VIC 38 A5
Wairewa VIC 43 K13 47 D8
Waitchie VIC 28 J5 41 F8
Waite Creek Settlement NT 90 D3
Waitpinga SA 61 J5 63 F8 65 K10
Waitpinga Con Park SA 61 J3
Wakool NSW 29 J8 41 F12
Walalkarra SA 68 C4
Walang NSW 22 G6
Walbundrie NSW 29 J12
Walcha NSW 25 J9
Walcha Road NSW 25 J8
Waldegrave Island Con Park SA 64 F4
Walebing WA 74 A3 76 J5
Walga Gunya WA 77 C8
Walgett NSW 24 F1 27 E14
Walgoolan WA 74 B7 77 J8
Walhalla VIC 45 C8 46 E2
Walitjara SA 68 A3 90 K3
Walka NT 79 J14 83 A7 90 H1
Walkamin QLD 11 D12
Walkaway WA 76 F3
Walker VIC 37 A14
Walker Flat SA 62 D6 65 J11
Walker Island TAS 52 K7 54 B2
Walkers Crossing SA 67 D12
Walkerston QLD 9 D8
Walkerville SA 59 F4 60 F2
Walkerville North VIC 44 H6
Walkerville South VIC 44 J6
Wall SA 62 D7 65 J11
Walla Walla NSW 29 J12
Wallabadah NSW 23 A8 24 K7
Wallabadah Nature Res NSW 23 A9 24 K7
Wallabi Group WA 76 F2
Wallabrook SA 38 B1 63 B11
Wallaby Island QLD 10 A6 16 G1
Wallace VIC 39 E11
Wallace Rockhole NT 90 G7
Wallacedale North VIC 38 G4
Wallacia NSW 21 G9 23 H8
Wallaga Lake Heights NSW 30 G5
Wallaga Lake Nat Park NSW 30 G5
Wallal QLD 15 E13
Wallaloo VIC 38 B7
Wallaloo East VIC 38 B7
Wallamba Nature Res NSW 23 C12
Wallan VIC 39 D14 42 H2
Wallan East VIC 39 D14 42 H2
Wallangarra NSW 7 K10 25 C10
Wallangra NSW 24 D7
Wallany SA 68 B4 90 K4
Wallarah Nat Park NSW 23 F10
Wallaroo NSW 32 A2
Wallaroo SA 62 H4 65 G8
Wallaroo Nature Res NSW 23 D11
Wallatinna SA 66 D2 68 C7
Wallaville QLD 7 A11
Wallendbeen NSW 22 K2 29 G14 30 B1
Wallerawang NSW 22 F7
Walleroobie NSW 29 F12
Walli NSW 22 G4
Wallinduc VIC 39 F9
Wallingat Nat Park NSW 23 C12
Wallington VIC 36 H4
Wallon QLD 5 H9
Walloway SA 62 F1 65 E10
Wallpolla Island VIC 40 A3
Walls of Jerusalem Nat Park TAS 52 A6 54 H6
Wallsend NSW 23 E10
Wallumbilla QLD 6 E6
Wallundry NSW 22 J1 29 F14
Wallup VIC 40 K5
Walmer NSW 22 D3
Walpa VIC 43 K10 45 B12 46 D5
Walpeup VIC 28 H3 40 E5
Walpole WA 74 K4
Walpole-Nornalup Nat Park WA 74 K4
Waltara NSW 20 D7
Walu NT 79 J14 90 H2
Walungurru (Kintore) NT 79 G14 90 E1
Walwa VIC 29 K14 43 A11
Walyahmoning Nature Res WA 77 H8
Walyinynga SA 68 A4 90 K4
Walytjatjata NT 68 A1 79 K14 90 K2
Walyunga Nat Park WA 72 F2
Wamberal NSW 20 B4
Wamberal Lagoon Nature Res NSW 23 G10
Wambool Nature Res NSW 22 G6
Wamboyne NSW 29 D13
Wammuta QLD 12 B4
Wamoon NSW 29 F11
Wamuran QLD 4 G4 7 F12
Wamuran Basin QLD 4 G4
Wanaaring NSW 26 D7
Wanagarren Nature Res WA 74 A1 76 J4
Wanbi SA 62 B6 65 J12
Wandana Nature Res WA 76 E4
Wandandian NSW 30 D6
Wandearah East SA 62 G3 65 F9
Wandearah West SA 62 G3 65 F9
Wandella NSW 30 G5
Wandering WA 72 C6 74 E4
Wandiligong VIC 43 E9
Wandilo SA 63 B13
Wandin North VIC 37 C11
Wando Bridge VIC 38 E3
Wando Vale VIC 38 E3
Wandoan QLD 6 D7
Wandong VIC 39 D14 42 H2
Wandoo Con Park WA 72 D4 74 D4 76 K5
Wandsworth NSW 25 F9
Wanganella NSW 29 H8 41 E13
Wangara WA 71 B3
Wangarabell VIC 47 C12
Wangaratta VIC 42 C6
Wangary SA 64 H5
Wangerrip VIC 39 K9
Wangetti QLD 11 C12
Wangkatjungka (Christmas Creek) WA 79 C12 81 K9
Wangoom VIC 38 H7
Wanguri NT 84 A3
Wanilla SA 64 H5
Wanjarri Nature Res WA 77 D10
Wankari NT 79 J14 83 A7 90 H1
Wanko QLD 15 E13
Wanna Lakes WA 83 D6
Wannamal WA 74 B3 76 J5
Wannarn WA 79 J13 83 A6
Wanneroo WA 71 A3 72 G2 74 C2 76 K4
Wanniassa ACT 32 H4
Wannon VIC 38 F4
Wannoo Billabong Roadhouse WA 76 C3
Wanora QLD 5 H8
Wantabadgery NSW 29 H14
Wanwin VIC 38 G2
Wapengo NSW 30 H5
Wapet Camp WA 78 E3
Wappinguy NSW 22 C7
Waragai Creek Nature Res NSW 25 E13
Warakurna WA 79 J13 83 A7
Warakurna Roadhouse WA 79 J13 83 A7
Waramanga ACT 32 G3
Warana QLD 4 D1
Waranga VIC 39 A14 42 D2
Waratah TAS 54 F4
Waratah Bay VIC 44 H6
Waratah North VIC 44 H6
Warburn NSW 29 F10
Warburton VIC 37 C13 42 K4 44 B5
Warburton WA 79 K12 83 B5
Warburton East VIC 37 C13
Warby Range State Park VIC 42 C6
Ward Island SA 64 G3
Wardang Island SA 62 H6 65 H8
Wardell NSW 25 C14
Wards Mistake NSW 25 F10
Wards River NSW 23 C11
Warialda NSW 24 D7
Warianna QLD 13 B10
Warilla NSW 23 K8 30 B7
Warkton NSW 22 A5 24 K3
Warkworth NSW 23 D9
Warmun WA 81 G13
Warmun (Turkey Creek) WA 79 A14
Warncoort VIC 39 H10
Warneet VIC 37 H10 44 E3
Warnertown SA 62 G3 65 F9
Warnervale NSW 20 B2
Warooka SA 62 H7 65 J8
Waroona WA 72 F7 74 E3
Warra QLD 7 E9
Warra Nat Park NSW 25 F10
Warrabah Nat Park NSW 24 G7
Warrabillinna SA 68 B5 90 K6
Warrabkook VIC 38 G5
Warracknabeal VIC 40 K6
Warradale SA 59 J2
Warraderry NSW 22 G2
Warragamba NSW 21 G10 23 H8
Warragamba VIC 41 K12
Warragoon NSW 29 K11 42 A6
Warragul VIC 37 G14 44 D6
Warrah Creek NSW 23 B8
Warrak VIC 39 D8
Warrakoo VIC 28 F2
Warrambine VIC 39 G10
Warramboo SA 64 F5
Warrandyte VIC 35 C7 37 C9 42 K3 44 B2
Warrandyte State Park VIC 35 B7 37 C9 42 K3 44 B2
Warranmang VIC 39 C9
Warranulla NSW 23 C11
Warrapura WA 83 A7
Warrawee NSW 20 C7
Warrawenia Lake NSW 28 D3
Warrayure VIC 38 F5
Warreah QLD 8 C2 11 K11 13 A11
Warrego Mine NT 89 G8
Warrell Creek NSW 25 H12
Warren NSW 22 A1 27 J14
Warren Con Park SA 60 D5
Warren Nat Park WA 73 F14 74 J3
Warrenbayne VIC 42 E5
Warrenben Con Park SA 62 J7 64 J7
Warrentinna TAS 55 D12
Warriewood NSW 20 B6
Warrigal QLD 8 C2 11 K12 13 A12
Warrill View QLD 5 J11
Warrimoo NSW 21 H8
Warrina SA 66 E6
Warringa TAS 54 E6
Warrion VIC 39 H10
Warrnambool VIC 38 H6
Warrong VIC 38 H6
Warroo NSW 22 F1 29 D13
Warrow SA 64 H5
Warrumbungle NSW 24 J2
Warrumbungle Nat Park NSW 24 J3
Warrupura WA 79 J14 90 H1
Warruwi NT 86 B7
Wartburg QLD 9 K12
Wartook VIC 38 C6
Warup WA 73 A9
Warwick QLD 7 H11 25 A10
Warwick WA 71 C2
Warwick Farm NSW 19 G1
WA-SA Border Village SA 68 K1 83 G7
Wasaga QLD 16 B2
Washpool Nat Park NSW 25 D11
Wasleys SA 60 A3 62 F6 65 H10
Watagan NSW 20 E1
Watagans Nat Park NSW 23 E9 23 E9
Watalgan QLD 9 K12
Watanobbi NSW 20 B2
Watarrka Nat Park NT 90 G5
Watarru SA 68 C2
Watchem VIC 40 J7
Watchupga VIC 28 K4 40 H7
Waterfall NSW 21 C11 23 J8
Waterfall Gully SA 59 H6
Waterford VIC 43 J9 45 A11 46 C4
Waterford WA 71 H4
Waterhouse TAS 55 D12
Waterhouse Con Area TAS 55 C11
Waterhouse Island TAS 55 C11
Waterloo SA 62 E4 65 G10
Waterloo TAS 50 J1 53 H9
Waterloo VIC 39 D9
Waterloo WA 73 G9
Waterloo Corner SA 59 A3
Waterman WA 71 C1
Watervale SA 62 F4 65 G10
Watgania VIC 38 E7
Watheroo WA 76 H5
Watheroo Nat Park WA 76 H4
Watinuna SA 68 B5
Watson ACT 32 C5
Watson SA 68 H4
Watson Island NT 87 J13 89 A13
Watson Oil Field QLD 14 H6
Watsonia VIC 35 B5 37 C8
Watsons Bay NSW 19 E7 21 B8
Watsons Creek NSW 25 H8
Watsons Creek VIC 37 B9
Watsons Creek Nature Res NSW 25 H8
Wattamolla NSW 21 B11
Wattamondara NSW 22 H3
Wattle Creek VIC 39 C8
Wattle Flat NSW 22 F6
Wattle Glen VIC 37 B9
Wattle Grove NSW 21 D10
Wattle Grove TAS 50 J2 53 H9
Wattle Grove WA 71 H7
Wattle Hill TAS 51 A10 53 F11
Wattle Island VIC 44 K7 46 K1
Wattle Park SA 59 G6
Wattle Park VIC 46 E6
Wattle Point VIC 45 C13
Wattle Range SA 63 B13
Wattle Vale VIC 39 B14 42 E2
Waubra VIC 39 D10
Wauchope NSW 23 A13 25 K12
Wauchope NT 89 J9 91 A9
Waukaringa SA 62 D1 65 D11
Wauraltee SA 62 H6 65 H8
Waurn Ponds VIC 36 H2 39 H12
Wavell Heights QLD 3 C4
Waverley NSW 19 F7 21 B8
Wayatinah TAS 52 D7
Waychinicup Nat Park WA 74 J7
Waygara VIC 43 K13 47 D8
Wayville SA 58 D2 59 G4
Weabonga NSW 25 J8
Weavers SA 62 H7 65 J8
Webbs NSW 22 C2
Webbs Creek NSW 20 F4
Wedderburn NSW 21 E12
Wedderburn VIC 41 K10
Wedderburn Junction VIC 41 K10
Weddin Mountains Nat Park NSW 22 H2 29 E14
Wedge Island SA 62 K7 64 J6
Wedge Island TAS 51 H10
Wedge Island WA 74 A1 76 J4
Wedge Islands TAS 53 H11
Wednesday Island QLD 16 B2
Wee Jasper NSW 30 D2
Wee Jasper Nature Res NSW 30 D2
Wee Waa NSW 24 F4
Weegena TAS 54 F7
Weelhamby Lake WA 76 G5
Weemelah NSW 24 C3
Weemol NT 87 F9
Weerangourt VIC 38 G4
Weerite VIC 39 H9
Weetah TAS 55 F8
Weetaliba NSW 22 A5 24 K4
Weetalibah Nature Res NSW 22 B5
Weetangera ACT 32 C3
Weethalle NSW 29 E12
Weetulta SA 62 H5 65 H8
Wee-Wee-Rup VIC 41 H12
Wehla VIC 39 A10
Weilmoringle NSW 6 K1 27 C12
Weimby NSW 28 G5 41 C8
Weipa QLD 16 E1
Weismantels NSW 23 C11
Weitalaba QLD 9 J11
Weja NSW 29 D12
Welaregang NSW 29 K14 43 B12
Weldborough TAS 55 E12
Welford Lagoon QLD 13 H10 15 A9
Welford Nat Park QLD 13 H9 15 A8
Wellesley Islands QLD 10 C4
Wellingrove NSW 25 E9
Wellington NSW 22 D4
Wellington SA 63 D8 65 K11
Wellington Nat Park WA 73 F9 74 F3
Wellington Point QLD 5 C8
Wellsford VIC 39 A12
Wellstead WA 74 J7
Welshmans Reef VIC 39 C11
Welshpool VIC 45 G8 46 H2
Welshpool WA 71 G6
Wembley WA 71 F3
Wembley Downs WA 71 E2
Wemen VIC 28 G4 40 D6
Wentworth NSW 28 F3 40 A4
Wentworth Falls NSW 21 K9 22 G7
Werakata Nat Park NSW 23 E10
Weranga QLD 7 F8
Wereneth VIC 39 G10
Werombi NSW 21 G11 23 H8
Werrap VIC 40 H4
Werribee VIC 36 E5 39 F13 42 K1
Werribee Gorge State Park VIC 36 B3 39 E12
Werribee South VIC 36 E5 39 G13
Werrikimbe Nat Park NSW 25 J10
Werrimull VIC 28 F2 40 B3
Werrington NSW 21 G8
Werris Creek NSW 24 K7
Wesburn VIC 37 C12
Wesley Vale TAS 54 E7
Wessel Islands NT 87 B12
West Beach SA 59 G2 60 G1 61 A5
West Bore No. 2 SA 68 B5
West Cape Howe Nat Park WA 74 K6
West End QLD 2 D1 3 E3 5 E8
West Frankford TAS 55 E8 56 F1
West Gosford NSW 20 C4
West Group WA 75 H12 83 J1
West Hill QLD 9 E8
West Hill Island QLD 9 E9
West Hill Nat Park QLD 9 E9
West Hobart TAS 49 C1
West Hoxton NSW 21 E10
West Island NT 87 J12 89 A12
West Island QLD 16 B1
West Island SA 61 K6
West Island Con Park SA 61 J7 61 K6
West Kentish TAS 54 F7
West Killara NSW 21 C8
West Lakes SA 59 E1 60 F1
West MacDonnell Nat Park NT 90 F7
West Pennant Hills NSW 19 C2
West Perth WA 70 A1 71 F3
West Pine TAS 54 E6
West Pymble NSW 19 D4 20 C7
West Ridgley TAS 54 E5
West Ryde NSW 19 E4
West Scottsdale TAS 55 E11
West Swan WA 71 C6
West Wyalong NSW 29 E13
Westbourne Park SA 59 H4
Westbury TAS 55 G9 56 H2
Westby NSW 29 J13
Westby VIC 28 J7 41 G11
Westdale WA 72 D5
Western Creek TAS 54 G7
Western Flat SA 38 A1 63 B11
Western Junction TAS 55 G10 56 J6
Western Port VIC 37 H10
Western River SA 63 J8 64 K7
Western River Con Park SA 63 J8 64 K7
Westerway TAS 53 E8
Westfield WA 71 K7
Westgate QLD 15 D14
Westmar QLD 6 H6
Westmead NSW 19 E2
Westmeadows VIC 35 A2
Westmere VIC 39 F8
Westminster WA 71 D3
Weston ACT 32 F3
Weston Creek ACT 32 F2
Westonia WA 74 B7 77 J8
Westwood QLD 9 H9
Westwood TAS 55 F9 56 H4
Wetherill Park NSW 21 E9
Weymouth TAS 55 D10 56 B5
Whale Beach NSW 20 B6
Wharminda SA 64 G6
Wharparilla VIC 41 J13 42 B1
Whealbah NSW 29 E9
Wheelers Hill VIC 35 F6
Wheeo NSW 22 K5 30 B4
Wherrol Flat NSW 23 B12
Whetstone QLD 7 J9 25 A8
Whidbey Isles Con Park SA 64 J4
Whim Creek WA 78 E5 82 C3
Whiporie NSW 25 D13
Whirily VIC 41 H8
White Beach TAS 51 H11 53 H12
White Cliffs NSW 26 G5
White Dam Con Park SA 62 D4 65 G11
White Flag Lake WA 77 H11
White Flat SA 64 H6
White Gum Valley WA 71 J2
White Hills TAS 55 F10 56 H6
White Hut SA 62 J7 64 J7
White Lake WA 79 J8
White Mountains Nat Park QLD 8 C2 11 K12 13 A11
Whitefoord TAS 53 D11
Whiteheads Creek VIC 42 F3
Whiteman WA 71 C5
Whitemark TAS 55 C9
Whitemore TAS 55 G9 56 J3
Whitewood QLD 13 B9
Whitfield VIC 42 E7
Whitsunday Group QLD 9 B8
Whitsunday Island QLD 9 B8
Whitsunday Islands Nat Park QLD 9 B8
Whittlesea VIC 37 A8 39 E14 42 J2 44 A2
Whitton NSW 29 F11
Whitwarta SA 62 F5 65 G9
Whoorel VIC 39 H10
Whorouly VIC 42 D7
Whorouly South VIC 42 D7
Whroo VIC 39 A14 42 D2
Whyalla SA 62 H2 65 E8
Whyalla Con Park SA 62 H2 65 E8
Whyte Island QLD 3 D7 4 D7
Whyte-Yarcowie SA 62 E3 65 F10
Wialki WA 76 H7
Wiangaree NSW 7 J12 25 B13
Wickepin WA 74 E6
Wickham WA 78 E4 82 C2
Wickliffe VIC 38 F7
Widden NSW 22 D7
Wide Bay QLD 7 C13
Widgelli NSW 29 F11
Widgiemooltha WA 75 B12 77 K11 83 G1
Widgiewa NSW 29 H11
Wigram Island NT 87 C12
Wigton Island QLD 9 C9
Wilandspey Con Park QLD 8 E4 13 B14
Wilban WA 83 F4
Wilberforce NSW 20 F6
Wilburville TAS 53 B9 55 J9
Wilby VIC 42 B6
Wilcannia NSW 26 H5
Wild Duck Island QLD 9 E9
Wild Horse Plains SA 62 G5 65 H9
Wildcat Bore SA 68 C6
Wilga WA 73 E11
Wilgarup WA 73 E13
Wilgena SA 64 A4 66 K4
Wilkatana SA 65 D9
Wilkawatt SA 63 B8 65 K12
Wilkie Island QLD 16 G4
Wilkinson Lakes SA 66 H1 68 F6
Willa VIC 40 F5
Willalooka SA 63 C10
Willandra Lakes World Heritage Area NSW 28 D5
Willandra Nat Park NSW 29 C8
Willangie VIC 40 G7
Willara Crossing NSW 15 K10 26 C7
Willare Bridge Roadhouse WA 79 B10 80 G5
Willatook VIC 38 H5
Willaura VIC 38 E7
Willawarrin NSW 25 J11
Willawong QLD 3 H3 5 E9
Willbriggie NSW 29 F11
Willenabrina VIC 40 J5
Willetton WA 71 J4
Willi Willi SA 68 B1 79 K14 90 K2
Willi Willi Nat Park NSW 25 J11
William Bay WA 74 K5
William Bay Nat Park WA 74 K5
William Creek SA 66 G6
Williams WA 73 C8 74 F5
Williams Island SA 64 J6
Williamsdale NSW 30 E3
Williamsford TAS 52 A4 54 H4
Williamstown SA 60 C5 62 E6 65 J10
Williamstown VIC 35 E2 36 D7 39 F14 42 K2 44 C1
Williamtown NSW 23 E11
Willis VIC 30 J1 43 F14
Willmot NSW 21 F8
Willochra SA 65 D9
Willow Crossing VIC 43 C12
Willow Grove VIC 44 D7 46 E1
Willow Springs WA 73 F12
Willow Tree NSW 23 A8
Willow Waters SA 65 C10
Willowbank QLD 5 H10
Willowie SA 62 F1 65 E9
Willowra NT 88 K6 90 B6
Willows QLD 8 H6
Willows Gemfield QLD 8 H6
Willowvale VIC 39 F9
Willung VIC 45 E9 46 F3
Willunga SA 61 E6 62 F7 65 K10
Willunga Hill SA 61 F6
Willyabrup WA 73 K11
Wilmington SA 62 G1 65 E9

Wilmot – Zuytdorp Nat Res 111

Wilmot TAS 54 F6
Wilora NT 91 C8
Wilpena SA 65 B10
Wilson SA 65 C10
Wilson Island QLD 9 H12
Wilsons Downfall NSW 25 B10
Wilsons Promontory VIC 44 J7 46 K1
Wilsons Promontory Nat Park VIC 44 J7 46 K1
Wilton NSW 21 F13
Wiltshire TAS 54 C3
Wiluna WA 77 C9 78 K7
Wimba VIC 39 J10
Wiminda NSW 24 E1
Winbin QLD 15 E11
Winburndale Nature Res NSW 22 F6
Winceby Island SA 64 H6
Winchelsea VIC 39 H11
Winchelsea Island NT 87 F12
Windamere Dam NSW 22 E6
Windarra WA 77 E12 83 D1
Windellama NSW 30 C5
Windemere VIC 39 E10
Windera QLD 7 D10
Windermere TAS 55 E9
Windeyer NSW 22 E5
Windjana Gorge Nat Park WA 79 A11 81 G8
Windomal Landing NSW 41 C9
Windorah QLD 13 J8 14 B7
Windsor NSW 20 F7 23 G8
Windsor QLD 3 D4
Windsor SA 62 F5 65 H9
Windsor Downs NSW 20 F7
Windsor Downs Nature Res NSW 20 F7 23 G8
Windsor Gardens SA 59 E5
Windurong NSW 22 A3 24 K2
Windy Corner WA 79 G11
Windy Harbour WA 74 J3
Winfield QLD 9 K12
Wingala NSW 19 D7
Wingarnie WA 75 C13 77 K11 83 G1
Wingeel VIC 39 G10
Wingellina (Irrunytju) WA 79 K14 83 B7
Wingello NSW 22 K7 30 C6
Wingen NSW 23 B9
Wingen Maid Nature Res NSW 23 B8
Wingfield SA 59 D3 60 F2
Wingham NSW 23 B12
Winiam VIC 40 K3
Winiam East VIC 40 K4
Winjallock VIC 39 B8
Winkie SA 62 B5 65 H13
Winkleigh TAS 55 E9 56 E2
Winmalee NSW 21 H8
Winnaleah TAS 55 D12
Winnambool VIC 28 H5 40 D7
Winnap VIC 38 G3
Winnellie NT 84 D3
Winninowie SA 62 G1 65 E9
Winninowie Con Park SA 62 G1 65 E9
Winnungra NSW 29 D12
Winslow VIC 38 H6
Winston Hills NSW 19 D2 21 D8
Wintawatu SA 68 A3 90 K4
Winthrop WA 71 J3
Winton QLD 13 D9
Winton VIC 42 D6
Winulta SA 62 G5 65 H9
Winya QLD 4 J3
Wirha SA 62 B7 65 K13
Wirra Wirra QLD 11 G10
Wirrabara SA 62 G2 65 E9
Wirraminna SA 64 B6
Wirrega SA 63 B10
Wirrida SA 66 H4
Wirrimah NSW 22 J3 30 A1
Wirrinya NSW 22 G1 29 E14
Wirrulla SA 64 D4
Wisanger SA 63 H8 65 K8
Wisemans Ferry NSW 20 E4 23 G9
Wishart QLD 3 G5
Wistow SA 60 J5
Witchcliffe WA 73 J12 74 H1
Withersfield QLD 8 H6
Witjira Nat Park SA 66 B5 91 K10
Witta QLD 4 G1
Wittenbra NSW 24 J3
Wittenoom WA 78 F5 82 F4
Wivenhoe Pocket QLD 5 J8
Woden Valley ACT 32 F4
Wodonga VIC 29 K12 43 B8
Woggoon Nature Res NSW 29 C12
Wokalup WA 73 G8 74 F3
Woko Nat Park NSW 23 B11
Wokurna SA 62 G4 65 G9
Wolfdene QLD 5 D11
Wolfe Creek Crater Nat Park WA 79 C13 81 K12
Wolfram QLD 11 D12
Wollar NSW 22 C6
Wollemi Nat Park NSW 20 K4 22 D7
Wollert VIC 37 A8
Wollombi NSW 23 E9
Wollomombi NSW 25 G10
Wollondilly River Nature Res NSW 22 J6 30 B5
Wollongong NSW 21 C14 23 K8 30 B7
Wollumbin Nat Park NSW 25 A13
Wollun NSW 25 H9
Wolseley SA 40 K1 63 A10
Wolumla NSW 30 J5
Wolvi QLD 7 D12
Wombarra NSW 21 C13
Wombat NSW 22 J2 30 B1
Wombelano VIC 38 C3
Womboota NSW 29 K8 41 H13
Womikata SA 68 A5 90 K6
Won Wron VIC 45 F9 46 G3
Wonboyn Lake NSW 30 K5 47 B14
Wondai QLD 7 D11
Wondalga NSW 29 J14 30 D1
Wondul Range Nat Park QLD 7 H9
Wonga Beach QLD 11 C12
Wonga Park VIC 37 C10
Wongalara Lake NSW 26 H7
Wongamine WA 72 D1
Wongan Hills WA 74 A4 76 J6
Wongarbon NSW 22 C4
Wongarbon Nature Res NSW 22 C4
Wongarra VIC 39 K10
Wongawallan QLD 5 C11
Wongianna SA 67 H9
Wongoondy WA 76 F4
Wongwibinda NSW 25 G10
Wonnangatta Station VIC 46 A3
Wonnangatta Station (site) VIC 43 G8
Wonnerup WA 73 H11
Wonoka SA 65 C10
Wonthaggi VIC 44 G4
Wonwondah East VIC 38 B5
Wonwondah North VIC 38 B5
Wonyip VIC 45 G8 46 H2
Woobera QLD 12 B4
Wood Wood VIC 28 H6 41 E9
Woodanilling WA 74 G5
Woodbridge TAS 50 J4 53 H10
Woodburn NSW 7 K13 25 C13
Woodburne VIC 39 F11
Woodbury TAS 53 C11 55 K11
Woodchester SA 60 K6 62 E7 65 K10
Woodenbong NSW 7 J12 25 A12
Woodend NSW 29 J12
Woodend VIC 39 D12
Woodford NSW 21 J9
Woodford QLD 4 G3 7 F12
Woodford Island Nature Res NSW 25 E13
Woodgate QLD 7 B12
Woodhill QLD 5 F12
Woodhouse QLD 8 B5
Woodhouselee NSW 22 K5 30 B4
Woodie Woodie Mine WA 79 E8
Woodlands WA 71 E2
Woodleigh VIC 37 K12 44 F4
Woodpark NSW 21 E9
Woodridge QLD 3 J5 5 E9
Woods Point VIC 42 J6 44 A7 46 C1
Woods Reef NSW 24 G7
Woods Well SA 63 D9
Woodsdale TAS 53 D11
Woodside SA 60 G5 62 E7 65 J10
Woodside VIC 45 G10 46 H3
Woodstock NSW 22 G4
Woodstock QLD 8 A5 11 H14
Woodstock TAS 50 G2 53 G9
Woodstock VIC 37 A8 39 B11 39 E14 42 J2 44 A2
Woodstock Nature Res ACT 32 C1
Woodvale WA 71 B2
Woodville NSW 23 D10
Woodville SA 59 E3 60 F2
Woodville South SA 59 F3
Woody Island QLD 7 B13
Woody Point QLD 4 D6
Woogoompah Island QLD 5 B11
Woohlpooer VIC 38 D5
Wool Bay SA 62 H7 65 J8
Wool Wool VIC 39 H9
Woolamai VIC 44 F4
Woolbrook NSW 25 J8
Woolgarlo NSW 30 C2
Woolgoolga NSW 25 F13
Wooli NSW 25 F13
Woollahra NSW 21 B8
Woollamia Nature Res NSW 30 D7
Woolloomooloo NSW 18 C3
Woolomin NSW 25 K8
Woolooga QLD 7 D12
Woolooma NSW 23 B9
Wooloware NSW 19 K4
Woolshed Flat SA 62 G1 65 D9
Woolsthorpe VIC 38 H6
Woomargama NSW 29 K13 43 A10
Woomargama Nat Park NSW 29 K13 43 A11
Woombye QLD 4 F1
Woomelang VIC 28 J4 40 G7
Woomera SA 64 B7
Woongoolba QLD 5 C10
Woonigan QLD 12 B4
Woonona NSW 21 C13
Woorabinda QLD 9 J8
Wooragee VIC 43 C8
Woorak VIC 40 K4
Wooramel Roadhouse WA 76 B2 78 K2
Wooreen VIC 44 F6
Woori Yallock VIC 37 C11 42 K4 44 B4
Woorim QLD 4 D4
Woorinen VIC 28 H6 41 F9
Woorinen North VIC 41 E9
Woornack VIC 28 H4 40 E6
Woorndoo VIC 38 F7
Wooroconda WA 78 F3
Wooroloo WA 72 E3 74 C3 76 K5
Wooroolin QLD 7 D11
Wooroonook VIC 41 K8
Wooroonooran Nat Park QLD 11 D13
Woosang VIC 41 K9
Wootha QLD 4 G2
Wootton NSW 23 C12
Worongary QLD 5 C13
Woronora NSW 19 J3
Worsley WA 73 F9
Wotto Nature Res WA 76 G4
Wowan QLD 9 J10
Woy Woy NSW 20 B5
Wreck Island QLD 9 H12
Wrens Flat VIC 42 H7 46 B2
Wright Island SA 61 J6
Wroxham VIC 30 K4 47 B12
Wubalawun NT 86 J7
Wubin WA 76 H5
Wudinna SA 64 E5
Wugullar (Beswick) NT 86 G7
Wujal Wujal QLD 11 B12
Wulgulmerang VIC 43 G13 47 A8
Wullwye Nature Res NSW 30 H2
Wumalgi QLD 9 F9
Wunara NT 89 H12
Wundowie WA 72 E2 74 C3 76 K5
Wunghnu VIC 42 B3
Wungu WA 79 B14 81 J12
Wunkar SA 62 B6 65 H12
Wurarga WA 76 E5
Wurdiboluc VIC 39 H11
Wurruk VIC 45 D10 46 F4
Wurtulla QLD 4 D1
Wuruma Dam QLD 7 B9
Wutan QLD 16 F1
Wutul QLD 7 F10
Wutunugurra NT 89 J10
Wy Yung VIC 43 K11 45 C13 46 D6
Wyalkatchem WA 74 B5 76 J6
Wyalong NSW 29 E13
Wyan NSW 25 C12
Wyandra QLD 15 F13
Wyanga NSW 22 D2 27 K14 29 B14
Wyangala NSW 22 H4
Wybong NSW 23 C8
Wycarbah QLD 9 H10
Wycheproof VIC 28 K5 41 J8
Wychitella VIC 41 K10
Wycliffe Well NT 89 J9 91 A9
Wye River VIC 39 J11
Wyee NSW 20 B1 23 F10
Wyee Point NSW 20 B1
Wyeebo VIC 43 C10
Wyelangta VIC 39 K9
Wyena TAS 56 D6
Wylie Creek NSW 25 B11
Wymah NSW 29 K13 43 B10
Wymlet VIC 28 H3 40 D5
Wynarka SA 62 D7 65 J11
Wynbring SA 66 K2 68 H7
Wyndham NSW 30 J4
Wyndham WA 81 D13
Wynn Vale SA 59 C6
Wynnum QLD 3 D7 4 D7
Wynyard TAS 54 D5
Wyola WA 72 A2
Wyola Lake SA 68 F3
Wyoming NSW 20 B4
Wyong NSW 20 B2 23 F10
Wyong Creek NSW 20 C3
Wyongah NSW 20 B2
Wyperfeld Nat Park VIC 28 J3 40 G4 65 K14
Wyrallah NSW 25 C13
Wyrrabalong Nat Park NSW 20 A2 23 F10
Wyuna VIC 41 J14 42 B2

Y

Yaamba QLD 9 G10
Yaapeet VIC 28 K3 40 H5
Yabba VIC 43 C10
Yabba North VIC 42 B4
Yabbra Nat Park NSW 7 J12 25 B11
Yabulu QLD 8 A4 11 H14
Yacka SA 62 F3 65 F10
Yackandandah VIC 43 C8
Yagga Yagga WA 79 E13
Yagoona NSW 21 D9
Yahl SA 38 G1 63 B14
Yakanarra WA 79 C11 81 J8
Yalamurra QLD 15 E12
Yalata SA 68 J5
Yalboroo QLD 8 C7
Yalbraith NSW 22 J6 30 A5
Yalca VIC 42 A3
Yalca North VIC 42 A3
Yalgogrin NSW 29 E12
Yalgogrin South NSW 29 F12
Yalgoo WA 76 E5
Yalgorup Nat Park WA 72 H7 74 E2
Yallambie NSW 20 E1
Yallaroi NSW 7 K8 24 C6
Yalleroi QLD 8 J3 13 F13
Yallingup WA 73 K11 74 G1
Yallock VIC 37 H12
Yallook VIC 41 K11
Yallourn VIC 44 E7 46 F1
Yallourn North VIC 44 D7 46 F1
Yallunda Flat SA 64 H6
Yaloak VIC 36 B2
Yaloak Vale VIC 36 C2
Yalwal NSW 30 C6
Yam Island QLD 16 A3
Yamala QLD 8 H7
Yamanto QLD 5 H9
Yamba NSW 25 D13
Yamba SA 28 F1 40 B1 62 A5 65 H13
Yambacoona TAS 54 A6
Yamboyna QLD 8 H7
Yambuk VIC 38 H5
Yan Yean VIC 37 A8 39 E14 42 J2 44 A2
Yanac VIC 40 J3
Yanac South VIC 40 K3
Yanakie VIC 44 H7 46 J1
Yanamah WA 73 F13
Yanchep WA 72 H1 74 C2 76 K4
Yanchep Nat Park WA 72 G1 74 B2 76 K4
Yanco NSW 29 G11
Yanco Glen NSW 26 J2
Yandaran QLD 7 A11 9 K12
Yanderra NSW 21 F14
Yandeyarra WA 78 E5 82 D4
Yandina QLD 7 E13
Yandoit VIC 39 C11
Yanga Nature Res NSW 28 G6 41 C10
Yango NSW 20 F1
Yaninee SA 64 E5
Yankalilla SA 61 H3 63 F8 65 K9
Yanna Ridge QLD 15 E13
Yannathan VIC 37 H12 44 E4
Yanneri Lake WA 78 H7 82 J7
Yantabulla NSW 27 C8
Yantara Lake NSW 26 E3
Yantbangee Lake NSW 26 F6
Yanunbeyan Nat Park NSW 30 E4
Yaouk NSW 30 F2
Yaouk Nature Res NSW 30 F2
Yaraka QLD 8 K1 13 H10 15 A10
Yarck VIC 42 G4
Yardanogo Nature Res WA 76 G4
Yarle Lakes SA 68 G4
Yarloop WA 73 G8 74 E3
Yarra Creek TAS 54 C7
Yarra Glen VIC 37 B10 42 J3 44 A3
Yarra Junction VIC 37 C12 42 K4 44 B4
Yarra Ranges Nat Park VIC 37 B12 42 J5 44 A5 46 D1
Yarra Yarra Lakes WA 76 G4
Yarrabah QLD 11 D13
Yarrabandai NSW 22 F1 29 C13
Yarrabin NSW 22 D5
Yarragon VIC 44 E6
Yarralena WA 73 A14
Yarralin NT 86 K3 88 B3
Yarralumla ACT 31 C1 32 E4
Yarram VIC 45 G9 46 H2
Yarramalong NSW 20 D2
Yarraman NSW 22 A7 24 K5
Yarraman QLD 7 E11
Yarrambat VIC 37 B9
Yarramony WA 72 C1
Yarranderie NSW 21 K13
Yarranderie State Con Area NSW 21 J13
Yarrangobilly NSW 30 E2
Yarrara VIC 28 G2 40 B2
Yarras NSW 23 A12 25 K11
Yarravel Nature Res NSW 25 J12
Yarrawonga VIC 29 K10 42 B5
Yarriabini Nat Park NSW 25 H12
Yarringully Nature Res NSW 25 C13
Yarrock VIC 40 K2
Yarroweyah VIC 42 A4
Yarrowitch NSW 25 K10
Yarrowyck NSW 25 G8
Yarto VIC 28 J4 40 F5
Yarwun QLD 9 H11
Yass NSW 30 C3
Yatala QLD 5 D10
Yatala Vale SA 59 C7
Yatchaw VIC 38 F5
Yathalamarra NT 87 C10
Yathong Nature Res NSW 27 K10 29 B10
Yatina SA 62 F2 65 E10
Yatpool VIC 28 F3 40 B5
Yattalunga SA 60 C4
Yatte Yattah NSW 30 D6
Yawalpa QLD 5 B11
Yea VIC 42 G3
Yeal Nature Res WA 72 G1 74 B3 76 K4
Yealering WA 74 E6
Yearinan NSW 24 J3
Yearinga VIC 40 K2
Yednia QLD 4 K2 7 E12
Yeelanna SA 64 G5
Yeerongpilly QLD 3 F3
Yelarbon QLD 7 J8 24 B7
Yeldulknie Con Park SA 62 K3 64 F7
Yellabinna Reg Res SA 64 A2 66 K2 68 J7
Yellagonga Regional Park WA 71 B2
Yellangip VIC 40 J5
Yellingbo VIC 37 D11
Yellowdine WA 75 B9 77 J9
Yellowdine Nature Res WA 75 B9 77 J9
Yelta VIC 28 F3 40 A4
Yelverton WA 73 J11
Yenda NSW 29 F11
Yendon VIC 39 E11
Yengo Nat Park NSW 20 G1 23 E9
Yennora NSW 21 D9
Yenyening Lakes Nature Res WA 72 A4 74 D5
Yeo Lake Nature Res WA 77 E14 83 C3
Yeo Yeo NSW 22 K2 29 F14
Yeoval NSW 22 D3
Yeppoon QLD 9 G10
Yerilla WA 77 G11 83 E1
Yering VIC 37 B10
Yerong Creek NSW 29 J12
Yeronga QLD 3 F3
Yerranderie NSW 22 J7 30 A6
Yerrinbool NSW 21 F14
Yetholme NSW 22 G6
Yetman NSW 24 B7
Yilliminning WA 72 A7
Yin Barun VIC 42 E5
Yinkanie SA 62 B5 65 H12
Yinnar VIC 44 E7 46 G1
Yinnar South VIC 44 F7 46 G1
Yirrirra WA 79 J13
Yirrkala NT 87 C13
Yiyili WA 79 C12 81 J10
Yokine WA 71 E4
Yolla TAS 54 D5
Yongala SA 62 E2 65 E10
Yoogali NSW 29 F11
Yoongarillup WA 73 H11
York WA 72 C3 74 C4 76 K5
York Plains TAS 53 C11 55 K11
Yorke Peninsula SA 62 H6
Yorketown SA 62 H7 65 J8
Yorkeys Knob QLD 11 D13
Yorklea NSW 25 C13
Yorktown TAS 55 E8 56 D2
Yornaning WA 72 B7 74 E5
Yornup WA 73 E12
You Yangs Reg Park VIC 36 E3 39 F12
Youanmite VIC 42 B4
Youndegin WA 72 A2
Young NSW 22 J2 30 A1
Younghusband Peninsula SA 63 E9
Youngtown TAS 56 H5
Youraling WA 72 B5
Yowah QLD 15 H11
Yowie Bay NSW 19 K4
Yowrie NSW 30 G5
Yudnamutana SA 67 J11
Yuelamu NT 90 D6
Yuendumu NT 90 D5
Yukan QLD 9 E8
Yulara NT 90 J4
Yuleba QLD 6 E6
Yulecart VIC 38 F5
Yulte Con Park SA 61 G5
Yuluma NSW 29 H11
Yulumba WA 79 A13 81 G11
Yumali SA 63 C8 65 K11
Yumbarra Con Park SA 64 C2 68 K7
Yumbarra Con Res SA 68 K6
Yuna WA 76 E3
Yundaga WA 77 G10
Yundamindera WA 77 F11 83 E1
Yunderup WA 72 G6 74 E3
Yundi SA 61 F6
Yundool VIC 42 C5
Yungaburra QLD 11 D12
Yungera VIC 41 C8
Yungngora WA 79 B11 80 J7
Yunta SA 62 D1 65 E11
Yunyarinyi (Kenmore Park) SA 68 A5 90 K6
Yurangka SA 68 B4 90 K5
Yuraygir Nat Park NSW 25 E13
Yurgo SA 62 C7 65 K12
Yuroke VIC 39 E13 42 J1 44 A1
Yuulong VIC 39 K9

Z

Zagai Island QLD 16 A3
Zanthus WA 77 J13 83 F2
Zeehan TAS 52 A3 54 H3
Zeerust VIC 42 C3
Zillmere QLD 3 B4
Zumsteins VIC 38 C6
Zuytdorp Nature Res WA 76 D2

List of abbreviations

CBD	– Central Business District
Con Area	– Conservation Area
Con Park	– Conservation Park
Nat Park	– National Park
Nature Res	– Nature Reserve
Rec Park	– Recreation Park
Reg Res	– Regional Reserve
Res	– Reserve

Legend

112 Australia Touring Atlas

Great Northern Highway, WA

Freeway / Divided Highway – sealed
Autobahn / Autostrasse
Autoroute / route rapide à chaussées séparées
Autostrada / superstrada

Freeway – future
Autobahn – im Bau
Autoroute – en construction
Autostrada – in costruzione

Major Highway – sealed / unsealed
Durchgangsstrasse – befestigt / unbefestigt
Route principale – revêtue / non revêtue
Strada di grande comunicazione – pavimentata / non pavimentata

Metroad
Metroad

Main Road – sealed / unsealed
Hauptstrasse – befestigt / unbefestigt
Route de communication – revêtue / non revêtue
Strada principale – pavimentata / non pavimentata

Minor Road – sealed / unsealed
Sonstige Strasse – befestigt / unbefestigt
Autre route revêtue / non revêtue
Altra strada – pavimentata / non pavimentata

Track, four-wheel drive only
Piste, nur mit 4-Rad-Antrieb befahrbar
Piste, utilisable pour véhicule à 4 roues motrices
Pista, praticabile solo con trazione integrale

Walking Track / Trail
Fussweg / Pfad
Sentier
Sentiero / viottolo

Total Kilometres
Totaldistanz in km
Distance totale en km
Distanza totale in km

Intermediate Kilometres
Teildistanz
Distance partielle
Distanza parziale

National Route Number / National Highway Number
Nationale Strassennummer / Nationale Durchgangsstrassen-Nummer
Numéro de route nationale / de route rapide
Numero della strada nazionale / Numero della strada di grande comunicazione

State Route Number
Staats-Strassennummer
Numéro de route d'Etat
Numero della strada dello stato

Tourist Route
Touristenstrasse
Route touristique
Strada turistica

Railway – in use / disused
Eisenbahn – in Betrieb / stillgelegt
Chemin de fer – en service / abandonné
Ferrovia – in esercizio / interrotto

Lake or Reservoir
See oder Reservoir
Lac ou réservoir
Lago o lago artificiale

Intermittent or Salt Lake
Periodischer oder Salzwassersee
Lac périodique ou d'eau salée
Lago periodico o salato

National Park / Reserve
Nationalpark / Reservat
Parc national / réserve
Parco nazionale / riserva

Regional Reserve
Regionalreservat
Réserve régionale
Riserva regionale

Conservation / Protected Area
Schutzgebiet
Zone protégée
Regione protetta

Aboriginal Land
Aborigines-Gebiet
Région d'aborigènes
Regione d'aborigeni

City / Major Town — Gawler
Gross- oder wichtige Stadt
Ville importante
Città grande o importante

Town / Community / Locality — Skipton
Stadt oder Gemeinde
Ville ou commune
Città o comunità

Homestead — 'Plumbago'
Gehöft
Ferme
Masseria

Tourist Point of Interest — Lookout
Touristische Sehenswürdigkeit
Curiosité touristique
Curiosità turistica

Mountain / Hill — Mt Brown
Berg / Hügel
Montagne / colline
Monte / colle

Camping Area (with facilities)
Camping (mit Einrichtungen)
Camping (avec équipement)
Campeggio (con equipaggiamento)

Rest Area (toilet/water tank in remote areas)
...and with overnight camping
Rastplatz (Toilette/Wassertank in der Nähe)
...und Camping (nur 1 Nacht)
Aire de repos (Toilettes/citerne d'eau à proximité)
...et camping (seulement 1 nuit)
Area di riposo (Gabinetto/serbatoio d'acqua a prossimità)
...e campeggio (solo 1 notte)

Outback Rest Area (no facilities)
Rastplatz (Outback; ohne Einrichtungen)
Aire de repos (Outback; sans équipement)
Area di riposo (Outback; senza equipaggiamento)

Picnic Area (city maps only)
Picknick-Platz (Stadtpläne)
Place pique-nique (Plans de villes)
Picnic (Piante di città)

Outback Fuel (diesel and unleaded available)
Tankstelle (Outback; Diesel und bleifreies Benzin erhältlich)
Station-service (Outback; diesel et carburant sans plomb disponible)
Stazione di servizio (Outback; diesel e benzina senza piombo disponibile)

Airport
Flughafen
Aéroport
Aeroporto

State Border
Staatsgrenze
Frontière d'Etat
Confine dello stato